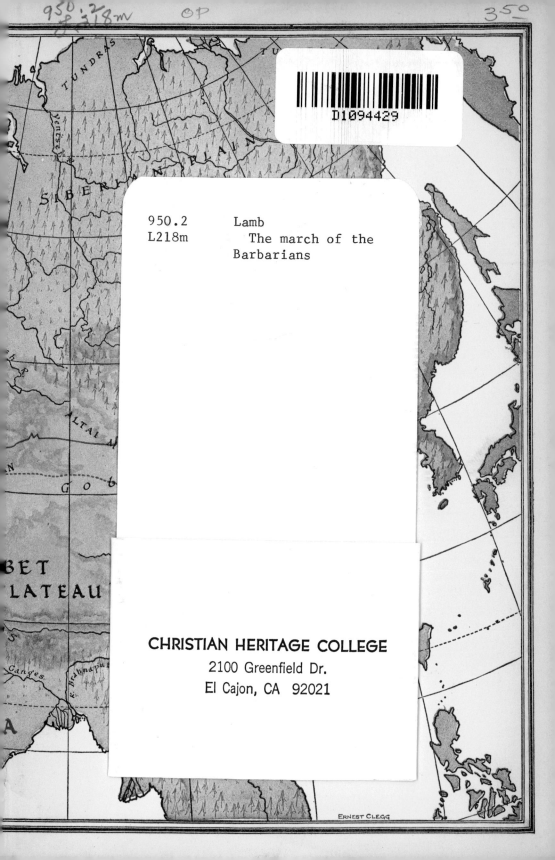

P+C

THE MARCH
OF THE
BARBARIANS

Xavier Hahn
4627 Lexington ave
Los Angeles

THE MARCH
OF THE
BARBARIANS

By
HAROLD LAMB, 1892-

THE LITERARY GUILD OF AMERICA, INC.

NEW YORK

PRINTED AT THE *Country Life Press*, GARDEN CITY, N. Y., U. S. A.

Contents

[v]

Contents

[*vi*]

Contents

Contents

I

The Steppes of Asia

I

The Steppes of Asia

THEY LIVED ALONG THE FRINGE of the great ice. We
know them only as shadowy groups of families, hunting their meat
below the edge of the glacial ice, under the flaring northern lights.

At this time, when snow still covered the higher ranges of Asia
and the last of the salt seas were drying up in the heart of Asia,
these men were cut off from the sun-warmed regions of the south.

In that south, as millenniums passed, civilization began to be.
It appeared in the river valleys where human beings could cultivate the fertile soil. It advanced when different races came into
contact, by making war on each other or by the intercourse of
trade. When one race mixed with another, a spark was kindled.
New ideas came into being, with children of new blood. . . .

From the Nile to the plain of the Tigris and Euphrates, and to
the river Indus, this belt of mother-civilization extended. It
reached across the Mediterranean to the sea dwellers of Crete.
The inhabitants of this mother-civilization gathered into cities,
in the centers of cultivated areas.

To protect themselves and their goods, they built walls around
the cities—the clay-brick walls of Kish rising with the stonework of
Mohenjo-daro, in India, some five thousand years ago.

A little later—a thousand years may signify many changes in the
affairs of human beings, while they are no more than an episode in
the implacable tenacity of nature—civilization appeared in the far

east, along the rivers flowing into an ocean then unknown, the Pacific. Chinese legends relate that men who had wrapped their bodies in the skins of animals and had lived like animals, knowing their mothers but not their fathers, advanced to civilization under the mythical Earth-Emperors Shun and Yu. These progressive men of China, it appears, rose to enlightenment by four steps: crops, matrimony, the calendar and cooking.

However that might have been, the Chinese became, like the city dwellers of Ur and Babylon, cultivators of the soil, bound to the soil. And they thrived.

Meanwhile the forgotten men in north Asia, roving somewhere along the frozen tundras, had developed a peculiarity. They had horses.

They still lived isolated from the civilized centers. They still hunted game and dressed themselves in skins. Sometimes they fished and wore fishskins to keep out the cold. They had domesticated the animals of this northern region, the reindeer, sheep and wild horse. Animal meat and milk nourished them, and they began to work hair into felts to cover tent poles and shelter them.

Of necessity they wandered in search of game, and grazing for their domesticated animals. Some of them kept to the virgin forests with their reindeer herds, building huts for shelter—the forest people. Others, living on horse herds, pushed down into the grasslands, sheltering themselves in felt tents—the steppe dwellers.

Their isolation kept them barbarians; their wandering made them nomads. And their horses could carry them at speed over the steppes.

The horse nomads had at this time a unique domain. It stretched from the arctic ice with its frozen swamps—tundras—down to what they called the great Snowy Mountains (Tibet and the Himalayas). And from the river valleys of the Celestial Empire (China) through the spinal barrier heights of mid-Asia on through a wilderness of grass valleys and forests to the far western barrier that the nomads called the Earth Girdle (the Urals). We know this immense domain vaguely as the steppes of Asia.

It is also known as central Asia, and sometimes as high Asia, because so much of it is elevated plateau land crossed by mountain ranges.

Actually, it is as varied as the climatic changes, which run from excessive cold to burning heat. And, more often than not, sweeping winds. The cold tundras, where the only grazing for animals is moss lichen, yield to the vast Siberian forests cut by swift rivers whose water is sweet. Below these forests stretch the grasslands—the high prairies where little rain falls. Toward the west, mountain ranges thrust into these open steppes. And in the ranges the barbarians came upon deposits of iron and silver, and some of the tribes learned to mine the deposits and work the metals after a fashion.

Southward, below the prairies with their rich grass, extends the arid area of the Desert (the Gobi), with its baked clay and windswept sand. Around the edge of the Gobi lie a chain of lakes, some of them the salty beds of ancient seas. The growth here is the gray wraith of tamarisk and brittle thornbush. Food for camels, not for cattle.

Still farther to the south rises one of earth's mightiest barriers: the Tibetan plateau, flanked by mountain ranges that are almost impenetrable, from Samarkand to the shore of the Gulf of Tongking.

So the horse nomads dwelt in the steppes and deserts that offered them a complete contrast between the good earth of the prairies and river valleys and the wastes of the dry lands. Possession of the good land meant life, while exile into the barrens meant inevitable destruction.

In consequence, the nomads of the steppes struggled for the fertile land. The victorious tribes survived, and the vanquished became their servants, or they perished. And, dwarfing these human wars, they waged an unceasing struggle with nature to endure. By such hardships their bodies were shaped.

As it happened, one of the most fertile regions lies southeast of Lake Baikal, where the prairies are moistened by the headwaters of rivers flowing into that isolated lake and into the great Amur River. This was a desirable region, a bone of contention among the nomad clans.

The March of the Barbarians

It is clear that these clans were confined to the steppes by natural barriers on almost every side: on the north by the arctic ice, at the northeast by the Khingan range that was like a palisade, with the heavy forests of Manchuria beyond it. Due south, the Tibetan massif rose beyond the clouds.

Only to the southeast, toward the settlements of China, and to the west through the wilderness of mid-Asia were the horse nomads able to penetrate the barriers that hemmed them in. Both these natural corridors offered grazing for their herds. The southeast corridor led into the highlands of China—the Chinese, who soon had reason to watch it, called it the North Gate. The western route led into the steppes that were to become Russian, and on into the valleys of Europe.

In the course of centuries, it was through these two corridors that the horse nomads proceeded to emerge.

But for the time being—for hundreds of years—the horse nomads of high Asia were isolated. The rest of Asia went on building dwellings and sailing boats and going to school. The horse nomads remained apart from all that, unaware of it.

After the first millennium before Christ the civilized peoples of the outer world became aware of the steppe dwellers. The Greeks knew that shadowy masses migrated beyond the edge of the known lands. And Greek writers of history invented names for them. Hyperboreans, dwellers beyond the north wind. The thoughtful Chinese christened them in other wise—"the rancid ones," and "devils."

In fact, the nomads of the unknown north were greasy. They coated their bodies with grease to keep out the cold. Their bodies were shaped by the hard earth and the bitter climate of the steppes. Lean flesh, hard skin with little hair; high cheekbones and eyes narrowed against wind and dust and snow or sun glare. Legs short and somewhat bowed to the body of a horse. Arms and shoulders powerful. They developed endurance against cold, and thirst. Those who could not endure, perished.

They had learned to ride their wild horses. They adapted their clothing to the horse, wearing trousers and short, soft boots at a time

[6]

when the outer world went clad in mantles and skirts and slippers.

And now they became skilled hunters. By degrees they discovered the best bow to use from the saddle, short and doubly curved. This bow was strengthened with horn, to give it power. They also fashioned a short lasso, at the end of a staff. For comfort in riding they put together a leather seat, a saddle. Having saddles, they contrived stirrups to rest their legs. At this time the rest of the world rode bareback, if at all.

By their skill in hunting and herding they nourished their families—with meat and the milk of animals, and the scanty grain that could be sown at the riversides. They did not learn to cultivate the soil, because the grasslands of their high plateaus could not be worked. They guided their herds toward grass, and they found grass only where water reached the steppes. Such country could not be irrigated. The nomads had to go where the water was.

They built no houses, because houses could not be moved, like their tents. And they made, out of wood and leather, only the light articles such as saddles chests and weapons that they needed and that could be carried on animals. What use to make anything for trade? At times a man might barter an arrow case for a leather sack. Or pay for a wife with sheep. Commerce, as such, had no meaning for them.

This routine of life remained almost unchanged among the horse nomads. Until a curious thing happened. They continued to exist as primitives of a bronze age, while civilization in the outer world progressed through the iron age. Below them, a few hundred miles away in Yen-king (the Great Court, now Pei-ping), the Chinese clad themselves in silks, and cultivated gardens. And with the generations, this gap grew greater between the barbarian and the civilized. Between the desert and the sown. Between the hunter and the sedentary worker.

Not that the steppe dweller became inferior, mentally. He was merely isolated from civilization—forced to struggle against the environment of a primitive terrain.

This isolation could not endure for long. Dry years on the steppes drove nomad tribes from watercourse to lake bottom, and, inevitably, to the edge of the cultivated lands beyond.

The March of the Barbarians

There, at some time, the refugees from the steppes first caught sight of the miracle of a man-made land—fields of waving grain, artificial lakes, markets filled with foodstuffs and riches. And that sight ended the isolation of the nomads.

In the beginning, they raided the cultivated lands to keep alive themselves. They darted in like wolf packs, to seize what could be carried off. Then they disappeared into the steppes, carrying their booty with them. They drove off cattle, loaded precious grain into carts.

So began the conflict between the desert and the sown, at the edge of high Asia. As instinctive at first as the night hunting of wolf packs. It was, in fact, a physical law that drove the nomad to raid. When the grass of the steppes failed, he drew from the cultivated lands what he needed to survive.

The Gods of the Ice

Behind the barbarians rode invisible fears. They dreaded the unseen forces of their northern region. The *kanun kotan*, their ancestors had called it—the land of evil gods. The north Siberian plain with its outcropping of black basalt that might have been carved by demon hands, its intense frost that made iron brittle and wood hard. In this frozen earth, the barbarians had found the carcasses of mammoths intact with ivory tusks.

The *kanun kotan* was cursed with long darkness, and with the *purga*, the arctic blizzard that drove snow through men's clothing, forcing human beings to lie with their heads toward the storm, wrapped in furs for two or three days until the *purga* ceased.

All these forces, the barbarians knew, were evil. The power that controlled them resided in the sky. In the *mongke tengri*, the Everlasting Blue Sky. The Sky was God.

To it they made sacrifices of human captives and white horses, on high places such as hilltops. These sacrifices were to avert the wrath of the Sky, and to draw down its benevolence. The sun was a lesser, living god, that rode across the Sky daily, before going to bed with his wife upon the earth at twilight.

The Sky showed its anger by destructive winds, by thunder and lightning. When it gleamed with a clear blue, it was well disposed toward men. In consequence, the barbarians had a liking for the color blue, and for white. Black was evil—the color of night, of rocks and of depths within the earth.

The earth itself was evil. Within its depths dwelt Erlik Khan, in eternal darkness and cold. Upon the surface of the earth, both good and evil forces were to be encountered. These spirits, or masters, resided in fire and in running water and in the winds of the high places. Care must be taken not to offend the "masters" of fire, or streams, or the upper air.

Only after death was a man's spirit released from the dominion of evil powers. Then he could dance in the red fires of the Gate of the Sky (the aurora borealis). He could ride through the blue vault of the Sky, where the wings of the bird of Heaven veiled the moon . . . or his spirit-life might choose to dwell with the "masters" of flames or water, or even in the form of an animal.

The animals themselves possessed "masters." A tutelary spirit watched over the reindeer, and over the bears of the forests. These animal-spirits must be propitiated and not offended by men. Such a spirit was the Blue Wolf, a legendary ancestor of one of the barbarian clans, the Mongols.

To deal with these spirits, the nomads had no priests. Instead they had a priest-doctor-magician—a *shaman*. The shaman examined the sick, and drove out the evil *kelets* (spirits) that caused sickness, or else the sufferer died. These steppe magicians presided at childbirth and at burials. They were called speakers to Heaven because in a trance they could send their spirits out of their bodies, to gallop up into the Sky. By piling stones together in a certain way they could bring on a storm.

They were cunning and unruly, especially among the forest tribes, and the nomads feared the shamans little less than the spirits they exorcised.

The steppe dweller was not stupid. He was simply shaped in a different mold than the so-called civilized dweller in the cultivated lands. He did not, as yet, know the use of writing. But he made up for that lack by a painstaking memory. He could not build a serviceable bridge across one of his mountain freshets; but he had learned how to swim his horses across by roping them together, and holding to their tails himself.

Circumstances had made him a hunter and a fighter, while the cultivator of the soil had learned the arts of peace. More than that, the steppe dweller had learned to adapt himself quickly to a new condition. Nature had given him little time to prepare to face a blizzard. When drought dried up the grass, he had to move himself, his family and his clan—those who depended on his judgment to survive—and his herds a hundred miles or more away from his familiar pastures. He could not afford the luxury of hesitation, he had no sovereign lord who might be disposed to answer his appeal for aid. Experience had shown him the futility of prayer to a god, even to the illimitable Sky. He acted first to save himself, and offered a sacrifice of the blood of horses or wine poured out to the *tengri*, the overhanging Heaven, when all was well.

The town dweller lacked this ability to adapt himself to a new condition. He depended upon his walls, his bridges, his irrigation, the fertility of his fields, and his weapons to defend all that. Besides, he was subject to the will of his liege lord, and to the priests of the local temple. This difference between the barbarian and the civilized, between the nomad and the cultivator, grew greater as time went on.

Meanwhile the nomad had been learning, very quickly, where his advantage lay. Instead of raiding the edge of civilization for a season's food supply, he penetrated deeper into the settled areas, killing off able-bodied men, taking away desirable women and young children that could be raised as slaves or warriors. He learned that his silver and gold had a trade value, and were not simply ornamental. The grape and rice wines of the towns made him pleasantly intoxicated; the gardens yielded sweet fruits. His women much preferred the silks of the market place to their home-fashioned woolens.

Also, from time to time, whole caravans laden with merchandise passed along the roads between the towns. Such caravans yielded him wealth when captured. With wealth, he could trade at leisure with strange merchants in yet-more-distant towns.

All this meant security to the nomad. And he acquired, very

quickly, a new concept of life. Conquest. He could gain security, even undreamed-of luxury, by one victory over the denizens of the cultivated areas. If the victory were great enough, it might serve him for a lifetime.

To gain this victory, he brought into play his skill as a hunter. He attacked the civilized areas beyond the steppes in much the same fashion as he had once stalked a herd of antelope.

And now—about three hundred years before Christ—a change took place in the fortunes of the nomads of high Asia. Until then their horses had served after a fashion for transportation. Now they were learning to maneuver on horseback in warfare. Their bows, used in the saddle, proved to be deadly weapons.

The horse archer had made his appearance in the steppes—a circumstance, at first little heeded, that was to have an astonishing effect. Elsewhere, in more or less civilized regions, some men were learning to ride horses, and other men used bows. The steppe dwellers did both at once. And nearly all the nomads did it.

Moreover in the civilized centers horses were still used more for drawing carts and chariots than for carrying men to war. The few horsemen in Egypt and Greece, for example, armed with short swords and javelins and riding without benefit of saddle and stirrups, were fairly harmless. Not so the steppe dwellers.

The riders of each clan became a natural army, capable of moving at great speed and of enduring hardships that would decimate an army on foot. These hordes—*ordus*, commands of riders—began to defeat the Chinese armies of defense, made up of heavy chariots and masses of spearmen on foot.

"The Tatars,"* a Chinese chronicler of the time complains, "make war a business. They eat the meat and drink the milk of their herds, which move about seeking pasture. Every man is skilled with his bow. In time of peace he takes life easily and enjoys it.

"On the other hand in China one class is opposed to another, so that many must slave for the luxury of those above them. Only by tilling the land and cultivating silkworms can food and clothing be

*Ta-ta was the Chinese word for the northern barbarians who were nearest to them. In time they came to apply it to other nomads—as did the Europeans.

had. Walls have to be built around towns to protect them. So, in time of peace, most men exist by laboring, and in time of war, no one is able to fight."

Elsewhere, to the west, the same phenomenon was taking place. The horse archer was emerging in the mid-region of Asia. Scythian tribes wandered over the Russian steppes, and Belshazzar, feasting, became aware of the coming of the horse archers, Medes and Aryans. The handwriting appeared on the palace wall.

The shadow of the horse archer was also stretching to the south, from the steppes. He was, at that time, a strange figure little heeded—a barbarian out of the wastelands, an energetic gnome living with his bow and his horse.

The Greeks called one such people *Skuthoi*, Scythians. The nomad who drank the milk of mares, making drinking cups of the skulls of his enemies, and slaughtering horses and slaves at the tomb of his chieftain—staking the dead men upright on the carcasses of the horses. The women of such a chieftain killed themselves with knives, so that their spirits could accompany him into the other world. This was in obedience to tribal custom. And it was done at the will of the wizards that Herodotus calls women-men—undoubtedly homosexuals.

The Scythian wore a pointed felt cap with flaps to protect his ears from the winds of the steppes. His loose, long trousers, tight-wrapped at the ankles, shielded his legs from thornbush, dust and snow. He looked much like a prototype of the modern aviator, except that he rode a small horse with close-cropped mane. "Small and ugly," the Greek historians called those mustangs of the steppes. But horse and rider could cover distances at surprising speed. The rider, wearing a crude armor of leather plates strung together, and wielding a long sword and lance, could inflict decisive damage.

Already the Scythian was filtering past the Greek palaces and the remains of Alexander's settlements in southern Asia. Without being aware of it, or caring, he was putting an end to the advance of Greek culture eastwards.

The horse nomad had a new weapon, a striking force new to

warfare. He could outdistance men on foot, and could kill them with his arrows at a hundred paces or more. And for seventeen centuries this weapon was to be the most dangerous in warfare. It was, actually, the Parthian arrow. Already it had made useless the Macedonian phalanx—Alexander's attacking force.

For the time being, the steppe dwellers moved without definite purpose. Individual clans and peoples merely migrated to warmer climates in the south.

Aryans

At least one people moved across the kaleidoscope of the steppes at this time toward the east and the rising sun. Tall men with blue or gray eyes and reddish hair. With long heads. They knew how to cultivate the soil, and they fought with long straight swords.

They were the racial cousins of the Scythians. One branch of them got as far as the Gobi, and the Chinese christened them the Yuë-chi. They were the Aryans (Iranians).

About these Aryans authorities have disputed hotly. They have been called Indo-Europeans, and the Great White Race. Some historians, in present-day Germany, have bestowed on them the ancient emblem of the swastika. But we know little about them. Even the place of their origin is disputed. Their birthland may have been the steppes of Russia.

It is certain that they became nomads and eventually horse archers like the other denizens of central Asia. Whether they were the ones who taught the eastern nomads to ride horses to advantage, or whether the easterners taught them, we do not know. Probably these western Aryans who had lived for a long time in the plains made use of their horses before the Asiatic barbarians, who were emerging from the forest belt and a primitive hunting economy just then. At least the early Chinese, who had reason to observe and to fear both of them, seemed to think so. But it is clear that the Asiatics were more skilled with bows. And it was not long before the eastern ordus broke the power of the Yuë-chi, who migrated closest to their homeland.

In their long wanderings, these blue-eyed and warlike men left behind them grave mounds scattered over the steppes. On these mounds they placed stone figures, a little larger than life size. These stone *babas*, or stone women—as the Russians called them later—all face the east. All stand in the same attitude with blank eyes toward the rising sun. And they have mystified archeologists ever since.

But these Yuë-chi, these blue-eyed devils who spoke the Aryan speech, struck a spark among the savage tribes of the steppes. A fresh spark of purpose and intelligence, falling into smoldering embers. They were dominant conquerors, inclined to rule where they conquered. They gave, as it were, a new purpose to the Asiatic tribes.

And they left physical traces of their passing. Blue eyes and reddish hair, tall bodies, among the steppe dwellers of Asia. We find such traces in the rock temples of mid-Asia, where the figures of tall men with European heads and light eyes are painted on the wall frescoes.

The outer world began to feel almost at once the spark of Aryan mentality, kindled in the wastelands. Leaders appeared among the horse nomads, to direct them in a mass toward the outer civilization.

The Great Wall

This civilization was no longer the gift of the great rivers. Irrigation had spread water through the lowlands; wheeled vehicles carried merchandise from settlement to settlement; ships felt their way along the shores of the oceans. Looms were at work. Glass and porcelain found their way into the channels of trade.

Increasing trade created wealth in the new merchant class. And a demand for luxuries among the rich. Caravans penetrated from India to Greece, to exchange incense and amber and woven silk for iron and gold. The walls of the metropolitan centers rose higher, to protect their wealth and their growing population of owners and slaves.

The steppe dwellers had not shared in this increasing culture. They remained as before, isolated. Until they began to find their way out of the steppes, under their new leaders. The first to appear were Huns—called in the beginning Huing-nu by the Chinese. Their chieftains, *kagans*, guided them along the easiest road to cultivated lands—from their homeland near Lake Baikal toward the North Gate, along the southeast corridor out of the steppes.

And now, to close this pathway, the Chinese emperors built the Great Wall across the hills, where their cultivated land met the prairies of the nomads. For a while this fortress line of twenty-one centuries ago kept back the barbarians. It served to turn them toward the west.

Here another road was open to them, and only one. It followed the grass of the prairies, just below the northern forests; it crossed the Mongolian plateau, to the passes of the Altai, following the rivers of mid-Asia and coming out of the heights into the immense, level steppes of the Kirghiz, threading through the low slopes of the Urals, to the grasslands of southern Russia. Thence it led on directly to the Hungarian plain.

No actual road, of course, existed. It was the natural corridor of grass—grazing for the herds. It passed for some four thousand miles through the wilderness where only nomads could maintain themselves. It might be called the road of the barbarians.

And over it the nomads went west. They started the long trek without knowing what would be at the end of it. For fifteen centuries this trek went on.

Something was happening in the steppes of Asia. The tribes, pent up within natural barriers, struggled among themselves for mastery. This struggle, wolf-like, knew no mercy. There could not be two rulers of the steppes. When a *kagan* of the Huns became strong enough to seize the fertile grasslands where herds could move from summer to winter pastures, the weaker tribes fled with their families and herds to another region. "There is one sun in the Sky," their proverb ran, "and one *kagan* on earth."

At times—usually for no more than a generation—the overlord of the steppes was powerful and farsighted enough to combine the turbulent masses into a brief empire. We are aware of shadowy and gigantic figures that ruled for a few years from the forests of Manchuria to the heights of mid-Asia. Seldom could such a conqueror bequeath his power to a son. Strife would break out again among the nomad masses, and the grazing lands would fall to new owners. But the steppe dwellers had discovered that when they were united under a chieftain strong enough to rule them, they could invade the outer world successfully.

With the regularity of human tides, masses of the horse nomads moved westward, in turn driving the original owners of the land before them.

So the Huns drove the Yuë-chi on, to crush the descendants of the Scythians in the west. There was no turn in the tide.

For a moment—for a generation or so—the farthest outpost of civilized Rome almost touched hands with the westernmost garrisons of the Chinese, then ruled by the Han dynasty. Until a new influx of horsemen from the steppes swept across these frontiers of civilization.

Rome itself succumbed to the invasion of Teutonic and Gothic peoples. But these in turn were fleeing from the approach of the Huns moving westward across the grasslands. For a generation Attila, a leader with keen political sense who had learned much from the Romans, formed an empire of barbarian peoples in the west. Deft and remorseless as he was, Attila created only the semblance of a government. It could not withstand the pressure of new migrations out of the east.

"Two-footed beasts," Ammius Marcellus wrote of the Hunnic invaders at the end of the fourth century, "small and beardless, and seemingly chained to their horses from which they take their meat and drink. They even sleep leaning on the necks of their mounts. Never do they cultivate a field, or touch a plow. They have no houses, their life is one of perpetual wandering . . . they are small men afoot, but in the saddle they appear gigantic."

The hunters of the steppes had discovered the plains of eastern Europe, a milder and a better land, where men were too weak to defend the soil. The road out of the east, the road of the barbarians where the stone *babas* stood guard over the burial mounds, had become a thoroughfare. Over the steppes new hordes pressed with their wagons. They were moving toward the sun, out of the land of the ice gods. They were fleeing from stronger masses beyond the horizon at their heels.

Instinct, stronger than reason, drove them on. Their wandering had only one purpose, to find and hold safe grazing land. To survive, in this tumult of *Völkerwanderungen*.

Their homeland, the high prairies around Lake Baikal in southern Siberia, had become a breeding ground of peoples, moving westward with the measured, unthinking force of a human avalanche. Like Scandinavia it spewed out human masses escaping from the blind forces of nature.

During the centuries after Attila vague rumors spread through western Europe, then in the throes of the dark ages and in the process of conversion to Christianity. These invaders out of the unknown east, the rumors said, were the harbingers of Antichrist, the precursors of those who would come to reap the last, dreadful harvest. For ages they had been pent up behind the barriers of Gog and Magog. Now they were emerging.

Had not the learned St Jerome prophesied that in the day of Antichrist a race polluted and unwashed, using neither wine nor salt nor wheat, would emerge from the land of Gog and Magog, bringing disaster with it?

It seemed to the western Europeans, our ancestors, that this prophecy was in a fair way to be realized.

The Human Tides and the Walls

These migratory masses emerging from the steppes crushed opposition with the savagery of thinking animals. After the Huns came the Avars and Bulgars. Like the Scythians of a thousand years before, they existed on horseback, moving with their herds. Their women bore children on the march, and no man could name the place of his birth.

"These barbarians," a western historian complains, "all resemble each other, but they resemble no one else."

Their impact telescoped the inhabitants of eastern and middle Europe, and scattered broadcast the seeds of modern Europe. The eastern Slavs were driven back toward the Dnieper and the Danube.

On that river the Avars pitched their wagon-ring encampments, sheltering their supplies and treasures, while their *kagan*, Bayan, measured the strength of civilization around him. The name of Bayan is pure Mongol, and his Avars were of Mongol descent.

The March of the Barbarians

At this time, about 600 A.D., three forces protected western civilization, such as it was. The vigor of the barbaric Franks and Germans, the fortifications of the Byzantine Empire—the survival of Rome, in Constantinople—and the unifying force of Christianity.

In 626 the wave of Avars broke and rolled back, at the walls of the imperial city, Constantinople. In 805 the remnants of them submitted to Charlemagne's Franks, and were baptized.

But already the Bulgars were moving in from the steppes to this western front. Six years later, Kroum, the Bulgar chieftain, made himself a drinking cup out of the skull of a Byzantine emperor who had stood in his way. Some of the Bulgars chose to remain inside the steppes by a wide river that was named, after them, the Volga. Others, penetrating what is now the Balkans, harassed the Byzantines until the kaleidoscope of peoples changed again.

This time the Magyars (the "Milk Drinkers" who were later called the Hungarians) emerged from the east. They were guided by a purpose more definite than the other Asiatics. They spoke a language akin to Finnish, and their chieftains were of a Turkic aristocracy.

For the first time western Europe had to defend itself against the keen intelligence of the steppe Turks, and during the next generations it had little success doing so. In 924 the Magyars wiped out the last descendant of the great Charles. The Byzantines were driven into the triple walls of Constantinople. It seemed as if the days of Attila had returned.

The stolid Germans broke the strength of the Magyars. The Hungarian king Vaik was converted, into St Stephen—and those indomitable horsemen retired to the high Hungarian plain. That circumstance proved important, later on.

The Hungarians now formed, with the warlike Slavs, a barrier in the east of Europe against fresh migrations from Asia. Barely in time, because the Byzantines, in spite of their wealth, their engineering skill and their invention of flame-throwing weapons, were becoming decadent. They were no more than the ghosts of Constantine's Rome, haunting the imperial city and the sea.

It was then the year 1000, when superstitious souls in the west believed their Christian world might end. It did not end, but it hung precariously in the balance, while a new striking force matured in the east.

For a long time other nomads had been making their way out of high Asia on foot. Forest dwellers, who made paths through the northern *taiga*, never emerging into the grasslands. Skin-clad hunters and fishers—some of them reindeer keepers. Men who kept peaceably to the snows.

Those who found their way westward were the Lapps and Finns. Others pushed to the east, and crossed ice-fringed water in their open canoes, carrying with them the carved images of animal totems, cared for by their shamans, their medicine men.

They crossed the strait now called Bering, and settled out of harm's way in northern America, becoming the ancestors of the so-called North American Indians.

No one paid any attention to them.

China's Yellow Earth

As the black earth of the Russian steppes had drawn the nomads into the west, China's fertile yellow earth drew them south and east.

The Great Wall had failed as a barrier long since. The early emperors had built it long enough and high enough to be invulnerable to the Hunnic tribes. But they forgot to watch it. The barbarians learned to break through where it was not defended.

Then began a movement as regular as the tides of the oceans, through the southeast corridor out of the steppes. When the Chinese city-states became degenerate, or divided by long war, the horse nomads would break in. To domineer for a few generations over the yellow-earth region of Shansi and the north.

"These barbarians," a Chinese relates, "did not number more than a fifth of the inhabitants of our prefectures. Their strength lay in their independence."

After tasting the luxury of the fertile land where rich grain grew, and the silkworm was bred, the nomads would be merged into the increasing mass of the Chinese. Their inroads brought a fresh lifeblood into the Chinese race. This conquest and assimilation went on without change, in the north. It seldom penetrated south of the Yellow River, and never beyond the Yang-tse.

So, to the nomads, the fertile region behind the Great Wall became a promised land. At the same time, they grew increasingly aware of the figure of the Chinese emperor, the Son of Heaven, who held all authority in his hands. In spite of the upheavals they caused, they remained in awe of the sublimated man on the Dragon Throne. He was, in effect, their ultimate lord—a perpetual viceroy of Heaven.

And at this time the Son of Heaven had become a splendid personality, remote from the sight of the steppe dwellers. Down in the south of China the T'ang dynasty reigned with victorious imperialism, surrounded by a shield of armies. Yet the occupants of the Dragon Throne were idealists who gave force and direction to life within the barriers of the Celestial Empire. They surrounded themselves with the grace of Buddhist art, delighting in sculptures of the human form—even the small clay figurines left in their tombs were human and graceful. In their realistic moods the T'ang monarchs built roads for pilgrims, and stored up grain against years of famine; they sent ambassadors to Indian kings, and their watchtowers stretched far into the west, beyond the Desert's sands.

To such benevolent patricians as these, the northern barbarians gave little concern. They knew the nearest of them as T'ou kiu, the Strong—or Turks. And also as slaves, because before the Turks had become horsemen, they had worked iron and dug the earth for forgotten emperors. Now these Turks wandered in tents, struggling to break through the northern barriers.

Beyond them, the T'ang rulers knew, hunters were emerging from the far northern forest belt, hunters of game whose dwellings were hauled about on wagons, who were called Mongols, or the Everlasting.

And beyond them, crossing the line of the Amur River, a still more savage people—who still clung to snowshoes and reindeer— the Tungus or Pig people. So the T'ang observers christened them.

It was only natural, in such circumstances, that when the first Turkish clans began to migrate out of the steppes, they should turn away from the strong armies of the T'ang, into the west.

II

The Emperors on Horseback

II

The Emperors on Horseback

IN THE THOUSAND YEARS SINCE the tribes of Huns had started to graze westward, nature had changed the surface of the steppes somewhat. There was now less snow on the mountain ridges. The lakes had shrunk, and become saltier.

During the fierce summer heat, the grass died more quickly. When the nomads changed their pastures they met dust storms that took toll of the herds. To the south, the sandy reaches of the Gobi began to encroach on the foothills. Winds whipped the long ridges of sand over outlying settlements.

When a crest of sand toppled over, it gave out a sound like the beating of distant invisible drums. The Chinese called these crests the *liu sha*, the moving sands—where evil spirits were accustomed to lure travelers away from the roads.

The steppes of high Asia were, in fact, drying up. This desiccation had two consequences. It moved the life-giving pastures farther north, increasing the gap between them and the cultivation of the outer world. And it forced greater numbers of the nomads to migrate in order to survive. Their homeland was yielding to the desert, and they looked more to the cultivated lands for their heritage.

And at this time the most formidable of the horse nomads, the Turks, were in movement.

[23]

The March of the Barbarians

The Adventuring of the Turks

The Chinese poet Li T'ai po called this new arrival, "The Frontiersman," saying of him: "All his life this man of the frontier never opens a book, but he knows how to hunt. He never draws his bow without killing. His whistling arrows can bring birds tumbling out of the air. When he gallops out into the plain he calls his falcon to him. The desert knows his courage."

Other Chinese made proverbs about this Turk. "A Turk in the saddle will care nothing for his own father." And: "A Turk is born in a hut, but he dies on the prairie."

In physical type the Turk came between the earlier Aryan (Iranian) and his eastern neighbor, the more savage Mongol. He was tall as the Aryan, and active. His skin, despite popular misconception, was white, in contrast to the browner Mongol. Often he had reddish hair and light eyes, with strongly marked features and a hairy body. The round-headed Mongol had a broad, bony face, and little hair.

He caught and tamed wild horses, but he also owned camels, cattle and a multitude of sheep. He even measured the years by the calendar of the Twelve Beasts.

His women shared his careless vitality; they clad themselves in Chinese embroidered silks; they tattooed, in the earliest time, their throats; they were lascivious, and bred many sons. They wore sables in cold weather, and they liked to listen to the music of flutes and drums, and bells hung on a staff.

The *kagan* of the Turks pitched his tent to face the east, where the sun rises. The standard pole before his tent bore a golden wolf's head, and he called his guardsmen wolves. He gave to each clansman a certain piece of land, but he reigned with undisputed authority over the clan. Each chieftain became as it were a monarch in little. The token of his authority was an arrow with a gold head, bearing his seal.

He refused to build citadels or monasteries, saying, "No! Houses and monasteries tend to make men mild in nature. Only the fierce and warlike can dominate others."

He had a Roman's sense of military discipline. The Chinese say that in the Turkish clans the best food was given to men of warrior age—the best of the captured women as well—and the young and the elders had to shift for themselves.

It is curious that, in this dour discipline, the Turkish clans shared with the stolid soldiery bred in the marshes of the western Tiber one extraordinary quality. Out of all the peoples, the Asiatic Turks and the European Romans only had shown the ability to create and rule a world dominion.

The Turks, however, never possessed the cohesion of the Romans. When they migrated from the drying-up steppes, their savage clans moved apart, each seeking a destination of its own. Guiding themselves by the stars, they crossed the wastes of the Gobi, moving south through the barrier of the Altai. Only the weaker clans took the eastern corridor leading toward the yellow earth of China—a circumstance fortunate both for the Turks and the Chinese who were then ruled by the splendid T'ang dynasty.

A poet, a man of T'ang, watching them pass, cried:

> " 'Ling-ling' their wagons squeal; 'siao-siao' their horses snort.
> The warriors ride with bow and arrows by their reins,
> Through their ranks run fathers and wives and children,
> Running through the dust that covers them, making them invisible,
> Holding to the garments of the men who are going away, as if to keep
> them back."

Savage and tenacious, the clans of the pagan Turks were moving south, toward the ice pass of the Father of Snow Mountains that led to the long valley of Samarkand. And here they came upon something new in the steppes.

The Five Cities

It was not altogether new. For some centuries civilization had been penetrating the southern barrier of the Tibetan ranges, to this *foyer* of the nomads.

By slow degrees a road had opened here across Asia. A road very different from the grass route of the barbarians, to the north.

It began at Tuen-huang, where the fertile earth of China ends. A caravan track leading out over the Gobi. Through the gray ghosts of tamarisks out into the blast of the wind over the dry clay where the only water lies hidden in the ground. A track made by the pads of camels plodding in line, laden, with horsemen riding at the head of their string, seeking a way through the dust, looking for the first green of the western hills across the waste land. Running past the oases of Turfan, along the line of hills to Kashgar with its gardens walled to keep out the dust. Up the winding trail to the shoulder of the Muztagh-ata, the Father of Snow Mountains. Sliding and stumbling down the pass through rocks molten in the sun's glare—or coated with winter ice—down to the red earth and water of the valley that leads to Samarkand. Past the domes of Merv, where the wild birds come down to water. Climbing through the dry grass up to the long plain of Iran (Persia), where the camels plod straight to the setting sun and a blue line of mountains stands on the skyline without drawing nearer or receding. The camels plowing through swift streams where no bridges are, heading to the west, going by moonlight to escape the day's searing heat in that dry air.

Such is the *Pe lu*, the great North Road, the ancient silk route. By this, eastern silk was brought to the ladies of imperial Rome and Byzantium. Silk to be dyed purple at Sidon or Tyre, or sold with ivory and jade to the merchants of Palmyra.

A southern route branched off into the sandy region of the Gobi, crossing lakes of dried reeds to the oases of Khotan and Yarkand. The *Nan lu*, the South Road, leading up to the gorges of the Roof of the World where devils echoed every sound and no water would boil to make tea. Over the wind-swept Kara-korum pass of black sand, over the snow passes above the fir forests of Kashmir, the sentinels of India. Or through the highlands to Balkh, the Mother of Cities.

Over these routes a thread of trade had been woven between the sedentary civilization of China and the cities of Persia, and the end of the sedentary Mediterranean world. A thin thread, often snapped and often repaired. And upon it, at the western end of the Gobi where the tree growth of the T'ian Shan meets the sands, cities had grown up around the oases. Here a civilization had developed, remote from the great empires. A kind of crossroads civilization, its shrines mixed with caravanserais, and its watch-towers of clay brick often unguarded. Around the five cities that rose by the oases and rivers, Bishbaligh, Almalyk on the way to Kashgar. And, to the south, Khotan and Yarkand. The Chinese knew it as the western region, and it might be called Kashgaria.

But it was really the Five Cities, changing only slowly with the changes in the outer world—holding to their seclusion and the heritage of the past.

These routes, too difficult for armies, became the fragile thorough-fare of trade, and the path of pilgrims. Alexander's Macedonians had turned back through India, at the foothills of the Himalayas, but Greek vases and sculptures were carried on into the mountains.

Red Buddhist bonzes followed, and Chinese disciples retraced their footsteps to visit the places sacred to Buddha in Kashmir. Persian artists arrived in the oases with the caravans of Chinese silk merchants.

The cities rose where the roads met. We know little about them except their names. But we are certain, from the language spoken there, that descendants of the wandering Aryan tribes survived in this hidden crossroads. It was here they left their portraits on the walls of the grotto temples, painted perhaps by Persians.

These wall paintings are like ghosts of remembered arts. A woman's figure might have been sketched in Pompeii—the draperies fall in Greek fashion about the Buddhist deities whose round faces have the grace of the Chinese artist's brush. The glowing reds and orange and green belong to a lost art—unless it survives in Tibet.

Here wandering Nestorian priests, carrying the ritual of Christianity into Asia, had their chapels beside Buddhist temples. Libraries preserved scrolls of sacred texts in Tokharian, an Aryan script.

To the refuge of the Five Cities came Manichaean missionaries, mild devotees of light as opposed to darkness. So the hidden cross-roads became a meeting place of the gentler religions, and of the three faiths persecuted elsewhere—Manicheism, Buddhism, and Christianity in Asia. An inscription uncovered on one of the walls reads: "This place, once filled with the fumes of blood, is now cultivated as a garden." A strange garden, almost Gothic, in Asia, where the dry red earth is shadowed by forest growth. These white-robed monks and courtly ladies cultivating flowers might have come to life out of a medieval prayerbook. In fact it is the legend-ary land of Prester John of Asia, often sought and never found by the medieval wanderers.

In the northern steppes trade did not penetrate, and the only art of the nomads was the crude ornamentation of gold clasps in the shape of animals, the silverwork upon saddles and bits, and the weaving of rugs.

It was in the Five Cities that the pagan Turks found culture at the threshold of the steppes. One of the great clans, the Uighurs (the Allies), driven out of the north, settled among the Five Cities in 860. They were tall men, who had been cattle breeders. Now they turned to cultivating the soil. They adapted an ancient alphabet, to write down their speech. They wrote with a Chinese ink brush as well as a reed pen, and they ate with Chinese chop-sticks.

We know little more of them than that. In this mid-region they interbred with the descendants of the Aryans. They accepted impartially the teachings of the Buddhists, the mild Manichees and the stray Nestorian Christians. They painted their own por-traits on the rock frescoes, and even exchanged ideas with the learned men of Tuen-huang across the Gobi.

In this way the nomads gained their first culture. The Uighurs became the secretaries and professors of the steppes. Odd, that this culture should have been one of peace.

The Turks, at Journeys' Ends

Other Turkish clans, filtering from the northern breeding ground, followed the fortunes of war. Except perhaps for the Kirghiz (the Fertile Fields), a people of great power, marked by their reddish hair. The Kirghiz had driven the Uighurs before them, and now they settled down to cultivate the warmer lands north of the Altai. From the Uighurs they learned to carry on trade.

The Emperors on Horseback

Not so the Karluks (the Snow Dwellers), who trekked with their herds, carrying a wolf's head as emblem of the legendary wolf chieftain, the first of their race. They carried with them the fear of the ice-world.

They said that long ago they had been shut up in an iron mountain, until one of them, the Forge-man, had hewn a way through the iron mountain and they had escaped. This meant nothing more than a tribal memory of the time when they had worked iron in the north, after heavy rains had laid bare the metal to them. By forging iron they had made weapons with which they fought their way to freedom.

Behind the Karluks pressed other clans, out of the northern obscurity—Naïmans and Kiraïts, who began to glean the new culture of the steppes.

Some Turkish clans penetrated the mountain barrier of the south—the long line of the Tibetan plateau, the Himalayas and the Hindu Kush. One clan seizing upon Ghazni became known as the Ghaznivids. Northern India fell to them.

Wherever they emerged, they dominated. They put an end to Iranian rule. It was the victory of Turan over Iran, of the militant north over the cultured south.

They passed into the gardens of Persia. From the highlands, some of them moved down to the palaces of Baghdad, to serve the Kalif there for a space, and then to be masters of his palaces.

It was the time of Mahmoud on his golden throne, the beginning of the reign of Turkish feudal lords. Because the Turk remained, as he had been, an aristocrat. He understood kingship, himself the king. He liked to stable his horse in a royal hall. There was no greater purpose in his ambition. But in his path there remained no power able to oppose him.

So with the appearance of masterful leaders, Turkish dominance grew rapidly, in a generation, only to diminish with succeeding generations—and then to start up elsewhere under a new leader. It was as if no Turk could establish an enduring rule, yet no generation could pass without the rise somewhere of a Turkish overlord.

The Turks ruled south of the Caspian as the Khwaresm-shahs, and in Syria as Atabegs (Father-lords). The greatest of them, the

Seljuk clan, moved farther west into Asia Minor. Under Malik Shah in the eleventh century, the Seljuks held an empire that penetrated the borders of Christendom. They rode through the hills of Palestine, and came within sight of Constantinople.

And in doing so they precipitated, much to their own surprise, a counter-attack by the militant Christians of western Europe. The warlike descendants of the Franks and Germans mobilized—knights in armor and bands of serfs—to march in a mass to the aid of Constantinople. And to gain back Jerusalem, which they had been told was trodden under the hoofs of the Turkish horses.

So began the long religious war between east and west known to us as the Crusades.

So for a generation or two, at the very end of the eleventh century, the three vital forces of the west were united in a purpose. The culture of the Byzantines, still clinging to existence within the walls of Constantinople, joined with the barbaric strength of the western Franks and Germans—with Norman, Lombard, Bavarian and Saxon and Provençal—in a flame of religious zeal.

The march of the Crusaders made a common fellowship of Christian priests, peasants and lords, and astute Byzantines. But that strange fellowship did not survive for long after the capture of Jerusalem.

The Black Stone of Mecca

The Turkish *khans*, the leaders of the clans, had been pagans worshiping—if anything—the power of the eternal Blue Sky. Because their conquests drew them to the south and west, they fell under the influence of Islam. This latest of world faiths was now spreading far beyond the Arabian desert, its place of origin.

The pagan horse nomads found much in Islam to satisfy them. Its rigid fatalism fitted with their understanding of the littleness of man's endeavor against the forces of nature; its simplicity appealed to their downright minds; its war propaganda seemed most reasonable to these makers of war. So they prayed toward the Black Stone of Mecca.

They followed the blind mysticism of the *shaiks* who exhorted and prophesied, rather than the rigidity of Koranic law. They preferred not to reason why; it suited them entirely to become "warriors for the faith." Mahmoud, raiding India, posed as a champion of the faith, but his incentive was plunder.

They remained, as they had been, a warrior caste, producing nothing. The high civilization of the Arab intellectuals afforded them only physical comfort. They clad themselves in the splendors of the kalifs of Baghdad, while they made war on each other, as they had done in former times in the steppes.

At this time they lacked a guiding intellect to direct them. Omar Khayyam, contemplating them, wrote: "Sultan after Sultan abode his destined hour and went his way."

Magnificent condottieri, war lords, chivalrous cavaliers, they seemed incapable of accomplishing more than to struggle for thrones. They called themselves by resounding titles—the Valiant Lion, the Glory of the Faith. They took the daughters of kalifs in marriage, they rode through courtyards where silver lions roared when the wind blew.

But they remained *au fond* the simple horsemen that the Chinese poet had admired long since; riding out with falcons on their wrists to new adventures.* Their women, who had once been as

---

*History is just now making clear the full impetus of this foray of the Turks into the outer world. The record of their acts is obscure, and often fails us. We are fully aware of them only when they come into contact with western Europe.

The persistence of their power is amazing. The Golden Horde that dominated most of Russia under the Mongols was largely Turkish, and was known to the Russians of that time as the Kipchak Ordu—the Court of the Desert Men.

Timur-i-lang (the Iron Limper, better known to us as Tamerlane), who attempted world conquest at the end of the fourteenth century, was a Turk of mid-Asia, ruling over Turks. The Manchus who conquered China in 1644 were northern barbarians, first cousins to the earlier Turks. In fact, only China during the Ming dynasty and Persia under the Safavids were ruled by dynasties of native rather than Turkish origin, after the Turco-Mongols.

India fell under the dominion of these adventurers when a Turk of Chagatai descent named Babar made his way into India and became the first of the so-called great Moghuls (Mongols).

As late as 1680, when the better-known Othmanli Turks of Constantinople were preparing to move on Vienna, a glance at the surrounding world would have revealed Tatar khans in the Krim peninsula, and in mid-Asia, the Mamluks still the ruling force in Egypt, the Moghuls in India—Manchus in China. And even in north Africa, the Turkish Deys of Algiers and Tunis.

Much of their story is lost, and much of it is being pieced together coherently today for the first time. The fact remains, as René Grousset points out, that only the Romans

free as the warriors, they were quite willing to confine to their beds and the harems of Islam.

A Chinese of the T'ang era said: "Look not at a woman's face; consider her actions. The beauty of women is recognized only by wise men."

A Seljuk Turk said: "Do not keep a woman hanging about the house; if you do, you may not be sick, but you will live in trouble. Never let a woman amuse herself outside the house; if she goes out, she will lose her honesty. . . . How many thousands of brave men have lost their peace of mind over women? How many thousands of high and well-known persons have been put, living, because of women, under the sod?"

These restless Turks, ruling as conquerors from Delhi to Bolghar and from Aleppo to Yen-king were, however exalted, tribal chieftains. They would submit to no authority, and they had no purpose to guide them—until at the end of the twelfth century Genghis-Khan subdued them and gave them in effect a design for living.

The propagandists of Islam had not as yet penetrated far into the steppes. Some of them reached the Bulgars, isolated at the edge of the northern forests by the river Volga—and the scientific-minded Moslems were amazed by the phenomena of the distant aurora borealis in winter, and the long white nights of summer.

Elsewhere, Arab merchants and zealous *hadjis* reached the crossroads of mid-Asia where the Uighurs ruled. They built mosques beside the Buddhist temples and ancient shrines of that refuge in the mountains. But the tolerant desert folk treated Islam as another, new faith of mankind. They did not yield to it.

Only to the south had Islam claimed the Turkish clans still wandering in search of conquest, still living in the saddle and struggling with each other—the Khwaresm-shahs at the edge of the Caspian, the Turkomans of the White and Black Sheep—the Kaizaks, or Wandering Ones (who gave their name later to the Cossacks of the European steppes).

and the Turco-Mongols were capable of world mastery. What the *populi Romani* did as an aggressive citizenry, the Turks managed to accomplish by the amazing exploits of individual families.

The Emperors on Horseback

In the great Russian plain, above the Black Sea, pagan shamans trundled in their wagons beside the preachers of Islam. Here the Turkish clans had forced each other farther into the west. The half-cultured Khazars were scattered by the savage Betchenaks, who were in turn forced on by the Kankalis (High Carts) and then by the Kipchaks (Desert Men).

With these last the Russian princes waged ceaseless warfare— barbarians struggling with barbarians for the black-earth prairies.

By the middle of the twelfth century, this conflict of isolated groups had spread in devastating fashion over the larger part of the known earth. The horse nomads, little changed by the outer civilization, had become war lords—if they were powerful enough. The smaller groups were no more than bandits.

This twilight belt of savage struggle extended even over China.

Cathay

By now the Great Wall served as little more than a landmark. A wave of horsemen had passed over it, coming this time from the forests of Manchuria. They had appropriated the north of China and settled down to live in luxury within its grain fields. They were the Khitans, or Cathayans. And their conquest became *Ta Khitai*, or Great Cathay.

They numbered not a fraction of the Chinese proper, then ruled by the Sung dynasty. The Sung were in their elder age of decadence, unable to maintain canals and roads, or to guard the great mass of their workers from drought and famine in the yellow-earth region. Still less were they able to drive out the barbaric Cathayans. They made the mistake of calling in other horse nomads, from the northern breeding ground.

These were a Tungusic, or Pig people, hunters who had fished through holes in ice not long since. They were ancestors of the later Manchus, and they wore their hair long and tied tightly at the back, the first pigtails to appear within the Wall. And they were accustomed to burn the carcass of a dog at the burial of a man, so that the dog could show the spirit of the man the way through the Sky.

Summoned out of their solitudes, they conquered the Cathayans who had become city dwellers and had grown wealthy with the labor of slaves. A remnant of Cathayans fled headlong into mid-Asia to set up an empire among the mountains—*Kara Khitai*, Black Cathay. There they found themselves neighbors of the Hsians, other refugees, no more than a collection of bandit clans on the slopes of the Tibet plateau.

Masters of Cathay, the Tungusic barbarians proceeded to drive back the Chinese who had invoked them. Ferocious as animals on a hunt, they forced the Sung to the south of the swift Yang-tse, the age-old refuge of the Son of Heaven. When they killed a Chinese noble, they disemboweled him and salted his flesh, carrying his body around with them. "Salted princeling," they called it. The Chinese called them "the fools of the North."

In his turn, their chieftain became emperor of Cathay. He could think of nothing finer than softly gleaming gold. And he named his dynasty the Kin, or Golden—himself the Ta Kin, the Great Golden One, seated on the throne with the dragon heads, the throne of Yen-king (the Great Court) within the wall.

The generations that followed him exulted in the luxury of the land. The horse herds abandoned by the Khitans they used for hunting. They did not notice that the Chinese peasants burned the tall, dry grass of the pastures, to kill off the horses. They had women with perfumed fingers to wait upon them, and musicians to soothe them, like caged birds.

In their turn the Kin became indolent, as the Cathayans had been. In ritual and in thought they became Chinese.

The Year 1157

It was now the twilight of the feudal age. Vital forces sank to a low ebb.

The impetus of Greco-Roman culture, penetrating Asia, had ceased at the mountain crossroads, in the shadow of the T'ian Shan. Western Europe had become estranged from it. A scholar attempting to make a Latin translation of Aristotle could be condemned as a heretic by zealous churchmen.

The lusty vigor of invading northmen—Normans and wandering Varangians—had spent itself. The impulse of Christianity among its last converts, Slavs and Scandinavians, had ceased to stir them to new activities.

Briefly, the flame of the Crusades had blazed up, moving men in the west as if by a miracle. It had fallen to embers. Although such a magnificent condottiere as Richard Lion Heart was still to run his course. The conflict of the Crusades moved toward exhaustion and the defeat of the west.

In similar fashion the impetus of eastern culture—moving into Europe after the collapse of Rome—had spent itself. Although it remained, perhaps, the chief influence on western minds. The greatest universities were at Cordoba in Arab-dominated Spain, and in Cairo; the Moslem Idrisi was making a map of the world upon silver, in Palermo. While the schools of Paris and Bologna were little more than classrooms for Latin catechism.

But the driving force had forsaken the Arabs. Islam had taken root where it had last penetrated. The brilliance of the kalifs of Baghdad had expired.

So, too, the ascendancy of Constantinople, that had seemed perpetual, was near its end. The imperial city was in the hands of adventurers, destined soon to be sacked by a wandering fleet of Crusaders.

The silk route, that ancient link between the east and the far west,* had been cut in a dozen places, overrun by Turkish condottieri. These Turks themselves had settled into stagnation—except for the Seljuks who still wandered, spurred into activity by the conflict of the Crusades. Not that the Turks had become degenerate. They had simply dismounted, taking root in a score of palaces.

They had become war lords, like the feudal nobles of Europe; landowners, served by slaves and protected by men-at-arms, many or few. The story of such war lords was the same, in Delhi or Paris: raid and siege, burning and seizing. The peasants got what

---

*It must be remembered that no such thing as a geographical boundary exists between Europe and Asia. Nor has it ever existed, in spite of the boundary stone that the czarist Russians placed in the Ural region.

In 1157 the dividing line between European and Asiatic civilization might have run from Venice to the Prussian forests. But Venice was half oriental, and the Finns at the end of the Baltic were assuredly Asiatics.

Europe was then no more than a distant peninsula of the known world, its peoples much more ignorant than the Asiatics.

food they could out of the earth, while their masters changed. They had no protection against plague or famine, or the muster-of-arms. They had no conception of any safeguard.

Beside the war lords, another class had grown in power. The merchant, who controlled supplies whether of grain or cloth or horseflesh, or slaves. These great merchants, often usurers, were Arabs for the most part, in Asia. Like the adventurous seafarers—Venetians—in Europe, they served as the advisers of kings and were capable of outfitting armies.

Above the cloud level, in Tibet, a new force was at work, in seclusion. Converts to the lord Buddha were building lamaseries as places of refuge.

Chinese civilization had reached a point of exhaustion. Li T'ai po had said of it: "We watch all things drift by, human souls and their doings, like the restless waters of the Yang-tse, floating by to lose themselves in the sea."

The reigning dynasty of the Sung had lost the vigor of the splendid T'ang period. It created clever paintings, and mused on its drift toward futility. Its artists shaped vases in the sensuous lines of women's hips. China, the ever-prolific, had become wearied of production.

This same inertia held the northern steppes in the year 1157. The great Turkish migrations had ceased. The era of primitive force seemed to have come to an end. The area of good grazing had diminished; the desert had encroached further toward the forest belt.

The movement of the immense patriarchal clans had slowed down and almost ceased to be. In previous centuries the nomads had grouped together, pitched their *ger* or individual tents in a wide circle that gave grazing room to the immense herds they tended. They had been then, in fact, the *ger-igren,* "people of the felt tents."

Now, in this feudal twilight, the tribal society had changed. Internal struggles had brought to supremacy individual warriors —*tarkhans.* These war lords of the prairies dwelt apart from each other. They protected their herds with armed followings, and the wealthiest of them became the aristocrats of the steppes, the *noyans*, or princes.

The social unit, instead of the great clan, had become the *usun*, the "bone" or family. Wealthy families with large horse herds could support a large following of armed riders, with slaves to do the menial work of the camp. Weak "bones" were driven to fare as best they could outside the lands of the aristocrats.

At that time no people held together in the northern prairies.

In that year the Mongols were scattered into small bands, following the local war lords in the grazing lands between the rivers southeast of Lake Baikal, the Onon and Kerulan. They were kept scattered by the activities of the Kin frontier generals, who paid the small but aggressive neighboring tribe, which happened to be the Tatars of the Buyar Lake pasturages, to raid the Mongol noyans. And these Mongol cattle lords had sunk so low that they depended on wandering Chinese merchants for supplies of grain and cloth and iron weapons.

It was in one of the broken-down families, the refugees, that a boy was born during this year of the Hare clutching a clot of blood in his hand. He came into the world with little else except the strong instinct to survive.

Genghis-Khan

His people, the Mongols, were scattered into small clans of perhaps a thousand families in all. His own clan, the Kiyat, had cast out his family. "Except for our shadows," his mother assured him when he was old enough to hunt for himself, "nothing clings to us. We have no friends. Except for a horse's tail, we have no whip."

His ancestors, it is true, had been *Borjigun*, Blue-eyed Men, legendary heroes of the steppes. His mother chanted the strength of the *Borjigun:* "Their voices rolled like thunder in the mountains. Their hands were strong as bears' paws—breaking men in two as easily as arrows. In winter nights they slept naked by a fire of mighty trees, and they felt the sparks and embers that fell on them no more than insect bites."

This boy had been named Temujin by his father at birth. The

father had looked around, and had christened the son after the first thing that caught his eye, which happened to be either a piece of iron, or a blacksmith at work with iron. Not for many years did the nomads greet him by the title of Genghis-Khan.

His father died, poisoned by enemies, before he was old enough to go on his first hunt. About that time the wealthier Mongol tarkhans were more widely separated by a raid of the Tatars who served the Kin.

The boy Temujin and his brothers hunted marmots and mice, to fill their bellies. They even caught fish in the streams—the last thing a Mongol would eat. When a stepbrother stole fish from him, Temujin and a blood brother killed the offender. They went to him outside the tents, one going before and the other behind. When the stepbrother saw them and knelt down, Temujin killed him with an arrow.

Temujin contrived to keep life in his body. And the impact of that life upon the civilized world was greater than that of any other man of the steppes. The force of twelve hundred years of the nomad migrations was compressed into the acts of this one Mongol.

This conquest of the known world by a barbarian who had never seen a city and did not know the use of writing has mystified people since his time. They have seen in him the scourge of God, loosed upon a civilization that had endured beyond its time. The Mongols themselves believed Genghis-Khan to be a *bogdo*, a spirit of the Everlasting Sky. Instead of a mystery, they accepted him quite simply as a miracle.

He himself did not believe in miracles. We can be certain from his acts that he did not at first anticipate his amazing victories over the forces of civilization. These victories convinced him, after the middle of his age, that with his Mongols he could achieve dominion over the other peoples of the earth. The Everlasting Sky, apparently, had given him this power.

Once Bela Noyan, a companion of his conquests, questioned him about it. "Men call you hero, and lord of power. What traces of such victory are there in your hand?"

Genghis-Khan answered: "This. Before I came to the seat of

empire, I was riding one day down a path. The path crossed a bridge, and there six men were lying, hidden, to attempt my life. When I saw them I drew my sword and rode at them. They rose, to meet me with a flight of arrows. But none of the arrows touched me. I killed the men with my sword and passed on unhurt.

"Riding back, I passed the place where I had killed those men. Their six horses were grazing, riderless, and I drove them to the place of my camp."

He did not say that divine aid had accomplished this. The arrows had missed him, so he had been able to slay the attackers and take their horses.

Many others have sought, after Bela Noyan, for the secret of his achievement. It was fate, they argued. Or a superlative genius. His life coincided with a vast exodus of the nomads, at a time when the surrounding powers of civilization were weak. He managed to terrorize all opposition. . . .

All this, that might have yielded the secret of another man, fails to explain Genghis-Khan, who was a simple barbarian, a man who did not leave his native steppes for the first forty years of his life.

His strange genius lay in his immense strength of will. This will was directed to one end, to overcome all opposition. He once asked his companions and commanders what they had found to be the greatest satisfaction in life. They thought it over, and answered in turn: "To ride out to hunting on a swift, good horse when the grass turns green and you hold a falcon on your wrist."

"No," the Mongol khan decided, "a man's highest joy in life is to break his enemies, to drive them before him, to take from them all the things that have been theirs, to hear the weeping of those who cherished them, to take their horses between his knees, and to press in his arms the most desirable of their women."

His Mongols had answered as nomads of the steppes, without other thought than their age-old enjoyment. Genghis-Khan had thought only of the joy of conquest.

In this lies the explanation of his strange character. Never was a man more shaped by the earth of his homeland. He did not change. But never had so strong a nature emerged from the steppes into the outer world. To understand this, it is only needful to look at his homeland, and the men who live in it.

The Mongols

They live apart, as did the first horse nomads. Men with long bodies greased to keep out the cold, and short legs shaped to a horse's body. They have senses keen as an animal's—they can see far in the night, they can tell where they are in the steppes by dismounting and examining the grass and moss of the ground.

Braced in their short stirrups, they ride watching the skyline. Beyond that skyline are enemies that may at any time hunt them away from their herds, and they cling to life with stubborn endurance.

A lance or long, curved sword hangs behind the rider's shoulder. A hand ax or horn-strengthened bow is in the case at his left hip; on the right side, a case of arrows ready to his fingers. He can draw those arrows and shoot them very quickly.

His forefathers were hunters, and the Mongol hunts methodically, knowing the habits of game—waiting concealed, or driving the herds of antelope and wild horses to pen them against a natural barrier, where they can be killed off. He needs the meat of the carcasses, and the hide. He even eats the intestines and drinks of the blood. He does this instinctively, without realizing that by this uncooked flesh he is hardening his body against the bitter cold of his plateaus.

For sport he trains falcons, flying them at winged game his arrows cannot reach. When he has food he stuffs himself until he chokes—obeying an instinct stronger than hunger.

As he eats to get full, he drinks to get drunk. But he has only fermented animal milk—mare's milk is the choicest—that is a food in itself and intoxicates slowly. When he is at ease, he likes to listen to the chants of the elder men, of the Blue Wolf, their ancestress, and the heroes who leaped their horses between mountain tops and fought with the kelets, the spirits. He relishes these ancient words of power chanted to the whine of the blind men's fiddles.

He is merry at such times, in the ger. For his home is still the beehive tent of layers of felt stretched around a framework of woven wands. This heavy felt of animal hair, oiled, or thickened with milk, keeps out the cold. The opening in the center of the dome lets out smoke, that blackens the inside. The outside is brightened with powdered chalk.

Especially in the spring when the herds drop their young, when the new grass comes, and milk and meat are plentiful, the Mongols rejoice in the fullness of their bodies. Then they mount their shaggy ponies and gather together for *ikhudur*, festival—slaughtering sheep and fat horses. Clumsily they dance, their hide boots stamping the ground.

The old men and the *bagaturs*—the venomous fighters, the slayers—sit by the *yurt* fires of thornbush and dried dung, exchanging the news of the steppes from the Mountain of Power to the frontier posts. The listeners fix the words in their minds, visioning the happenings, so that they can repeat them in their home tents.

For they care nothing for written words. They have no skill in arts that do not concern the feeding of human bodies or the care of herds.

Such matters as the building of walled towns and the payment of taxes, the science of medicine and the complexities of a priesthood dwelling in pagodas, are problems of the outer world, not of their inner world of the steppes.

Of nights, they do not look too long at the moon, because they know that Sky-walker has a lasso that might noose a man who looks at him too long. Those of them who have come out of the forests—the *oyin-igren*—believe that the Sun, that other Walker-around, drives reindeer across the path in the Sky. White reindeer, or dogs, they do not know which.

When the *kele* of sickness invades their yurts, they summon a shaman, to drive out the devil with drumbeat and dance. For the shamans can speak to the Sky; they know the ways of the spirits. The fear of destructive spirits is still in these Mongols. To stumble on the threshold of a tent means that misfortune may come to that tent. To bring wet boots inside means to risk the blows of thunder or lightning from the Sky. The Mongol will not dwell in a camp that has been struck by lightning.

The March of the Barbarians

On the inside of the tent entrance he draws crude figures or places images of felt there. Before he will eat himself, he rubs the food across the lips of the images.

When the *buran*, the black wind of the north, sweeps the prairies, he rolls himself in sheepskins and deer hides, lying close to the fire of his domed tent, and he outlives the storm. He is not aware that this cold and the long winter nights would touch him with arctic madness, hysteria, if he did not amuse himself until he choked with laughter, at these festivals.

When women, more sensitive than men, fall victim to this hysteria, they tear off their clothes and wound themselves with knives. In the sunlight of the mild spring there is no madness, and the Mongols rejoice. They place their tents on the wide wagon frames, *kibitkas*, and move down toward the lowlands south of the Mountain of Power. Oxen draw the kibitkas over the prairies at a slow pace.

The Mongols do not know that these prairies are shrinking, drawing back farther to the north, away from the sands of the Gobi, and that they themselves are drawing farther away from the habitations of civilization.

One of the first Europeans to venture among them, in their homeland, was a Franciscan friar, William of Rubruk, and—although he saw them three generations later—he gives clear testimony of the isolation of their life in the steppes. He said he felt as if he had entered another world when he came among the Tartars, as he calls them.

"The Tartars have no city of their own," he relates. "And they are ignorant of the future. Yet each chieftain knows the limits of his pastures and where he ought to let his herds feed in winter and summer—when they come down to the warmer plains of the south. Such pastures as have no water are reserved for winter, when there is snow on the ground.

"The houses in which they sleep are covered with white felt, over a framework of wattled rods. Sometimes the felt is brightened with paintings of vines and birds and beasts. They are mounted upon wagon frames, and I measured the distance between the wheels of one to be twenty feet. I have counted twenty-two bullocks dragging one wagon-house. Their household goods and treasure they put in chests upon higher carts drawn by camels, that can cross rivers without harm.

"When the living-houses are unloaded from the wagons, their doors are always turned to the south, and the carts with the chests are drawn up in two rows, about a stone's throw away.

"The married women get the more beautiful carts made for them. One rich Mongol or Tartar will have from a hundred to two hundred such carts with chests. When the camp is pitched, the house of the first wife is placed on the west of the Mongol's—the others stretch toward the east, a stone's throw apart. When I met such a camp on the move, I thought that a great city was traveling toward us. I was astonished at the immense droves of oxen and horses and flocks of sheep, though I saw very few men to herd them.

"One girl is able to drive twenty or thirty carts. The ground is quite level, so they fasten the carts and wagons together, and the girl sits on the front of the leading cart, guiding the cattle, while all the rest follow. They travel slowly—only as fast as an ox or lamb can walk.

"When the house is on the ground, the bed of the master is placed opposite the door. Over the head of the lord hangs an image or puppet of felt, which is called the master's brother. When they meet together for drinking, they first sprinkle some of the wine or milk over this idol. After this a servant goes out of the house with a cup and sprinkles thrice toward the south, kneeling, in honor of the fire; then toward the east, in honor of the air, and the north, for the dead. Then he carries drink to the lord and his wife who sit on a bed. In winter they have excellent drink of rice, millet or honey mead; in summer they drink only the mare's milk which always stands by the door. Beside it is a minstrel with his fiddle.

"When the lord has more than one wife, she with whom he slept the night before sits beside him that day, and the other wives must come to her house to drink. The gifts the lord gets that day are put in her chests.

"As the lord drinks, one of the servants shouts 'Hai!' and the

[*43*]

minstrel begins to play. When they make a great feast, the guests
all strike their hands together, and dance to the music—the men
before the lord and the women before the lady of the house. At a
feast after a victory they sometimes get beastly drunk.

"When they want to honor a person, three of them take a full
cup, moving toward him, singing and dancing and stamping with
their feet until he has finished the cup. . . .

"The men make bows and arrows, and saddles. They build the
houses and carts, take care of the horses and milk the mares. Of felt
they also make cloths, to put under their saddles.

"During winter they wear at least two fur garments, one with the
fur inward, the other with the fur outward. Their breeches are
made of skins, and they often line their garments with silk shag,
which is exceeding light, soft and warm. . . .

"Out of the horns of mountain sheep they make their large
drinking cups—of such amazing size that I was hardly able to lift
a pair of them with one hand. The Tartars are most excellent
hunters, and they get a great share of their food by the chase. They
have falcons, gerfalcons and other hawks in abundance, which
they carry on their right hands, and cast off after game.

"The women all sit astride on horseback, like men, binding
their mantles round their waists with sky-blue sashes, and they
bind another scarf around their breasts. . . . No man can have a
wife unless he buys her, so many maids are mature before marriage. Widows never marry, as they believe that they who have
served a man in this life shall do so in the next. Hence arises an
abominable custom—that the son sometimes marries all his
father's wives except his own mother. For the household of the
father and mother always devolves to the youngest son. He has to
provide for all his father's wives.

"The women employ themselves in guiding the wagons, loading
pack animals, milking cows, making butter and dressing skins—
in which they use sinews finely split and twisted into long threads.
They likewise make sandals and socks and other garments, and
felts for the tents. They never wash their garments, saying that it
would offend God to do so. They are amazingly afraid of thunder,
turning all strangers out of their dwellings and wrapping them-

selves up in black felt until it is over. When they wash their hands or heads, they fill their mouths with water which they squirt out gradually on their hands. . . .

"When anyone lies sick in bed, a mark is made on the house so that no one may enter—as no Mongol ever visits the sick man, except his own servant. When nobles of the great court are sick, watchmen are placed at a distance all around, so that no one may enter the vicinity. They dread that evil spirits, or bad winds, might enter along with the visitors. They consider their magicians, or people who practice divination, as priests."

The Frontier

In the no-man's-land between the steppes and cultivation, there are only the crossroads towns where Chinese traders come. Corrals for animals, with huts of dried mud brick, and perhaps a small temple or painted Buddhist shrine.

At times the nomads drive in horses and sheep. Or they sell their winter's catch of furs, marmot and sable and mink, to the traders, who cheat them. The traders have iron fire-strikers, Chinese silks and lacquerwork, embroidery, thread and silver set with pearls and turquoises, to catch the eyes of the nomad women.

On their part, the Mongols despise the merchants, traffickers of the "hat and girdle people," as they call the town dwellers. But to the Mongols themselves the hat and girdle were important emblems. To take off their wide-crowned felt hats, to loosen their girdles and hang them over their shoulders, was a sign of submission. The men of the tribes did that, when the tribal council chose a new chieftain, and raised him, protesting, upon a carpet of felt for all the eyes to see him and know him. To others than their elected chieftains—the khans—the Mongols had no least inclination to submit.

They knew that in earlier times many tribes had gone forth beyond the steppes, to make conquest or to serve new masters. But the elder Mongols had little good to say of that.

"Why go ye forth to the east and the west?" they complained. "Why go ye with lust for war? What comes of it, save that your blood is shed like water, your bones heaped up like mountains, your strong sons bear the yoke of slaves, your clean daughters are defiled?"

These elder spokesmen were contemptuous of the Cathayans who had left the forests to dwell within walls. "They have a throne. And what does that mean? They have thousands of women and musicians and mummers. They spend their hours in hawking and riding about; they fill themselves with wine, keeping worthless persons about, to amuse them. And in this way they have fallen into the dirt."

Better, the elder men argued, to be as the Mongols were—free, owing service to no one. Free as the wild fowl that flew, crying, over the lakes. Wandering, without the need to settle down. "In winter, may we eat toward the south," they chanted, as they drank. "In summer may we eat toward the north. May we find plenty of wild swine and deer in the hunts."

To live otherwise, as civilized people, within walls, was to become softened and weak—fit only to be in bondage, to labor under a master, to be ruled; while the nomads were hard and enduring, capable of ruling.

This pride of the nomads actuated all they did. They fought savagely to keep their personal liberty. At the same time, they coveted the rich possessions of the civilized areas. Such possessions meant security and endless feasting.

The Mongols longed to bring into the steppes and to have for their own the thousands of women, the cartloads of grain, the trained hawks and limitless wine the Cathayans and the Golden people enjoyed. . . . They did not think that they, the Mongols, descendants of the Blue Wolf, would ever fall into the dirt.

For a while the Mongols waver between the frontier and the fastness of the inner prairies. In the north there is safety from enemies. But there the wind of the ice-world awaits them, and the long nights that breed madness. The line of the Borjigun is broken; they have no longer the mighty Borjigun to lead them, the Blue-eyed men of power who were like strong, unbroken rocks and rushing torrents.

They have only the steppe aristocracy, the noyans and the

owners of the greater horse herds, as well as the tarkhans who have the right of keeping the spoil of battle. These are willing to raid and fight along the frontier, to keep the ancestral grazing lands between the Onon and the Kerulan waters where the dark slopes of the Burkhan Kaldun, the Mountain of Power, rise over the plain. Here the cattle grazes.

The masters of the sheep herds, lesser aristocrats have to seek different ground; they have feuds with the cattle breeders, and they live closer to the earth—hunting for game.

Beyond them, the forest hunters have less claim to distinction. They are more savage, their *beki* or chieftain half a magician who speaks with spirits. The Uriangut and Oyrat are forest tribes. They have seen the *Vairgin*, the Reindeer Spirit, moving at nights through the tree growth.

Least of all, the black-boned people who cultivate the earth in the northwest desire to move from the wilderness. They have taken root in the earth. They have no slaves, taken in battle, to serve them. The shadow of starvation lies over them.

"The earth," it was said of them, "was bitter to them, and the sun did not shine into such a place."

The old, orderly pastoral existence, in which the families of the steppes had their appointed places in grazing and hunting within the usun, the blood clan, had ended. The clans no longer formed a people for mutual protection. Conflict divided them, and except for the wealthy herd owners they were close to starvation.

"The younger ones," the chronicler Rashid says of them, "failed to obey the wise words of their elders. Many began to steal, to rebel and to rob. The horse herds and cattle were given no quiet. The best horses, ridden incessantly, were giving out, and had to be slain."

With the thinning of their herds, the Mongols are reduced to hunger. The security of the old nomad life is ended, in a turmoil of intertribal conflict.

The Women

More than the men, the steppe women cherish their freedom. They are mistresses of the yurts, the care of the family property lies upon them. While the men are off on a hunt, or raid or war, the women have to manage as best they can, not knowing what the next day might bring.

The Mongol women of that time wear garments like men—sheepskin-lined boots with high heels, often brightly painted. Their breeches and the wide coats folded over their breasts are much the same, except that they manage to find silk to wear, if possible. Only their hats look different, for they do not like the wide felt brims that can be turned up during the heat, and turned down over the shoulders in a storm.

To tend the herds, they have to ride like their men, to make stages of seventy miles in a day. The only veils they wear are the white cloths hanging from below their eyes over their breasts to shield them from dust and the ceaseless wind. They can kill wolves with arrows, and they often go with their men to war. Sometimes they join in the fighting.

With them rests the success or failure of the family economy. Their hands must press the felts, and split cords from dried tendons of slaughtered animals, curing the hides with salt. Or preserve the precious milk by shaking it in leather sacks until it curdles. They gather dung and make it into fuel cakes, stacking it to dry.

The tent furniture is no more than can be carried on animal-back; lacquered chests, iron pots and leather sacks for barley and dried meat. Often, on long journeys, some of this dried meat is carried under the saddles, so the warmth and friction of the horse's back will soften it. Dried milk curds, put in a sack with water, and shaken into liquid by the riding, make a meal at need—when the riders cannot dismount to cook.

Everything must be put to use for the family. The women are covetous of goods from the outer world. From unraveled hemp or horsehair they plait supple lariats for the riders.

Inside the ger, they portion out the food and prepare it. When guests appear they sit ceremoniously at the feet of the husband, on his left hand, the side of honor because it is next his heart—the right side of the tent entrance.

Each wife has a tent home of her own, and servants in the wealthier families. When the master dies, the first wife has little time for mourning—she is the head of the house, responsible for its affairs, unless a grown son or brother takes over her duties.

If the dead man be the head of a clan, the first wife rules the clan until his successor is appointed. Then the new chieftain may take the widows of the dead man for his wives.

The young girls of the ordu, the encampment, are not leisurely creatures. Their duty is to aid the elder women, and they do not become important until they are bought or stolen in marriage. After that, they may bind up their long hair, shaving it across the top of their foreheads, and wear a birch diadem with flowers—of gold, if the husband be rich. And this husband will not be one of their own intimates. The law of the steppes requires men to marry outside the clan. So the brides leave their own ordus, to breed and raise their children among strangers.

Honor comes to them with the birth of the first son. Not before. "Young girls," a Mongol proverb relates, "have long hair and short intelligence."

Living beside men, in the ever-moving camps, handsome girls must protect themselves or be taken by the men. "Lacking a mother," a proverb runs, "a girl becomes loose."

Not that that is a stigma in the eyes of the steppe dweller, who cares more for the *jeldn*, the woman experienced at love, than for a timid girl. Even when she is mistress of a yurt, the nomad woman must be ready to deal with wanderers, especially cunning shamans who offer her love spells. Often she is carried off in a raid, to become the property of another man and give birth to his children, until she is redeemed from captivity, or taken by another raider.

She has the vitality of a splendid animal, and the patience of one who pits her body against the blind forces of nature. She must nurse her strength herself, for physicians do not enter the steppes. She is fortunate if she is not weakened by dysentery or broken bones before she is thirty. Yet there is a merry and mischievous spirit in her, and the creatures of the yurt who look to her for nourishment come for her guidance in misfortune. "Every mouth," the Mongols say, "must be fed."

"It matters not so much," the steppe dwellers admit, "if a man lose his father, if he have a mother."

The March of the Barbarians

The mother of Genghis-Khan was taken by raid from another tribe. She bore sons to his father, Yesukai. After Yesukai's death, by poison, she kept life in the boys. She taught them the legends of the Borjigun, putting into their minds the power of their ancestors, while they were adolescent.

Bortai, the first wife of Genghis-Khan, brought him something of wealth—a sable cloak given him at their marriage. She saved him from ambush by his enemies. When she was carried off by Tatars in a raid, she gave him a bastard for his eldest son. But by the sagacity of his mother and the devotion of his wife, Genghis-Khan survived.

The Miracle

In all of this lies the explanation of the strange nature of Genghis-Khan. He was hunted through the steppes, until he came to realize that his only safety would be the destruction of his enemies. He trusted only his companions of those early, outlaw years—those who had drunk the headwaters of the Kerulan with him. One had sucked stiffened blood from his throat when he was wounded. Another had watched over him while he slept in the snow. The chosen ones became *andas*, brothers in arms, united by the blood they had drunk from the other's veins.

Outside this narrow circle of warriors, he trusted no one except Bortai and the sons he bred.

His suspicion was that of a hunted animal. When he had the power to do so, he scattered the neighboring tribes, tracking down their leaders and slaying them. Those who were of the lineage of the great khans, he suffocated in felt cloths, or strangled, so that he did not cause their blood to run. For that would be a sin, liable to be revenged by the power of the Sky.

Those who came to him of their own will and offered to serve him, he cherished—and watched. And he had one quality dear to the nomads. He gave away all he possessed, at times, to those who fought for his life. "He will get down from the horse he rides," they said, "and bestow it as a gift."

The steppes chanted the strength of his chosen companions. "They are his hounds—they feed on human flesh. They are held by him in a leash of iron. Their heads are hard as bronze, their teeth gnaw into rocks, their hearts are iron. Night dew is their drink, and the winds speed them when they ride.

"When he unleashes them, they throw away their whips and carry curved swords in their hands. Then the foam flies from their mouths, and they are filled with joy."

Here we see the clearest side of his genius. He could judge men with extraordinary skill, and use them. He did not spare them—his leash was really of iron—but he rewarded them immensely. Like most Mongols, he had the patience of a hunter. By degrees—it was never easy—he learned to hold his own sharp temper in check. Unlike the mass of nomads, he had an inflexible determination.

He was not satisfied with a victory. He felt no security until the steppes were cleared of all leaders strong enough to resist him. Driven by his own fear of disaster, he enforced his will on the broken tribes by a discipline from which there was no escape. He told one of his commanders: "If any one fails to obey you, send him to me to be judged, if I know him. If not, put him to death at once."

This military discipline had never been so enforced in the steppes. Nor had men been so bound, before, to serve one commander.

They came to fear this tall man with the catlike eyes and the long beard. At the same time they wondered at his continued victories. A shaman said: "The power of the Everlasting Blue Sky has descended on him. Here on earth, he is its agent."

The Year 1206

The aristocrats of the steppes who had survived these tribal wars assembled around their fires and discussed who should be chosen as leader. Not without argument did they agree on the Mongol who had prevailed in the battles. But no one else was willing to serve as khan. Two noyans of the oldest families went to him, and said: "We have made up our minds to name you Khan. When you are Khan, we will obey you. We shall stand in the front of battle against your foes. When we take captive beautiful girls, we will give the best of them to you. When you hunt, we will start earliest into the field, and the beasts we bring down we will take to you. If at any time we disobey your word or do injury to you, then take from us our wives and possessions, and turn us out into the waste-lands."

The Mongol took them at their word, without comment. His first act was to protect himself by organizing the *keshik*, the Khan's Guard of chosen men, devoted to himself.

He allowed the nomads who followed him no more idleness. To their accustomed, haphazard life he gave a purpose. Instead of a coalition of tribes—the ancient pastoral *ulus*—he formed an army; a permanent army of horsemen, with tribes merged into regiments. Into this army he drafted the best of the men able to ride, over fourteen years of age and less than seventy. Able-bodied men not chosen for the army were given the duty of caring for roads and transport animals. The weaker sort of men, armed only with sticks and whips, cared for the herds. The work in the home encampments he left to the women, the boys and elders.

The new regiments of the *kul* or center of the army kept at home —the Guard went with the Khan. The *jun-gar*, or Left Wing operated in the east, the *barun-gar*, the Right Wing, in the western regions.

The nomads grew accustomed to the new routine of continued warfare. Women, immature boys and household slaves kept up the yurts, with a new sense of security. While the army, led by this strange, inflexible Mongol, was absent from the home grazing lands, they were safe from raids. This army cleared the steppes from the Altai to the forests of Manchuria. It broke up the power-ful Kraït Turks.

The officers commanding the new units were kinsmen of the warriors in the ranks. Sons began to take the places of their fathers. By degrees all the former tribesmen—the Urianguts, Oyrats, Merkits, the reckless Tatars, and the superior Kraïts—coalesced into the regiments of the great Ordu.

Now in the spring and autumn they were allowed to go on the tribal hunts, to kill game for food. Spoil taken in battle was divided evenly and sent back to the home yurts. A new economy appeared in the steppes—a military economy, regulated by the cautious

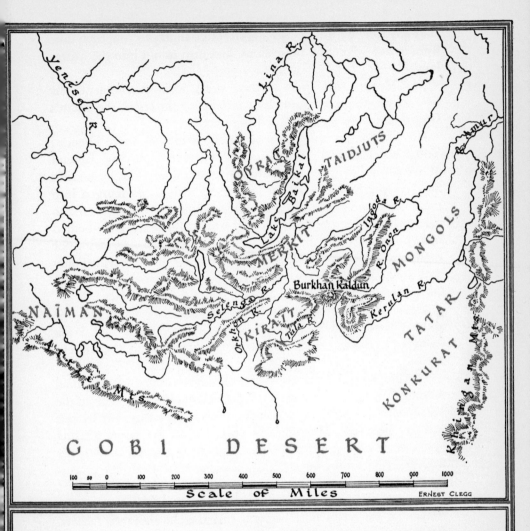

Grazing lands of the nomad clans of the Lake Baikal region which formed the confederacy under Genghis-Khan. The Mongol khan made the nucleus of his army from these clans. The burial site of the nomad khans was on the sunny or south side of Burkhan-Kaldun (the Mountain of Power) between the headwaters of the Kerulan and Tula Rivers.

Mongol, who was suspicious of everything that did not serve him. The other tribesmen began, naturally, to call themselves Mongols.

In the year of the Leopard, which is 1206 A.D., their leader summoned a *kuriltai*. To this council of the blood aristocrats came all the commanders of the army, to the home grazing lands of the Mongols at the headwaters of the Onon. And there they named him Genghis-Khan. The meaning of this name is doubtful. It may signify the great khan, or the bright-shining khan. Genghis-Khan never took the title of khakhan or emperor. The title of khakhan signifies supreme ruler—derived from the Turkish *kagan*. Genghis-Khan allowed no titles among his new subjects. The only distinctive terms were *Sechen*, Wise, and *Bagatur*, Valiant.

There Genghis-Khan made a promise to those he called his venomous fighters.

"My warriors are dark and sturdy as the many trees of a forest. I shall refresh their mouths with sweet sugar. I shall hang brocades upon their shoulders, and seat them in the saddles of swift geldings. They shall drink from clean and pleasant rivers, just as their horses will graze upon high, rich grass. From the new roads which serve my people, all harmful things shall be cleared, and no thornbush or weeds shall grow in their pasturelands."

He had been thinking over the mouthings of the soothsayers. Whether he believed them or not, he saw the advantage to be gained by prophecy.

"The Sky," he informed his followers, "has appointed me to rule all the generation living in felt tents."

He was then forty-nine years of age. And he kept his promise to his nomads—probably to a greater degree than he himself had expected. This poetic chant of his, put into words they understood, and fixed in the minds of the listeners without a word written down, became his testament to them, because he succeeded beyond their utmost expectation.

Dreading the outbreak of old intertribal feuds, he made it a crime to quarrel—for one who called himself Mongol to strike another. And the predatory tribes themselves were fast disappearing into the Banners (the regiments—the Thousands) of the new army of the steppes.

"From this time," he told those who listened, "I shall speak words of mercy, and I shall distribute the Thousands of men among those who aided me in this labor."

And the shaman Geukchu said of him, before the assembled noyans and bagaturs, "The power of the Everlasting Blue Sky has descended on him. Here, upon earth, he is its agent."

This, to the listeners, appeared most reasonable. Hereafter, in all the acts of the Mongol chieftain, the power of the Sky might be expected to appear. Had he not raised his family above others among the Mongols, and raised the Mongol clan above the other tent-dwelling peoples? Was he not the offspring of the legendary Blue Wolf, heritor of the Borjigun? Invisible, the guardian spirits of the waters and the forests would bear him company where he went.

How much Genghis-Khan himself believed this, we do not know. But from that day he acted upon it. Incurably superstitious, like all the nomads, he fought against his superstition. He had the shamans make their predictions before him; he scrutinized the lines in the thigh bones of sheep that they burned in fire. But he shaped his own plans. He would believe nothing outside his own experience.

He demanded loyalty among those who served him—the loyalty of a vassal to his master. It became known in the steppes that traitors who brought their lords captive to the dark khan of the Mongols would be put to death. On the other hand, Genghis-Khan was merciful to those who fought to the end for their masters. Upon such tested loyalty he put great value.

"You fought for three days," he said to one Kiraït, "to give your lord time and space to escape. Serve me in this way. Be my companion."

The steppe dwellers understood and appreciated this code. Genghis-Khan had no moral inhibitions in dealing with an enemy. Trickery and treachery were weapons to be used as well as steel. But to his own followers he kept his word. "A word spoken at sunrise and forgotten at night is faithless," he told them. "I have promised you mercy. Be content."

His supremacy over the tribes did not satisfy him. In the west

[*54*]

and south were peoples of the forest who harvested grain and dealt with merchants. The material goods of these peoples gave them security; this wealth was a permanent thing, and might give them power over the tent dwellers. He sent his eldest son to subdue the forest people, the Kirghiz. And he gave to this son the western forests—a circumstance that had great consequences thereafter.

The intelligent Uighurs made submission after a brief struggle. Among the captives from the Naïmans, Genghis-Khan encountered a lettered Uighur, Keeper of the Seal, Tatatunga by name. He was brought forcibly into contact with writing for the first time—discovering that Tatatunga could make written signs that preserved the spoken Mongol words. And Genghis-Khan ordered that the younger sons of his family should be taught this writing.

He summoned learned Uighurs to talk with him, and he learned much from Arab merchants who could describe the outer world. As with the soothsayers of the steppes, the savage Mongol listened to them, storing up knowledge, without following their advice.

The Ride Against the Walls

It was inevitable that the Mongol who ruled the steppes and the Golden Emperor who reigned behind the Great Wall could not exist side by side. The Kin dynasty had endeavored to drive the nomads further into the northern wastelands. Now the nomads struck back at the wealth of the cultivated lands.

Genghis-Khan moved with the caution of a stalking animal. He took pains to rid his people of their awe of Cathay and its Golden Emperor. "The Son of Heaven," he told them, "should be an extraordinary man, but this one is unworthy a throne." And he spat toward the south.

Before turning against the Kin empire, he subdued the strange bandit kingdom of Hsi-Hsia on his flank. This gave him experience with his new formations of massed riders, and it cleared his flank. He led the former nomads—now the horsemen of a disciplined army—through the Great Wall with the care of a shepherd tending a flock. He took no chances.

In at least one respect he changed the accustomed tactics of the nomads. Hitherto, the Banners or regiments of the steppe dwellers had been loosely knit. Genghis-Khan doubled the number of riders in such a formation. So, in an attack a new Mongol regiment charged with weight and the power of close formation. In this way the Mongol commander had fewer units to handle.

The Kin commanders had planned to attack him; so he struck them first. He unleashed the speed of his horsemen, and led them in nomad tactics that they understood—in wide circling movements that cut off the slower and more numerous armies of the Kin.

For the first years he was content with driving off the herds and the spoil gathered up by the Mongols after a victory. On the march he put his divisions through maneuvers, never relaxing his rigid discipline. Carefully he avoided the strong, walled towns of civilization, retiring swiftly beyond the Wall with his gains.

Then, when he felt sure of his mounted divisions, he apportioned them under the command of his four sons, so that they would be able to strike from four directions at once. The armies of the Kin, moving blindly in quest of the Mongols, were broken by this swift concentration. The Mongol had clear information about the enemy. He was well served by his "eyes and ears."

And barbarian forces, enlisted under the Kin, went over to the victorious nomads, realizing that this was no raid of tribesmen snatching at booty, but the methodical advance of a conqueror.

Those who submitted were well treated—in spite of the tales of a holocaust wrought by the Mongol horsemen in Cathay. Genghis-Khan was quick to seize the advantage these new recruits gave him. He judged men at a glance, and accepted them. In the five years that his columns threaded through north China, it became apparent to the Kin soldiery that the Mongols could not be resisted.

Only the walled cities remained to be taken. Against these, the old Mongol used terror as a weapon. He announced that no lives would be spared in a citadel that resisted a Mongol siege. Carefully he launched his divisions in their first siege operations. In this he profited from the advice of the Kin officers who had joined his standard. And resistance was crushed with inhuman, methodical massacre of all lives within the walls.

From this destruction, the Mongols retrieved only the things that might be of use to them in the steppes—the foodstuffs to be carted away, strong young slaves to serve them, woven stuffs and precious metals and weapons. The rest was torn down, kindled into conflagration. Genghis-Khan had determined to leave no walled structures that might shelter men against him in the future. Once he had taken away the harvested grains, he was willing to let cultivated lands be overgrown with grass that could feed horse herds and cattle.

"Since the beginning of the world," a Chinese exclaimed, "no nation has been as powerful as these Mongols are now. They annihilate empires as if they were tearing up grass. Why does Heaven permit it?"

It was not, however, any heavenly force, but the ceaseless vigilance of a savage mind that permitted it. Genghis-Khan recognized the value of knowledge possessed by the Kins and Cathayans. They understood matters that his eyes had never seen. And with instant, naïve curiosity, he grasped at that knowledge. He ordered the philosophers of China to march with him and to talk to him in his tent. At the same time he commandeered artisans and engineers for his army.

Great herds of cattle were moving out to the prairies; cartloads of grain creaked over the new roads leading out of China. The barrier of the Great Wall was broken down for all time. And Genghis-Khan could be sure that his people, the Mongol *ulus*, would never lack food while he lived.

Whether he himself spoke the name, or others, we do not know. But at this time the family of the Mongol conqueror began to be called the *Altyn Uruk*, the Golden Family.

The Roads to the West

His subjection of most of north China brought Genghis-Khan no elation. He knew that that work was unfinished, and he placed the Left Wing of the new Mongol fighting machine there to make an end of resistance.

And he took pains to clear his other flank, in the mountain ranges of mid-Asia—twelve hundred miles away. By now he could rely on his divisional commanders, and two of them waged a curious warfare among those mountains. They announced that they had come to bring religious freedom to oppressed sects. Peacefully, they galloped past the mosques and Buddhist shrines, and Nestorian chapels of the Five Cities. And the little people of the shrines greeted them, refusing to take arms against them.

So the war in the mountains became a man hunt—congenial sport for the hard-riding Mongols—in pursuit of the ruler of Black Cathay, the war lord of the mountains. He was cornered and slain with his followers before the mass of the people knew what was happening. And the triumphant Mongols sent back twenty thousand white horses to Genghis-Khan in the steppes.

They laughed and danced in their tents, telling about the success of their man hunt. And from that time it became part of the Mongol strategy to liquidate any ruler who dared make a stand against them. Such a man was condemned to death by man hunt.

"Do not become too proud," Genghis-Khan warned his *tuman-bashis*—division commanders—by courier. "Pride brought Wang Khan of the Kiraïts to the end of his life."

He was struggling, as at first, to hold in check the brutal reactions of his people. To the Mongols, human life outside their clans had no value. The Mongol conqueror saw value in it at times—as in the skill of Chinese engineers who could build siege engines, and bridges over mountain freshets.

"In war," he told his people, "be like tigers; in peace, like doves."

Ceaselessly, he tried to teach them the iron restraint that he had learned. And watchfulness. "In daylight," he is believed to have told them, "hunt with the wariness of an old wolf. At night, with the keen sight of a raven. Swoop upon your enemies like hawks."

The March to the West

Ironically, it was sheer accident that turned his attention to the west, beyond the mountains. Otherwise he might have spent the last years of his life in the steppes, content with a nomad's empire and the tribute from north China.

The Emperors on Horseback

But the old Mongol had become interested in trade. Moslem merchants described to him the wealth of Islam in the west, and what Genghis-Khan heard, he remembered. He sent merchants and Mongol ambassadors to the nearest of the western powers, the Khwaresm-shahs who ruled from Samarkand to Baghdad. That reckless monarch saw fit to allow the merchants to be plundered and killed. He was foolish enough to execute the envoy the Mongol khan sent to his court to demand the punishment of those who had slain the merchants.

To the Mongols, the person of an ambassador was sacred. To a Mongol like Genghis-Khan, the injury could only be wiped out by war.

He prepared cautiously, trusting nothing, and eliminating every chance of failure that he could visualize. Perhaps he had intended this conflict to be; if not, he seized upon it without an instant's hesitation. Here was a new Golden Emperor to be destroyed, with the immense armed forces of Islam; a power residing beyond the mountain barrier of mid-Asia, as the Golden Emperor had sheltered himself behind the Great Wall.

First, information. The old Mongol questioned traveling merchants until he was satisfied that he knew the strength of the Islamic shah and the geography of the world beyond the mountains. Spies were sent ahead, to provide information later, and a screen of scouts was ordered through the mountain passes.

Second, morale. Genghis-Khan went alone to a height near the Mountain of Power and took the covering from his head, the girdle from his waist. For hours he communed with the spirits of the high and distant places, and he came down with a message. The Everlasting Blue Sky had granted victory to the Mongols.

Third, mobilization. He took only some fifteen divisions of ten thousand men. But these were veterans of the Kin campaigns, and were strengthened with Turkish Uighurs and bands of the powerful Kirghiz, brought in by his eldest son, Juchi. The long march from the steppes through the ranges was slow, orderly. In the ordu of Genghis-Khan a young, fair wife, Kulan, was included, with a geographer of Cathay and learned minds of the Uighurs.

They made their way over the ranges methodically, tending the

The March of the Barbarians

remount herds and the wagon trains. How methodically they moved, we learn from the account of a Taoist, Ch'ang-Ch'un, who followed, at the order of the Khan. On the heights of the Yin Shan, beyond the place of White Bones—where a nomad army had perished in forgotten times—passing Sairam Lake, Ch'ang Ch'un entered a ravine cut by mountain torrents.

"When he accompanied the Great Khan," Ch'ang Ch'un relates, "Chagatai, the second son of the Khan, built the first road through this ravine to the west. He broke down the rocks of the slopes and built no less than forty-eight bridges of wood wide enough for two carts to pass over, side by side."

The Terror

The Moslem forces had expected to meet a horde of barbarians. They met, instead, disciplined divisions, maneuvering in silence with amazing speed, according to a plan carefully prepared by the old Mongol.* These divisions appeared out of the night, striking with blasts of steel-tipped arrows and heavy bows. Although they outnumbered the Mongols, the armies of the Khwaresm-shah were scattered in a few weeks. The Shah himself became a fugitive, like his former rival of Black Cathay, with a Mongol man hunt at his heels. His life ended in an island of the Caspian where the Mongol horsemen could not reach him—he died of exhaustion and terror.

*By now the Mongol man power had been mobilized into a national army for at least a dozen years. To a man the Mongols had become professional soldiers. They were opposed, in the Kin and western campaigns, by fragments of regular armies, court guards, and the immense feudal levies of the time.

It is not true, as some historians relate, that the Mongols achieved conquest only over decadent empires. The Turkish Khwaresm-shahs were a young military power; the Seljuk Turks were still to arrive at their full strength, and were at that time engaging the Crusaders on even terms. The Georgians, Kipchaks and Russians were warlike peoples accustomed to victory. The Mongols were, in nearly every case, outnumbered by the enemy.

They had the advantage of their permanent military organization. Their regiments, unlike most of the feudal forces of the time, were able to maneuver in close formations. Their officers were recruited from the *keshek* (the Guard) which served as a military school for chosen youths, under the eye of the Khan.

As evidence of their discipline, we find no accounts of individual bravery among the Mongols in these campaigns, while the Moslem accounts relate the exploits of various heroes such as Jelal ad-Din. The Mongols remain anonymous in their obedience to the orders of the military genius directing them.

The Emperors on Horseback

The scattered armies were given no chance to reform. Genghis-Khan was trusting to speed of movement; he had brought the tactics of the hunt into warfare in the west. Cities were stormed, or tricked into surrender and demolished in a few days.

For the first time the Mongols devoted themselves to inspiring terror. Confronted by superior numbers of a warlike race utterly alien to the steppes, they waged a war of extermination against the multitudes. They led out the peoples of walled towns, examining them carefully and ordering the skilled workers—who would be useful—to move apart. Then the soldiers went through the ranks of helpless human beings, killing methodically with their swords and hand axes—as harvesters would go through a field of standing wheat. They took the wailing women by the hair, bending forward their heads, to sever the spine the more easily. They slaughtered, with blows on the head, men who resisted weakly.

In some places, the Moslems say, not even the dogs and cats survived the passing of the Mongol horsemen. Terror fell on the cultivated lands of Islam like a pall, interrupting communications, sending the living into hiding. It paralyzed the will to resist. And it lasted for years.

"A man of Nisapur," the historian Ibn Athir relates, "told me that he watched, hidden in a house, through an opening. When the Mongols appeared to kill someone, they cried each time, '*Allah-ilahi!*' (in mockery of the Moslem cry). When the massacre was over, they led away the women after pillaging the houses. I watched them mount their saddles. They laughed, chanting in their speech, and shouting '*Allah-ilahi.*'

"So great was the dread that Allah put into all hearts," Ibn Athir continues, "things happened that are hard to believe. Someone told me that a Tatar rode alone into a village with many people, and set himself to kill them, one after the other, without a person daring to defend himself. I heard also that one Tatar, wishing to kill a prisoner of his and finding himself without a weapon, ordered his captive to lie down. He went to look for a sword, with which he killed the unfortunate, who had not moved.

"Someone said to me: 'I was on the road with seventeen other men. We saw a Tatar horseman come up to us. He ordered us to tie up our companions, each man to bind the other's arms behind his back. The others were beginning to obey him, when I said to them, "This man is alone. Let us kill him and escape." They replied, "We are too much afraid." "But this man will kill you," I said. "Let's do for him, and perhaps Allah will preserve us."

" 'Yet, by my faith, not one of the seventeen dared do it. So I killed the Tatar with a blow of my knife. We all ran away and saved ourselves.' "

The systematic slaughter went on. And the Moslems began to whisper that Genghis-Khan was a scourge of the supernatural, an implacable being, the Accursed.

From one city all the inhabitants were led out, separated into groups and told to bind each other's arms. When they were all trussed up, the Mongol soldiery surrounded them and killed the masses with arrows—men, women and children, without discrimination. Then the Mongols retrieved their arrows.

The prisoners taken at the siege of Bokhara were not slain. They were conducted to Samarkand, and tied in groups, to be driven toward the walls to form a human shield for the first ranks of the Mongol attack on that city. And the captives of Samarkand were led off, to serve in the assault of Urgench, the city of the Khwaresm-shahs.

These captives were driven to the task of filling up the ditch around the great city, and then to undermining the walls. The Mongols stormed the walls and fired the outer quarters of the Moslem metropolis with naphtha. But the multitudes penned up within the city defended each street, until the Mongol dead lay piled between the buildings.

The Mongols then drove their horde of captives to dam the Amu River that flowed past Urgench, and divert its course. They forced their way into the streets from the bed of the river, and the defenders of the city surrendered.

These survivors were driven out into the fields and separated into three groups. The artisans and skilled workers were sent east, to labor for the conquerors; young women and children were kept to become slaves; the rest were killed methodically. The chroniclers say that each Mongol soldier put to death twenty-four of the inhabitants of Urgench. There were about 50,000 Mongols at this siege.

Many Moslems had hid themselves among the ruins and the piles of the slain. They did not escape, because the Mongols destroyed the dam before leaving. The river water flooded the ruins, wiping out all trace of life.

Here, the chronicles relate, the two eldest sons of Genghis-Khan quarreled. Juchi, the first-born, wished to keep the city undemolished, since it might belong to him thereafter. Chagatai insisted that no city could be spared after causing the death of Mongols. Urgench vanished, in actuality, from the face of the earth, and two centuries passed before the Amu River found its way back to its old bed, flowing again into the sea of Aral.

At times, after the Mongols sacked a town, they rode off, only to appear suddenly a few days later, to put to death the survivors who had returned to the ruined houses. So the people of Islam who lived through the terror learned to avoid all town sites, leaving them to the scavenger birds and dogs that fed for a while on the decaying bodies.

Along the belt of Arabic-Iranian civilization, four fifths of the population was eradicated. The slaughter was methodical, without evidence of sadistic torment. At times men who were known to have wealth were tortured to make them give up their treasures— whether real or imagined. No towers of skulls were built as monuments to the Mongol terror.

Genghis-Khan deliberately turned the rich belt of Islamic civilization into a no-man's-land. He put an end to the agricultural working of the land, creating an artificial steppe here, on the frontier of his new empire. Making it, he thought, suited to the life of his own people.

The Way Back

From the years 1218 to 1222, his Mongols overrode the southwest of the known world with meteorlike rapidity. Over the Pamirs, through the long fertile valley of Samarkand, into the heart of Persia. Along the Persian highlands to the unlooked-for waters of the Caspian that the Mongols called the Sea of the Ravens. On to the good grass plains beyond, and the cities of Tabriz and Mosul. Doubling back past the snow peaks of the Hindu Kush, through the bare heights of the Afghans, down to the river Indus.

Two of his divisions made an incredible march up through the gorges of the Caucasus, breaking the armed resistance of the war-like Georgians. They debouched into the Russian steppes, where the wandering Kipchaks (Desert People) had been looking for them to appear from the north. They drove the Kipchaks back to the lands of their ancestral enemies, the Russian princes. At the river Khalka the Mongols swept over the stalwart soldiery of the Russian princes of Kiev and Galicia. They turned south to raid the Krimea—and then were recalled by an order of the Khan. They turned back reluctantly across the steppes, over the old road of the barbarians—the route of the Huns and Turks—scattering the Bulgars dwelling along the Volga, and the Kankali Turks of the Ural.

They brought back with them a wealth of horseflesh and precious things, and tidings of the rich grazing in the Russian steppes. One of them, the *tuman-bashi* Subotai, left with the determination to return and invade the unknown west. Subotai, called *Bagatur*, the Valiant, had hunted the Khwaresm-shahs into the Caspian; now he had set his mind on returning, to ride into Europe beyond the Danube.

Throughout this havoc the youngest son of the old Mongol appears—Tului (the Mirror)—as the most daring spirit of the ordus. To him was given the task of destroying great cities, with the stone-casting and fire-throwing machines that the Chinese engineers had brought from the east. This fire artillery, in which gunpowder may have been used, added to the terror of the Mongol assault. Tului, seated on a golden throne, directed the storm that never ceased until a walled city was taken. To the Mongols who served under him, he became the incarnate spirit of victory.

Once the military strength of the Moslems had been broken, Genghis-Khan turned his mind to the future care of the new lands.

He left his four sons and generals in command of the divisions of the army—and even established a school of war for young Mongol officers. For he was determined to keep the control of his vast conquests in the hands of the Mongol *ulus*.

One commander, Shiki Kutaku—who had endeared himself to the Khan as a boy when he had tracked and slain a herd of deer for meat during a heavy fall of snow—had been defeated by Turkish horsemen in the Afghan hills. This had been the only check to the Mongol invasion. Genghis-Khan received the defeated general without anger.

"Until now," he said, "Shiki Kutaku has always been successful. He has become too accustomed to victory, because he has never known the cruelty of misfortune. Now, he will be more cautious."

And in his pursuit of the Turkish army, which he broke up later on the banks of the Indus, Genghis-Khan turned aside to examine the ground where his general had been worsted. Here he blamed the young Mongol commander severely for choosing a bad position for combat.

After the passing of his armies, the Khan gave order that all fighting should cease. No men could take up arms where the Mongols ruled. This nomad peace, terrible but effective, put an end to the feudal warfare and the battles between princes that had harried the Islamic lands before the coming of the Mongols.

Behind the Mongol *tumans* appeared the organizers of the conquests—mandarins of Cathay to take the census of the survivors, Uighur secretaries to write down the lists of human beings and houses and cattle herds—the *darugashis*, to administer the new roads and the courier post that carried news to the Mongol homeland.

This nomad government of the old Mongol, devised in the heat of his campaigning, accomplished the three things he desired: an orderly peace, the collection of wealth, and communication with his steppes. "An empire," Yeliu Ch'u-tsai said, "has been conquered in the saddle."

Genghis-Khan was intensely curious about the Moslem world and the nature of the new lands. He tried to find a direct road home, through the passes of the Himalayas, across the Tibet plateau—the shortest way. Wisely, he turned back from the snow of the higher passes, realizing that no army could cross this roof of the world. With miraculous skill, he led his tumans back in safety, toward the long road of Samarkand.

At Bokhara he questioned the strange readers of the Koran about Islam, the religion of his enemies. He agreed that the teachings of Muhammad were good, except for the pilgrimage to Mecca. Why should men go to one place to bow down, when the Sky stretched over all the earth? He could see no sense in that. But he exempted the teachers of Islam from taxation. He was not making war against a religion. But he felt in these callers-to-prayer, and these ascetics who could govern crowds with a word, a strength that he did not understand. Here was a force that could control men, and it was useless to try to slay it with weapons. He had had the arch-shaman Geukchu killed, but there were thousands of other shamans, wizards, who might or might not be able to summon to their assistance the powers of kelets, the strength of thunderstorms, even the lightning of the Sky itself. Could they do so? The old Mongol did not know. But he pondered this dark, intangible force that was in its way as great as that of his tumans. With ghostly fingers, the fear of the old ice gods touched his mind.

He felt his body weakening with age. He did not have much time to decide this vital question. Was the power of the shamans and priesthoods greater than his own—could he destroy this danger, or must he conciliate it, shrewdly, warily, winning it over to aid his four sons after his death? Could this power, perhaps, prolong his own life? He did not know, but he wasted no time in trying to find out. He had questioned the Moslem speakers-to-Heaven without finding them dangerous. Now he remembered that his commander of the Left Wing, in China, had reported that he had encountered certain Reverend Ones, Taoists, who might be speakers-to-Heaven. "From what you tell me," the old Mongol had answered, "they appear to be truly speakers-to-Heaven. Clothe them and feed them well, and if you find others of the same sort, gather them together, and give them the liberties of tarkhans."

Now he sent for one of these mysterious strangers. In far-off

The Emperors on Horseback

Honan a messenger of the Khan wearing a gold tiger-tablet of authority appeared to a certain elderly and revered Taoist, Ch'ang Ch'un, saying "Your name is esteemed by men, and the Khan hath sent me, a special envoy, across mountains and lakes to summon you, and not to return without you."

And he repeated to the master Taoist the message of Genghis-Khan. Yeliu Ch'u-tsai, the Chinese secretary, had phrased it for the Mongol:

"From the northern barrens I have come, eating the food of common men, and wearing only one coat. The people who dwell in felt tents are my children, and their thoughts and mine are the same. When they struggle in battle, I am with them.

"In seven years I have accomplished the task of conquering for them the forces of the world, and my supremacy is acknowledged. I have few talents, therefore I am fond of intelligent men, treating them as my brothers. And I fear that I am not able to rule wisely. To cross a river, we make use of rafts and poles. So, to govern an empire, we must use the advice of wise men. Your sanctity is cloudlike, above other men. You are separated from me by mountains and spaces of sandy deserts. Do not be afraid because of that. Think of the welfare of the people, and come to my side, and communicate to me how my life can be preserved."

So Ch'ang Ch'un made the journey across Asia, finding himself, to his embarrassment, at one time in the company of twenty singing and dancing girls who were also being convoyed to the Khan's tent. In fact they were there attending on the Mongol conqueror when Ch'ang Ch'un entered the pavilion and stood without fear before the face of Genghis-Khan.

"You, who obey no king's command," the Mongol said, "have come to me. I am glad. Have you brought the secret that will prolong my life?"

Ch'ang Ch'un did not hesitate. "There are ways of protecting life," he explained, "but no elixir to preserve it."

This frankness pleased the Khan, who ordered food and drink to be given the ascetic.

"It is not by my will," Ch'ang Ch'un said boldly, "but by the will of Heaven that I have come."

[67]

The old Mongol could appreciate this. Here was a power without fear. "Engrave his words on your hearts," he told his sons, "for they are worthy to be meditated upon."

Nor did he show any anger when Ch'ang Ch'un made clear that, to live to an advanced age, a chieftain should sleep alone at night, not in the arms of painted girls. Nor should he destroy life in others.

As it happened, they were then on the return journey through the mountains, and the Mongols indulged in a hunt for relaxation. Although he was nearly seventy years of age, Genghis-Khan rode in the hunting ring, and was thrown from his horse when a boar charged him. The boar swerved aside and did not harm him.

"That was a sign of warning," the Taoist told him. "You have done ill to take life. If Heaven had not intervened, the boar would have gored you."

The old Mongol thought this over, and answered, "I understood that myself. I know your advice is good. But we Mongols have grown accustomed from our earliest years to ride, and to hunt with arrows. It is not easy to change our habits. However, this time I have engraved your words on my heart."

But two months later he was in the saddle again, hunting. It was not, indeed, easy to change his ways. It seemed to him that Ch'ang Ch'un possessed no secret power, but still had to be conciliated. And he gave the aged Taoist a decree freeing himself and all his disciples from taxation and harm. It was best to have the support of the speakers-to-Heaven in the conquered lands. With mutual respect, without yielding to the other, the aged conqueror and the ascetic parted, not to meet again.

A greater foreboding preyed on Genghis-Khan. They were marching back, around the Roof of the World, chasing the wild ass and the antelope before them. The distant divisions were being called in, for reunion. After five years they would see the home prairies again. His three sons came in to the great ordu, Tului, Chagatai from his duty of mending roads—he had just repaired a broken bridge of boats for Ch'ang Ch'un—and Ogadai. Juchi, the eldest, rode in from the northern steppes, driving a gift of twenty thousand white horses before him for his Khan. And to his sons

Genghis-Khan spoke of the future. "To destroy your own blood kin," he said, "is to put out the fire on the hearth. I intend to give to each of you a nation, but one must rule over the others, and they must obey him as you obey me now."

This he said to Juchi, as well as the three younger ones. To Juchi, the first-born, and bastard—born of the imperial mother Bortai when she had been raped in a tribal raid. Genghis-Khan had won her back, yet she had been delivered of her first son on the way to rejoin him. The men escorting her had made a cradle lined with the only soft stuff they had, fresh dough. This was to carry the child, on horseback. And Genghis-Khan, seeing her son for the first time in this fashion, had said, "Well, he comes as a guest." So they had given him that name, Juchi, the Guest. The father had said nothing against Bortai, his wife, nor had he made less of Juchi than his other sons. Because Juchi had never forgotten the manner of his birth, and had kept apart from the others, Genghis-Khan had allowed him to go to the most distant land, the western steppes. But more than once Juchi had clashed with the others— in the war along the border of his new lands.

Now the three others protested, hearing that Juchi was to be master of an *ulus* like their own.

"Is he to be like to us, he who comes from Merkit blood?"

The father heard them out in silence, and an elder Mongol, who was Chagatai's adviser, answered them:

"You three were yet unborn, and every *ulus* was torn by strife, when your mother was stolen. Since then your mother has labored to create an empire. She brought up you boys hoping that you would be men. She was bright as the sun, and strong as the deep ocean. How can you speak so of one who was like that?"

Juchi, however, did not stay, after that, with the Mongol who was not his father. He left the great Ordu to go back to his steppes. When Genghis-Khan summoned all the Mongols to a kuriltai, a general council, the next year, Juchi did not appear. Instead, he sent a message that he was sick.

Until then no one had disobeyed a summons of the Khan. The old Mongol waited, without comment, until it was certain that his eldest son was not on the way to the meeting place by the mountain lakes. Then he questioned the Mongol officer who had brought the message.

"Is it true," he asked, "that Juchi is too sick to ride?"

The noyan who had come from the north answered with care. "When I left his side, he was hunting."

This, Genghis-Khan understood, meant disobedience. And he could not pass it over. He gave command to his other sons to prepare to march north, into Juchi's steppes, to punish the rebel. Before they left the mountains, word reached them that Juchi was dead.

Genghis-Khan did not delay to mourn. "In spite of all our expectation," he said, "death will come." He turned back toward the lakes. The kuriltai had been ordered, and must be held. But he grew more silent then, and did not go again to hunt on the march.

On the homeward hunt, the far-flung units of the Mongols came together. Subotai appeared, to give an account of what he had seen at the threshold of Europe. In the grasslands they met again, after years, to feast and to quaff mare's milk while the minstrels chanted at the night fires. Here Genghis-Khan held the council— with his three sons, with his blood relations and the Mongol noyans who had served him. Outside the pavilion of the Khan stood the Mongol standard with the nine yak tails, and the white falcon poised above them—the white bird that with outstretched wings had seemed to Christian observers like a cross.

In this kuriltai, the Mongols listened to the words of the Khan. They were reluctant to speak themselves because they were convinced now that the power of the Sky had descended on the old man who led them. "The Blue Sky," they whispered, "has ordered him to govern all peoples."

Genghis-Khan thought it to be time to divide this new heritage among his four sons—the four who were born of Bortai. He had a nomad's conception of wealth. He apportioned among his sons what seemed most desirable to him. Men to serve his children, herds upon which these men subsisted, and fertile lands upon which the herds could thrive. He wasted no thought on gold or silver. Walled cities and the industry of townsmen, with all their possessions, were, in his mind, only incidental to the all-important grazing lands and the caravan routes over which trade could pass.

Lacking maps, or any sympathy with previous property rights, the old Mongol simply gave his sons certain tribes, with vast areas of river beds and mountain ranges beyond the steppes. He had obliterated the old frontiers.

He had conquered the greater part of Asia. Now he divided up his conquest as a nomad might have divided his heads of cattle and herders.

But he gave the army to Tului.

For he held in utter obedience an invincible army. With it, he had conquered more of the earth's surface than any other man. From the Pacific to the Volga his word was law; his roads were being opened from the Persian desert to the edge of the Siberian *taiga* where the first horse nomads had existed.

This conquest Genghis-Khan intended to be complete and to endure. He had welded together into a new nation the people who dwelt in tents. And he meant them to rule over the limits still to be conquered upon the earth.

Above this nation would be the Mongol clan, the tarkhans and noyans, companions of his early struggles. He intended them to remain as they were, nomads, masters of civilized men.

And above them would rule his family, the *Altyn Uruk*, the Golden Family—his sons and their sons, with all his blood kin and the offspring of their wives. Among them the empire of the steppes would be divided, like the cattle and men of the old pastoral days.

At the head of the Golden Family there would be, eventually, the one who would reign as khan, sitting on the strip of gray felt where Genghis-Khan sat now. Abiding in the steppes, this successor would hold the mastery of all human beings.

Such was the purpose of the Mongol conqueror. Before he could complete it, he died in a campaign against rebels, in 1227, the year of the Pig, within the hills of Hsia.

III

The Book of the Kuriltai

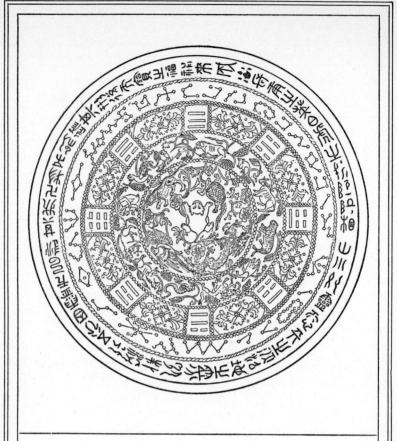

THE CYCLE OF THE TWELVE BEASTS

THIS CHINESE CYCLE OF TIME *forms the ornamentation on a mirror of the T'ang dynasty. In the center the four cardinal points of the compass are indicated; then the cycle of the twelve beasts—Mouse, Ox, Panther, Hare, Dragon, Snake, Horse, Goat, Monkey, Cock, Dog, Pig. Outside the circle of the eight mystical trigrams, the astronomical mansions of the moon are indicated. All these entered into the Chinese calculation of time and portents—a cycle of Cathay.*

III

The Book of the Kuriltai

IT WAS AUTUMN, when the steppe grass turned brown. Before the coming of the strong winds, the pines around Lake Baikal were still mirrored in the waters. The Mongols, bringing home the cart on which lay the body of Genghis-Khan, were riding through the red dust toward the cold air of the prairies.

"He was an eagle, flying past us," they said, "crying out, seeking its prey. Never had he home or abiding place before."

The casket was drawing nearer to the Yakka Ordu, the great camp where the domed yurts of gray felt stretched away to the skyline, by the waters of the Kerulan. It seemed strange to the riders that the tall man of seventy years with the wide, bent shoulders and the gray cat's eyes should lie motionless in a casket jolting over the ruts.

On the journey across the red soil of China, they had killed all the people of the countryside who had seen the cart passing. They did not wish any enemies to see the death cart of the Khan.

But here in the Mongol tent city, the news could not be hidden. The sons of Genghis-Khan and the lords of outlying tribes and army divisions were riding in daily from the prairies. "The strong stone," they said, "is broken. The eagle that once flew before us has fallen like a colt that stumbles." And they asked, "Has he in truth left his people?"

For each day of four days the casket was left in a yurt of one of

[75]

the four imperial wives of the Khan. And the mourning wail was heard:

"In the time of grass thou didst nourish me,
O my Khan!
In the winter's wind thou didst warm me.
Now is the water gone from the sweet lake whereby I sat,
And the shade from the garden wherein I dwelt,
O my Khan!"

Each wife remained carefully within her own household, as tribal custom ordained. Even Kulan, the youngest one, the last imperial wife, obeyed the custom. Each waited her turn to mourn when the casket crossed her threshold. They wailed for the old man who had bred their many sons and daughters—and through them the seed of the sons, the young grandchildren—who had been inexorable in life, and who had conquered what pleased him of the far lands of the earth.

The question whispered around the yurt fires in that time of mourning was, where will the spirit of Genghis-Khan find its abiding place? For the life of the Khan had not been snuffed out by giving him grease instead of food for nourishment, as if he had been a common old man, past his useful years. Nor had he been slain by a weapon, directed by the will of the Everlasting Sky.

For the present, now that he had ceased to breathe, the spirit-life of Genghis-Khan resided in the blood of his body. This blood had not been shed, so it must be pent up there inside him still.

The question that agitated the Mongols was, would this *suldë*, this spirit-life of the Khan, depart quietly to the Sky, whence it had come in the first place to visit the earth? Would it descend to the cold, subterranean region of Erlik? Or would it take up its abiding place somewhere on the earth itself, among his people—in fire or in running water, where lesser spirits dwelt? The Beki would tell them the answer.

The Beki was the oldest of the forest people, the Uriangut, who alone could breed reindeer, and who were in close communion with the spirits of the forests. Genghis-Khan had appointed the Beki, the aged shaman-chieftain, to ride on a white horse, to clothe himself in white, and to sit in the highest place in a public gathering. The Beki was to choose the good years and the favorable moons of the years for undertaking things.

Now the Beki announced the day for the burial. He rode in his white furs with the princes and commanders, when Genghis-Khan was trundled upon the funeral cart. Out of the encampment, across the prairies, to the valley beneath the sunny side of the hills of the Burkhan Kaldun, the Mountain of Power.

There, the Beki reminded the Mongols, the Khan had once admired a tall tree, saying that its shade would be a good resting place for an old man. And there the grave was dug beneath a lofty pine rising from a grove of young trees.

In the space hollowed out beneath the roots, a miniature wooden yurt was built. In this, dishes of meat and cooked grain were placed, with a bow and sword and the bones of the war horse last mounted by the Khan. The bones had been carefully burned with fire.

During his lifetime Genghis-Khan had enjoyed having a bevy of some twenty young and slender girls about him, to make music and dance. But now, in the grave yurt, he sat on his accustomed strip of gray felt, facing the south and his grazing lands, without the girls.

Then the grave was closed, and the fresh earth trodden by the hoofs of the horses. The funeral cart was broken up, and incense burned in the grove. The Beki and the elder Mongols decided that the forest men, the Uriangut, should be the guards of the grove until the young trees should grow high enough to conceal the pine that marked the grave. Then the question in the minds of the assembled men was answered by the Beki, who spoke words of power:

"Now has the spirit-life left the body of Genghis-Khan," he said.

"To what place," they asked, "has it taken its way?"

"Into the banner," he told them, "of the Mongol tribe."

To the elder Mongols this seemed most satisfying. The suldë of Genghis-Khan would reside in the great standard of the nine yak tails that was carried with the army. There it might be expected to guide and protect them.

"Now," added the Beki, "wherever men can hear, let the name of the great ancestor never be spoken aloud."

The March of the Barbarians

This, also, could be easily understood. To speak aloud the name of Genghis-Khan would be to attract the attention of the suldë residing in the standard of the nine tails. The Mongols turned away from the grove in the Mountain of Power, and mounted their horses to ride back over the prairies, with word of the burial.

But some in the encampment did not believe that the suldë could be within the great banner. And among the doubters was the mother of Kubilai.

In that year of the Pig, the boy Kubilai was thirteen years of age. He was heavier than his brothers. He had brown eyes and dark hair. "How dark he is," Genghis-Khan, his grandfather, had said once, without approval.

Kubilai had feared his grandfather more than the thunder that came down from the sky. That was because the dreaded Khan had been away from his homeland, at war in the western regions, for the greater part of Kubilai's life. The boy was nine years old before he was taken to see the face of his grandsire, when the main army of the Mongols was returning slowly from its conquests, north of Samarkand.

Then Genghis-Khan had been preoccupied with hunting. And he had taken the boy Kubilai along, to initiate him at his first hunt by rubbing grease and meat on his middle finger, before he used his bow.

Genghis-Khan had turned to those around him. "The words of the boy Kubilai are full of wisdom. Heed them well—heed them, all of ye."

And this had been written down by the secretaries as one of the utterances of the Khan. When Kubilai's mother heard of it, she flushed with exultation. But Kubilai was not talkative; he used words sparingly. Kubilai Sechen, they called him—Kubilai the Wise.

He was still attached to his mother's yurt. Not yet had he been given his first wife, to breed his sons.

Now that Genghis-Khan had been shut up in his grave, Kubilai's mother was troubled by misgiving. She said nothing about it, but the adolescent boy knew that she was holding her anger in leash.

Siyurkuktiti Begi,* his mother, was daring and brilliant. She had come from the Kiraït clan, Turkish in descent. In the time before Genghis-Khan dissolved the great clans, the Kiraït had been plains nomads, superior to the forest people, or the herders of sheep. They had lived on their horse herds, and so had been part of the steppe aristocracy. But like the Mongols, their neighbors, they had been weakened, poverty-ridden—unlike the Mongols, they had been forced to take the less desirable grazing land near the edge of the clay barrens.

Siyurkuktiti, then, had the hard endurance of the steppe women. She had known no security. Her possessions had been no more than the portable things that could be carried on animals—the clothes she embroidered herself, iron utensils, bits of carved ivory made into barbaric jewelry, boxes of birch, and perhaps a prized mirror of polished silver. She had pressed felts with her hands and stripped cords from sinews.

But she had beauty, a quick wit, and the skill to guard herself against danger. For she had been the niece of Wang Khan of the Kiraïts, who had died of his wounds in fighting the Mongols, a Nestorian Christian who was called, after his death, the Prester John of Asia. Siyurkuktiti had listened to the bearded Nestorian priests who quartered themselves in the tents of her clan and mumbled the news of the caravan tracks. She dreaded the wandering shamans who came, like the shadows of her ancestors, to threaten and to beg for alms.

Some of these shamans were long-haired women-men, who relieved their grotesque lusts on each other. And others defiled boys during the séances in the yurts when their spirits went out of their bodies. They belonged to the dark elder world from which Siyurkuktiti tried to escape.

Her other neighbors had been the more intelligent Uighurs,

---

*This name is difficult to transliterate into English. In the Syriac chronicle it appears as Sarkothani Bagi. The European friars who reached the Mongol court rendered it in Latin as Serocten, and Surukti. Professor Pelliot, translating from the T'oung Pao, has it Soyorghachtani-bagi (Chinese into French). Rashid's chronicle (Persian) from which this is translated has Siyurquqtiti. Begi (Persian, Bayki) is a title equivalent to Princess.

merchants who traveled with wandering minstrels and sold her, to her delight, lengths of silken brocade from Cathay.

Siyurkuktiti listened to the minstrels who told of far-off things, and she rubbed the roughened skin of her face with sour cream, to soften it. She was desirable, and she had been given as a girl to Tului, the youngest son of the Mongol conqueror. Because she was his first wife, the sons she bore him would be his heirs.

The incessant campaigns of the Mongols had kept Tului in the saddle, and she had gone with him—unwilling to stay in the home yurts of the Golden Family. Now her own yurt had become splendid with the spoils of Cathay—with hangings of silk sewn with pearls, and incense to burn in silver braziers. But this did not content Siyurkuktiti. She put golden flowers in her plaited hair, with a crest of heron's plumes.

"But," she warned Kubilai, her third son, "the whip you lose is always the one with the golden handle."

She wanted her sons, in this new empire of the Golden Family, to have a security she had not known. She wanted them to be strong enough to survive, no matter what happened.

Kubilai, although born in a felt tent, had grown up in what seemed to his mother to be luxury. He knew the gleam of alabaster, and the feel of smooth jade stone. She dressed him in Chinese satin, and white fox bellies. For his father had been the *Naukar*, the favored one of Genghis-Khan, always kept at the side of the Mongol conqueror.

"I do not think thy words are at all wise," she laughed, "but *he* said they were, and what he has said is so."

And, to make them so, Siyurkuktiti did a daring thing. She had her son taught to write, and to read the written words. Genghis-Khan and Tului had not been able to read.

But scholars, Siyurkuktiti knew, entered a world apart from ordinary living and doing. They could trace at their fingers' ends the words of wise men. They conceived ideas that had nothing to do with ordinary happenings. Elsewhere, kings and lords could draw on this fund of stored-up wisdom.

"Riding astride a calf," the elder Mongol women told her,

The Book of the Kuriltai

"does not make a boy a nomad. Ekh! Reading words does not make a scholar."

"*Ugë*—" the mother of Kubilai retorted—"talking to stupid ears is like sprinkling corn over a cow's horns!"

To her large household—for now, as Tului's first wife, she had soldiers to watch her herds, and maids, and waiting men to carry her messages, and slaves who were captives brought from the wars to do her menial work—she added two scholars.

One was a Uighur, a hardheaded educated merchant from a caravan city. The other a Chinese who said little but did miraculous things with a brush and slab of ink. Under their tutelage, Kubilai began to learn what his eyes had never seen, and his mother was satisfied, to that extent.

The thing that irked her like a thorn in the flesh was the fact that Tului had not been chosen khan, to succeed his father.

For Genghis-Khan had spoken plain words, that would be obeyed without question. As tribal custom demanded, he had given to his youngest son Tului the home grazing lands of the Mongols. Tului was *Utchigin*, keeper of the hearth. He had the steppes from the Great Wall to beyond Siyurkuktiti's homeland. And the greater part of the army.

"It has ever been the way of the Mongol and Turk," she reminded Tului, "from the oldest times that the father in his lifetime divides up among his elder-born sons his riches and flocks and herds and followers. Whatever is left belongs to the youngest son who is called Utchigin. For he must guard the foundation of the house of his father.

"It is known to all of us that Genghis-Khan thought to entrust the rule of the empire to you, but in the end he said, 'It is better that thou have the home Ordu and care for my army. So wilt thou be easier in mind. And in the end, since thou hast so many thousands of warriors, thy children shall be mightier than all the other princes.'"

These words that his wife had treasured in her mind, Tului had thought of no more.

But he did not have the throne, the Khanate. Genghis-Khan had given that to Ogadai, Tului's good-natured and hard-drinking brother.

This, to Tului's wife, was a bitter thing. For Tului had had the right to the throne. Ogadai himself she liked—everyone liked Ogadai. Yet Ogadai's first wife, a loud-spoken barbarian, she hated.

Siyurkuktiti said nothing about her anger. It seemed to her as if the words of a man now dead had raised a barrier between her sons and their birthright. And she resolved, quietly, to break down this barrier.

She said nothing of this to Tului. He would have thought her mad, to question the words of Genghis-Khan. Besides, Tului loved his brother.

Tului's name meant the Mirror. He was gentle with his family, and both violent and reckless in war. Being the youngest son, he had grown up, in actuality, in the saddle beside Genghis-Khan. Indifferent to danger, he had been chosen to lead where the hazard was greatest—and now he commanded the Guard, and the banners of ninety thousand men.

"Tului Khan," the chronicler Rashid says, "was the fourth son of Genghis-Khan, the youngest of those that men called the four who cannot be shaken. That is, they were as four strong pillars. And Genghis-Khan used to call him *Naukar*—him whom we trust. He had no match for bravery and wisdom in war. His father asked the daughter of the brother of Unuk (Wang Khan) the king of the Kiraït people for him when he was still a child. Her name was Siyurkuktiti Begi, and she became the first and best-loved of the ladies of Tului Khan, and mother of his four leading sons, who like the four sons of Genghis-Khan were as four pillars of the realm."

When he was not drunk, Tului's loyalty to the family could be passionate. And, drunk or sober, he would not forget that he was the keeper of the hearth—as he liked to say—in the House of Genghis-Khan.

" 'Be ye of the same mind,' he said to us," Tului told Siyurkuktiti, " 'and hold together.' And he commanded each of us to bring him an arrow. Then, taking all the arrows in his hand, he bade each of us try to break the bundle. No one had the strength to break the arrows. Then he told me, the youngest, to take them one by one. I broke them very easily.

" 'Why,' he asked of the others, 'were you unable to break the arrows I gave you?'

" 'Because they were many together,' they answered.

" 'Then why has your youngest brother been able to break them?'

" 'Because they were divided when he broke them, one at a time.'

" 'So it will happen to you,' he then said. 'While you are together and of one mind, you will endure. If you are separated, you will be broken.' "

This, to Tului's wife, was evident. And she made no response.

"He also said," Tului assured her, "that his descendants will clothe themselves in stuffs embroidered with gold; they will nourish themselves with fine meats, and will ride on magnificent horses. They will press young and lovely girls in their arms, and they will not think of him to whom they owe these enjoyments."

To Tului, it was unthinkable that they should forget.

To Siyurkuktiti, his wife, it seemed that Tului had become the servant of a dead man's words. And that the family he thought of was not his own sons.

Moreover, Tului had changed. Little more than thirty-five, he had become like the shell of a man. A cup of grape wine was never far from his hand. Mixed with this, he drank raw spirits that darkened his face and made his head steam. The skin was drawn over his bones, and when he slept he would start up, shaking. His nights, he spent with strange women brought back from his last campaign, who exhausted his strength.

To the boy Kubilai this father, who gave directions to a multitude of men, was a stranger. He feared him almost as much as the dead grandfather.

The First Gathering

For two years after the burial of the great ancestor, the Mongols waited, uncertain how they were to act together, and who would summon them to action. The members of the Golden Family, scattered in distant grazing lands, assembled their new herds.

"Each went to his home, as they had agreed," their chronicler, Rashid, explains, "and for two years they rested. So for these two years there was no one to rule them, and they bethought themselves that if they had need in some matter, no one would be able to act as ruler."

Then a vague uneasiness stirred in them. Isolated from each other, they could not talk together. And the voice of Genghis-Khan no longer spoke to them. True, the suldë, the spirit-life of the Khan, might reside in the nine-tailed banner standing in the ancestral grazing land. But it did not give them advice, as formerly. Unquestionably the Beki and his shamans carried on intercourse with the Sky. Yet the Everlasting Sky appeared to have no definite message for the Mongols. If need arose, who would give commands?

Without doubt, there should be a living person, to rule in the place of Genghis-Khan—one of the Golden Family, chosen by the family to be its head. Tului realized this. And in the late winter of 1229, the year of the Ox in the calendar of the twelve beasts, he sent out couriers to summon his blood kinsmen to a gathering.

Genghis-Khan had warned his sons to meet regularly at such a gathering, or kuriltai. "He who remains in a distant place, and does not come," the Khan had said to the Mongol clans, "will be like a stone fallen into deep water, or an arrow shot among reeds. He will disappear." ·

No one stayed away from the first kuriltai.

"When the grip of cold was broken, and the first of spring came on," the chronicler Rashid relates of this year, "from every region all the imperial sons and the chieftains turned their faces toward the old-time yurt, and the great Ordu."

Generals and war lords rode in from north China, where war was still waging. An uncle appeared from the long white mountains of Manchuria-way, fetching with him the chieftains of the Tatars and the freshly conquered Liao-tung (Iron Men.)

From the western forests, at the edge of the Russian steppes, three thousand miles away, came a youngster, Batu, with his brothers—the offspring of Juchi—at the head of their forest people. The people and the western land had been Juchi's heritage.

From his appanage, the high ranges of the southwest, from the

Altai to the distant valley of Samarkand, came Chagatai, the eldest surviving son, with his Uighurs and Black Cathayans and long-limbed Turkomans in their striped robes. Camel strings carried his baggage, and his carts were drawn by plodding yaks.

Chagatai—the Wild Horse—was, as his father had been, a nomad to the core. Cautious, sparing of words, he cherished tribal customs. He drank alone, and he punished savagely. He craved new women, but—as with Tului—no woman could influence him. A sorcerer kept at his side, feeding his superstition with magical tricks.

Although the Wild Horse brooded over the supernatural, men dreaded his anger. He was unyielding as the stone of his mountain gorges. In his dominion no guards kept the roads or the city gates. It was said that a virgin could go unattended, carrying a jar of gold pieces in safety from one end of his lands to the other.

Ogadai, the second brother, rode in from his lands at the headwaters of the Yenisei with his Kirghiz and Turkish clansmen, silver gleaming in their wolfskins. And he came in a gilded wagon with a canopy held over him by his horsemen. For Ogadai liked to sit at ease, with a touch of splendor about him. He had a gift of laughter, and enduring good nature. But his gray eyes missed little that went on, and his temper could be savage when he was aroused.

Beside him, her arms weighted with bracelets and her head with heron's plumes, rode his chief wife Turakina. Heavy and dominant, she made much of her dignity. She had been the wife of a Merkit chieftain killed by the Mongols, and Ogadai had claimed her. "She had a man's appearance," a chronicler says, "so that only Ogadai found her beautiful." Ogadai liked to indulge Turakina's whims, and she had many.

The dry spirit of Chagatai and the flaming temper of Tului had this in common: both were dominant natures, unable to yield to another; both had behind them years of devastating warfare, and massacre; and both of them loved Ogadai.

At first not one of the three knew what to do. Tului, keeper of the hearth, welcomed his brothers joyfully to the kuriltai by the dark waters of the Kerulan. "*Ahatou*," he greeted them. "Look— the smoke of the hearth has not died out. It has not ceased to be."

The March of the Barbarians

After the last kinsman had dismounted and gone the rounds of the different ordus, Tului played host to the assembled clans. He trundled in wine by the cartload and sheep by the thousand. He summoned noyans, *begs* and tarkhans to the feasting pavilion.

In the mornings that followed, he staged races. Horses from the different clans were matched, with small boys—the smallest and lightest that could manage the racers—riding them, without saddles, a dozen miles out into the plain and back. At noon the three brothers sat down to drink. Knowing Ogadai's fondness for wrestling, Tului paired off warriors against shamans before him. The champions, stripped to the girdle, grappled and kicked until bones were broken, or one was thrown so heavily he could not rise.

Through the night, the Mongols drank together with glad hearts. They knelt in the long kuriltai pavilion, stuffing their bellies with meat, until they went out to vomit, to make room for more. Under the smoking torches they told stories, or watched a Chinese shadow play.

For the Mongols, with food to fill them and drink to warm the blood in their heads, were utterly carefree. When one emptied a goblet of rice wine or corn spirits, others at his side pulled back his ears, to stretch his throat wider. When the three brothers drank, musicians struck their cymbals together, while the pipes wailed, and drunken chieftains, unable to contain themselves, stumbled up and danced, beating their sharp heels into the ground.

In this imperial feast, no one knew what word to say, to elevate another to the seat of Genghis-Khan, whose suldë, no doubt, was observing this festival. Most of the noyans favored Tului, to whom Genghis-Khan had bequeathed the bulk of the army.

"He is the mightiest one," they said, "and the lords of the Right Wing and the Left Wing are his men."

"Truly," others agreed, "the Mirror is the trusted one, yet the Wild Horse is the elder and the life of the old buck is strong in him."

"When the great ancestor," observed one who had been close to the Khan, "pondered the natures of his sons, he thought now of Ogadai, and now of the younger Tului. Although it be the Mongol way from ancient times that the yurt and the first home of the father shall be ruled by the youngest son, yet *he* said that the work of the khan is a hard task—let Ogadai perform it. And the task of caring for the precious things and the armies that he had gathered, let Tului perform that. So he said, and his words are not to be changed."

In silence, they assented to this. Who could be found idiotic enough to disobey a command of the great ancestor?

"*He* also said," another put in, "that any of us desiring counsel should go to Chagatai, and whosoever sought wealth and such goodly things should betake himself to Ogadai, and any who yearned after the seizing of nations should follow Tului."

And they returned to their cups, until the slaves of the gate had to lift them and steady their feet in the hour before dawn, when they went back to the yurts of their wives. This they did for forty days.

No woman could sit in this kuriltai. Turakina waited impatiently for messengers from the kuriltai tent. Siyurkuktiti listened nightly to the inebriated Tului, without revealing her anxiety. If her husband became khan—and she knew that the majority of the congress wanted him—it meant in all certainty that the sons of her body would reign after him. And Tului could not live long.

Both Tului and Chagatai were persuading Ogadai to accept the title of khakhan or supreme ruler. The scarred Mirror rose and spoke with authority in the kuriltai.

"By the power of the Everlasting Sky," he exclaimed, "our father became the great Khan. And by his command the succession must be thine."

Sparing of words, Chagatai assented. "Ay, so."

Ogadai answered: "It is true that the wish of the father is all-compelling. Yet have I uncles, and an elder brother. And, beyond all, is the younger brother Tului better fitted to shoulder this task. For by the ways and the laws of the Mongol, the youngest son of the greatest house shall stand in the father's stead and shall rule his yurt. And your Yakka Noyan is the youngest son of this great Ordu. At every hour of the day and night, he attended the father, and heard of the laws-to-be. With him present here, how can I sit in the throne-seat of the Khakhan?"

The March of the Barbarians

What would have been the result of the rivalry between the brothers to elect another, is uncertain. But a wiser brain than theirs was present in the kuriltai. It belonged to a philosopher of Cathay, and it forced the issue.

Yeliu Ch'u-tsai

A man thirty-nine years of age, unusually tall, with a long beard and mustache—the Chinese nicknamed him Long Mustache— Yeliu Ch'u-tsai had learned to hold both his tongue and his temper. Descendant of a Cathayan prince, and son of a father who had served the Kin dynasty faithfully, Yeliu Ch'u-tsai had devoured books as a boy. An expert mathematician, he had experimented with calendars. He had a strange hobby, puzzling out geography for himself, and not content with the Chinese system of astronomy, he had worked out new calculations of his own. Yeliu Ch'u-tsai had a genius for applying abstract thought. He could put aside his books, to deal just as effectively with human problems. At twenty, he had been governor of Yen-king.

When the Mongols captured this city, his tall figure and deep voice had caught the eye of Genghis-Khan.

"The Kin were enemies of the Cathayans," the old Mongol observed to him, "and so it happens that I have avenged you."

"My father and I," Yeliu Ch'u-tsai replied, "have always served the Kin. How, then, could they be our enemies?"

This straightforward answer pleased the Mongol Khan, who took the young minister into his service, believing that if the Cathayan could be faithful to the Kin dynasty, he could be trusted to aid the Mongols. The barbarian Alexander had found an Aristotle. At first Genghis-Khan called on Yeliu Ch'u-tsai for astrological predictions, and the Cathayan used his wit to good purpose.

Once when he had selected a day for the departure of the Mongols on the western expedition, it snowed to a depth of three feet. Genghis-Khan, doubtful at this, asked Yeliu Ch'u-tsai to explain the meaning of the omen.

"It signifies," the Cathayan answered at once, "that the lord of the cold northern region will conquer the king of the warm south."

And this proved to be the case. A certain Tangutan, famous

for his skill at making bows, was contemptuous of the learned Cathayan. "What business has a man of books," he demanded, "among a fellowship of warriors?"

"To make bows," Yeliu Ch'u-tsai retorted, "a woodworker is needed; but when it comes to governing an empire, a man of wisdom is needed."

Genghis-Khan heard of this reply, and it pleased him. Still, he was careful to check the Cathayan's predictions by the ancient augury of the tribes—by placing the shoulder blade of a sheep in fire and studying the cracks that appeared on it. He made use of Yeliu Ch'u-tsai's brains as he availed himself of planks to build a bridge to cross a river that could not otherwise be crossed. He demanded only one thing of his adviser, integrity. And that rare quality Yeliu Ch'u-tsai possessed.

The philosopher was a match for the inflexible conqueror. Yeliu Ch'u-tsai could read the matter-of-fact Mongols like a written book, but they never understood him. He was a follower of Confucius, serving an ideal of conduct so vague that for the barbarians it did not exist.

Once, in the defiles of the lower Himalayas, Genghis-Khan dreamed that a miraculous animal shaped like a deer but green in color and with only a single horn appeared in his path. Disturbed, he called upon Yeliu Ch'u-tsai for an explanation of the phenomenon.

"It cried out in a human voice," he asserted, "saying, turn back —quickly."

"That strange animal is Kio-tuan," the Cathayan answered gravely. "He knows every language, and he loves living men. He has a horror of slaying. His appearance to you is a warning. You, the Khakhan, possess the power of Heaven, but the living men of the earth are your children. You are responsible for them."

Whatever he may have thought of this, Genghis-Khan turned back from his intended march through the Himalayas.

So Long Mustache rode the whirlwind of carnage, and tried to rein it—laboring to bring order out of the chaos of destruction. While he did so he mapped the geography of the unknown western regions, and collected herbs and cuttings of fruit. When an epidemic attacked the Mongols, he enjoyed a philosopher's revenge. He dosed them with rhubarb and cured them.

He was made Chinese secretary, and he found himself placed beside the two other advisers of the old Mongol. Mahmoud Yelvadj, a wise Turk, and Chinkai, a Uighur, an elderly man of letters—a Christian nicknamed Lord Colony by the Mongols. And the Mongols respected these three men of wisdom, who had won their way out of captivity by showing no fear. Even Tului listened to Long Mustache.

When the kuriltai buzzed with argument after forty days of indecision, Yeliu Ch'u-tsai spoke to Tului.

"The day that is to come," he said, "will be the twenty-second of the eighth moon. And it will be auspicious for the naming of the khakhan."

Silently Tului considered, and shook his head. "No one is ready," he objected. "Let it be put off to another day."

"After tomorrow, no day will be auspicious."

And when the council convened the next morning, Yeliu Ch'u-tsai sought out the brooding Chagatai. "Prince," he said quietly, "you are the eldest. But you are also the subject of the khakhan. Unless you bow first to the khakhan-to-be, who else will dare proclaim him?"

He had invoked the tribal law, and Chagatai could be influenced by a point of law. His hesitation vanished as the Cathayan led him toward Ogadai.

"What are we doing?" Chagatai cried. "The father himself commanded that Ogadai be seated in his stead!"

There was silence in the pavilion, while the Mongols who had argued for Tului and the army, and those who had wished for Chagatai and tribal law, watched the three brothers intently. Chagatai seized the right arm of the surprised Ogadai. And Tului, never slow to act, ran forward to grasp his left hand. "Come on, ox," he laughed.

Ogadai, massive as a bear, resisted, until an uncle pushed through the crowd to grasp his waist, and these three kinsmen carried him toward the throne seat covered with gray felt.

The Book of the Kuriltai

They forced him down on it. Chagatai took off his cap, and loosened the girdle from his hips, throwing it over his shoulder. Then he bent his knee three times before Ogadai. "Ogadai," his harsh voice proclaimed, "you are khakhan."

Hearing this word spoken, the noyans and chieftains of tribes took off their girdles and headgear and knelt before their new khakhan. Hastily, Tului filled a goblet with wine and offered it to his brother, now his ruler with immutable power over the different branches of the *Altyn Uruk*, the Golden Family, over the chieftains who were the steppe aristocracy, over the Mongol clans, the personal army of the former khakhan, Genghis, and all the peoples who dwelt in felt tents, and—distant from them—the peoples of the earth itself.

"Look, O my Khakhan," he said as Ogadai drank mechanically, "they stretch out their necks to thee, and hang the cord of servitude upon them."

The hundreds who knelt gave tongue, calling Ogadai by the name of Khakhan. A keeper-of-the-door went out into the sunlight, to pour wine from a goblet toward the four quarters of the sky. When Ogadai came out, to kneel to the Everlasting Sky, the waiting thousands hailed him. Amazed, Ogadai listened to the salutations of the inscrutable Yeliu Ch'u-tsai and that tolerant soul, Yelvadj. "I told the father," he objected, "I could not argue with him about his choice. But I feared that my sons and their sons would be worthless, and unable to sit on the throne. Then *he* said, 'if all the sons of Ogadai and their sons turn out worthless, can it be that of all my descendants one worthy enough will not be found?'"

These words were heard and remembered. But their immediate effect was to draw from the assembled nomads an oath that they would never place anyone upon the throne except a member of Ogadai's house, so long as there remained of his descendants a morsel of flesh large enough—if thrown into grass—to keep cattle from eating of the grass.

This oath, taken together by the Mongol nomads, contemptuous of written documents, was utterly binding—not only upon themselves, but upon future generations.

The March of the Barbarians

A wave of rejoicing went through the encampment. The clansmen settled down to drink in earnest. Their khakhan had been chosen, and the future provided for. Yeliu Ch'u-tsai, who had brought it about, understood what had been in the mind of Genghis-Khan. Neither Tului nor Chagatai would have submitted to the other for long. Yet both were devoted to Ogadai, and both would aid him to rule. So the three brothers would be united in support of the throne. In Ogadai's ordu, Turakina held herself erect in pride, beholding herself as empress.

And Siyurkuktiti, the first wife of Tului, heard that the boy Kubilai and his brothers had been deprived of the birthright that she had sought for them. Instead of closing her tent to grieve, Siyurkuktiti robed herself in white floss silk, and brushed her hair until it shone. She put rice powder on her cheeks and darkened her eyelids with kohl, and went out with her slave maidens to greet the Mongol noyans and rejoice with them. Only she said nothing of what she kept hidden within her.

The tribesmen who saw her thus commented that she carried herself like a majestic woman. Tului, they admitted, was fortunate in his chief wife.

So in the year of the Ox was held the first coronation of the nomad peers.

Ogadai Khakhan

A methodical and good-natured animal, an illiterate, who trusted little beyond his own senses, except his two brothers; who remembered clearly the years when he had had to sleep, wrapped in furs, under the snow, and to stifle his hunger with grass chewed to a pulp. Ogadai, in middle age, was too old to change, and he had no slightest inclination to go to school to learn. He feared only one thing, the spirit-life of his father that hovered about the great Ordu. He desired most of all to stuff himself with hot meats and sugared fruits.

His first command was to hold three days of mourning for Genghis-Khan—a mourning feast. Steaming horseflesh, sizzling, torn mutton and roasted beef were to be set before every man, with bowls of mare's milk and wine.

The Book of the Kuriltai

To propitiate the spirit-life of his father, he selected forty girls young enough to be virgins. Picking them out from the families of the chieftains, he had them dressed in Chinese garments and adorned with glowing precious stones.

Then he had them led to the grave near the Burkhan Kaldun, where the body of Genghis-Khan sat under the roots of the giant pine, with the bones of his war horse. Forty of the best white stallions were brought to this tree where the Reindeer Tribe kept watch.

The Beki made the sacrifice. The fair girls were strangled, and the horses slain, to go to serve the soul of Genghis-Khan.

After this Ogadai emptied the carts that stood on a rise by the encampment. These carts had been there for months, unguarded. Out of them came bars of silver, chests of pearls, carved ivory, and cinnabar, gleaming jade figures, and soft, beaten gold, rolls of silk, heaped-up precious stones—the spoils of the last campaigns, still undistributed. They had been left unguarded because theft was at that time unheard of among the Mongols.

He made a gift of this treasure to the multitude at the kuriltai. "Our Khakhan," he said, "raised our imperial house with great trouble. Now is it time to take the burden from the peoples, and to give to all peace and prosperity."

"The Khakhan, your father," Yeliu Ch'u-tsai warned him, "conquered an empire in the saddle, but it cannot be governed from the saddle."

Ogadai was not ready to admit that. It had been the conception of Genghis-Khan that the nomads were to make slaves of the settled peoples. Once masters of the land itself, the nomads were to remain free from settled habitation, while the surviving townspeople labored within walls to support them.

Assenting to this, Yeliu Ch'u-tsai pointed out that conquest was one thing, administration another. Yearly taxes had to be levied, and supplies stored in granaries. Communications had to be kept open, and judgments given. "To make a vase," he suggested, "you avail yourself of a potter. To keep accounts and records, learned men should be used."

[93]

"Well," Ogadai demanded, "what hinders thee from making use of them?"

Yeliu Ch'u-tsai admitted that most of the educated men he needed were Cathayans imprisoned, or in slavery. And he asked for a *yarligh*—a written command—to free them so that they could hold office.

He also persuaded Ogadai to appoint officers who were not of the army, in conquered regions, where human carcasses still littered the public squares. He argued that the civilian population should be judged before being executed, and the Khakhan conceded this.

Instead of general looting, the Cathayan argued that a regular tax would bring greater supplies and treasure to the Ordu. Ogadai was skeptical about that, when Yeliu Ch'u-tsai predicted that a tax of one animal in a hundred upon the nomads, and one tenth of their produce, in wine, rice grain, salt, upon the conquered settlements would fetch in yearly over 500,000 ounces of silver to the treasury of the Ordu. But as what the Cathayan predicted usually came to pass, Ogadai agreed to experiment with that arrangement.

Most vital of all, he kept the hard-working Chinkai as Secretary of State. No yarlighs were to be effective unless they bore Chinkai's seal. Mahmoud Yelvadj he selected for his minister, and Yeliu Ch'u-tsai for his governor of north China.

Ogadai had ideas of his own. When the first merchants from the caravan routes arrived at his Ordu, hastening to offer their carpets and plate and curios to the new khakhan, Ogadai accepted everything at the merchants' valuation, which was exorbitant. When the officers of his personal treasury protested that he was being swindled, he admitted it. "These men came," he said, "expecting to make a profit from me. And I do not wish them to go away disappointed."

A beggar appeared weekly before the Khakhan, always asking for a balish of silver. And Ogadai ordered it given him, after he asked the beggar what he wanted it for. "To pay some debts that I owe, to buy me some new garments, and to drink my fill," the man answered boldly.

The Book of the Kuriltai

And Ogadai discovered presently that his officers were not paying the spendthrift. He ordered his Mongols to pay the petitioner
two balishes of silver. Every time, he said, that they failed to pay,
the amount would be doubled.

"He makes good use of the silver," the Khakhan explained,
"and there are just as many balishes handed around as before.
Eventually this one will come back to your coffer from which you
took it."

He had all a nomad's craving for possessions that he could use,
and indifference to stored-up wealth. And he was angered when
his officers objected to his giving away the precious metals. "I cannot take such things out of the world with me," he cried. "You are
trying to injure me. Am I not to have a good name for giving—
when that is the only thing about me that will endure?"

Somehow Ogadai learned of a custom of the Kin, or Golden
Emperors, that interested him immediately. Every year, it seemed,
search had been made through the lands of the Kin for the loveliest
of the young girls. Those who were shapeliest, with melodious
voices and sweet breath, were sent to the Court, where the most
alluring were chosen, some fifty of them, to wait upon the Emperor. They tended him, they fetched wine at his pleasure, they
rubbed his limbs with sandal, and they slept by his couch, until
he made choice of those who were to sleep with him. This struck
Ogadai as a kingly and meritorious custom, and he asked Yeliu
Ch'u-tsai to arrange it for him, now that the Mongol khakhans
had made themselves greater than the Kin emperors.

Long Mustache objected. Knowing that the Mongols favored
Chinese girls who were daintier and more sophisticated than the
nomad women, he foresaw a yearly conscription of the young
women of Cathay.

Ogadai was not pleased. "The great ancestor said that no delight
was equal to the joy of seeing vanquished people lying at your feet,
while their fine horses are led forth for you, and the wailing of
their women resounds in your ears. Above all is the joy of lying
with the shapeliest of their young women—crushing their soft
breasts and warm thighs in your arms. Why should this be denied
me?"

[95]

"Have you not twenty-eight such girls already?" the Cathayan demanded. "Does not that number suffice you? You will only make trouble if you go further."

Pondering this, Ogadai agreed. But he insisted that Yeliu Ch'u-tsai requisition all the horses of north China—in spite of the instant objection of the Cathayan philosopher that his people, unlike the nomads, had few horses and that these were needed for agriculture.

Before his death Ogadai increased the number of his bedfellows to sixty. Seldom did he sleep without experiencing the delight that different girls could yield. It did not seem to exhaust his strength. The Mongols had in them the vitality of generations of tribal life in the grasslands. Sexual weakness and abnormal sexual acts were outside their understanding, as yet.

In the Yasa, the code of law of Genghis-Khan, fornication was punished by death, whether the guilty were married or not—likewise sodomy, deliberate lying, and magic.

The Yasa had been dictated by Genghis-Khan from time to time, and traced on leaves of gold by his secretaries. These leaves of the Law were only to be touched by the children of his house, who brought them forth at the councils. They were the Bible and the code of the nomads, immutable as fate. Ogadai himself could not perform an act contrary to the Yasa.

"If the descendants born after me," Genghis-Khan had said, "keep to the Yasa and do not change it; for a thousand and ten thousand years the Everlasting Sky will aid and preserve them."

Neither Ogadai nor his brothers could read the tracings on the gold leaves. But they had the careful memory of the illiterate for the spoken word, and they knew every saying of the Yasa—or, at least, Chagatai did. The Wild Horse had the duty of enforcing the law.

Yeliu Ch'u-tsai understood better than they what Genghis-Khan had tried to do. Before then the nomads as a whole had had no written laws. Genghis-Khan had become acquainted with the laws of civilized peoples, and had ignored them as worthless. He had made up his own code, out of tribal customs and the inhibitions that he hoped would hold his Mongols together, as a clan, through all changes in fortune.

The Yasa forbade anyone to urinate into water or the ashes of a fire, or to wash garments in running water. (A sanitary measure—for the Mongols spent their lives in camps.)

It forbade any Mongol to eat in the presence of another, without sharing his food. No one was to satisfy his hunger more than another. And a Mongol riding by a group who were eating could dismount and take his share of the food without asking permission or being opposed. (A measure to preserve tribal hospitality. The possession of food had meant life itself among the nomads.)

Clothing must not be washed, but must be worn until it shredded apart. (A memory of their early poverty.)

Nothing, the Yasa decreed, must be called unclean. All things are clean, and no distinction exists between clean and unclean. And men must respect religious faiths, without being bound by any one faith. No one was to take sides, between the different sects.

In this new law of the nomads, a Buddhist was the equal of a Christian, a Taoist, or a simple pagan. In this simple requirement the sagacity of the Mongol conqueror made itself felt. He had come into conflict with some of the religions of civilized peoples—or rather, emerging from his desert, he had discovered that his enemies in the settled regions were all devotees of religions. He foresaw the probability of further conflict. Above all, he understood that the paganism of his nomads was their natural belief, and best suited to them. He told his people that other doctrines gave reverence to the same immutable God of the upper regions, the power of the Everlasting Sky. Not for any altruistic reason but to insure the survival of his family and clan, he demanded of them religious tolerance.

He had exempted from taxation and forced labor the teachers of Tao. This privilege he had extended, in the Yasa, to philosophers and lamas, to Buddhist bonzes, and even Moslem callers-to-prayer. He had been suspicious, however, of the magic practiced by the native shamans. But there remained in the Yasa traces of native superstition. It was forbidden any man to step over a fire, or to walk in running water during the spring and summer. (This to escape troubling the tutelary spirits of fire and water.)

If a yurt were touched by lightning, all the dwellers in that yurt were exiled from the clan for three years. They could return only after being purified by passing between two fires. (Lightning was unquestionably the visible force of the wrath of the *tengri*, the Sky-Heaven.)

The Yasa imposed a death penalty for disobedience to an order, for any attempt of a lesser man to use the authority that belonged to the Khakhan alone. And for evidence of quarreling—even for spying upon another man, or taking sides with one of two who were disputing together. (This to put an end to the ancient feuds of the nomads, who had maintained a state of tribal warfare for centuries.)

On the other hand, it forbade the use of high-sounding titles or any exploitation of rank. Those who held rank were to be addressed only by their given names. The Khakhan himself had no other title.

If any man were accused of wrongdoing, he must testify as to his guilt or innocence. In this way he would judge himself. But if it were discovered afterward that he had lied, he was to suffer the death penalty for lying.

During his lifetime, Genghis-Khan had managed to eradicate crime among the Mongols. He made disloyalty, lying, failure to share their acquisitions punishable, under the Yasa. Having undreamed-of abundance, they had no incentive to steal. And the Yasa bound them to keep peace among themselves. Beyond that, they were loyal to family ties and to the vestiges of tribal customs.

The Yasa, so ideal for the pastoral aristocracy of the Mongols, worked hardship enough on subject peoples and those enslaved by the wars. It was a one man's family code. "It was a sort of religion with them," a Moslem chronicler relates, "and they adhered to it until God destroyed them."

The one thing Genghis-Khan had not foreseen was that the Mongols would change their nomadic life. Nor had he allowed for the effect of education on a simple people. He had thought, it appears, that they would learn, and still remain nomads. Yeliu

Ch'u-tsai, perhaps, was the first to perceive that these barbarians, impervious to force, could be educated.

Chagatai, Keeper of the Law

No tutor kept closer to the side of his charge than Chagatai to his younger brother, the Khakhan. Chagatai's zeal for enforcing the letter of the Yasa annoyed Ogadai, who had an idea that all ranks of his people, women and captives included, were entitled to share in the new prosperity of his reign.

Once when the two brothers were riding back to the Ordu, they observed a Moslem—hence a subject, not entitled to Mongol privileges—standing in a stream making ablutions before his prayer; a palpable infringement of the Yasa—polluting running water in the summer. And Chagatai disliked Moslems. He said the offender should be killed.

Ogadai saw that the Moslem was a poor sort, and harmless. The Khakhan dismounted to examine the water, and slipped a bar of silver into it, unnoticed. Then he said to the impatient Wild Horse that the culprit had better appear before the throne of the Khakhan the next day for judgment. Was not that the thing to do?

"Say," he whispered to the Moslem, "that you lost a balish of silver in the stream, and you were hunting for it."

At the next day's hearing the Moslem gave his testimony as Ogadai had prompted him. The Khakhan sent officers out to the stream to verify his words. They returned with the bar of silver, and Ogadai argued that the culprit, being poor, had a right to go into the water for his silver. And, pleased with his conniving, he gave the Moslem ten balishes more.

Chagatai could enforce the law against himself without mercy. Once when he and Ogadai were both drunk they mounted horses to ride over the prairie, their attendants trailing after them. As they rode, Chagatai had an impulse to match his mount against his brother's, and he challenged Ogadai, who accepted promptly. Ogadai lost the race.

That evening, in his ordu, Chagatai—whose head had cleared by then—began to reflect that he had challenged the Khakhan of the world to a contest, and had bettered him at it. So, he, Chagatai, had lacked respect for his Khakhan, and by coming in first he had slighted the dignity of his brother. He felt himself to be guilty on two counts, and he meditated through the night as to what must be done to atone for his offense.

The next morning Ogadai was roused by servants who said that Chagatai Khan, with his sons, his sorcerer, his officers and household troops, was standing before the entrance of the Khakhan's tent.

Amazed, and rather uneasy, Ogadai went out to face his brother. Chagatai had bared his head and put his girdle over his shoulders.

"Yesterday," he said, "I lacked respect for the Khakhan. At this hour I have come to be judged, with my people. I am ready for the punishment. It should be a beating with cudgels. It might be death."

Ogadai looked at him. "Don't be a fool. You are my brother."

Only after argument did Chagatai accept his pardon. He stipulated that he must *k'o tow* before the tent entrance, and make a gift of nine times nine horses, and that the scribes of the judgment court must go through the great Ordu crying out his pardon. He told them what to say: "The Khakhan gives Chagatai his life, so that all the people will know that Chagatai beats his head on the ground to thank the Khakhan for his mercy."

Rarely did Ogadai show the savagery in his nature. Once a tribe tried to avoid obedience, and they never forgot their punishment for so doing.

The Oyrats—the Wood People, one of the first to be taken under the Mongol yoke—heard that the Khakhan intended to marry their girls off to the men of another tribe. Disliking that and yet fearing to protest, the Oyrats quietly and quickly betrothed their girls within the tribe itself. Several marriages were carried out.

Ogadai, learning of this, gave order to assemble all the unmarried girls of the Oyrat older than seven years, and those who had been married within the year.

Four thousand of them appeared, in their festival garments, in the plain by the Ordu. Their families waited anxiously in the background while the Khakhan bade his officers range the girls in two long lines. He walked between the lines, picking out the young women who seemed most desirable to him.

Those he kept for himself. His second choice he gave to his higher officials. The most desirable of the remaining girls he turned over to the keepers of prostitutes. Then he signed to his guards and the onlookers. "Help yourself to the rest," he urged them.

While the fathers, brothers and husbands watched, the men rushed on the girls, snatching at them and carrying them off. No one dared protest.

The Oyrat men had attempted to disobey the Khakhan, and they had learned their lesson, without bloodshed.

Turakina, his empress, was the first to suggest that Ogadai might live in more splendor. Other kings of the earth, she pointed out, had palaces with tiled flooring and perfumed sleeping chambers, while Ogadai the Khakhan continued to dwell in the tents of his ancestors, as if he were still a keeper of herds.

Ogadai replied that these yurts were now spacious and hung with silk.

The Golden Emperor, Turakina retorted truthfully, housed his slaves in better buildings. But she could not reconcile Ogadai to living within walls. Had not the great ancestor warned the Mongols that they were born to wander, and never to settle down? To build houses like townspeople or merchants would be to anger the suldë of his father, and he would not do it.

He did, however, cover the poles of his great pavilion with beaten gold. And he built out in the prairies a long, curving wall of mud bricks. This he could use to pen wild game, when he hunted. Like all Mongols, Ogadai was passionately fond of the chase.

Perhaps, then, he wished that Turakina were not so demanding. She quoted the law to him, and she made no secret of her ambition. When she left her yurt, she rode in a sedan chair under a palanquin like a mandarin—or like Ogadai himself—with a mass of black slaves in red robes going before her. At her side she kept a cunning Nestorian priest who wrote spells, and a bold-eyed slave girl named Fatima who haled from Persia. Sometimes it appeared as if Turakina had a court of her own. Well, she was entitled to that.

Tului's wife, on the other hand, used the newest importations from Cathay to make herself comely. Like smooth jade, she gleamed when she rode at the left hand of her redoubtable husband. Always she spoke in a low voice, approving what Tului and Ogadai did. And she did not cease from taking heed of their comfort. Ogadai found it pleasant to watch Siyurkuktiti and listen to her.

The Downfall of the Kin

Meanwhile Ogadai went to war. He might have remained in the great Ordu on the ancestral grazing lands. Tului urged him to do so, saying that the new Khakhan should sit in the center of his dominion, ordering all things, while he, Tului and the Mongol noyans carried on the work of conquest for him, as Genghis-Khan had planned.

This Ogadai would not do. He preferred the comfort of a throne seat to a saddle, but in the saddle he meant to be.

Before the first kuriltai was dismissed, the Mongols had made their plans for a further thrust against the civilized powers. Tului burned with anxiety to be in the field, while the veteran commanders only waited for the order to start back to the frontiers.

Some were found who argued that they already possessed grazing lands enough to last the nomads for untold generations. They had penetrated to the Great Ocean (the Pacific). They had conquered the west, for a hundred marches (about 3300 miles), and in the south they had come to the great Snowy Mountains (the Hindu Kush). Their outposts held the edge of the Sea of the Ravens (the Caspian). They had demolished the great cities in their path, tearing down the walls so that in many places they could graze their horses there. They had broken the armies of the civilized peoples so far, and slain masses of the town dwellers. Other multitudes had become their slaves, to tend their herds and do hand labor for them. They had enough—so argued the Chinese councilors, and the Uighurs.

Moreover, said they, the great ancestor had reined his horse back at the Snowy Mountains. And he had summoned back the two Orluks—the Eagles—from the steppes of Russia. He had not commanded them to go on to further conquests, but to make certain of what they now held—as far as the hoofs of Mongol ponies had trod. Why should they go farther?

To these hesitators one made answer who had taken no part in the election or the festivities. Subotai Bahadur, the surviving Orluk (Eagle) of Genghis-Khan—Subotai whose cunning had brought ceaseless victories to the Mongols. He was a Mongol of the older type, of the Reindeer people, silent, insatiable and remorseless. And he spoke for the elder Mongol noyans, the commanders of the victorious army. He said that their work was not yet done. While enemies existed with unbroken strength in the world, the Mongol dominion was not secure.

In the far corner of Cathay by the sea, he reminded them, the Golden Emperor still lived in his citadel. And beyond, to the south, lay the empire of ancient China, still untouched.

While under the setting sun, he declared, dwelt warlike barbarians who mocked at the Mongol name—Russians and other Christians of that far peninsula, Europe. He himself had entered their lands, only to be recalled by Genghis-Khan. But now he, Subotai, would not turn back until he had crossed the Danube River and conquered the west.

Subotai spoke with authority. And the Mongols assented to his words. Ogadai gave him a princess of the Golden Family to wife and appointed him to go with Tului against the Kin.

But more than any argument was the instinct that drove these Mongols toward the south and the warmth of the sun. They had been weaned in the wind-swept steppes, and the fir forests of Sibir—these Mongols, Arlats, Taidjuts, Tatars, Oyrats and Urianguts. Subotai himself came from the Reindeer keepers. Like their forebears, they were driven to escape from the region of long night and of the frost gods. They wanted to leave behind them the homeland where the wild birds cried and the black basalt rocks, shaped by demon hands, rose out of the plain.

This second attack on civilization was planned by Subotai and the veteran army commanders—by what might be called the General Staff of the Mongols. Ogadai and Tului merely expressed their wishes as individuals. And Subotai planned only cautious moves at first.

Young Batu was sent back with his westerners to reoccupy the grazing lands as far as the Urals—part of the heritage of his wayward father, Juchi. A small army was detached to bring Korea into subjection; another, under the Mongol general Charmaghan, was sent to obliterate the resistance of the Moslems in north Persia. All this was no more than consolidation of their conquests.

Subotai planned it. It would be their first campaign without the guiding genius of Genghis-Khan. But Genghis-Khan, it seems, had advised them what to do, before his death. Moreover, he had broken, in his last year, the power of the Hsians on the flank of China, so the way would be open for them to move south into China.

And this was to be the effort of the main army, to conquer the last strongholds of Cathay.

Only a corner of Cathay remained. The Ta Kin, or Golden Emperor, driven out of Yen-king and the north, had settled himself in fertile Honan, behind the broad Yellow River. Here, however, the Kin were protected by strong natural barriers—the Yellow River in the north, the chains of the Blue Mountains and the strong fortress of Tung-kuan in the west, and the Yang-tse in the south.

The Kin still possessed great wealth, and immensely strong cities. Their new capitol Kai-fong-fu (Nan-king, the Southern Court) had within its forty-mile circuit of walls some four million souls. So the Kin, although warlike enough, had not prepared large armies to take the field. They were making ready to hold their lines of defense, knowing by experience that rivers and fortified walls could stop the Mongols where armies of maneuver would be wiped out.

And Subotai was correspondingly unwilling to risk his main army against a river, flooded plains, and walled citadels. Genghis-Khan had laid down the rule that the Mongols must keep to the strategy of the steppes, avoiding loss of life and needless battles.

Such strategy demanded that an enemy must be maneuvered, if possible, into a position where he would be helpless, before the Mongols launched their main attack. Such maneuvering could best be carried out by a pincerlike movement of two armies, concentrating at the proper time on the enemy.

It seemed out of the question to accomplish anything like that against the Kin, who were arrogant in their confidence that, after a dozen years, they could keep the Mongols out of Honan. Moreover, with the ocean at their backs, their defense would be desperate—a circumstance that made the Mongols wary.

Their difficulty had been solved for them by Genghis-Khan. When he felt himself dying, the old Mongol had advised Tului how to destroy the Kin. The Kin, he had explained, must be invaded, not in the strongly defended north and west, but from the south where they would expect no enemy to appear. The Kin armies would be facing north, along the Yellow River. So a Mongol army must circle them and break through in the southwest.

Ogadai agreed. This hazardous part of the maneuver fell to Tului as usual. Ogadai and Subotai took command of the Left Wing of the Mongol army that had been occupying northern Cathay. With their siege engines they advanced slowly against the Yellow River line of defense, reducing the frontier citadels while they waited for Tului to make his circle and close the other half of the pincers.

Tului asked Subotai how to proceed against the Kin when he reached them.

"They are town-bred people," the Mongol Eagle said, "and so they cannot endure fatigue. Harry them enough, and you will find it easy to overcome them in battle."

Tului remembered this and acted on it when the time came. Since no large army could penetrate where he had to go, he took a small force—three divisions, 30,000 horsemen from the veteran *kul* or center, with two experienced generals to command the other two units. With them, he disappeared.

That is, he marched south, across the barren end of the Gobi. He passed through the abandoned Great Wall that had become a

Mongol thoroughfare by now, and passed into the mountain ranges. He moved far south. Across the dark pine ridges the snow peaks of Tibet were visible on the skyline when he turned eastward. Climbing through the trails of Szechuan, he emerged unexpectedly into the valleys of the neutral Sung empire. Moving rapidly now, he crossed the upper Wei. Gaining the consent of the Sung powers to make the march that he had already made, he turned north, threading through highlands where no armies had maneuvered before them.

No one had opposed him, because no one had expected him to appear from this point of the compass. Now the Kin generals hurried south to meet him with their main forces.

It was autumn, the cold severe. Tului's mounted divisions had been thinned by the severe march. He withdrew promptly, separating his divisions, and the Kin armies climbed after him, reporting to the court at Nan-king that they had gained a victory. But Tului seized their baggage trains and maneuvered into higher and still more difficult ground. Winter storms swept both armies— the Mongols, protected by their felt capes, enduring better than the hard-driven Kin. Supplies failed, and the masses of men were near the starvation point. The Mongols ate flesh from dead horses and human bodies. From the heights they made sudden attacks on the nearly exhausted enemy.

The great numbers of the Kin could not protect them against such cavalry thrusts in broken country. Meanwhile Ogadai and Subotai had crossed the line of the Yellow River, in the north. The garrisons of the Kin cities were mustered to face this new danger, while the main army was recalled hastily. It could not free itself, however, from Tului's incessant attacks, and its withdrawal became a hurried retreat. Tului had carried out Subotai's suggestion brilliantly.

On the northern front the Kin commanders tried to cut the dikes of the rivers, to flood the country around Nan-king. But Subotai's advanced detachments reached the dikes first and stopped the flooding. His forces drove the Cathayans back toward their capitol.

The surviving portions of the main army of the Kin arrived

almost within sight of Nan-king as they retreated before Tului. They were caught between Tului's columns and Subotai's advance, and hemmed in.

The Mongols, by sheer maneuvering, had crippled the enemy's main force and penned it like a herd of cattle to be butchered. Refusing to surrender, the Cathayan army was annihilated in a prolonged and bitter conflict.

And the millions in Nan-king found the Mongols preparing to besiege their city. Ogadai, rejoicing, welcomed his brother into his tent, to listen to the story of his long march. Tului said casually that the success was due to the endurance of his men.

Now that the maneuvering was over, and siege warfare begun, Ogadai left the command with the implacable Subotai. Midsummer heat held the region, and the stout Khakhan longed for the cool air of his prairies. He trekked back through the Wall, taking Tului with him—after demanding gifts from the Golden Emperor, who now besought him for terms of peace. Ogadai asked, characteristically, for unexpected things—among them a certain scholar, descended from Confucius, and a quantity of girls skilled in making embroidery, with men-servants experienced in hunting with falcons. And these were sent him.

But Subotai refused to abandon the siege, saying that he had heard nothing of peace.

Just after he left the Great Wall, Ogadai was stricken with a deadly sickness. In Yeliu Ch'u-tsai's absence, there was no physician to be summoned, and Ogadai called in the *kams*, the shaman-magicians, to drive out the demon that tormented him.

The shamans sealed the tent of the sick man and sat down to their drums. They drew water from a spring, and they swept out the yurt with birch seedlings made into a broom, to cleanse the earth. They poured wine and milk of a goat into the water, heating it in a wooden bowl over the embers of a dung fire. With this liquid they washed the afflicted parts of Ogadai's body—to wash away the demon that had fastened upon the Khakhan's flesh.

Then Tului, who sat watching in silent anxiety, took the bowl from them. He spoke an invocation to the Everlasting Sky—that its power might heal Ogadai.

For Tului believed, as his brother believed, in the magic of the shamans. He drank the liquid in the bowl, saying, "Thou knowest that I have more of blood guilt than he, for I have slain more men and made slaves of multitudes. Or," he added, "if it is for his beauty Thou seekest him—he is more hideous than I. Let him live as he is, and take me in his stead."

It seemed to him quite reasonable. If the evil kelets craved a life, they should be satisfied with Tului's as much as Ogadai's. And Tului, who had watched so many thousands die, was terrified at thought of Ogadai dying.

But Ogadai recovered, and they resumed their journey toward the Ordu. They had come in sight of the dark hills at the headwaters of the Onon, when Tului sickened swiftly. Within a few days he was dead.

The shamans felt justified of their magic. They explained that Tului had drunk the sickness that was in Ogadai.

The Widow

Ogadai, however, comforted himself by drinking wine. The young brother had gone through the Gate in the Sky, his suldë would be companioning with that of the father which dwelt in the yak tails of the standard. There was no help for it. The smoke still rose from the ancestral hearth in the grasslands by the Kerulan. But the Keeper of the Hearth had left Ogadai.

He experimented with new wines of Cathay, seasoned with cloves and sugar. When he drank, the coldness left his limbs. Warm blood sang in his head. His feet moved as if they were dancing of their own accord. His ears heard his own voice. At such a time when he was entirely drunk, the Blue Wolf of his ancient clan would appear in the yurt, and Ogadai felt a sense of power. The voices of his girls chimed like tiny bells, and their white skin gleamed like smooth satin. . . .

Chagatai had come back to the Ordu, when the hard-riding couriers brought him word of Tului's death. Chagatai forbade Ogadai to drink more than six goblets a day. The Khakhan was too fearful of his elder brother's anger to disobey. Besides, Chagatai told off an officer to be with Ogadai when he ate or drank, to see that he kept to the six allotted cups.

And Ogadai did keep to them. But he had larger ones made, to double the amount of wine and spirits. The officer noticed the change but said nothing to Chagatai.

It was not so easy to evade Yeliu Ch'u-tsai. The wise Cathayan knew that drink and dysentery had carried off Tului. Until a generation before, the nomads had drunk little except their inevitable fermented mare's milk. Now, with jars of liquor stored about them, they craved intoxication.

One day Yeliu Ch'u-tsai brought his master an iron jar in which spirits had been standing. He showed Ogadai how the iron had been corroded by the spirits. "If it does this to iron," he warned, "judge for yourself what it must do to your intestines."

The demonstration impressed Ogadai, and he drank less. "I grieved for Tului," he said, "so I drank more than my share of wine."

At the Ordu, he often found Siyurkuktiti in his presence. The widow of Tului made no trouble in her mourning. She listened to the shamans and the bonzes who came to console her, and gave them gifts impartially. It stirred Ogadai's heart to see her in mourning. He urged her to ask for anything she wished—he would not deny her. She asked for an officer who served the Khakhan to attend her. The man was valuable, and Ogadai did not wish to give him up. Then, with a flash of temper and tears in her eyes, Siyurkuktiti cried:

"Tului was loved and desired of me. See! For whom hath Tului sacrificed himself? For whom hath he died!"

Ogadai, troubled, considered. "The right is with Siyurkuktiti Bcgi. Let her forgive me. Her wish is granted."

When this reached the ear of Turakina, the first wife of the Khakhan made trouble about it. Was the Khakhan, she demanded, like a weak reed, to bend at the breath of a woman's anger? Her sharp words made it seem as if Ogadai had been belittled by Siyurkuktiti.

And the Khakhan made test of Tului's widow. Without consulting her or the princes of the Golden Family, he gave two thousand warriors of the Suldus clan to his own son.

Then the chieftains of the army who had belonged to Tului, the commanders of thousands and tens of thousands, came together to the yurt of Tului's widow, before her sons and the other princes of the Golden Family.

"Those two thousand of the Suldus are ours," they said, "by the mandate of Genghis-Khan. Now Ogadai gives them to his son. How can we endure such a thing? How can we alter the word of the yarligh of Genghis-Khan? Indeed, we shall bring this before the face of the Khakhan."

Siyurkuktiti spoke to them quietly: "Truly have you spoken. Yet think! Are we lacking in riches that have been handed down to us? No—nor is anything owing to us. And, beyond that, the army and ourselves belong now to the Khakhan. We are his to command, and he knows what must be bidden, and we shall bow to his will."

When they heard this, the chieftains stood silent. Everyone who heard was satisfied.

Especially Ogadai. "When shall I see," he demanded of the princes, "another among the race of women like to her?" For a while he pondered, and decided that the fittest thing would be to make an offer of marriage to Siyurkuktiti Begi. He offered to marry her to his eldest son, Kuyuk. (It was a tribal custom for a brother or a nephew or, at times, a son to take the wives of a man who had died.)

Kuyuk, Ogadai reflected, was morose and solitary, and troubled besides by the evil kelets of sickness. Siyurkuktiti would be a blessing for him, and the marriage would unite his own house with Tului's house.

When his envoy made the proposal to Siyurkuktiti, she thanked him and explained that she had no wish for another husband. "How can one do otherwise than obey the will of the Khakhan?" she said. "Yet it is my one desire to bring up these children of mine to manhood, striving to make them mannerly, and keeping them from hating one another, and growing apart—so that out of their fidelity a good work may come."

This wish of a mother moved Ogadai greatly. He felt that he should grant her all Tului's heritage—the homeland and the hearth of the Mongols, the nucleus of the first tribes, and the bulk of the veteran army. For he thought her modest and chaste as well as wise. And Siyurkuktiti received her husband's appanage gratefully from his hand.

"Since some of her children were very young when their father died," Rashid says, "she guided them and made every effort to train them—and to guard the great chieftains and war clans that they had inherited from Genghis-Khan. And these commanders, seeing her equal to all things, never strayed from her ordering."

The death of Tului, while Ogadai lived, had removed her sons from the prospect of leadership in the Golden Family. But Siyurkuktiti had managed to keep them in power, and she herself had become the head of the house of Tului. Instinct, surer then Yeliu Ch'u-tsai's sagacity, warned her that weaklings could not survive in this new world of the Mongols.

Ogadai Builds Himself a Palace

After returning from the Cathay campaign, Ogadai no longer held out against Turakina's importunity. He had quartered himself in the comfortable yamens of Cathay, admiring their courtyards and garden pools. And he did not feel inclined to return to tent life. If Turakina wanted palaces, palaces she should have.

True, the great ancestor had advised him to keep moving, and not to settle down. Ogadai compromised, shrewdly. He would have palaces enough to keep moving between them.

"He bent his thoughts," Rashid relates, "to the designing of all types of buildings."

For his town residence, he selected the grasslands where a river branched, south of Lake Baikal. Here he had a wall of dried mud put up, to mark the townsite, and to corral his horses.

It was known as *Kara-korum*—Black Walls—and also as the *Ordu-baligh*, or Camp-city.

"Since from the region of Cathay," Rashid explains, "he had brought back craftsmen who were masters, he bade them raise up in the yurt of Kara-korum—where he liked to reside—a palace solid of base and lofty of pillar, befitting a monarch such as he. Its sides were the length of an arrow's flight, and they adorned it with paintings and sculptured figures, and he made it his throne seat. Then the order went forth that his brother and son and the other princes of the imperial House were to raise up palaces of their own by it. All of them obeyed, and when these edifices were finished and joined together, great throngs came to look upon them.

"Then the Khakhan bade that the most skillful goldsmiths should make festive fountains for the wine hall in the shapes of beasts such as elephants, lions and horses. They were filled with wine and mare's milk, and before each one was a basin made of silver, so that the wine and mare's milk would flow out into the basins.

"And he gave command that each day five hundred wagons, drawn by six oxen, and filled with wine, grain and meat, should arrive at his palace, and be given out from his storerooms."

A day's ride from his desert metropolis of Kara-korum, Ogadai built a banquet pavilion. When he was inclined to feast, he would go thither. Only for a month, in spring, would he reside in his palace.

"All the people," Rashid says, "would put on garments of the same color. For a month he would busy himself with pleasures in the palace, and set open the door of his treasure house, to let high and low profit from his bounty. Every nightfall he would pit his bowmen and his archers and wrestlers one against the other, and he would flatter the winners and give them gifts."

Farther out on the prairie, he had Persian artisans—since Kara-korum had been entrusted to the Chinese—build another palace at a place where he heard the gamekeepers of a long-dead king had dwelt. He visited this in the spring when the wild beasts were astir after the winter, and he called it *Kurt chagan* (the White Wolf).

For a summer residence Ogadai selected a site by the Blue Lake, where the wild birds gathered. Here he had a great pavilion pitched, the outside studded with gold, and tapestries hung within

—a tent that could hold a thousand people. This he called the *Sira Ordu*—the Golden Camp.

The winters he passed at the hunting wall, with a large part of the army, who served to drive the game.

"For a month they made a human ring," Rashid relates, "to drive the game against the barrier—the warriors standing shoulder to shoulder in a circle. First Ogadai with his chosen companions would enter and amuse himself killing the game. When he was sated, the princes and chieftains would go in, in order. After that the common people and soldiers would hunt—until the remaining animals were freed for next year's chase, and the stewards divided up all the game so that no man remained without his portion. After nine days' feasting, each tribe returned to its own yurt."

The Salvage of Cathay

Long before Ogadai's palaces were finished in the prairies, the cities of Cathay had crumbled beneath Subotai's attack. A generation before this, when the Mongols first rode into Cathay, they had avoided the cities, knowing little of siege warfare. Now they had engineers to serve them, to sap and to mine.

Around Nan-king, Subotai had built a counter-wall, fifty-four miles in circuit, with wooden towers that rose above the wall of the doomed city. Siege machines creaked and thudded on each wall. The firepots of the Mongols kept the roofs in the city smoking; but the Cathayans had the *ho pao*, the fire machines that wrought destruction with gunpowder. They thrust long iron tubes through holes in the walls into the Mongol trenches. Then the powder in the tubes exploded with a roar, making a black and smoking crater in the earth. The Mongols had a healthy fear of the *ho pao*, until they learned how to use the machines themselves.

For six days Subotai assaulted the walls, after captives had piled bundles of brush against them, and human bodies rose with the brush. He sat quietly in his tent, hearing the tidings that were brought to its entrance. He had a thin, reddish beard and small eyes, and the skin was lean on the bones of his head. No written words or maps littered the tent; he carried the plan of the country and the positions of his regiments in his mind. And he was implacable as death itself.

A Kin general among the captives condemned to death asked to have Subotai pointed out to him. The Mongol stepped forward.

"Thou who hast not a moment to live," Subotai demanded. "What dost thou wish of me?"

"It is not chance but destiny that makes conquerors such as thou," the captive answered. "Having seen thee, I am ready to die." And he was killed.

When the attack failed, the Mongol leader waited patiently for starvation to do his work for him. The multitude inside the walls ate what remained of horseflesh, and made soup of saddle leather and human bones, mixed with green weeds. Flesh was taken from the bodies of the sick and slain prisoners. Then plague thinned the ranks of the living. . . . Subotai let it be known that he would consider terms of peace, and the Kin, snatching at this hope, sent out armfuls of their treasure to him. Whereupon Subotai did withdraw his forces far beyond sight of the walls.

He wanted to rest his men in camps remote from the plague. When he was ready, he attacked again. A division of Chinese troops from the Sung empire aided him.

The Kin emperor, young and stout, bewildered by calamity, wrote to the Sung, "The Mongols have taken Hsia and forty kingdoms. After the Kin will come the turn of the Sung. You do evil, in aiding them."

This Golden Emperor was unable to realize that his dynasty had come to an end. At his birth he had been the overlord of millions who were, in different degree, his slaves. They had reverenced him as the child of an all-powerful Heaven. Now he still wrote verses and amused himself with music and girls on a pleasure barge upon the lake of Nan-king—until the Mongols drained the lake.

He left the city with his courtiers, to assemble a new army. But he found the other cities ruined, or hopeless, and he threw himself into a fortress to escape the Mongol horsemen. Women put on the garments of men, to defend his life when they heard that the Mongols had broken through the walls of Nan-king.

The Book of the Kuriltai

Giving up the seal of state, he bade his kinsmen carry on the dynasty if they survived. Then he ordered the wives who still accompanied him to be slain, and the tower in which he had taken refuge to be filled with straw. Bidding his servants set fire to the straw, he hung himself.

Before his servants could sprinkle the waters of oblation over the ashes, the Mongols were swarming through the place, with the Sung soldiers. And the Sung commander carried off a vase of the ashes, to take back with him to the imperial temple of the Chinese.

The Golden Emperor, who had longed to write verses, had become a handful of ashes in an inscribed urn. Survivors of his family committed suicide by jumping into the river, or they were hunted down and slain.

The Kin dynasty had come to an end. It was Yeliu Ch'u-tsai who preserved its culture and the surviving human beings who no longer had a protector.

Yeliu Ch'u-tsai, as usual, had been following where the Mongols looted. Before fire could destroy what they left behind, he and his Cathayan servants gathered up many things tossed aside by the Mongols—sheaves of maps, books of brush paintings, old coins. And always the valuable stacks of rhubarb.

When he heard that Nan-king had fallen, he hurried to Ogadai and did an amazing thing. He knew that most of the population of Honan had taken refuge in the great city, and he asked the Khakhan to order his commanders to spare the lives of the several million survivors.

Until then the Mongol army had devastated any walled habitation that resisted it. Subotai was preparing to let his regiments loot and massacre within Nan-king as a matter of course. Its stubborn defense enraged the Mongol leaders.

And Ogadai refused at first to break the long-established custom.

"Do you want to lose," the Cathayan demanded, "the results of ten years of warfare?"

The land of Cathay, he asked, what was it worth in itself without the inhabitants who raised grain and rice, and made silk from worms and mulberry leaves?

The March of the Barbarians

Still Ogadai refused.

"Then think of this," his minister argued. "The treasure you have taken from Cathay, the gold, the fine objects and the splendid iron of its swords and arrowheads, all that is no more than the work of the hands of its artisans. If you put an end to this generation of men, you will get no more treasure made."

Ogadai conceded that this was true. And he ordered Subotai to spare the civilian population. The Cathayan armies had been annihilated, with their officers, and the members of the imperial family were being exterminated. But the peasant farmers, the artisans of the towns, and the scholars survived the storm. Yeliu Ch'u-tsai made certain of that, by distributing banners to them inscribed with the yarligh of the Khakhan. He took pains to summon back refugees from the mountains before they could develop into outlaws.

And he promised Ogadai that the time would come when he could collect a million ounces of silver yearly in revenues from Cathay. Ogadai was satisfied, because Yeliu Ch'u-tsai had never failed to keep a promise.

But many of the Mongol nobles at Kara-korum were not satisfied. They had been amazed at first at the amount the yearly taxes brought in; now they complained to Ogadai that the taxes were too light. If taxes produced so much wealth, why not double the taxes, and have twice as much wealth?

Government, Yeliu Ch'u-tsai warned them, must be saving. It could not be avaricious. "These taxes," he cried, "are already too heavy if they go to enrich grasping men."

It needed more than courage to fight the battle Yeliu Ch'u-tsai was waging for Chinese civilization. Only steel-like purpose—as inflexible as Subotai's—and extraordinary presence of mind enabled him to convince the conquerors that he was right. Added to that, he had to have at his fingers' ends a knowledge of the countries as great as theirs.

Already the Cathayan had established schools in Yen-king and elsewhere to teach the boys of the Mongol princes something of geography, astronomy and history. He explained that it was possible to know things about a country before they visited it, and to anticipate the movements of the planets—to which they paid superstitious heed. Once the teaching began, Mongols whose sons were still illiterate often brought them in to the new schools.

"*Chikin khudlchi, nüdn ünchi,*" the elder Mongols reminded them. "Ears deceive—eyes reveal!"

A period of grim reconstruction set in. Mongol officers in occupied territory were more than mere governors. They were nomads who cared only for the immediate moment, and most of all for gain. They enforced, in agricultural Cathay, the customs of the steppes. If bandits robbed along the highways, they collected the amount of the loss from the nearest villages—and they commandeered horses for the post stations that linked together the new empire.

Frequently the heads of Chinese villages, forced to produce a tax assessment in silver, had to borrow from Moslem moneylenders. In the course of a year exorbitant interest would double the amount of the debt. If another year passed without payment, the debt and interest would double again, and the usurers would take the farm animals from the community in payment. The people would then abandon their homes, or sell their children as slaves—going off to become part of the drifting human tide that began to move in the wake of a war.

Yeliu Ch'u-tsai convinced Ogadai that these debts of harassed communities ought to be shouldered by the public treasury. "These people," he told the Khakhan, "are your children."

Ogadai had a fresh idea. "I am told," he said to Yeliu Ch'u-tsai, "that in Cathay they stamped money out of a worthless stuff, paper. They used this paper instead of coins. Why cannot we print money in this fashion?"

The Cathayan smiled. "True—it was done once. And they called the minister who did it Lord Scrap-paper. After a while, with this same precious paper, it took ten thousand *taels* to buy one cake. Do you wish that to happen to us?"

Paper money, he explained, had one peculiarity. If you printed a little of it, it was indeed precious paper—as the Chinese called it—but if you printed overmuch, the paper would be worth nothing at all. No more than one hundred thousand paper notes, for as many ounces of silver, he said, should be issued. And, in fact, he held the issue down to fifty thousand.

To this, Ogadai paid little heed. That was Yeliu Ch'u-tsai's affair, and the Khakhan was more interested in the evening's shadow plays and wrestling bouts.

Yeliu Ch'u-tsai had a bitter conflict with the Mongol nobles who had begged overlordship of captured districts from Ogadai. The Khakhan was quite willing to parcel out his new empire in this way, but the wise Cathayan saw the danger in creating a feudal state.

"Give them gold or woven stuffs," he advised. "Anything but land."

"I have promised," Ogadai objected.

"Then give the princes and the grandees a year's tax from these districts. But never let the land and the population go from your hand."

He won his point, but he made more enemies. When he passed judgment on a murderer who had killed a priest, Ogadai lost all patience and gave order that Yeliu Ch'u-tsai was to be imprisoned. After a few days, he began to miss his minister, and sent word that the Cathayan was to be released. Yeliu Ch'u-tsai would not move out of his cell.

"You named me your minister," he sent word to Ogadai. "You arrested me. So—I was guilty. Now you give me liberty. And so I am innocent. But how am I to manage the affairs of the empire?"

"A thousand words slip out of me in a day," the Khakhan replied by messenger, "and how can I answer for all of them? The truth is, you are innocent, and you are restored to your rank."

In the spring of the year 1235, the year of the Goat by Mongol reckoning, Ogadai summoned a second kuriltai—this time to the housewarming of his Kara-korum palace. And his first toast, at the first evening's banquet, was to Yeliu Ch'u-tsai.

"Behold him," he challenged. "He stays by my side, yet he brings in stores of gold and precious things from afar. Has any other ruler of men a minister such as he?"

And he appointed Yeliu Ch'u-tsai governor general of Cathay.

The occasion was one to warm Ogadai's heart. Turakina sat in splendor at his left hand, and hundreds of his kinsmen faced him down the long wine hall. From the gleaming elephants and horses, wine and mare's milk flowed into the silver basins. All the feasters were robed in blue silk, the blue of the Sky. When he lifted his cup to drink, a whole orchestra resounded musically.

Ogadai had sent for wrestlers from Persia, and Charmaghan had shipped him back thirty, of which one named Pila caught Ogadai's eye by his enormous physique. Ogadai wagered that Pila would throw any steppe-born wrestler, and he won his wager when the giant Persian broke the bones of an army champion.

Pleased with his find, he gave Pila a girl who was strikingly handsome. Some time afterward he asked this girl how she found the Persian as a lover—the Persians for some reason having a reputation in that respect among the Mongols.

"May my lord's anger not be upon me," she begged, and confessed, "Pila will have nothing to do with me."

Rendered curious, Ogadai asked his wrestler why he had not enjoyed the girl.

"To the court of the Lord of the World I came," Pila explained. "And I have not been bettered by any other wrestler. Thy servant wished to keep his strength unspent, so that he would keep the favor of the Lord of the World."

Ogadai laughed and said he would like to see some offspring of that same strength, and that Pila could forget about his reputation.

Around the pavilion of this second kuriltai new faces appeared. Caravan merchants, aware of the wealth flowing into the mud walls of Kara-korum. Venturesome lamas, wandering out of Tibet to see the face of the nomad emperor. Shrewd minds, probing for profit in the simplicity of the barbarians.

Increasingly now, Ogadai was subjected to subtle propaganda. But he was protected by the astuteness of Ch'u-tsai and Yelvadj. And his own native shrewdness sometimes turned deception against the deceiver.

The March of the Barbarians

A stranger prostrated himself before Ogadai's throne seat, crying that he had a portent, a warning out of the spirit-world, from the suldë of Genghis-Khan (knowing well that the Mongols would obey any imaginable command from the great ancestor).

In a dream, he said, the old Mongol had appeared to him, saying, "Go thou on my behalf to my sons, and bid them exterminate the Moslems, who are an evil race."

Ogadai, as usual, pondered this. "Did my father speak to you by an interpreter?" he asked.

The man shook his head. No, the mighty conqueror had appeared alone to him.

"And do you understand the Mongol speech?" Ogadai asked.

"Nay, as the Khakhan perceives, I speak only Turkish."

"Then you lie, because my father spoke only Mongolian."

And Ogadai had the man killed.

Even the aging and irascible Chagatai was content at this kuriltai. The Yasa was obeyed. All the members of the Golden Family were present to hear the wise words spoken. The testament of the great ancestor was being fulfilled—the victories of the last years had obliterated Cathay and pushed the Persian frontier beyond the Caspian. Korea had rebelled, but Korea could be brought to hand, now that the Kin were out of the world.

Years of peace in the Mongol homelands had strengthened the army; the new wealth had filled the yurts like well-stocked granaries. The horse herds had grown beyond counting. True, the Wild Horse did not much approve of Ogadai's new buildings in Karakorum—he preferred the felt tents himself. But so long as Ogadai continued to dwell in the steppes, he might build what he wanted. That was the nomad way, to take the treasures of the cities into the plains.

The Mongols knew they were ready to attack again. And this would be on a greater scale. No one knows who made the decision, but it was Subotai's old ambition to make the main thrust into the west, to destroy the distant, warlike Christian nations in their peninsula beyond the Danube. The Eagle had been making his plans to do so.

The Left Wing, as a matter of course, would resume its advance into China—this time against the empire of the Sung beyond the Yang-tse. Another division would make an exploratory raid into Kashmir and north India. But the main army, under Subotai's direction, would go west.

To this the shamans and lamas agreed, perforce. Such was the intention, clearly to be seen, of the suldë residing in the Mongol banner, which in turn was actuated by the power of the Everlasting Blue Sky.

Turakina discussed it with her favorite, Fatima, and approved. For Ogadai—after Tului's death—would remain in Kara-korum with her. Instead of the Khakhan, her eldest son Kuyuk would go. Kuyuk had gained no victories as yet for the Mongols. He was still a pigmy beside such giants as Ch'u-tsai and Yelvadj, or Subotai. And he needed military glory if he was to govern Mongols. Let Kuyuk command, in this new march across the face of the earth.

Ogadai wanted to go, but everyone joined in urging him not to do so. They had almost lost their Khakhan in the Kin campaign, and they were not willing to take such a chance again. Better to let the youngest of his house, the brilliant grandson Kaidu, ride with Subotai, to learn from him.

Chagatai announced that two of his house would go, two of his sons. So there would be a pack of the young cubs, to sharpen their teeth in this venture. He did not realize that this would breed trouble. For the nominal command—Subotai being the actual brains of the undertaking—was given not to Kuyuk but to Batu, because the attack was to start from Batu's lands in the west, and because Batu was eldest of the younger generation.

Yeliu Ch'u-tsai approved, after a hot debate with Ogadai. Ogadai had argued it would be good to make up the army of invasion out of the Left Wing veterans and the Chinese levies, while he summoned Batu and the westerners—the Kirghiz and Turkish elements—to carry on the conquest of China. Ogadai, rather shrewdly, wanted to fight easterners with westerners, and vice versa.

"It will not do," Ch'u-tsai protested. "The distances are too great—you cannot march the Turks down to the China Sea, and send the Chinese into the steppes they do not know."

The March of the Barbarians

Actually the astute Cathayan wanted to keep the still barbaric Turks as far as possible from his beloved China. Also, he sent the war faction of the Mongols west, where it would be off the scene for some time. (In reality, it was gone for five years.)

Siyurkuktiti, who had more influence than any other woman, acquiesced in the plan. Ch'u-tsai had promised to find a better tutor for her son Kubilai. She also let the old Turk Yelvadj urge upon her that the Mongols should indeed go west, along the road of the barbarians, of the Turks. Let them keep to central Asia, and rule from the saddle—build palaces to their hearts' content—but make allies, not enemies, of the Moslems.

"To hold the caravan roads," Siyurkuktiti agreed. Was she not a friend of the Moslems? Had she not dwelt with them in the apple orchards of Almalyk, while her sons were taught? Was not her first-born, Mangu, more familiar with the west than Kuyuk, Turakina's eldest? Yelvadj could not but agree that Mangu was better fitted to command than the dour Kuyuk.

And Mangu would go with the army of invasion. So Siyurkuktiti managed to keep a son in the forefront of both the Chinese and the Turkish factions. Because she told Kubilai, her next-born, that he could not go. He would remain to keep the ancestral hearth and acquire knowledge with the young students.

Observant and quiet, Kubilai made no protest. Kubilai Sechen had become a man. He had his first wife, the Lady Jamui, a small and mild girl of the Konkurat (Chestnut Horse) tribe, noted for its beauty—being interbred with the Cathayans. As Siyurkuktiti had known them, Jamui knew the traditions of the nomads. She did not seclude herself, or bind her feet with Chinese affectation, but she tinted her cheeks and perfumed her throat, to please her husband.

No longer did Kubilai live in a yurt. His house was built of hewn cedar, with tiled floors, like a Chinese yamen, with a screen to keep devils from entering the door. There appeared at this door a man unknown to Kubilai.

The stranger was an elderly Chinese, barefoot. His servants carried writing materials and the rolls of books—little else. His name was Yao Chow, and he had come at Siyurkuktiti's request to live with the young Mongol. He did not say that Ch'u-tsai had singled him out to come.

Oddly, Yao Chow made no obeisance to the son of Tului. He seemed to exist apart from the house, yet to be a human factor in it. Smiling, he admitted that his work was to write books for impoverished people to read. But others spoke of Yao Chow as *linya*—doctor of learning.

"It is necessary for you to learn the principles of government," he told Kubilai presently.

The Mongol laughed—he had a quick sense of humor. "I can manage, as it is."

Yao Chow did not seem to think so. There were many princes of the blood, he explained, Mongol as well as others. And few who could rule men with inner certainty.

Kubilai had little interest in this. What concerned him just then was his new wife, his hunting falcons, the trees he had ordered planted about his yamen. In a curious way the *linya* seemed to approve of that.

"Yet it might be," he said, "that you will rule the world."

For a moment Kubilai thought of his grandfather and Yeliu Ch'u-tsai.

"But first," said the maker of books, "you must learn to govern yourself."

IV

The Book of the Western March

IV

The Book of the Western March

IN THE SUMMER OF 1236 the new Mongol army mobilized to subjugate the far west region of Europe. Like a gathering avalanche, it moved leisurely at first.

Couriers rode along the route to be followed by the army assembling cattle herds. The road was cleared of obstacles, bridges built over the swifter rivers, and forage stored at regular intervals. Good grassland along the route was marked off, to be kept for the grazing of the tumans—the divisions—when they should arrive.

Then ox-drawn wagons creaked along the route, loaded with the shaped timbers of the war engines and munitions. With these went a corps of Chinese engineers, under command of a *k'ung pao*, a master of artillery. With him went sacks of saltpeter and sulphur, the ingredients of the new and still mysterious fire weapon.

When the grass was dying north of the Gobi, the tumans assembled from the different ordus and route-marched to the west. They had sixty degrees of longitude to cover, and they took their time about it.

The riders of the tumans carried complete personal equipment. Each man had one or more remounts. He had a felt cape and sheepskin-lined fur jacket for protection against the cold. For the horses, he had a lariat and picket ropes (which served to attach to the wagons, to draw them through swampy ground or up grades), sacks of barley and a nosebag, a pot for the rider's cooking, a short ax, a bag of salt, wax, a file and needle and thread.

"The leaders must have the men show them," the Yasa of Genghis-Khan commanded, "all the articles to be carried into battle. They must look at everything down to the needle and thread; and if in this inspection they come upon a soldier who lacks something, they are to punish him."

Nothing in the mobilization was left to chance. The army went equipped for a march of several years. Heavy tents, for shelter during storms, were carried in the regimental wagon trains. The Mongols never knew the luxury of winter quarters, because they were expected to operate in snow and extreme cold. The steppe-bred horses could forage at need for themselves, digging under light snow with their hoofs to get at grass or moss.

Moreover, the divisions of Subotai's army were made up from the peoples of the forest belt in the mid-west. They were Turks for the most part, Kirghiz and Uighurs, Karluks (Snow Dwellers) and roving Turkomans. There was only a nucleus of Mongols, to stiffen the discipline of the new army.

Few weapons could be seen, while they route-marched. Their chief arm, their bows—the horn-strengthened, double-curved Turkish bow for power, and the short hunting bow for rapid handling from the saddle—were put away, oiled in their cases. The bow case hung low on the left hip of the rider, while the arrow case was on the right side. In action, the warrior could draw and fire his arrows with a slight movement of his hands, with startling rapidity. And he was equipped with three kinds of arrows, ranging from the long, light flight shaft, to the heavy, armor-piercing arrow with sharpened steel head as broad as three fingers. Braced in his stirrups, he could fire a burst of these heavy arrows from the Turkish bow at a gallop. And he could fire to the rear almost as easily.

But on the march these steel-tipped arrows were carried on the pack animals. The peculiar long Mongol sword, light and slightly curving—a forerunner of the nineteenth-century cavalry saber— was carried, oiled, in its leather sheath behind the rider's left shoulder.

Some Banners—regiments—were issued light lances with tufts of horsehair below the points, or long hooks, to pull antagonists from the saddle. But these hand weapons were seldom used. They were instruments of the final killing, after arrow fire had broken the resistance of the enemy. They were to the Mongols what the bayonet is to the modern rifleman.

Like the weapons, armor was light and serviceable—strips of oxhide that had been boiled and shaped to the rider's shoulders and body, often with a split apron of leather hanging from his belt over his knees. All leather was lacquered, to keep dampness out. Iron bands strengthened the helmets without making them heavy, while a soft leather drop, studded with iron, protected the neck.

Many of the Banners had armored their horses with leather that guarded the animals' bodies without interfering with movement. Rarely, bronze and light iron plates shielded the horses' heads. Only the regiments of the *keshak*, the Guard Corps, had shields for defense. And these were intended for use on foot, at night.

Such metal as he had in his equipment the Mongol was expected to keep polished and oiled. His equipment as a whole was planned for actual service, and for one purpose—swift movement, and power in striking during that movement.

A discipline as unyielding as iron held together this mass of men. Death was the penalty for turning back during an action without an order—as it was for failing to give aid to an injured squad mate, and for neglecting to pick up any equipment dropped by a front-file man.

These squads of ten had been in service together for years. The individual rider knew where his comrades were, and what they would do under all circumstances. The *ung-khan* or squad leader was responsible for the welfare of his nine men; the leader of the first squad commanded his hundred, and so on up to the general commanding a tuman of ten thousand. If the officer of a regiment were killed, the leader of the second hundred would take over his duties without hesitation.

Underlying this discipline was the equality of all ranks. Once a

campaign had begun, peacetime rank ceased to be. A dispatch
rider, on the road, could order a tuman commander to dismount,
and take his horse. A veteran Guardsman had privileges above
officers of other branches of the service.

"A man of my bodyguard," Genghis-Khan announced, "is
superior to a regimental commander of another division. If a
regimental commander of the outer line disputes or fights with a
keshaktu, he shall be punished. Who deserves losing his head shall
lose it; who deserves a beating shall have it."

As a rule the commanders were kinsmen of the ranks serving
under them. And Banners were recruited from a single clan—
preserving a vestige of the old tribal unit. The officers spent a lifetime with their men. Failure on the part of an officer meant dis-
grace for the remainder of his life. Anyone from the ranks might
succeed him.

Most of the officers now in the army had grown up under the
star of victory. "They shielded me," Genghis-Khan had said, "in
snow and in rainy nights as well as in battle. My descendants must
cherish them as a monument of my making, and not offend them."

A generation of victory had given the ranks unshakable confidence in their leaders. They believed that the spirit-life of Genghis-
Khan had entered the standard of the army, with its nine white
horsetails. To this confidence was added a sense of safety. The first
rule of the army was to bring the ranks back alive. In proportion
to the terrible loss of life they had caused, the Mongols had suffered
very little. Officers had been trained to be jealous of the safety of
their men.

The ranks felt equally confident of the highest command. The
mounted bowman in the foremost patrol knew that he was moving
in accordance with a definite plan that would destroy the enemy
by strategy rather than hand-to-hand fighting.

The strategical skill of the Mongols had been developed in the
stress of war. They had learned to keep track of an enemy's movements, while trying to conceal their own. In this maneuvering they
had learned not to depend on commands given by voice, which often
cannot be heard in the uproar of moving mounted men. Regiments
signaled their movements by raising black or white ensigns—by

raising and lowering colored lanterns at night. They used whistling arrows, with a hollow pierced head for other signals.

They could hide, at times, their formation behind a drifting smoke screen.

With the armed tumans advanced other branches of the service —interpreters to deal with the tangle of languages, Chinese physicians and Mongol shamans to minister after their fashion to the sick, and the darugashis, the Road Managers, who were to take inventories of the captured areas for the great Khan at Kara-korum. There was even an officer in charge of a lost-and-found department.

And behind the army, cattlemen and carpenters worked to build the corrals and huts of the *yam*, the stations of the horse post that was to link the new west to their homeland.

This host of a hundred thousand men or so (it had not yet been reinforced by Batu's divisions on the Volga) was marching without maps or compasses, or knowledge of what lay at the end of its road, to face many times its number of potential enemies scattered over hundreds of thousands of square miles. Yet it marched with implicit confidence, without thought of defeat.

The mounted columns moved at ease out of the plains, through the passes of the Altai, and into the *taiga*, the dense forest growth of Ibir-Sibir. Snow held the forest, but the stores and cattle awaited the tumans along the route. Detachments were thrown out to hunt for game, which grew scarcer as the forest changed to the fir and birch of the west.

By now all the different contingents of the Right Wing, the *baran-gar*, were on the line of march. Some women rode with them, in the ox-drawn kibitkas, to cook the meat on the march, and to serve the men in this solitude of Sibir where no towns were seen.

At times, in the camping places, they had theatricals to amuse them—actors in false beards and the costumes of legendary kings singing the shrill chants that the tribesmen knew by heart.

Threading through the low summits of the Urals, the columns began to descend into the western steppes. They crossed rivers on the ice, and the hunters went out to the flanks on skis that carried them swiftly over the deep snow. . . . With the melting of the snow, and the first grass, they came on lean horses to the concentration point near the gray Volga.

There they were met and inspected by Subotai and the princes who had spent the winter in the yurts of Batu, methodically going over the reports of the merchants and spies who pieced together for them the picture of the western regions—its thoroughfares and grazing lands, and especially the defenses of its cities and politics of its princes.

"For you will not find one nation at peace with another," the spies announced, "nor one chieftain who does not raid his cousins. Nay, even their archpriest is at war with their great emperor."

Subotai was insatiable in asking about the details of these quarrels. A master of strategy, he knew the importance of keeping an enemy divided.

The End of the Russians

Batu, Khan of the Golden Horde, lived under a cloud. In a way, he had become an exile.

He was a bastard's son, and his father, Juchi, had felt the shame of being born of another father. In his later years Juchi had kept away from the other brothers, in the western steppes, where some said that he meant to create a dominion of his own. . . . Upon Batu, his son, this shame rested. Ogadai had granted him willingly enough the khanship of the forest people, in the west. And he had given him the nominal command of the new expedition.

Batu, who had kept to the nomad life of his father, had welcomed Subotai and the imperial princes shyly. He had come on foot to greet his mighty guests, and had slaughtered cattle to feast them in his pavilion that shone with cloth-of-gold, on the bank of the Volga, so that men called it the Sira Ordu (the Golden Horde).

He was mild before his guests, uncertain of them when his impetuous cousins teased him. They laughed at him, good-naturedly—although Kuyuk felt jealous because Batu held the higher command.

"Why, behold," they said, "Batu is splendid. There is no prince anywhere so magnificent as he."

This nickname stuck, and Batu became known among the Mongols as *Sain Khan*, the Splendid Khan. Under his amiability, however, there was a stubborn pride. The son of a bastard, he could never reign as khakhan. Still, he meant to hold power among them.

Especially the madcap sons of Chagatai—a contrast to their father—mocked Batu's good nature. Baidar, and Bouri, a grandson, lived only to hunt and make war. And Kaidu, the fledgling of the lot, Ogadai's grandson, imitated them.

"Batu Sain Khan," he cried, "is a good host. Why, he stuffs us robbers with his best meat. His manners are such that he will never be angered at us."

Kaidu had caught Subotai's eye. The aging master of war saw in the wild youngster the spark of the Mongol genius for warfare. And he instructed him patiently. The one thing Kaidu lacked was patience.

Batu felt that he was beholden to Ogadai, who gave him the command of these great ones. Yet he did not know how he was to make them obey him. He was anxious lest they try to take away his beloved grasslands. Fortunately, with Subotai at his side, he had no need to fear them as yet.

Subotai did not hurry. He and his Mongols were amazed at the vast extent of the Russian plain and the richness of the grass. Wild grain sprang up miraculously from the black earth. Here was an ideal land for the horse nomads. And they understood why Juchi and Batu had clung so persistently to these western steppes.

In that early summer on the Volga, Subotai did not move farther west. His first thought was to clear his flanks. At the same time he welded together the tribal regiments that served Batu—the Bashkirs of the Turgai region and the Kirghiz of Sibir—stiffening them with the steel of Mongol discipline. In doing so he thrashed the Bulgars on the upper Volga—destroying their age-old trading center of Bolghar.

To the south, he sent Mangu, to break up the wild Kipchaks.

The March of the Barbarians

Mangu and his men rode by the stone *babas*, the mark of another race upon the steppes, indifferently. By now he and his Mongols were accustomed to meeting the images of strange gods. The Kipchaks gave way before him as foxes take shelter at the coming of a wolf. Some of the nomad Turkish tribesmen submitted to the Mongol yoke, but most of them fled westward, toward the Dnieper. Mangu let them go, and turned back to hunt down the bandits that had infested the lower Volga.

Not until the first heavy snow covered the steppe did Subotai move against the Russians.

For it was a law laid down by Genghis-Khan that Mongol armies of invasion, emerging from the steppes, should advance by stages. When the conflict was ended in the first zone, the survivors there were rounded up. With their horse herds, the men were conscripted and led or driven on by the ordus, into the next zone.

Here the refugees were used as a human screen by the Mongols, at need, in an attack. By this, the lives of the Mongol contingents were protected. And in the first zone, at their rear, no mass of men remained to rise in rebellion. A few guard posts scattered along the roads could maintain order—aided by the terror of the invasion.

In this way Subotai herded the remnants of Bulgars and the Volga men into mounted bands, trained them, and led them into Russia. Before that he sent envoys to demand submission from the Russian princes, as the price of peace.

The strange Mongol emissaries, appearing at the gates of the towns, were put to death by the Russians.

As if enraged beyond caution by this, Subotai struck into the northwest straight toward the larger Russian cities. Apparently, he was doing a senseless thing—turning aside from the open steppes, where the nomad raids had gone before, into the forested regions. And he attacked in December 1237, when the cold was bitter.

Actually, the Mongol leaders had reasons of their own for doing this. By striking their first blow against the stronger region, where the Russians might have defended themselves, given time, in the forests, the Mongols cleared this difficult ground of defenders before the Russians realized their purpose. The open steppes were a thoroughfare for the nomads; they let the south wait.

And by moving in midwinter, they could cross rivers on the ice. The Russians would not expect them, and would be collected, with stores of grain and meat, in the towns. As for the forests, the Mongols cut a way through, wide enough for three carts to pass abreast, at need.

"They advanced," the chroniclers say, "as if driving game in a hunt."

The Russians had settled down for the winter behind the wooden walls of their cities and hamlets. They were a turbulent, warlike people—their princes descendants of the Variags (Swedes) of the north. Their cities of the fertile Riazan region had thrived from the slave and fur trade, and they carried on unending feuds. Their log walls had been sufficient to check the raids of Kipchaks and Bulgars, and the Slavs had the foolish hardihood of brave men who had never been far from home.

They were warriors on horseback, rather than horsemen. They rode in crude iron armor, followed by the mass of the *smerdi*, the stinking ones, the Finns and armed peasantry on foot. Heretofore they had fought hand to hand with swords, and they knew no other method of warfare.

They had had a warning of the Mongol peril, when the army of the southern princes was annihilated by Subotai on a raid at the river Khalka in 1222. This warning went unheeded.

An eclipse of the sun, at the end of that summer, caused them more concern. "There was a sign in the sun on the third day of August," the monks of Novgorod wrote in their chronicle. "The sign was of this kind: there was a darkness on the western side of the sun; it became like a moon of five nights."

Along the frozen rivers, the Mongol columns moved north, sending envoys ahead to bid the Russians submit to the great Khan and pay a tithe.

"They sent their emissaries," the Novgorod chronicle relates, "to the *Kniazes* of Riazan, a sorceress and two men with her, demanding from them one tenth of everything: of men and Kniazes

The March of the Barbarians

and horses—of everything, one tenth. And the Kniazes, without letting them into their towns, went out to meet them, saying, 'Only when none of us are left alive, then all will be yours.' And the Kniazes (the Noble-born) of Riazan sent to Yuri of Vladimir asking for help, or himself to come. But Yuri neither went himself nor listened to the request of the Kniazes of Riazan, but he himself wished to make war separately.

"But it was too late to oppose the wrath of God."

The Russian princes, seemingly incapable of understanding their danger, would not move to aid each other at first. When they did move, sluggishly through the snow, they had no knowledge of what was going on elsewhere. The Mongol mounted divisions swept over them, piecemeal.

The wooden walls of Riazan crumbled under the bombardment of the Mongol siege engines. Before the Russians realized that the walls had failed, the Mongol horsemen were in the city.

Riazan became a slaughterhouse. Men were hunted through the red snow of the alleys, and thrust on stakes to wriggle out their lives. Priests who had shut themselves up in the churches were exterminated like sheep. The women who had sought sanctuary with them were violated and killed.

"No eyes," a chronicler mourns, "remained open to weep for the dead."

In swift succession Suzdal, Rostov and Yaroslavl were stormed and destroyed—the Mongol columns following the frozen rivers from citadel to citadel. Moscow, then a small town on the steep cliff (today the height of the Kremlin) where the Moskva River joins the Neglinnaya, was burned. "And the men of Moscow," the Novgorod chronicle explains, "ran away, having seen nothing."

Along the Kolomenka River a Russian army suffered "a bitter and violent death."

Vladimir, the largest stronghold of fertile central Russia, was broken into while its princely families were crowding into the Church of the Holy Mother of God, barricading themselves in to gain time to have themselves shorn like the monks and taken into the monastic order in these last moments of their lives. Crowded into the sacristy of the church, they were burned.

The Book of the Western March

The Grand Prince Yuri, who should have rallied his vassals in time to meet the Mongols, was not even in the city. He was approaching when he heard that Vladimir had been destroyed.

"And Kniaz Yuri," the chronicle adds, "sent out Dorozh to scout with three thousand men; and Dorozh came running, and said: 'They have surrounded us, Kniaz.' And the prince began to muster his forces about him, when behold, the Tartars came up suddenly, and the Kniaz, without having been able to do anything, fled. And it happened when he reached the river Sit, they overtook him and there he ended his life."

This tale was repeated elsewhere. The feudal levies of the princes, marching out of their log and dirt fortifications, moving slowly through the snow, were struck before they realized they were in danger by a fire-power that crippled them from a distance. The Mongols divided into two columns, and took cities, as it were, in their stride.

"Thus did God by means of these men," the chronicle adds, "take from us our strength, and put into us perplexity, and a dread as if of thunder."

The Russians were valiant enough. Their best men died, surrounded, fighting hand to hand. The Mongols let the fugitives go, as their custom was, to be followed later through the forest paths and eliminated, or added to the growing bands of slaves. There was no escaping the swift-moving detachments. The heavy Russian horses were outpaced by the steppe-bred mustangs.

In the month of February twelve walled cities were obliterated. In the short space between December and the end of March, the free peoples of central Russia vanished. And the sturdy and turbulent independence of the Variag-governed Slavs ceased to be. The word Slav had meant "Glorious." Now the territory of the Slavs became a vast prison-zone, and it was destined to be that for a long time to come.

Another change took place. The destruction of the city-communities drove the survivors out into the smaller rural hamlets, where they turned by necessity to agriculture to sustain their lives. The animal-like *smerdis* raised food for the children of the slain warriors.

[*137*]

The March of the Barbarians

The snow was melting and the spring rains setting in when Batu's column moved north through the pine and birch woodlands toward the Baltic and Novgorod the Great.

Northern Russia escaped by good luck. The powerful merchants' republic of Novgorod had made no attempt to aid the cities in the Riazan region—perhaps because the merchants were willing to see their rivals destroyed, more probably because they had no inclination to march out of their own city-state of breweries, bees and forests.

By the edge of Lake Ilmen, near the Baltic, the free men of Novgorod had carried on a prosperous trade with the German Hanseatic ports, quarreling and fighting sturdy little duels with the Swedes and the Teutonic Knights who competed with them for the northern fur trade. (From the edge of the Baltic south, the militant Germans were pressing against the Slavs, with the smaller peoples, Poles, and pagan Lithuanians, caught between the greater masses. The Prussians were at that time savages, the lawful prey, for slaughter or conversion, of the Teutonic Knights. This centuries-long conflict of Germans and Slavs for possession of the eastern marches of Europe was interrupted rudely by the Mongols.)

Batu's division made toward Novgorod from ruined Pereyaslavl. By then the snow had gone and the invading horsemen found themselves in a labyrinth of swamps and dense forest growth. By rare fortune—for the Novgorodians—it rained almost continually that spring and summer. The wet, and lack of grazing, worked hardship on the Mongol horsemen accustomed to the almost rainless prairies of high Asia. Before they sighted Lake Ilmen they turned back, wearied by the constant rain, within sixty miles of wealthy Novgorod.

Batu turned back by Subotai's advice. That experienced general realized that he had forced his divisions through a hard campaign in the midwinter cold. Their horses were in bad condition. So he turned all the units of his army to the south, leaving only guard detachments in the ravaged central Russia. Now he had need of the good grazing in the southern steppes.

Moreover, the Mongols had discovered that the Slavs of the cities were unlike the Asiatic nomads. They would not or could not be drafted into the mounted regiments of the Ordu, to learn the Mongol method of warfare. They were useful only as sappers and laborers. The Mongols, therefore, would have to make their attack on the next zone of resistance without Russian conscripts, and Subotai, the ever-cautious, took time to prepare for the next move.

It took him longer than he expected.

In that summer of 1238 he followed the grass south, putting his horses in condition. Curiously the Mongols explored the fertile steppes around the Black Sea. Here, where the grasslands stretched to the salt inlets, they discovered an ideal coast, sun-warmed, suitable for cattle.

Some of them investigated the Krimea and came face to face with a strange variety of Christians. These spoke an unknown tongue, they wore no boots and they lived by barter, like the Arab caravan merchants. They proved to be Venetians, and since they did not appear in arms against the Mongols, they were not massacred. Instead, they bought Russian slaves and loot from the nomads.

At the same time Subotai's detachments penetrated the heights of the Caucasus far enough to establish contact with the other Mongol army, of north Persia. The two commands, meeting after four years, exchanged information and parted.

The Mongols were putting central Russia in order, methodically as usual. The darugashi, the governor for the Khakhan, estimated the yield of grain in the southern black-earth region, and the value of the furs—the sable, miniver, black and silver fox and beaver— that came out of the north. These, and hides and tallow, with the silver of the Ural region, and the human beings to be sold as slaves or kept to pay taxes, made up the wealth of Russia.

Since he found almost no coined money in Russia, the darugashi planned to have his new subjects pay a tax in beasts of the five kinds—sheep, horses, cows, oxen and hogs. Already he had begun, with his Uighur and Chinese secretaries, the census of human souls, the building of granaries along the courier roads that did not exist as yet. He had to establish contact between this new empire of Batu and the court of the Khakhan in the far east. . . .

While this was going on, Subotai was delayed by something he could not prevent—friction between the members of the Golden Family. They had advanced nearly a thousand miles from the old frontier of the Urals, they had won most of the Russian plain for Batu. Batu's golden tents and his numerous wives accompanied the army. It seemed to Kuyuk and to the sons of Chagatai that Batu had enough of an empire already. But Subotai, the inflexible, would hear of no halt in the march toward Europe. Nor would Kuyuk, the unyielding, consent to act as divisional general for the Sain Khan, the son of a bastard.

Mangu on the other hand—on Siyurkuktiti's advice—was kind to Batu. And Mangu had been gaining victories in the fertile south. Mangu had conscripted a division of the strong Kipchak Turks— although the greater part of the Kipchaks, some 40,000 tents, had fled westward with their chieftain Kutyan headlong across the rivers, up to the Hungarian plain. This aged Kutyan knew the Mongols of old, and he put as much space between them and his people as he could.

This escape of a powerful enemy, who was certain to warn Europe of the coming attack by the Mongols, irked Subotai. But Kuyuk and the unruly princes would pay no attention to his protests. They wanted to be back in Kara-korum with the ailing Ogadai. Batu, in this crisis, called for a kuriltai of the leaders of the army, only to be mocked by Kuyuk and his sympathizers. And Batu sent a message of protest to the Khakhan in Kara-korum.

"O Khakhan, my uncle! By the power of Heaven," he wrote, "we have overcome the eleven nations. When the armies turned back, a feast was held for all the princes. I am the eldest, so I drank one or two cups of wine before the others.

"Then were Kuyuk and Bouri angered. They rose from the feast and went out, mounting their horses. They abused me. Bouri cried out, 'Batu is in no way superior to me—why does he drink before I drink? He is no more than an old woman with a beard. With one kick I could knock him down and roll him over.'

"Kuyuk said, 'Nay, he is an old woman with a sword and armor. I shall order him to be beaten with a stick.'

"And another one called out to fasten a wooden tail to my body behind. Such was the speech of these princes when, after the war with the different peoples of the west, we gathered to deliberate upon important matters. And we had to break up without discussing affairs at all. Such is my message to you, O Khakhan, my uncle."

After months the riders of the horse post brought a reply from Ogadai, indignant at this family dispute which held up the work of conquest. The Khakhan censured his son Kuyuk severely, adding that Bouri and Baidar would be judged by Chagatai. "As for you," Ogadai reminded Batu, "do not boast so much of your victories. They were gained by Subotai."

More than that, Ogadai recalled Kuyuk and Bouri and the others. They left with their followers for the long trek back to the Gobi. But, being in no mood to be called to account before Ogadai, they went at a foot pace, hunting on the way.

Batu, worried, would have followed. Mangu had heard from his mother that Ogadai had fallen sick, and the master of the Golden Horde wanted to protect his own interests—at least to return to his headquarters on the Volga. "I cannot keep you from going," Subotai said to him, "yet I will not turn aside until I have watered my horse in the Danube."

Knowing that his own men would not follow him from the war, Batu had to stay with the sixty-year-old general. But it seemed to him that they risked defeat by advancing. The immense area behind them held within it peoples who had been stunned but not destroyed by the Mongol inroads. The detachments Subotai had left to guard their communications, perhaps 50,000 men, did not number more than a fraction of the surviving populations. He and Subotai could not have mustered more than 90,000 men for a new campaign.

Besides, after the flight of the Kipchaks, Europe would be warned, and armed and ready. For two years the Mongols had delayed in the steppes north of the Don.

Subotai, however, would not listen to objections.

The Court of the Golden Heads

Subotai struck again in December 1240. This time against elder Russia, where trading centers had grown up around Kiev, the mother of cities. For centuries here the southern Slavs had been in contact with Byzantine culture—the Dnieper and the Black Sea being the way to Constantinople. But here in the southwest the prince was at feud with his rivals. And, as in the devastated north, their neighbors gave them no aid.

Mangu and Batu led this new invasion, across the frozen Dnieper. The worried master of the Golden Horde and the silent son of Tului had become fast friends. And Subotai could not trust Batu to lead without a wiser head beside him.

They were struck by the first sight of Kiev, with its gilded domes and white walls reflected in the river. And they christened it the Court of the Golden Heads.

Mangu had sent the Kievans the usual summons to submit, adding, "If you do otherwise, we know not what will happen. Only God knows."

Recklessly the city men slew the Mongol envoys bringing the summons, and closed their gates when the first horsemen appeared with the ruins of the river hamlets smoking behind them.

"See how the little pigs," the Mongols laughed, "have gathered in their pen to be put to death."

The capture of Kiev was followed by its utter devastation. The Russians ran from the wall into the churches, and the flat roof of one, crowded with people, caved in on the frantic multitude beneath. The great Church of the Tithe was torn apart by the Mongols—only heaped-up stones remaining on its site. The Byzantine mosaics and the treasures of the sanctuaries almost vanished. When Kiev was at last rebuilt, it was only a shadow, the chroniclers say, of the lost city.

The Grand Prince Michael escaped toward Poland, but the charred bodies of his people lay unburied in the dismantled walls, until the stench of them drove human beings from the place.

After the fleeing nobles, the Mongols followed, driving the Kipchaks and Slavs ahead of them. Wives of the boyarins who had never worked with their hands labored at grinding grain and watering the Mongols' horses. "It was strange," a chronicle relates, "to see those who had commanded servants doing the work of servants."

The Book of the Western March

The pursuit of the Mongols reached the barrier of the Carpathian Mountains, and halted for a few days to rest the horses.

Batu had a fondness for the Russians, and wished to spare them. He admired one of the first captives, Oleg the Handsome, whose blue eyes and long yellow hair held something of a woman's charm. When Batu tried to caress Oleg, the Russian thrust him away, and in time Batu killed him. At the sack of Kiev, he had spared the bold Dmitri, called the Galician. Dmitri became his intimate, and urged him to have nothing to do with the western peoples.

West of the Carpathians, Dmitri said, militant barbarians would be met with—people of the forests and the cities; proud kings and bishops who were no less than kings—hosts of mail-clad knights and men-at-arms trained in war. There monasteries and churches were to be seen as formidable as castles. Swift rivers now filling with the spring thaw, and dangerous marshlands, and towns strengthened by citadels—all these would be obstacles to the Mongol horsemen.

Moreover the inhabitants of this middle Europe were accustomed to make war for the glory of their God—Slavs beyond the Dnieper, Poles, dour Croats and Magyars, Bohemians, Hungarians, aided by the Teutonic Knights and French Templars who had come to serve against the invading pagans. And behind them the twin powers of the German Emperor and the Church of Rome, then engaged in a war of their own.

(The Mongols encamped outside the barrier of the Carpathians were confronted by what was until recently Poland, Rumania, Hungary, and Jugo-Slavia, with the southern Germans, Austrians and Czechs. And behind these the twin powers of the Third Reich and Italy.)

These Europeans had had ample warning of the Mongols' approach. They were mustering their armed strength as far away as Bohemia, in the midwinter snows. But they were moving slowly, not yet united. They heard that a Mongol raiding detachment had penetrated as far as Sandomir in Polish territory, to seize captives for information. Kutyan's Kipchak tribesmen had described the Mongols and their method of warfare to the King of

Hungary. The Kipchaks were in such fear of the Mongols that they consented to be baptized en masse by the Hungarians, to join the army of that strong nation.

Moreover, Russian refugees, thronging across the Galician plains, had come into the Polish courts with tales of the sack of Kiev. These tales grew in the telling, until the Europeans assured each other that a horde of demons was on the march toward them. A certain Ivo of Narbonne wrote down gravely that these pagans had the heads of dogs, and that after they had fed upon the bodies of the dead, vultures would not touch the bones. Young and lovely women, Ivo added, after being ravished by the dog-headed Mongols, had their breasts torn open and were kept for dainty eating thereafter.

A Friar Julian had made two journeys into Russia, and had written to his bishop, Salvius of Perouse, that the Mongols would move against Germany, and that they talked of conquering Rome and the lands beyond.

But of the true nature of the invaders, of their method of warfare and their purpose, the Europeans were ignorant. Like the Russians they trusted blindly in their ability to defeat any numbers of pagans.

They paid no attention to the formal letter Batu wrote to Bela, king of the Hungarians. For one reason, it was written in the Uighur script and no one at the court could read it.

But the Kipchaks could read it, and the same Friar Julian had it read to him. It had a consequence amusing as we look back on it but grim enough at the time. It was, in fact, a Mongol trick.

"I am *Sain*," it began, "the messenger of the Lord of the Sky [the Khakhan] who has authority over the earth. He has given me power to raise up those who submit to me and to crush those who defy me. I am surprised that you, King of Hungary, have paid no heed to the envoys I sent to you. . . . It may anger you to submit, yet it is best to do so."

So far, the routine summons to surrender to Mongol rule. Now follows the barb:

"Word has come to me that you have taken the Kipchak, our servants, under your protection. Cease harboring them, or you

[*144*]

will make of me an enemy because of them. They, who have no houses and dwell in tents, will find it easy to escape. But you who dwell in houses within towns—how can you escape from me?"

Now Batu had interpreters enough about him—a little later he even sent a message by a captured Englishman who spoke seven languages. He could have had the letter written in Russian or Hungarian. Instead he used a script that only the Kipchaks could read. (And this was not by accident, because after the campaign he wrought more deviltry by letter when he got possession of Bela's state seal.)

The natural consequence was that the Hungarians suspected he was sending a secret message to the Kipchak Khan, who actually desired nothing more than to stand with the Hungarians against the Mongols. This led to the rumor that the Mongols had sent the Turkish Kipchaks on ahead, to betray the Hungarians. Then it was discovered that the letter stated that the tribesmen would escape, while the Europeans who dwelt in houses would be exterminated.

A worthy Austrian archduke who had volunteered for the campaign was impelled to kill the Khan of the Kipchaks and throw his head out of a window. The net result was that the Kipchaks, who would have been valuable allies, fled to the mountains and raided the Hungarians like wolves.

The Ride of the Four Columns

It was then February 1241—Subotai and Batu were resting their horses in the Galician plain, outside the barrier of the Carpathians, questioning the captives brought from Sandomir. Subotai has learned much from spies and the obliging Venetian merchants. He and his commanders have pieced together, out of this information, an exact picture of the lands that lie ahead of them, and the human forces gathering to oppose them. Subotai assures Batu that it will not be safe to hold the Russian plain unless this strength of middle Europe is broken.

Batu is doubtful, because they are going against odds of two and three to one, and defeat in the west would be disastrous to him.

The March of the Barbarians

Subotai is counting upon speed to avoid defeat. The Mongol horses can maneuver at a speed that is two to three times that of the enemy. He plans to divide his army into four columns, to break through and around the line of the Carpathians. His four columns will be able, he believes, to find and obliterate the Christian points of mobilization. In this march, or rather headlong ride, they will meet again at the point where the main European strength is gathering, at Pest on the Danube. Some of them, at least, will get there if they keep up their pace.

Because Batu is doubtful, Subotai keeps the Sain Khan with him, in command of the main body. The flanking columns he gives to the impetuous warriors, Kaidu and Kadaan. (Mangu has been recalled to Kara-korum.)

His timetable calls for his columns to arrive at the rendezvous on the Danube on March 17.

He sends the Mongols of the right-flank column off first, in the beginning of March. This is a strong division, with some thirty thousand riders under command of Kaidu. It has, besides, the longest circuit to make, to the north around the great arc of the Carpathians. Here the snow is already leaving the ground.

For the first week the flying column moves slowly, passing through Sandomir, ruined by the Mongols' winter raid. Dividing into two, it feels for the first resistance, and finds the Poles gathering to the standard of Boleslas the Chaste, with the Slavs of Prince Mieceslas.

The Mongols, in close formation, attack at Szydlow. Separating the two commands of the Polish army, they drive Mieceslas with the survivors of his Slavs to the west, while Boleslas flees south toward the mountains. This is March 18.

Kaidu pursues to the west without the waste of a day. Coming to the town of Kracow, they find the inhabitants deserting it. They storm Kracow and burn it—March 24. Throwing a bridge of boats and planks across the Oder, the column strikes into German territory, takes Breslau and finds that resistance is forming to the north, at Liegnitz.

Here Henry the Pious, Polish Duke of Silesia, musters his Germans, with the Margrave of Moravia, and contingents from the palatinate of Kracow—about 30,000 in all, strengthened by a force of Teutonic Knights. A little to the south, good King Wenceslas—the jolly monarch of the Christmas song—is coming up with a powerful array of his Bohemians by forced marches to join Duke Henry.

With this strength confronting it, the Mongol flying column increases its pace to reach the army at Liegnitz before the Bohemians can come up.

On the morning of April 9, the Polish-German army moves out of Liegnitz to try to join forces with the Bohemians. Headed off by Kaidu's advance, it takes position on level ground. The men-at-arms, on foot, move forward against the first Mongol formation, which retires before them. Other Mongol regiments appear on their flanks, surround them and begin to cut them down with arrows.

Two divisions of Poles charge, to extricate the unfortunate infantry. They find themselves plunging into clouds of evil-smelling smoke that blinds them and conceals the Mongols. Out of this smoke appears what seems to be a great cross with a long beard—in reality the Mongol standard with its long tails. The fighting is heavy, at close range in this smoke screen, when a strange rider gallops past the Polish ranks shouting *"Byegayce*—fly!" The Polish horsemen draw back in confusion and are broken by a Mongol charge.

Seeing this, Duke Henry charges with his reserve of horsemen, his Silesian and Polish armored knights, and the mounted Teutonic crusaders. Mongol reserves appear on their flanks, and they are overwhelmed by numbers. Henry turns to escape with four companions, who are killed beside him. He is caught, his head cut off.

Few of the Christians survive the field of Liegnitz. The right ears of the dead are cut off by the Mongols and packed into sacks, to be counted later, while Kaidu moves on to the town of Liegnitz. Finding it deserted by its people, he burns it.

Wenceslas and his Bohemians hear of the catastrophe while they are still a day's march distant. They turn back hastily, taking up a position in the defile of Glatz, in the hills to the south.

The March of the Barbarians

The Mongols reconnoiter this position and find it too strong to attack. After resting their horses, they move slowly aside, into Bohemia, destroying the towns in their way.

When he learns of this, Wenceslas hastens back to defend his homeland. But the movement of the Mongols is only a feint. Turning about, they quicken their pace, and pass through the defile of Glatz unopposed, heading into the fertile valleys of Moravia. Before an army can be gathered to defend it, Moravia is overrun and sacked by Kaidu's riders, who keep on, down to Hungary.

The good Wenceslas of Bohemia writes to Frederick, the German Emperor, that he has driven away the "Tartars."

In the space of a month, this northern column has covered more than four hundred miles, fighting two decisive battles, destroying four cities, and breaking up all resistance in Poland and Silesia from the river Vistula to Liegnitz. And now it forages through the valleys of Moravia, watching the Bohemian army, and waiting for orders from Subotai.

"Know," Ponce d'Aubon, Master of the Templars in France, writes to his lord, the saintly Louis of France, "that the Tartars have destroyed the country that was of Henry, the Duke of Poland, and killed him with many of his barons, and six of our brothers, with three knights and two sergeants and five hundred of our men-at-arms. Three of our brothers escaped.

"And know that all the barons of Germany and the clergy and those in Hungary have taken the cross to go against the Tartars. And if these be vanquished, by the will of God, the Tartars will find none to stand against them, as far as your land."

Now Subotai is moving, to keep to his timetable. As soon as Kaidu starts off, he releases his second column, to skirt the barrier of the Carpathians and head down along the small river March toward Pest.

This second column has a long way to go. It is mounted on fast horses, and as it goes it keeps in touch by courier with Kaidu to the north.

Then Subotai starts a third flying column, this time to sweep to the south through Galicia. Its duty is to clear the southern flank

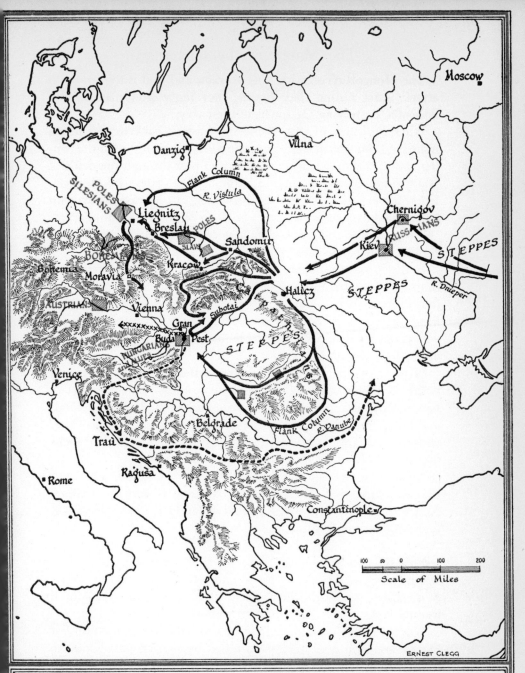

Campaign of the Mongols against Middle Europe: Winter of 1240-41

Concentration, at the end of the summer, 1240, east of the Dnieper. Capture of Kiev and Chernigov, early December. Concentration against middle Europe, January-February 1241 between the headwaters of the Vistula and Halicz. Movement of the four columns began the first of March. The main column with Batu and Subotai forced the Carpathians March 12, and reached the assembly point at Pest on the Danube March 17. The main battles were fought to the west of Sandomir, and near Liegnitz and on the river Sayo where the Mongols trapped the army of the Hungarians and their allies. In these six weeks (first of March to middle of April) the Mongol flying columns had crushed four European armies before they could concentrate, and had driven off a fifth – the Bohemians. The next summer concentration was in the Hungarian plain.

Route of main army across the Danube, in midwinter of 1242 . xxxxxxxx⟩

Raid of Kaadan down the Dalmatian coast and withdrawal through the Balkans after news of Ogadai's death was received ▬ ▬ ▬ ▬ ▬

and rejoin the other divisions near Pest on March 17. It is led by Kadaan.

It also has a long way to go. Like the second column, it follows an arc like one of the pincers of a pair of ice tongs—the points of the pincers to come together at Pest March 17. It breaks up into smaller detachments to glean what forage it can in the snowbound, wooded country. It raids the towns for food but passes by the stronger castles, breaking up the small armed forces it finds in its way.

The rivers along its route through Transylvania are not yet swollen by melting snows and the spring rains. The Mongol riders discover fords if they can, or they swim the current, their horses roped together, the men swimming beside them, holding to their leather kit sacks, inflated with air. They can stop for nothing because they must cover more than forty miles a day through snow.

The startled inhabitants of the countryside are aware only that the forests seem to be alive with pagan horsemen, passing like specter riders to an unknown destination. At least once a bit of comedy is played out.

In the rich town of Rudan, near a silver mine in the mountains, the people see Mongol patrols filtering by. The townspeople are sturdy Germans, and they muster their men-at-arms to go out and give battle to the invaders. The Mongol detachment left to screen the town withdraws in a feigned retreat. They play their part so well that the Germans believe they have driven off the enemy.

Well content, the German men-at-arms about-face and march back to town, to celebrate their victory. Scattering through the taverns, they put aside their weapons and settle down to beer in the good Teutonic fashion. By the time they are well drunk, the Mongols come back through the open gates of the town, without striking a blow. They round up the Count Ariscald and six hundred men-at-arms and take them along into the forest, giving them axes to do pioneer work.

Some towns close their gates, and the defenders line the walls to watch the Mongols—until arrows, shot from a distance by the strange horsemen, begin to strike them. Astonished, the Christians take shelter, holding up dummies to watch the steel shafts smash through them. At times the Mongols release a volley of arrows that rises like a cloud and descends on the people within the walls. Or they fire flaming arrows into thatched roofs before riding on.

But the southern column, forcing its way through wooded hills, lags behind its schedule.

Meanwhile Subotai has moved with the rest of the army, the main column some 40,000 strong. He takes Batu with him, and the smaller engines, dismounted and roped to sleighs.

Ascending the barrier of the Carpathians toward the pass known as the Russian Gates, he finds the heights held by a frontier guard of Hungarians who have felled trees to block the road. The Mongol advance forces the pass but is delayed in clearing the road. On March 12 Subotai is through the heights. Taking command of the advance division, he begins the pursuit of the retiring Hungarians, and the pursuit is frightening in its speed.

Down from the pass, out into the Hungarian plain, Subotai's tumans gallop 180 miles in less than three days. On March 15, two days before the appointed rendezvous, his patrols reach the bank of the Danube.

On the 17th Batu appears with the mass of the central division. And the second column comes in, feeling its way down the Danube. It brings word of the progress of Kaidu in the north, and the assurance that Subotai's right flank is clear. The third column due in from the south is still missing, but the Mongols have two columns united in front of Pest, ready to give battle to Bela and his Hungarians.

The End of the Hungarians

Bela, king of Hungary, is at that time seated in council with his barons and prelates to discuss the danger of a possible Mongol invasion through the Carpathians. They are in Pest, across the river from Buda, where their army is mobilizing, when they are interrupted by the appearance of the Count of Zolnuk, commander of the frontier guard. He reports to the assembly that the frontier of the Carpathians no longer exists—that the Mongols are here at Pest at his heels.

Subotai finds the gates of Pest closed, and he is too wise to attempt to cross the broad Danube. So he explores the country, trying to draw the Hungarians out on his side the river.

Bela, just as cautious—startled by the appearance of the invaders at his doorstep—issues orders that no one is to venture out against the Mongols. A fighting bishop, lord of Ugolin, disobeys the orders. He sallies out with his armored riders against the detachments of leather-clad pagans who are gathering forage in the villages beyond the walls, under his eyes.

The mailed Christians charge the groups of strange riders, who drift away, apparently frightened. Ugolin and his men press the pursuit with shields dressed and lances down, and find themselves sinking into marshy ground over which the lighter Mongols have made their way safely. When the Christians, burdened by their heavy armor, try to extricate themselves, they are caught under the fire of the Mongol arrows. Three of them get back to Pest, with the impetuous bishop. The rest are left dead in the swamp.

Not until April 4, when the bulk of his army has crossed from Buda, does Bela move out of Pest.

This—although Bela and his barons reck little of it—is the day after the missing left wing of the Mongols has appeared at the rendezvous on the Danube. And Subotai has heard that his flying right wing has shattered the Poles in the north. He withdraws his Mongols at a walk, to lead Bela well away from Pest.

And the Hungarian king follows as if led by the hand. The Christians have a great array, because Koloman, the king's brother, has brought up the contingents of Slavonia and Croatia, and a force of French Templars has joined them: perhaps a hundred thousand in all—barons, bishops, knights, crusaders and men-at-arms, with a backbone of sturdy infantry. As they advance, they grow more confident.

The Mongols are barely to be seen retreating. Their main body has disappeared. Certainly they are weaker in numbers than the Hungarians, and apparently they have no desire to stand and fight.

On the sixth day the Hungarians camp in the plain of Mohi. Ahead of them winds a swift river, the Sayo; beyond that, dark forests. To either side rise the vine-clad hills of Tokay, and wooded heights. It is the evening of April 9, and already Duke Henry has fallen at Liegnitz in the north.

The Hungarians pitch their tents in the plain of Mohi, build their fires and water their horses in the river. They are experienced men, not to be caught unawares. Their scouts push into the brush beyond the river without seeing any Mongols—only the tracks of horses are visible. A Russian captive, escaping from Batu's camp, finds his way to the Hungarians and warns them that the invisible Mongols are, in fact, camped a few miles farther on.

So the Hungarians take precautions against surprise. They are protected by wooded hills on either side. But they encircle their camp with a ring of wagons, roped together. Koloman himself goes with a thousand men to the only bridge over the Sayo, between them and the Mongols. This advance keeps watch while the main body within the wagon ring turns in for the night.

Before dawn the Mongols are in motion, returning to the river from their camp five miles away in the brush. One column, under Batu, approaches the stone bridge over the Sayo. The other, with Subotai commanding, makes for the river lower down, to flank the Hungarian camp.

At dawn Batu's riders rush the bridge, and are checked by Koloman's thousand Hungarians. The Mongols bring up seven catapults and rake the bridge with heavy missiles. The Hungarians are driven back, and the Mongol horsemen come across, to deploy into the plain.

Meanwhile, undiscovered as yet, Subotai is fording the Sayo— throwing across a bridge of beams and tree trunks to aid the crossing.

In the camp, the Hungarians come out of their tents to find the strange horsemen massing on the higher ground around them. The Mongols move silently, without molesting the Hungarians, but they encircle the camp steadily.

The Hungarian cavalry goes out against them and charges in a mass. The Mongols seem to drift away before the Christian charge, closing in on its flanks and sweeping it with volleys of arrows.

Crippled by the fire that it cannot return, the Hungarian charge breaks up, sways back to the camp in confusion. By now Subotai's column is coming up, closing the circle about the camp where a multitude of armed men is elbowing about restlessly, hungry, bewildered, staring at the ranks of dark horsemen closing the avenues of escape from the camp. The Mongols open fire with volleys of arrows from the higher ground upon the Hungarians.

Again the Hungarian leaders, Koloman and the adventurous Ugolin, rally their mounted men to charge out of the wagon ring. But few are willing to follow them this time. The Templars go out to a man. And again they are cut to pieces and herded back, without the Templars, who died fighting.

The multitude in the camp is unsteady now, with no leadership to direct it. Bela, unskilled at soldiering, is helpless—Koloman wounded. Then the Mongols move down the slopes, firing flaming arrows and naphtha into the close-packed Hungarian ranks. At the same time the ring of horsemen opens, toward the west, where the level plain runs back to the Danube. The Hungarians move toward the opening uncertainly. The first of them get through the opening without harm. Then they begin to run.

They lose all formation as they press through the tents toward safety, cutting the tent ropes to clear a way. Bela thinks at first that his army is advancing on the enemy; then, seeing the retreat, he joins it.

The Mongols cease firing and draw back, allowing the Hungarians to march out unmolested. They move on either side, at a foot pace, waiting.

Nearly a hundred thousand men are pushing toward safety, and their leaders cannot stop them now. It does not matter that safety lies beyond the Danube, six days' march away. They push toward the opening in the ring of horsemen.

For two days the slow and terrible flight lasts. The Mongols, waiting until they see men exhausted, ride in and kill them like sheep with their hand weapons. Some of the Hungarians are herded into swamps, to be killed more easily. Bela, unrecognized, escapes by the speed of his horse.

Bodies are heaped up on the ground for the space of the two

days' march. Seventy thousand, it is said, die there, with Ugolin and two archbishops and the greater part of the Hungarian nobility. The survivors are fugitives, hunted through the hills, drugged by fear. Bela's flight ends in a monastery in the higher Carpathians, where he finds his fellow monarch of yesterday, Boleslas the Chaste, also a refugee.

The wounded Koloman, passing through Pest, warns the inhabitants to cross the Danube and escape to the west if they can. Instead, they try to defend their city. It is stormed and burned by the Mongols, and its people slain.

"However great their multitude may have been," the chronicler Thomas of Spalato wrote of the Germans and Hungarians, "still greater in that battle was their hardihood. But no people in the world knows as much as the Mongols, especially in warfare in open country, about how to conquer an enemy either by daring or by knowledge of war."

The battle on the Sayo had an aftermath in a kuriltai on the other side of the world. Batu reproached Subotai, saying, "When we fought, together near the river Danube, I lost my friend Bahatu and thirty men by your fault, for you were late in reaching the battle."

"You know well," Subotai answered, "that where you crossed, the river was shallow and you had a bridge already built. You have forgotten that where I crossed the river was deep, and I had to build a bridge."

Batu admitted that Subotai was right in this, and he yielded credit for the victory over the Europeans to the old Mongol general. He took for himself, however, the royal pavilion that Bela had abandoned on the field of Mohi—its splendor appealed to his taste for luxury.

Europe, in the Summer of 1241

Kaidu, hearing that the campaign in Hungary was won, came down with his column. On the way he made a feint at the mass of Bohemians of good King Wenceslas and the armed host of the Duke of Saxony. He took and burned the city of Brunn. He called in the flying division which had been thrown out on his right flank and had swung far north through the Lithuanians and Prussians, almost within sight of the Baltic. Then he rejoined Subotai and Batu on the Hungarian plateau.

There the grass was fresh, and the Mongol horses could find good grazing. Subotai gave command to rest and to complete the occupation of Hungary. The Mongols would use the Hungarian plain for the base of their next advance, as they had used the Russian Ukraine in the last summer.

In four months—Kiev was taken December 6—his commands had overrun middle Europe from the Dnieper to the Vistula near the Baltic. In two months he had conquered the lands from the Carpathians to the Danube. Within three days, his columns had annihilated the armed forces that warlike Poland, Hungary, Brandenburg, Saxony, Silesia and Bohemia had put in the field against him. Their fortresses were obliterated, their cities burned and villages sacked.

His Mongols had been heavily outnumbered, yet they had suffered so little loss of life that their divisions were intact, and they were ready for the next advance against the Germans and Italians. The Mongols had accomplished this by their discipline and speed of movement, and by the brilliant handling of their leaders.

In this disastrous invasion of the winter of 1240-41, the people of Europe, not the horsemen from the steppes, were the true barbarians.

For dread of the invaders seized on Europe. The shock of the disaster seemed to affect the westerners like some unlooked-for catastrophe of nature. They could not understand it.

Their feudal lords and the church dignitaries had been swept aside like men of straw. Their will to resist had been broken.

"A great fear of this barbaric race spread even into far-off lands like Burgundy and Spain where the name of Tartar was unknown until then." As far as the North Sea this dread made itself felt. Danish herring fishers failed to put to sea that year, and the price of herrings went up accordingly in England.

The Mongols had appeared at so many points within those weeks that the Europeans fancied they must be as numerous as some vast horde. The destruction they caused could only be explained, in European minds, as an act of God's anger.

The good queen-mother of France demanded of her son, the saintly Louis, "My son, what wilt thou do?" And he answered with true piety: "The heavenly consolation remains to us that when the Tartars come, we will either drive them back to Tartary, or we will be elevated ourselves to the blessedness of the chosen souls."

Refugees who had escaped from the ruins of towns made their way west, babbling of deserted habitations and men surviving like animals in the hills.

In Paris, the monk-chronicler Matthew entered a record in his huge book: "Swarming like locusts over the face of the earth, they have wrought terrible devastation to the eastern parts, laying it waste with fire and carnage. They are inhuman and beastly, rather monsters than men, thirsting for and drinking human blood. They are without human laws, knowing no comforts—more ferocious than bears."

Matthew of Paris had all the ardent imagination of a writer far from the scene of battle. But a more curious and discriminating mind echoed his thoughts. Frederick of Hohenstaufen, then Emperor of Germany, addressed a warning that was an appeal to "France, that nurses an intrepid soldiery, to warlike Spain, to England, powerful in its men-at-arms and ships. . . .

"A people," Frederick said, "issuing from the uttermost parts of the world, where they had long been hidden under a frightful climate, has suddenly and violently seized upon the countries of the north, and multiplied there like grasshoppers. . . . It is not without a manifest judgment of God that they have been reserved . . . as a chastisement for the sins of men and, perhaps, for the destruction of Christendom.

"This ferocious and barbarous nation knows nothing of the laws of humanity. They have, however, a chief whom they venerate, and whose orders they blindly obey, calling him the God of earth. . . . At the least sign from their chieftain, these men rush with impetuous valor into the midst of perils. . . .

"Up to the present time they have had no other armor than rough and ill-joined plates of iron. But already—and we cannot utter it without a groan—they are beginning to equip themselves better from the spoils of Christians; and soon the wrath of God will perhaps permit us to be shamefully massacred with our own weapons.

"The Tartars are mounted on the finest horses, and they now feed on the most dainty meats, and dress richly and with care. They are incomparable archers."

Frederick, head of the Holy Roman Empire, and closest to the line of the Mongol advance, was the one to urge an alliance of the European princes against the invaders. He was the temporal head of Christendom, as the aged Pope, Gregory IX, in the Lateran palace, was the spiritual head. Together, they could have collected forces that might have withstood the Mongol attack. Refugees from the conquered area were crowding into the valleys of Bohemia, and into northern Italy, while the luckless Bela sent appeals for aid from his hiding place to both courts.

But the pope and the emperor were locked in their long strife for supremacy. Frederick, aware of the peril of the Mongol advance —"Of those matters we have been informed for a long time," he observed, in June 1241—suggested a truce. The papal powers would have no truce.

Gregory made the gesture of allowing a crusade to be preached against the Mongols—he had already preached a crusade against Frederick—and said that he grieved for the Hungarians. His Welfs spread the rumor that Frederick's envoys had been seen among the Mongols, and that the Emperor himself must have summoned the invaders into Europe. A rhyming commentator of the day wrote:

> *"Emperor Frederick by his act*
> *Made them come, to attack*
> *All Christianity."*

With the papal forces determined to carry on the civil war, Frederick refused to move against the Mongols. "If I march against the Tartars," he said bluntly, "I will expose my own states to attack. . . . After pacifying Italy I will march against the invaders."

To the envoy of Bela who besought him for aid, the aged Gregory answered: "If Frederick who calls himself emperor returns with a contrite heart to obedience to the Mother Church . . . that will allow you to be aided."

And Matthew of Paris lamented: "Great was the anger of God toward the Christians to permit such feuds to be."

In July Frederick wrote to his brother-in-law, Henry III of England: "If the Tartars penetrate into Germany and find no barriers to their progress there, other nations will suffer from the terrible scourge. . . . Use your diligence, therefore in giving aid, for this people (the Mongols) have left their own country intending to subdue all the west, and to destroy the faith and name of Christian."

The summer was passing, without an adequate defense being prepared against the Mongols. Two Swabian barons, obedient to Frederick, led a force of some 4,000 men-at-arms eastward, and checked an exploring detachment of Mongols. Yaroslav of Sternberg brought 500 Bohemians to the defense of the strong city of Olmutz. Sternberg, an experienced captain, kept the people of Olmutz within the walls, and kept the Mongols out—making one sortie at night and killing a number of the invaders. But the Mongols made no attempt to besiege Olmutz.

Then, in August, the aged Gregory died, leaving Europe without a pope. The conflict between the religious and the civil power ceased in Italy.

Meanwhile the Mongols began to assemble their commands to resume their march westward across the Danube, with no European army in the field to oppose them.

The "Carmen Miserabile"

During the summer the Mongols had regained their strength in the high valleys of Hungary, replenishing their horses on the *puszta*, and making the most of the rich grazing. This, like the Russian plain, was a country well suited to their needs. And they found the Magyars to be descendants of Turkish nomads, speaking a language akin to their own. They were joined by the Kipchak tribesmen who had watched the annihilation of the Christian armies and were ready now to make submission to the victors.

Meanwhile Batu had been doing some more letter writing. His men had found the state seal of Hungary on the battlefield of the

Sayo, and the Sain Khan concocted with his interpreters a forged missive in Hungarian that he stamped with the royal seal:

"Do not fear the rage and savagery of these dogs," his letter ran. "And take care not to quit your towns. Although WE abandoned our camp because WE were taken unaware in it, WE expect with the aid of God to retake it soon, sword in hand. Content yourselves then to pray to God that WE may be permitted to vanquish our enemies."

This was signed by the Mongols with Bela's name and circulated among the Hungarians. It helped to keep them quiet in their villages where the Mongol patrols could get at them more easily. These patrols were scouring the countryside, methodically rounding up the cattle and horse herds, assembling captives in bands and putting them to work. The greater part of the peasantry they left unmolested in the fields at that time, because they wanted the crops cultivated and the harvest gathered in. From Moravia to Transylvania, the same systematic garnering of supplies and liquidation of the people went on.

A certain Roger, canon of Varadin, left an account of his hide-and-seek with death that summer, in his *Carmen Miserabile:*

"While the Tartars sacked Varadin," Roger relates, "I hid in a neighboring forest. I escaped that night to Pont-Thomas, a German town on the river Koeroesch, and, thinking myself still in danger, I left there to take shelter in a fortified island in the river. When I heard a little later of the sack of Pont-Thomas, I saddled the horses again, and left the island, turning aside into a forest.

"The next day the island was occupied by the Tartars, who cut down all they found alive there. Several of the people escaped into the wood along the bank. After three days, thinking that the enemy had gone off, they went back to look for food. But they were found and massacred by Tartars hidden in the houses.

"After that I wandered in the forest without any supplies. Hunger forced me to go back at night to the island, to search among the bodies. I carried off cautiously some meat and grain hidden in the ground. For five days I got along in this way, hiding in daylight in ravines and the hollows of trees.

[*159*]

The March of the Barbarians

"When the Tartars promised not to harm any people who went back to their homes, I did not put any trust in their words. I decided it would be better to go into one of their camps than to try my luck in a village. I gave myself up to a Hungarian who had gone into the service of the Tartars. As a great favor, he consented to let me join his own servants.

"While I remained with him, half-clothed, taking care of his wagons, I looked on death every day. One day I saw a large number of Tartars and Kipchaks coming in from every direction with carts loaded with spoil, driving great flocks and herds in front of them. I found out that the night before they had killed the people of all the villages around there. They had not burned the grain, or the fodder, or houses. That made me think they meant to pass the winter in the neighborhood, and my guess was right.

"They had only let the villagers live long enough to get in the crops and cut the hay. They had not waited until these unfortunates began to use what they had gathered in.

"After that the pagan princes ordered us to leave the country, and we all began to march off with the horses, the herds, and the wagons loaded with booty. The Tartars themselves dismounted and went through the forests on foot, to try to discover anything they might have passed by when they came in.

"The army, retiring slowly in this manner, emerged from the forests to find a multitude of other Tartars and captives waiting in camps already prepared. Leaving Hungary behind, the united army entered the country of the Kipchaks. Now it was not allowed, as before, to kill cattle for meat for the captives. We were only permitted to have the intestines and the hoofs and heads of the beasts which had been slaughtered to feed the Tartars. We began then to be afraid that they meant to put us to death—the interpreters admitted that this was so.

"I thought over how I might escape. Pretending to leave the road to empty my bowels, I plunged suddenly into the brush. My servant followed. I made my way into a deep ravine, and covered myself up with boughs—my servant hiding not far off.

"We stayed stretched out like this, as if we were in our coffins. For two days we did not dare raise our heads. We listened to the harsh cries of the Tartars who searched out animals in the wood, or called to captives who had hidden themselves. Finally the ache of hunger forced us to come out of our hiding.

"Almost at once we saw a man. Seized with fright, we started to run—he going off the other way. Then we looked at each other, and stopped. None of us carried arms, and we made signs that we wanted to speak to the other man. After that, we talked over our sorrowful experiences with him and debated what we ought to do.

"Strengthening ourselves by our trust in God, we went out to the edge of the wood and climbed a high tree. We saw that the open countryside, untouched by the Tartars on their arrival, was now utterly desolate. We started out across this barren land, where the bell towers of the churches guided us, and we were happy if we found any onions or garlic in the gardens of the ruined villages. Otherwise, we had to subsist on roots.

"Eight days after leaving the wood, we came to Albe. There we found nothing but human bones, and the stain of Christian blood on the walls of the palace and the churches. Ten thousand paces from there stood the country house commonly known as *Frata*, near a forest. Four miles within the forest we came to a high mountain where many refugees, both men and women, had gathered. They rejoiced over us, with tears in their eyes, and questioned us about the dangers we had come through.

"They gave us some black bread made of meal flavored with dog's flesh, which seemed to us the most delicious food we had ever eaten. We stayed a month in this place, not daring to leave it. But we sent out often to try to find men farther off, to learn if the Tartars had not remained somewhere in the country. For we feared always that their withdrawal was only a pretense, and that they would return to kill those who had escaped their savagery. Although the need of food forced us to go down continually to the villages that had once been inhabited, we did not leave our refuge, actually, until after the return of Bela, our king."

Roger's story was that of a half-million survivors of the invasion. And by degrees these men, physically weakened by hardships, began to lose hope of resistance. They understood that it would be useless. Instead, they began to have a gray and terrible hope that they would survive under this strange yoke of the pagans. The slaughtering ceased when resistance ended. Roger himself relates that after his return to human habitations he and his fellow refugees found "peace and a market, and a judge to decide disputes."

Other chroniclers testify that the Magyar men brought their daughters in to these markets, to exchange them for cattle and meat. The Mongols found the Magyar girls desirable and not very different from their own women.

The Mongol darugashis were at work. The census takers were tabulating the resources of Hungary. Like Russia, the Hungarian plain was being made over for occupancy by the steppe dwellers. The Bulgars and Kipchaks were being taken into the ordus, like the Georgians and Armenians of the Caucasus. Mongol coins began to circulate in the markets.

And the Hungarians were coming to know their strange masters a little better. They realized that talented men—artists and goldsmiths—were being expressed to the east, to a place called Karakorum, along with the captured treasures. The more attractive girls fared well as prostitutes.

The Mongols no longer destroyed churches. For the walled monasteries and cathedrals had been centers of resistance, and they had been burned in the attack because burning was the simplest way to get rid of them. True, commanders of the Christians had been put to death in an unusual way, being suffocated in felt cloths. But this was because the steppe dwellers did not desire to have a brave man lose his blood. They wanted him to serve them, intact, in another life. Batu had ordered the right ears of all the Christian dead at Liegnitz to be cut off; this, however, was their way of taking a rough toll of the casualties.

Wealthy captives were tortured at times, to make them confess where they had hidden their riches, whether real or imaginary. This practice, Roger and his fellows knew, was not confined to the Mongols in that age.

It became increasingly clear to the Hungarians that so long as they paid the tithe to the invaders—and the agents of the Mongols provided them with coins to pay this tenth—and served in the requisitioned work, they could enjoy peace, if not security. It was the first experience of western peoples with the nomad peace that forbade conflict between the subjects of the great Khan.

After what they had witnessed, Roger and his mates were slavishly willing to obey commands. They whispered among themselves that if a man obeyed, he was safe.

Not so the Poles and Germans. For it was the custom of the Mongols to preserve everything that might be useful to them in the conquered areas, even to the carts and human beings—but to obliterate life in the next zone that resisted them. In this way they created an artificial desert along their frontier. This devastated area would not sustain an army, they thought, advancing to attack them.

Although the Hungarians did not realize it, they were being taken into the Mongol yoke, while the zone destined to be destroyed would be immediately east of them, across the Danube.

A strange tenacity, this—a survival of the nomad instinct to safeguard themselves against the unknown forces of the world. These steppe dwellers of a generation before were appropriating everything that might be useful to them, and drawing it homeward with them, as beavers drag sticks to a dam. They were taking, not gold or gleaming jewels, but the linens woven in Europe, and the best iron, the brains of educated men. And they prayed that they might have the souls of the talented dead!

The steppe dwellers were moving stubbornly, and at the moment irresistibly, toward the sun.

When he received a summons from the Mongols to submit, Frederick laughed and said that he might be qualified to serve as keeper of the great Khan's falcons.

Ice on the Danube

At the end of autumn, frost gripped middle Europe. Snow began to close the roads over the mountains. The harvests were all stored under roofs. And Subotai was ready to begin the winter campaign.

He chose the winter, as in Russia, because the larger rivers could be crossed on the ice, and because hostile mobilization would be hampered by the snow. But he moved slowly, his eyes on the west.

The March of the Barbarians

No armies, apparently, had gathered there to resist him—certainly his occupation of the Danube had gone unchallenged. And when puzzled, he became cautious.

He thrust out two columns, one to the north, under Batu, the other toward Venice, under the young *tuman-bashi*, Kadaan—the same who had commandeered the six hundred drunken Germans at Rudan that spring.

Faced by the icebound Danube, Batu made a test of the ice without risking his own men on it. His advance guard drove a large herd of cattle down to the edge of the river and withdrew, leaving the animals there. After two days the Europeans on the other bank ventured to cross, to gather in the great herd and drive it to their side of the river. And Mongol scouts, watching from the heights, saw that the ice held this multitude safely. Whereupon, on Christmas Day, as it happened, the Mongol horsemen rode across it.

They headed toward the great city of Gran, where French and Lombard merchants gathered with the citizens behind the wooden walls, instead of evacuating the place. Bringing up thirty catapults, the Mongol engineers battered a way through the walls, and Gran was taken before its people realized the siege had begun.

The merchants set fire to their wooden warehouses, but the Mongols, angered by this destruction of useful goods, burned them over slow fires to make them confess where they had buried their other valuables. Three hundred noble-born Austrian and Hungarian women were taken in one building. They put on their court garments and asked to be brought before Batu—pleading with him that they were willing to become slaves and serve the Mongols. Instead, Batu ordered them to be stripped and then killed—their rich garments, unstained by blood, were carefully preserved.

With Gran smoking behind them, the Mongol advance guards circled Vienna and pushed on as far as Neustadt. They were checked by an army of Bohemians and Germans, and Batu turned south to join Kadaan—Subotai remaining on the Hungarian side of the Danube, with the mass of the Mongols, waiting for the German or Italian armies to materialize in force.

One detachment passed along the edge of the Tyrol, as far as Udine, at the end of the Adriatic, within a short distance of the

Venetian lagoons. The Mongols were filtering through the new line of defense, as they had penetrated Poland in February, feeling for the centers of resistance.

Meanwhile Kadaan had been pursuing a monarch. The Mongol spy service had discovered that Bela, king of the Hungarians, had survived the holocaust at the Sayo. And by Mongol custom, the ruler of a hostile nation was to be put to death.

The list of their executions was by then a long one—from Wang Khan of the Kraïts to Gutchluk of Black Cathay, and the Golden Emperor, to Muhammad the Khwaresm-shah and Sultan Jelal ad-Din, to the Volga chieftain Kutchman, and the Grand Prince Yuri of Riazan, and Henry of Silesia. Some of these had been hunted down for months, but no one had survived.

Bela had moved from his monastery in the Carpathians to the Austrian court. He fled thence to the Dalmatian coast, in February 1242. The Mongol hunters traced their quarry down to the shore. Bela fled out to sea, to one of the islets along the coast. This checked Kadaan—his horsemen were not familiar with such a great expanse of water, over which they could not swim their horses—until he commandeered other ships and began to search through the islands. Frightened, Bela had himself transported back to the coast.

Kadaan picked up his trail again there and began to work down the coast, slaughtering the small army of captives he had brought with him from Hungary when they hindered his march.

First Bela sought refuge in the fortress of Clissa. Then, hearing of the approach of the Mongol horsemen, he rode to Spalato, where nobles of the Hungarian court had flocked. Fearful, even in that strongly defended port, he fled on to Trau.

Kadaan's advance appeared before Clissa and fired a volley of arrows into it before dismounting and climbing to the assault. Learning that Bela was no longer within its walls, the pursuers went on to Trau. There they sent a messenger who spoke Slavonic into the town.

"Kadaan, a lord of the unconquered army, bids you know," the messenger announced, "that you will share the punishment of one who is not blood kin to you, if you do not yield him into our hands."

But Bela had taken to the sea again, sailing out to a small island off Trau, where the Mongol horses could not follow him.

Kadaan ravaged the coast to the south, and his men attacked the ships that had escorted Bela out, when they were driven ashore by a storm.

Beyond the Danube Subotai waited, ready to move into western Europe at the first appearance of a hostile army. Then, at the end of February 1242, a courier from the other side of the world reached the camp of the old Mongol general, and put a stop to all operations. The courier carried a gold tablet of command, and the message he brought to Subotai was this:

The Night at the Blue Lake

More than four thousand miles away, the Khakhan, Ogadai, had lingered in his summer quarters by the Blue Lake where the waterfowl gathered. The wild geese, abandoning their summer haunts in the tundras, passed south, crying out. Clouds of sand grouse swept by, on the heavy winds, between the gusts of hail. And Ogadai drank in his gold-studded pavilion. Even after the first flurries of snow, he stayed at the lake to hunt. At times, after a drinking bout, he lay speechless and weak. But he would not follow the birds toward his winter palace.

His elder brother Chagatai was no longer at his side. Chagatai—the Wild Horse—was feeling his age. A nomad at heart, he kept to his mountains in mid-Asia. He had opened new roads through the ranges, winding down to the Five Cities, joining the different Mongol dominions together. His granaries were full. His people kept to the Yasa of Genghis-Khan. With nothing to concern him, Chagatai built artificial lakes by his mountain camps, so that like Ogadai he could watch the bird life gathered there. And he listened to the messengers from the western army telling of the fortunes of his warrior son and grandson, Baidar and Bouri.

Then too the Wild Horse had fallen under the influence of a wizard who could subdue the spirits of the high and distant places, and invoke the stars—a wizard named Sakaki.

Sakaki could lay an enchantment on a city that would keep fires from burning, and he could summon into Chagatai's tent of nights an army of fire-spirits, armed with flaming weapons. If a man doubted Sakaki's power, he forced him to kiss the tail of a dog.

Once, when a flight of herons passed overhead, Chagatai had lifted his bow to shoot at the birds, when the wizard touched his arm. "Which would you like to see fall?" he asked.

Glancing up at the herons, Chagatai saw that there were five. "The first, and the last," he said, "and the middle one."

Whereupon Sakaki made a sign with his finger on the ground, and struck his hands together. The three herons that Chagatai had picked out fluttered and fell into the grass. Chagatai bit his fingers in astonishment. He could not understand the power of the wizard, and he feared him. Sakaki was careful to keep the old Mongol away from his brother's court. . . .

The burden of administration in the east had fallen upon that wise Cathayan, Yeliu Ch'u-tsai. With Ogadai ailing, his task was doubled, and he had little time now to play the dozen lutes that were his hobby, or to write verses to his confreres. He had to struggle against plausible strangers who came to Ogadai's feet with schemes for aggrandizement and still more fabulous profit.

And he had to tread, with great care, a middle ground between the ideas of the elder Mongols and Turks, who believed in government from the saddle, and the growing Chinese element that sought to convert the Mongol khans to the ritual of the Chinese empire.

On the nomad Mongol side, Turakina, the favored empress, was gaining the ascendancy—because Ogadai was still patient with her whims. And Turakina saw no reason why the Mongol court should not wax more wealthy—herself the fountainhead of the new prosperity. She was partial to a shrewd Moslem, Abd ar-Rahman who pledged himself to collect two million ounces of silver yearly from the conquered areas in China, if he could be given the tax administration that was in Yeliu Ch'u-tsai's hands.

Against Abd ar-Rahman's scheme the Cathayan argued passionately, knowing what grinding oppression would come to the Chinese with the farming of the taxes.

"Are you trying to stand against us?" Ogadai demanded fretfully. "Do you weep for those people?"

"I weep," Ch'u-tsai replied, "because the misery of the people begins from this moment."

When Ogadai lay on his couch in the Golden Camp, without rising, Turakina came to Ch'u-tsai's quarters to ask how the government was to be carried on, with the great Khan lying helpless.

"For thirty years," the Cathayan answered, "I have carried it on, by doing what was reasonable and punishing what was wrong. The Khakhan trusted those affairs to me."

"But now that he is ill," Turakina suggested, "new edicts are needed."

"Without a decree of the Khakhan, nothing can be altered."

The Cathayan would concede nothing to her growing insistence, or to the whispering of her adherents. Ogadai recovered a little as winter settled down on the steppes. But he would not leave the tent camp for civilized quarters. And against Ch'u-tsai's urging he rode off to hunt again.

When he mounted his horse, a Mongol shepherd came to his stirrup, to complain of a wolf that had been killing sheep. Hearing that, the Mongol beaters assembling around the Khakhan carried up to him a wolf they had just trapped and bound. For a moment Ogadai stared at the gray beast twisting in its cords.

Then he ordered a flock of sheep to be given the shepherd as a reward, and on an impulse of his own he told the beaters to release the captured wolf.

"I will let him go," Ogadai said gravely, "so that he will go back to the other wolves of the pack and warn them of the danger that came to him. Thus, they will all leave the countryside."

Those who heard Ogadai did not know if he were still drunk, or if a whim had seized him. They freed the wolf and let it go—only to see it seized by a pack of dogs before it could get clear of the camp. The dogs killed the wolf.

Ogadai seemed depressed by this happening. Dismounting, he went back into his pavilion and was silent a long time. He refused to think of hunting. "My strength fails," he said at last. "I thought that the Sky might be willing to let me live longer, but I see now that no one can run away from his end. It is not a good omen, for me."

He took to drinking again, in his couch. At the beginning of the twelfth moon he sat late to drink one night with two companions, one being the sister of Siyurkuktiti, the other her nephew who had come on a visit from Cathay. Ogadai welcomed them, and emptied cups of hot and cold wine with them. That night he died in his sleep.

At daybreak, when other women found Ogadai's body, the wailing began, and accusations against the two who had sat with Ogadai in the night. Some said that Siyurkuktiti's sister had poisoned the Khakhan.

Ilchidai Noyan, a powerful chieftain of the Jelairs, spoke against this.

"What scattered words are these?" he exclaimed. "The Khakhan hath ever drunk too much of wine. Why then should we give our Khakhan a bad name, saying that he died at the hand of another? For his hour was upon him. Let no man speak such words again."

The Mongols who heard Ilchidai nodded their heads in agreement. Ogadai, their Khakhan, had ascended to the throne seat of empire, they remembered, in the year of the Ox, and now that twelve years had passed, he had died in that same year of the Ox. It seemed fitting enough.

As their custom was, they kept the news a secret. That daybreak, when Ogadai lay lifeless by the Blue Lake, orders were given to close the post roads. No merchants or strangers were allowed within the gates of Kara-korum; no Mongol could leave the Blue Lake encampment except the couriers who carried the tidings to the blood kin of the Golden Family. Travelers on the roads were halted at the stations, and the couriers went through on racing horses. One quested for and found Kuyuk, loitering near the Gobi; another, with a gold tablet that gave him the authority of a khakhan, galloped across Asia in midwinter, sleeping in the saddle as he went, to carry the tidings to Subotai and Batu.

The March of the Barbarians

Ogadai had died on the eleventh of December 1241. The courier arrived at Subotai's quarters on the Danube late in February. He had covered nearly five thousand miles of snow trails in two months and a half.

And this courier brought a summons to Batu and the chieftains of the house of Genghis-Khan to ride back to the Mongol homeland, to a kuriltai of the blood kin. To disobey such a summons was, to Subotai, unthinkable.

Now it was Batu's turn to object. Ogadai's death had been a release to him. By it the bastard's son had become the eldest of the house of Genghis-Khan—for Chagatai was aged, his health broken by heavy drinking. More than that, Batu commanded the victorious army of the west. His domain had grown with each yearly campaign. He had no desire now to quit the Danube to journey back to Kara-korum to help elect one of his cousins of the house of Ogadai to the great Khan's throne. Certainly not Kuyuk, who had called him an old woman with a beard. Batu wished, therefore, to carry on the war. Had not that been Ogadai's command?

Subotai, indifferent to politics, answered that the Yasa, the word of Genghis-Khan, summoned them to the homelands. He thought no more of his own ambition to penetrate beyond the Danube. Back they must go. And he ordered the evacuation of Europe.

Kadaan was called off from his man hunt. The great Ordu about-faced and began its slow march eastward to the steppes. But Subotai took pains to make the Europeans understand that this was no retreat.

To screen his movement, Kaidu was sent with a flying column, to circle Vienna and carry off loot from the Germans. As they went, Kaidu's riders proclaimed, "We are called away, and we spare the Germans war."

The Mongols decided to abandon the Hungarian plateau zone. They stripped that plain of its herds, driving the cattle eastward. This zone, in which they had been settling, was to be turned into a desert. Kadaan's army was ordered back through the Balkans— to crush the Serbs and Bulgars there. In its passing, it burned

Belgrade and compelled the Bulgars to become tributaries of the Khakhan. Then it rejoined Subotai in the Russian steppes.

Their new frontier was to be the end of these grasslands, at the line of the Balkans, the Transylvanian Alps, and the Carpathians. With their wagon trains, they disappeared into the east. Europe had been granted a truce.

What would have happened if Ogadai had not died? Would western Europe have escaped the Mongol yoke?

This much is certain. Subotai had come into contact with the German military power, and it was part of the Mongol plan of conquest not to leave a defiant enemy uncrushed. It is clear also that the steppe dwellers felt little desire for the hilly country beyond the Danube, with its small valleys and rivers. They had been drawn toward the steppes of Russia, the Polish plain and the Hungarian plateau.

That they would have destroyed Frederick and his war bands, there can be no doubt. And the French chivalry, led by the hapless Louis, might have fared no better. The European monarchs had proved themselves incapable of acting together. In numbers and individual bravery, the Europeans were at least the equals of the Mongols, but they had shown themselves helpless before the maneuvering of the Mongol cavalry divisions, directed by a strategist like Subotai.

As it was, Subotai's campaign had a decisive effect on the growth of eastern Europe. His armies had decimated and scattered the western Slavs and Magyars. The zone around Hungary had been half depopulated; crops had not been sown that summer, and famine and typhoid thinned the surviving peoples. On the other hand the Germans beyond Bohemia had escaped with little harm. Districts like Silesia and fertile Moravia were repopulated in time by German settlers.

Teutonic Austria gained the ascendancy over the sadly mixed survivors of Hungary. The Turkish element in Europe—Bulgars and Kipchaks—were driven into that refuge of minorities, the Balkan mountains, or they were drawn into the orderly mass of the Golden Horde, in the steppes.

By this upheaval of peoples the Mongols changed the racial

map of that part of Europe, not by interbreeding. The steppe dwellers avoided settling in those lands; they were still nomads by temperament, and they withdraw with their gleanings from the captured lands, leaving almost no descendants there. The children of the women they took east with them grew up in the steppes.

For Batu withdrew to the Volga banks before settling down with his Golden Horde.

In their retreat, the Mongols disappeared from the ken of the Europeans. The westerners, in that summer of 1242, were left stunned. They felt helpless and uncertain. They asked themselves who the "Tartars" were, and whither had they gone. What purpose had brought them out of the east? When would they strike again? The eastern churches inserted a new prayer in their litany, to be "delivered from the fury of the Tartars."

A new Pope, Innocent IV, coming into the Lateran, warned the Europeans to fortify themselves against the Mongol peril. He heard that the pagan invaders had appeared north of the Holy Land. And that Russia was no more. He advised his peoples to obstruct all roads leading into the east. And he sent his missionary friars after the retreating armies, toward the unknown empire beyond the steppes, "to exhort them from ceasing to slaughter mankind."

But at the same time merchants like the Polo brothers began to explore the caravan routes beyond the ruins of Kiev, to resume their trade with the pagans.

Batu stopped at the line of the Volga, where the courts of his twenty-six wives awaited him. All his life he had been little better than an exile from the Golden Family. Now he had under his gilded domes the spoils of the European war; he had a domain that was a sea of grass; he was safe from any enemy, with food enough to keep his people from hunger indefinitely. He reigned, a Sain Khan in truth, over an empire more suited to the nomads than Cathay. And he made up his mind to do something unheard of.

He told Subotai that he would not go to the kuriltai.

"You are the eldest prince," Subotai said. "It is not wise to refuse."

Batu made an excuse—the gout in his leg kept him from going.

"The great ancestor said," Subotai reminded him, "that those who do not appear at the gathering of the blood kin will be like arrows shot into reeds. They will disappear."

Then Batu agreed that he would make the journey east. But when Subotai departed with his followers, the Sain Khan did not come after him. Instead, he sent word that his gout was worse and he could not come.

The kuriltai was held without him.

V

The Book of the Three Great Ladies

V

The Book of the Three Great Ladies

TURAKINA DID NOT KNOW what to do when Ogadai ceased to breathe. She lost no time in going to talk to Yeliu Ch'u-tsai. The Khakhan no longer existed—how was the work of the throne to be carried on?

"The Khakhan who is now dead," he assured her, "left a will. We can do nothing but conform to that. We cannot let strangers put their hands on the government now."

Turakina had hoped he would say something else. But the iron in the Cathayan would not yield to a woman's dominance. Exasperated, the widow took counsel with her advisers, who reminded her that by Mongol custom the first wife of a dead chieftain cared for his people and his possessions, until his successor could be named. She herself was now head of Ogadai's house. Authority, then, rested in her hands.

"The empire," Ch'u-tsai objected, "was the property of the dead Khakhan. How can you own what was his?"

No longer, he pointed out, were the Mongols a clan disposing only of their flocks and herds. The elder Mongols, the *sechens* and *bagaturs*, discussed the matter among themselves and petitioned Chagatai to take the throne seat. But the Wild Horse refused, feeling himself to be weak and aged. Moreover, Chagatai knew that Turakina held to her right by tribal law. He agreed that, as the widow, she should rule until another was elected by the kuriltai.

[*177*]

The March of the Barbarians

Meanwhile Abd ar-Rahman, her Persian minister, opened his coffers to make gifts to the kinsmen of the Golden Family. To increase the gifts, Turakina issued a decree by which Abd ar-Rahman became minister of the empire, with authority over Ch'u-tsai and the other officials. She signed the decree with her hand-print.

"Such orders cannot be executed," the Cathayan stormed. "Does the imperial widow mean to reward my services of twenty-five years by death?"

He was inflexible in his determination. And Turakina had no wish to dispense with Ch'u-tsai, who had been with Genghis-Khan and Subotai, a founder of the empire. Ch'u-tsai had devised a government for the Mongols by which they had grown wealthy, while the subject populations could still survive. He had joined the cities to the steppes in a new manner. So she praised him and treated him with respect.

Then Chagatai, the maker of laws, died. Turakina felt herself more secure in her power. Abd ar-Rahman made plans to double the taxation, in spite of Ch'u-tsai's protests. And the Cathayan withdrew from the government, grieving.

For the first time a woman's hand guided the Mongol world. The woman was Turakina, unlovely—except in the eyes of the dead Ogadai—and more than sixty years of age. But Turakina had the vitality of the steppe women who endured beyond the child-bearing age.

Moreover, she had matured before the years of the conquests. Like Ogadai she had the instincts of a nomad. And she was a shrewd manager. "She was wise," the chroniclers admit. And they add: "She reigned according to her will."

Being a woman, she had more than Ogadai's adaptability. Because she could ride astride a horse for a day's journey, it did not seem to her that she should ride so like common people. She preferred to be carried in state, which meant in a canopied sedan. She could sleep by a yurt fire of dried dung, but she chose to dwell in the Kara-korum palace that had braziers and sleeping quilts upon a floor of stately tiling. She had a conviction that power was her due. Was she not head of the house of Ogadai, the empress-dowager, ruler of the Golden Family? Even Chagatai had admitted that.

And Turakina, lined and brown with the weather, hardened by years of nomad strife, became more of an aristocrat than her husband. She had no patience with the frippery of singing girls and hot wine; she wanted security and power for the children of her body—the children who now formed, in her thoughts, the Golden Family. The outside populations—which she had never seen—were so many slaves to be made to labor for her family. Turakina had few misgivings, and no inhibitions. She felt herself quite capable of directing the course of this new empire, founded in the saddle, which could not be governed from the saddle.

Like the older Mongols, Turakina was at heart a pagan. True, she liked to have the desert priests officiate outside her doorway— the bearded and dirty Nestorians of mid-Asia beat their plates and went through the dimly remembered ritual of the Mass, while the shamans of the forest people doctored the sick of the Golden Family with drums, and invocations to the spirits of the upper air. But the practical Mongol grandmother remained incurious as to her own spirit-life.

Her main concern was her growing family. The blood kin of the house of Ogadai had increased swiftly. Now that they were sheltered from the Siberian blizzards, and gorged with food, the young men of the great house bred many sons. These were no longer killed off by the tribal feuds and hardships of the winter hunts. Even Kaidu, the reckless grandson, returned unscathed from the western war.

And these young men, with unlimited herds and lands of their own, increased the number of women they took to wife—healthy girls who bred easily, being bound no longer to the toil of the yurt that had made Turakina's body lean and hard. Also, the returning warriors brought back with them sturdy Magyar girls, slender Persians, and prattling, quick-witted Chinese. A youth like Kaidu had four sons, already, tumbling about the pavilions of his wives, and Mongols in middle age might have forty sons—a certain nephew of Genghis-Khan boasted of a hundred children. They nicknamed him the Centenarian.

Each boy, when he matured, demanded his own establishment with women and serving men, cattle and land, by tribal law. Then there were daughters to be given in marriage. And all of them hungry for the new wealth.

Turakina, in this incredible prosperity of her family, provided marriage payments and estates for all her growing blood kin. She discovered that it was possible to commandeer wealth in a simple way. If Turakina stamped a bit of Chinese paper with the state seal she had entrusted to Abd ar-Rahman, strange merchants would appear, to yield her with infinite respect hundredweights of silver, and sacks of gold coins, for such a scrap of paper.

These gleanings of coins the Mongol dowager handed over to the throng of descendants that clustered about her knees. Then, too, by speaking a word to Abd ar-Rahman, she could bestow an appanage on a grandson—miles of fertile land, with villages of slave-souls ready to labor with plow and forge and silk loom. There was, apparently, no limitation on this wealth she could bestow through the arranging of Abd ar-Rahman, at the suggestion of her adroit confidante, the Persian Fatima.

"For Fatima," a chronicler relates, "knew the secrets of the great princess."

She did not bother, now, to consult Yeliu Ch'u-tsai, who had retired to his house in Kara-korum. Ch'u-tsai still objected harshly to this easy acquisition of wealth by the house of Ogadai.

"The throne has bad counselors," he lamented. "Avarice dominates the court; the public charges are sold; the prisons are full of honest men whose only crime was to object to the lawless grabbing of silver."

In the fifth moon of the year of the Dragon, Ch'u-tsai died of this grieving. He had served Genghis-Khan, Ogadai and Turakina for thirty years, and when his life's work was taken from him, he died.

Abd ar-Rahman's intimates hinted to Turakina that the man who had been the chief servant of the khakhans for so many years would have wealth stored up in his house.

"And such wealth," they added, "should be brought back into the house of Ogadai."

Turakina hesitated. She—who lived in awe only of the suldë of

Genghis-Khan—had felt an abiding respect for the Cathayan minister. But she had heard whisperings about the treasures stored in his home, and Turakina was curious. She ordered Ch'u-tsai's quarters to be searched.

Abd ar-Rahman's agents found no treasure of the kind they sought. There was a little coined money, the dozen lutes that had been Ch'u-tsai's diversion, shelves of ancient manuscript books, and other volumes written in the Cathayan's fine calligraphy, a collection of old coins and several pieces of jasper, with inscriptions carved on stone and marble—nothing worth while, to the searchers.

One other woman Turakina watched with jealous eyes: Siyur-kuktiti Begi, also the widow of a son of Genghis-Khan and head of a great house. No one was more comely to look upon than the Begi, who dressed herself so carefully in new fashions, who had refused out of modesty to take Kuyuk, Turakina's eldest son, for a second husband. Siyurkuktiti Begi bowed her gleaming head to the Yasa—she was younger in years than Turakina and obedient to all Turakina's wishes, and she seemed to care for nothing except the education of her sons. Still, she thought that her sons were as much a part of the Golden Family as the sons of the house of Ogadai.

"She was the greatest woman in all the world," Rashid says of her. "Since some of her children were very young when their father died, she made efforts to have them trained, and she taught them good ways—never letting trouble come between them. And after that, she kept the hearts of their ladies in friendship, one for another. And she guarded as well the great chieftains and armies that they had received from Genghis-Khan and Tului.

"Just as the mother of Genghis-Khan trained him, when he was left a young child at the death of his father, and held the army together for him and led it until Genghis-Khan grew strong and won his way to empire—just so was Siyurkuktiti Begi, in the training of her children. They called her the Princess because no other was like to her."

When Turakina had sent Kuyuk, her eldest, to win military fame with the western army, under Subotai's wing—and no Mongol prince could hold the respect of the steppe dwellers unless he had led them in war—this other great lady also sent her eldest, Mangu, to the western regions.

And Mangu came back with a brilliant record. He had led campaigns and taken cities. "Ay, he slew and he looted," the elder Mongols said, "and he took with his hand great grazing lands for us."

Kuyuk had not distinguished himself by such feats. Moreover, Mangu had become the fast friend of the Sain Khan Batu—now master of Europe—while Kuyuk had quarreled with Sain Khan.

Turakina said nothing of her jealousy, unless to the attentive Fatima. For the Princess made no claim before the chieftains and noyans that Mangu should be honored above Kuyuk.

The imperial widow asked the princes and great chieftains to elect the son of her loins, Kuyuk, the first-born of Ogadai, to the four cushions of the Mongol throne.

One obstacle stood in her way. Ogadai had named a grandson, Shiramun, to succeed him—Shiramun (Solomon), a smooth-cheeked boy, born of another woman. This Turakina would not endure. Shiramun might have been Ogadai's favorite, but he was too young, she pointed out, to sit in the seat of the Khakhan.

"Shall a grandson be chosen," she demanded, "while a son lives?"

The Mongols yielded to her wish. They had pledged obedience to the house of Ogadai. And Siyurkuktiti Begi made no objection.

When Batu failed to appear in his homeland for the election of Kuyuk, Turakina commanded that the second kuriltai of the Golden Family be held without him, on the shore of the Blue Lake.

"No one," a chronicler relates, "ever beheld such an assemblage before."

For a few weeks, in 1245, the encampment at the Blue Lake became the metropolis of the world. Two thousand white felt tents were pitched there, around the Sira Ordu, yet the throngs that crowded in had not space to dismount within the borders of the camp, and the plain became alive with cavalcades seeking quarters.

Doctors of learning from Cathay ate by the open fires in the steppes with shaven mullahs of Samarkand, and red lamas out of

Tibet. Chinese ministers and Manchurian lords brought their gifts to the new Khakhan, with the Judge of Judges from Baghdad, and the silent envoys of the Old Man of the Mountain.

Twenty reigning princes waited outside Kuyuk's threshold, to do homage. Some of them had made the long journey from the far west—the Amir Arghun from Khorasan, Sultan Rukn ad-Din from the Turks of Asia Minor, and two brothers of the Atabeg of Aleppo. From the Caucasus appeared Sempad the Constable of the Armenians, and his enemy, Kilidj Arslan (the Red Lion), the Sultan of the Seljuks. And David, pretender to the throne of the Georgians.

The Grand Prince Yaroslav had come from Russia—Batu had sent him to represent him.

Subotai appeared, and then, weary of politics and ceremonial, asked permission to depart to the war in China.

All the members of the houses of Ogadai, Tului and Chagatai came in from their far-off domains to the feasting and the dancing of Kuyuk's kuriltai.

Never had they beheld such evidence of the growth of the nomad empire that stretched now over more than half the known earth—over six thousand miles from the rising to the setting sun, and roughly two thousand from the polar ice down toward the torrid lands of the sun. Except for the barbarians at the end of Europe's peninsula, and the ancient dynasty of the Sung in southern China, the Mongols knew of no powers able to stand against their progress. The chain of their victories had been unbroken. . . .

Yet there was a restlessness and a fear in the sons of the three great houses, even while they feasted. Batu had failed to come to the kuriltai of his blood kin. And they remembered the saying of Genghis-Khan: "He who remains in a distant place and does not come will be like a stone fallen into deep water, or an arrow shot among reeds. He will disappear."

They were in dread of Kuyuk, as well. He allowed no one, now that he was khakhan, to approach nearer to him than the stables without permission, or to speak before he spoke. He had a nature as inexorable and majestic as his grandsire's.

Some of the elder Mongols thought that the suldë of Genghis-Khan had left the great standard and entered the sickly body of

Kuyuk. They seemed much alike in their grimness. The Mongols felt uncertain of the future. They did not know in what direction they would be ordered to move.

What Friar John Saw

Close to the entrance of the Khakhan's pavilion waited a strange figure: a man with a coarse brown robe knotted about his hips by a rope—a man with the top of his head shaven and his bare feet thrust into sandals. He spoke no intelligible language, and he had no friends in the multitude that waited with him.

Still, he was given a good place by the door because he claimed to be the envoy of the spiritual lord of the distant Christians. He was, in fact, the nuncio of the Pope, the Franciscan friar, John of Plano Carpini, the first European to arrive of his own will at the nomad court—a stout, shrewd man, full of energy, who had come in, to the amazement of the Mongols, astride a donkey.

He had explained himself to Batu, back on the Volga: "That we were messengers from our lord the Pope, the father and lord of the Christians, going to the Tartar nation, to desire peace and friendship between the Tartars and the Christians. And, as the Pope wished the Tartars to become great, he admonished them by us and by his letters to embrace the faith of Christ, without which they could not be saved. That the Pope was astonished to hear of their monstrous slaughter of mankind . . . and admonished them to repent of what they had done, and he asked them to say what they meant to do."

After hearing this, Batu had dispatched the friar east, by swift relays, to arrive nearly exhausted, in time for the coronation.

"We beheld," Friar John wrote, "an immense tent, with the Tartar lords and their men riding about it, amusing themselves. The first day they were all clothed in white robes; the second day —when Kuyuk came to the great tent—they were dressed in scarlet. The third day in blue, and the fourth in rich robes of *baldakin* [brocades from Baghdad]. Many of them had upon their saddles and the trappings of their horses as much as twenty marks of gold.

"At noon they began to drink mare's milk, and they kept on

The Book of the Three Great Ladies

drinking amazing amounts until evening. They invited us to drink with them, treating us with ale, as we did not drink mare's milk—so much that we made them understand it was hurtful to us, when they desisted.

"They gave to us, and the duke, Yaroslav, the place of honor. . . . When Kuyuk came out of the tent he was greeted with a sound of music, and was saluted with beautiful rods tipped with scarlet wool. . . . They told us that four thousand envoys had come to him with gifts. Among the gifts were samites and silk girdles wrought with gold, and a canopy covered with precious stones, and numbers of camels having trappings of *baldakin*, with horses caparisoned in leather or iron links. . . . We were asked what gifts we had to offer, but we were unable to present anything."

To the Mongols, in the full tide of the great festival, the appearance of this strangely robed envoy who had no gifts—who besought the Khakhan to change his nature, instead of submitting to him—was an astonishing riddle. The voiceless Carpini (he had a companion, a Pole, to interpret for him) was sent to Turakina, to be inspected by the dowager.

"We were in distress," Carpini adds, "for food and drink. But God sent to our aid a Russian goldsmith named Cosmas, who was favored by the emperor. He got us some food. And he showed us the imperial seal, which he had been employed to make. It is thus inscribed:

GOD IN HEAVEN: ON EARTH KUYUK, KHAN BY THE POWER OF GOD: THE SEAL OF THE RULER OF ALL MEN.

"While we were at his court, this emperor raised a standard of defiance against the church of God, the Holy Roman Empire, and all the Christian nations of the west, unless they should be obedient to his commands. The intention of the Tartars is to subdue all the earth, in eighteen years, and they have only abstained from this purpose of late because of the death of Ogadai Khan. Of all the nations, they are in some fear only of us, and on this account they are now preparing to make war on us."

[*185*]

The March of the Barbarians

While they puzzled over this envoy who looked like a beggar, Friar John was making shrewd use of his eyes—studying the Mongols and asking questions about their methods of war. When the Khakhan's secretaries inquired if the Pope had people about him who could read their answering letter, in Mongolian or Russian or Arabic, Carpini had to explain that no one in the papal court could read such a missive.

When the Mongols urged him to take their envoys back with him to the papal court, Carpini objected, for reasons of his own. ("I was not willing to do so," he explains in his journal, "for this reason: they might see the wars and quarreling that went on among the Christians, and so would be more encouraged to make war on us. Also I feared that the messengers were meant to act as spies, to examine the approaches to our land.")

The amusing point is that Carpini himself was carrying out a spy's mission.

He suggested that the Mongols explain to him what they wanted to say, and that he himself would write it down. The secretaries were aghast at such ignorance in handling such a missive. Chinkai, the Uighur minister, and a half-dozen scribes finally dictated the Khakhan's response, word for word, making Carpini repeat it to them from his Latin writing. Still dissatisfied with such unscholarly procedure, they gave him a written copy in Persian, in case anyone in the west might be found to read it.

"Take heed," they said, "that it be understood."

Their reply read:

"The Khan of all the great peoples, by the power of the Everlasting Sky. Our order:

"We command this, that follows, and send it to the great Pope so that he may know it and take note of it.

"After taking counsel with the kings of your dominion, you have sent us an offer of submission which we have had from your envoys.

"If you wish to act in accordance with your words, come yourself, you who are the great Pope, with the other kings, and we will make you acquainted with the commandments of the Yasa.

"For the rest: You say that it would be good for us to become

Christians. You say that yourself, and require it of us; but we do not understand that demand.

"After that: You have told us this, 'You have attacked the country of the Magyars and other Christians, and that astonishes me. Tell me in what way they were to blame.' We do not understand those words. Genghis-Khan and Ogadai the Khakhan have made known the commandments of the Sky. But those people did not wish to believe the commandments of the Sky. Those people, of whom you speak, had a strangely arrogant bearing, and they killed our envoys. The people of those countries were then, according to the will of the Everlasting Sky, slain and annihilated. If it was not by the will of the Sky, how could they have been killed and conquered?

"And when you say: 'I am the Christ, I pray to God, I complain of, and have no care for, other folk'—how do you know what is pleasing to God, and whence do you gain the power to pronounce such words?

"By the will of the Eternal Sky, all the earth from the rising to the setting sun has been given us. How could anyone go against the commands of the Sky? You ought to say now, sincerely, 'We will be your subjects, we will put our power at your service.' You should come in person, at the head of the kings, and no one should be missing, to offer your services and your homage. Not until then will we recognize your submission.

"And if you do not respect the commandments of the Sky, and do otherwise than these our orders, we will know that you are our enemies.

"There is what we want you to know. If you do otherwise, how can we know what will happen to you? Only the Sky will know."

It was signed with the red seal that Genghis-Khan had used on orders that sent his commanders to subdue new lands.

Kuyuk

Turakina gave the bold friar fox-skin robes to wear during his homeward journey, so that he would not die of the cold. He was not summoned to Siyurkuktiti's camp, but even in his brief visit he heard of her—"the greatest lady among the Tartars and the most honored, except the mother of the emperor, and more powerful than any subject save Batu."

Nor was he admitted to kneel before the throne of Kuyuk. Like the envoys of the Kalif of Baghdad, and the ministers of the Old Man of the Mountain, the nuncio of the Pope was excluded from recognition, because Kuyuk meant to exterminate those three dignitaries by war. And the shrewd friar understood well enough the significance of this treatment.

He only saw Kuyuk pass at a distance—"a man of middle size, exceeding careful and grave in his manner—hardly ever seen to laugh. It is his custom never to speak face to face with a stranger, no matter how high in rank, but always to hear, as it were, and to answer through a third person. . . . For despatching affairs, both public and private, he has agents, secretaries and officers of all kinds except lawyers; since every question is decided by his will without strife or argumentation."

Frail in body, Kuyuk's implacable determination contrasted sharply with his father's animal-like tolerance of things as they were.

"Kuyuk was by nature feeble in health," Rashid declares, "and seldom free from ailments. In spite of that, from the hours of sunset to sunrise he occupied himself with goblets of wine and fairy-cheeked creatures, lovely in body. So his sickness ever waxed greater, nor would he leave off from so doing. . . . In the days, he was a prey to melancholy, without the desire to speak or to hear. . . . In the giving of gifts he exceeded all bounds, and he desired his name to be raised beyond that of his father, but his time was too short."

The father, impatient of his son's sickness, had put him aside for a favored grandchild. The son, resenting the slight, longed to excel his father. Ogadai had talked with beggars and peddlers—Kuyuk would speak only through a minister to a suppliant kneeling before the throne.

The portrait is clear: of the new Khakhan racked by illness, driven by the intensity of his purpose, keeping apart from his fellows, and filling the wakeful hours of the night with wine and women.

No doubting his strength of purpose. He gave away five hundred wagonloads of treasure; he commanded that all yarlighs bearing the sacred red seal of Ogadai should stand approved without being referred to him. He put to death the financial juggler Abd ar-Rahman, and summoned back the old ministers of integrity, Chinkai, the Christian Uighur, and Yelvadj, the pagan Turk.

His Mongols complained of the influence of the Persian slave woman Fatima upon his mother. "A little more," they said, "and she will become the ruler of the great Khanate." And they warned Kuyuk. "This slave woman will work her sorcery on thee, and on thy brothers."

Kuyuk ordered Fatima to be taken by force from his mother's tents, and stripped and flogged naked until she confessed to sorcery. Her Mongol inquisitors then made certain that the evil power, the kelet within her, would not escape to do further damage when she died. They sewed up the openings of her head and lower body, and threw her into a river to drown. This enraged Turakina, but Kuyuk paid no heed to her anger.

And, with decision as swift as a sword stroke, he led the nomad empire in a new direction.

Like Genghis-Khan, he believed that the steppe dwellers must remain in the steppes, to rule the outer world. The throne must be at Kara-korum, in the Black Walls. And the learning of the steppes, the teaching of the Uighurs and the Nestorians—who remembered the Christian letters and ritual only dimly from the last days of the apostles—must suffice.

Thus curiously did Kuyuk lean upon the advice of the forgotten men, the Christian converts of Asia, while he sent defiance to the Pope at Rome.

As Turakina had wished, he meant to rule from the saddle, treating the civilization of China and Islam as the foremost enemies of Mongol dominion. He would carry on the warfare of the desert against the towns.

In this he departed from the policy of Ch'u-tsai, who had sought to bring the learning of civilization into the desert. (Already the great Cathayan had established academies, with Chinese, Uighur, Persian and Arab instructors, to educate the Mongol youth.)

[*189*]

And Kuyuk intended to force the Mongol yoke upon all the civilized earth, to go beyond where the Mongol horses had trod. The power of the Sky had raised him to this high place, but he meant to occupy it alone—"Kuyuk, Khan upon earth."

His clairvoyant mind became aware of the danger of dividing dominion as Genghis-Khan had done among the four branches of the Golden Family. He would do away with the four great *ulus*, and concentrate them in one—making an end of mighty fiefs to be handed down from father to son. No longer could the Centenarians and the growing throng of imperial princes wax stout on the slave labor of their appanages. They must labor themselves, to strengthen the empire, to increase the army.

Kuyuk did away, by a stamp of Chinkai's seal, with the multitude of beggars along the new Mongol roads, and with the throng of idle women swelling the camps. They were put to labor for the horsemen of the army.

In these forceful measures, Kuyuk had the aid of his wife Ogul Gaimish, who was favored by Turakina and who imagined herself the First Lady of this one-man administration.

Kuyuk could be politic in his family chastisement. He was careful to seize upon nothing that belonged by tribal right to the house of Tului—to Siyurkuktiti, and her now popular son Mangu. He needed their influence in what he planned to do. He asked Siyurkuktiti herself to distribute to the Mongol noyans the largesse of the five hundred wagonloads.

"For the sake of my health," he announced cryptically, "I intend to journey to the pasture of the river Imil."

There dwelt Batu. And Batu had rebelled against the Yasa; he had remained away from the kuriltai. He had built up a dominion that he meant to hand down to his sons, against Kuyuk's desire.

Kuyuk sent a summons to his cousin to come to a kuriltai in the homeland.

"My foot pains me," Batu answered, without stirring from his steppes.

Before proceeding against outer enemies, Kuyuk moved against Batu to bring him into submission to the throne. And he moved with the Banners of the Right Wing and Center, with the imperial guard, with the members of the house of Tului and their household regiments, with his mother and all of the court.

One mind had penetrated Kuyuk's purpose. Siyurkuktiti Begi understood, and she saw, at long last, an opportunity to act for her sons.

"Kuyuk was angered," Rashid says, "and in his heart he plotted against Batu. . . . But since Siyurkuktiti Begi was aware of his plan, she sent a secret message, and she warned Batu."

Far off in China, in that year, Subotai felt the weakness of his age coming over him. Whether he knew of Kuyuk's purpose to lead Mongols against Mongols is uncertain. He asked permission of the Khakhan to retire from the Left Wing, to his yurt in the steppes by the river Tula.

There he put away the insignia of his rank and took to sitting on the sunny side of his yurt, watching his herds go out to grazing. He died there at the age of seventy-three—he had been sixty-eight when he turned his back on Europe.

Tradition says that he had been victor in sixty-five battles and had conquered thirty-two nations. He had been the spearhead of the Mongol march, and no commander of men except Genghis-Khan, whom he served, had accomplished such results in war. The Mongols called him the Unfailing. "He was a soldier," the astute Carpini said, "without a weakness."

The Two Roads to the Lake of the Eagles

Strings of laden camels plodding down the great North Road— dust sweeping away from them. Lines of horsemen, their faces bound in cloths, bending against the whirling sand. Over the drumming of the wind across the shifting crests of the sand dunes, the reverberation of the saddle drums of the Mongols beat to drive away the evil spirits of the wasteland. Dark masses of wagon tents, roped together, human beings sheltered under the felt domes . . .

Kuyuk was crossing the edge of the Gobi, rounding the wooded summits of the Altai, going down to the caravan crossroads of the Five Cities, with his armed host.

They were crossing the sands in the region of the White Bones,

The March of the Barbarians

where an army had perished in a time before the memory of the Mongol clans. On one of the wagons lurched a wooden chapel, ornamented with crudely painted figures, a chapel of the Nestorians.

Kuyuk's horsemen were bound beyond the Five Cities, through the Gate of the two mountain ranges, to the river Imil that had been one of Ogadai's grazing grounds, in the heights of mid-Asia.

The river Imil flowed into the Lake of the Eagles, beyond the Gate.

And Batu, approaching from the west, was crossing the expanse of steppes and lakes that gleam blue and yellow, like the fertile fields of a mirage. He must have known of Kuyuk's destination, because he was in sight of the Lake of the Eagles where wind whips the water into surf, breaking white against the shores.

Here, at the mouth of the Imil, Batu waited with his tens of thousands.

Until a courier appeared from the east, from the great North Road, riding with his face and body bound with cloths, leaning against the wind. The courier carried a golden tablet of command, and he would not dismount before he reached the entrance of Batu's tents.

When they asked him what word he brought, he said, "The Khakhan is dead of his sickness."

To Batu it must have seemed as if fate had given him back his life.

In their camp at the edge of the Gobi, the women tried at first to hide Kuyuk's death. For once Turakina hesitated, debating with Kuyuk's widow what they must do.

They ordered the roads closed, and travelers stopped at the post stations. They were far from Kara-korum and almost within Batu's reach. Between the two armies stood snow-capped mountains and the pass known as the Gate.

Then the two women sent to Batu Khan, saying that Ogul Gaimish, the widow of the dead Khakhan, would now rule, but they wished Batu to come to them, to advise them.

The Book of the Three Great Ladies

The Sain Khan replied that he was resting his horses by the lake. "And my foot pains me," he added, "so I may not ride."

Siyurkuktiti, more adroit than they, seized this opportunity. "Batu Khan," she told Mangu, "has lived long. He is indeed the *Agha* of all the grandsons of Genghis-Khan, and in the kuriltai no created being will turn aside from his word. Now that the others will not go unto Batu, though he be the lord of them all, and suffers from his ailment, go thou to him as one inquiring of his health."

Whereupon Mangu and his younger brother Kubilai rode up from the sands, over the pass to the lake. With them they took their household officers.

The Sain Khan greeted Mangu warmly. Had they not shared victories together a few years before? Had not Mangu's mother sent him timely warning? He made a feast for the younger princes, and praised them.

There followed a pretty play of politics, with true Mongol caution. First Batu sent couriers to the women's camp in the Gobi, saying that, now Mangu and Kubilai were at his camp, the other grandsons should come, and a kuriltai be held there.

Turakina and Ogul Gaimish replied that it was not the custom to hold a kuriltai except in the homeland of the Mongols, by the waters of the Kerulan. Meanwhile Ogul Gaimish must be regent.

They claimed their rights by tribal law, and the elder Mongols in both camps assented. Batu was in a fair way to put himself in the wrong. But at this point Siyurkuktiti took the initiative, without hesitation or mercy. "The four sons of Genghis-Khan," she announced, "remain no longer on the earth. Is not the Sain Khan lord of the grandsons? Is he not revered, and much honored? Who has the right to turn aside from his word at this time?"

Both Turakina and Ogul Gaimish had the right, as they well knew. They were dowager and regent of all the Mongol clans. And these same clans had sworn an oath, not to be broken, that they would obey the house of Ogadai so long as a morsel of its flesh remained.

Siyurkuktiti did not argue. She had Batu and the west to support her, and she was popular with the home army of the khakhans. "Did not the great ancestor say," she demanded, "that if the descendants of Ogadai should prove unworthy, *someone* will be found to take the throne?"

She knew the danger of delay, and she must have known that an election held in the homeland would be decided by Mongol tradition, and would go against her. She wanted the election now, in the armed camps of mid-Asia. And she understood perfectly that Batu, the dweller in the west, the son of a bastard, could never hope to be named khakhan.

While the aged Turakina struggled with jealousy and anger, and Ogul Gaimish—less clever than Siyurkuktiti—consulted shamans, the mother of Mangu acted. She mustered her household troops and Cathayan counselors, and rode up from the Gobi to the mountain pass. Two of Chagatai's sons followed her.

Now she had the greater part of the two armies with her, and she sent back word that the kuriltai would be held in Batu's camp by the Lake of the Eagles.

When she dismounted at Batu's tents, the lord of Europe greeted her with appreciation.

"I see in Mangu, thy son," he said, "the signs of maturity and power. He has the training and experience to be khakhan."

For these words and this opportunity, Siyurkuktiti had waited nineteen years. Both Mangu and Kubilai were fit to rule because she had schooled them, remorselessly, with the patience of a steppe woman, to take themselves in the course of years the heritage that had been denied her drunken husband Tului.

She had won, in the conflict with her rival, Turakina, and the superstitious Ogul Gaimish. Her enemies understood that she had won. Turakina sent envoys to Batu's tents to represent the house of Ogadai, saying, "Batu is lord of the princes, and his command is binding upon them, and none shall turn aside from his counsel."

And the two widows started their return journey to Kara-korum, bearing Kuyuk's body with them. Turakina's last gesture had been shrewd, and the final decision of the kuriltai remained in doubt. For Batu was now torn between his loyalty to the memory of Genghis-Khan and the solicitation of Siyurkuktiti.

Once the kuriltai was seated in Batu's pavilion, the possibility of armed conflict ceased. The princes and noyans had come as his guests, and they were free to make their decision as they judged best. No one of the house of Ogadai sat in the assemblage, nor had Kaidu consented to come.

Batu presided, but refrained for a while from speaking. Mangu also was silent. Many of the older chieftains resented Kuyuk's arbitrary act in taking away their family dominions—they no longer felt blindly devoted to the reigning house of Ogadai. But they were all steadfast in their loyalty to the Yasa of Genghis-Khan and to Mongol custom.

Old Ilchidai, the Jelair chieftain, put forward the claim of the house of Ogadai bluntly. Twenty years before, he said, they had pledged themselves never to elect a khakhan who was not of Ogadai's line, while a morsel of flesh of the family remained.

Batu did not answer him. Kubilai, now a mature man, took the word.

"As thou hast said, we did," he answered. "But the descendants of Ogadai were the first to go against the will of Ogadai, for they raised Kuyuk to the throne, when Ogadai had chosen the boy Shiramun for his successor."

Then, the chieftains of Ogadai's side argued, let the boy Shiramun be named now, as was most fitting.

To this Mangusar, a general who had served under Tului, objected grimly. "The work of the Khanate is not for a child's hands." The work of the Khanate was the labor of war, and a man able to lead in war must be selected. He named Batu as the eldest of the surviving princes.

Then Batu spoke. Sitting at the head of the lines of attentive men, he talked to them thoughtfully, reminding them of Mongol tradition and the Yasa that was their final law. He refused to let his name be put forward.

"Among the princes," he said, "it is Mangu who has the experience to become our khakhan. He has seen much of good and evil; many times he has led the armies to war. Great was his dignity and severity of bearing in the eyes of Ogadai. For the Khakhan sent him with me and my *uruk* toward the Kipchak land and the countries beyond, and we conquered them. It was Mangu who broke the strength of the Kipchaks and Circassians and turned their countries into a grazing land for us. It was his hand that made captive the chieftain of the Volga."

And Batu retold the tale of Mangu's victories, his eyes on the elder chieftains.

"After that, in the year of the Ox, Ogadai Khakhan sent out his yarligh that the princes return, and when they reached there, the Khakhan had died; and the yarligh then decreed that his son's son Shiramun should be his heritor."

Again Batu reminded his opponents of their mistake. "Yet Turakina Khatun changed his command, nor did she heed it, and she set up Kuyuk as our head."

Skillfully he reminded them of the nomads' law. "By command of the Yasa, and the custom of the Mongols, the heritage of the father falls to the youngest son. So the heritage of the Khanate should have fallen to Tului, the keeper of the hearth—my good uncle. And the son of Tului is Mangu. Out of the family of Genghis-Khan what other grandson is there who, with a clear mind and wisdom, can lay his hand upon the land and the army? In ability, he stands out from the other princes. At this time, he is most worthy of the Khanate."

When Batu ceased speaking, no one raised a voice against him. Whereupon he commanded that the feasting begin, and he wrote to the great ladies of the house of Genghis-Khan: "The one who has seen the Yasa and the yarligh of Genghis-Khan with his eyes and heard them with his ears is Mangu. It is for the good of the army and the people [ulus] and us who are princes that we make him khakhan."

At first, as the custom was, Mangu refused. While the feasting went on, Kubilai spoke to him persuasively. The younger brother had set his heart on the election of the taciturn Mangu. And another cried out to the assemblage:

"We have all given the binding of our word to agree to the will of the Sain Khan, Batu. How then does Mangu alone refuse? Is he not to keep to his word?"

And Mangu consented to serve the Mongols as their khakhan.

The House of Genghis-Khan

Borjigun
Traditional } Ancestors

Yesukai
m. Oyelin Yakki

Temujin m. Bortai
[Genghis-Khan]

Juchi   Chagatai   Ogadai
m. Turjakina

Tului
m. Siyurkukteti

Batu   Birkai   Baidar   Kuyuk   Kadaan   Mangu   Kubilai   Hulagu   ArikBuka
            Bouri   m. Ogul Gaimish   m. Kutuktai   m. Jamui   m. Dokuz

Sartak   Kaidu   Chingkim   Abaka

                                                 Timur   Arghun

House of Juchi   House of Chagatai   House of Ogadai   House of Kubilai   House of Hulagu
(Golden Horde)   (Chagatai khans)   (Ogadai khans)   (Yüan Dynasty   (Il Khans of Persia)
                                                     of China)

Genghis-Khan and his descendants, from 1200 A·D· to approximately 1500 A·D· The names of the khans are given in Italics. Only the names of people mentioned in this book are given in the table. The great khakhans are shown in large letters; those who came to head individual nations or empires in medium letters.

There remained the coronation. Batu ordered that strong armies should go with Mangu and Kubilai to Kara-korum, while he sent invitations to the blood kin to come to the seating of Mangu.

"This thing," he wrote, "has been done in such a way that it cannot be undone. Had any other than Mangu been named, the work of the Khanate would have suffered. And if the sons of the family will think about it and cast their eyes into the future, they will understand that the rule has passed from the line of the former Khakhan—for the work of the Khanate cannot be done with the small strength that lies in the arms of children."

Still the members of the house of Ogadai would not come to the ceremony. Riders passed over the steppe roads, between the tent cities, and the heads of the clans sat down to discuss the situation with the princes by the night fires.

For the steppes were troubled with uncertainty. In the almost empty palaces of Kara-korum, the widow Ogul Gaimish called in her conjurors, and wrote out hastily orders for great sums of money from the Moslem merchants. There was whispering and argument against Mangu, but no one came forward with a just word to say against him. Batu retired to his beloved Russia—his gout apparently ceasing to trouble him. And Siyurkuktiti, dreading delay, sent a message to Batu:

"For two years we have sought to seat Mangu upon the throne, yet the children of Kuyuk and Chagatai have not come."

"Set him on the throne," Batu wrote, "and take the head from any living being who turns aside from the Yasa."

The End of the House of Ogadai

As anxious as any hostess, Siyurkuktiti arranged the last details of the ceremony—making gifts to the guests who dismounted at the imperial camp. On the day itself, she set the stage for the kuriltai. She consulted astrologers—worried because black storm clouds hid the sky in the early morning. But the sun came out at the hour of the ceremony.

Deftly she arranged the seating of the Mongols, putting Birkai, Batu's brother—who limped with the family gout—upon comfortable cushions. And she made certain that her younger son Kubilai would be noticed. She made him sit before Birkai—"that all should hear the speech of Kubilai."

Mangu she placed at the entrance, to welcome his guests, and Hulagu, the third brother, she put by the table—"to see that no one spoke or made answer in unlawful words."

Then, hidden behind a curtain, she watched while Mangu was led to his throne seat.

It was the fulfillment of her desire, the sublimation of her four sons, with Mangu, the head of the house of Tului, the khakhan.

When Mangu spoke to the princes and noyans who stood massed below him, their girdles thrown over their shoulders, he spoke in a fashion that surprised them.

"I would like," the quiet man said, "to have rest settle down on all the kinds of life. It is my yarligh that on this day no creature lay a burden on another. They shall all find pleasure in it, and have goodly things to share. Let the domestic animals be free today of their riders and their packs. Let them be unbound. Make no blood run from animals that are to be eaten. And game, the feathered kind or the grazing kind, shall be safe from nets and arrows. Birds can fly where they will."

The elder Mongols thought that this was a mild speech from a khakhan. While they feasted in a pavilion of cloth-of-gold, a gift from the old Yelvadj to the new Khakhan, with wagonloads of wine and mare's milk trundling up to the entrance, a shadow crept over the feast. A mule driver appeared, begging to speak to the new Khakhan. This man said he had been searching for a wandering mule, when he fell in with a company of riders escorting loaded carts toward the kuriltai. A boy of the company had asked the mule driver to help him repair a broken cart, and the man had noticed that the cart was filled with weapons. The others, he discovered, were loaded in the same way, and he heard that the riders had come at orders of the princes of the house of Ogadai, to kill Mangu and the feasters when they had drunk too much at the kuriltai.

Mangu and the others did not pay much attention to this harangue, but the mule driver stuck to his story. He had come three days' journey in a day to warn the Khakhan. Then Mangu ordered the old general, Mangusar, to bring in the riders with the carts.

When these arrived at the feast, they were welcomed. Mangu, undisturbed, asked them to sit down with his people. He told them the story of the mule driver. "Such talk," he said, "is not easily to be believed. Yet it is needful that no suspicion lie upon you. For suspicion does not die away with time. It grows. So, if you are blameless, those who have spoken against you will be heavily punished."

Under such direct questioning, the noyans of the house of Ogadai could not deny that there had been a plot against Mangu. Ogul Gaimish and the mother of Shiramun, the boy who had been named khakhan by Ogadai, were calling upon the princes and noyans to hold to their oath of fidelity to the house of Ogadai.

Mangu considered the problem. The officers who had been caught with the weapons had struck no blow. They had told the truth. In what way were they guilty? He decided to let them go, when he noticed old Yelvadj standing at the back of the pavilion, saying nothing.

"Why don't you speak?" he asked irritably.

"What can I say in this place?" Yelvadj responded. "If the Khakhan will be pleased to come with me to my garden, I can show him how such a garden is cultivated. I will pull up for him the tough, strong trees with the deepest roots, and I will plant young and weak cuttings."

Again Mangu considered, understanding the parable. He ordered the officers put to death, their sons to be appointed to their places.

Swiftly and inexorably he dealt with the conspiracy, stepping aside himself to let the old general Mangusar administer the family purge. He had Ogul Gaimish and the mother of Shiramun taken and brought to Siyurkuktiti's camp. And his mother showed the captive women no mercy. She ordered the hands of Kuyuk's widow to be sewn into a leather sack, and she called in Mangusar to judge her.

The Mongol general had Ogul Gaimish stripped naked, and accused her of sorcery.

[*199*]

"How can you look on a body," she cried defiantly, "that none but a king has seen?"

Mangusar had her twisted into felt cloths and flung into water to drown. The shamans who had served her, and the mother of Shiramun, went the same way.

"How could that evil woman, viler than a bitch," Mangu said of her later, to the envoy of Louis of France, "know the ways of war and peace? How could she settle the great world in quiet?"

Mangu's armed searchers hunted down the members of the rival family. Chinkai, the aged Christian Uighur, their minister, was put to death. Bouri, their friend, was seized and sent to Batu, who nourished an old grudge against him. Brought into the presence of the Sain Khan, Bouri explained moodily, "I was drunk when I called you an old woman."

"You remember too well," Batu retorted, "the words you spoke when you were drunk." And he had Bouri put to death.

Messengers of the Khakhan found Kadaan—Bouri's companion in command during the European campaign—alone in his camp. "My friends have all gone," he said to the messengers. "Now my turn comes."

He was removed from his people to a grazing land far from Kara-korum. The youthful Shiramun was given to the care of Kubilai, who asked for him, and took him off in safety toward China. Only Kaidu escaped the taint of conspiracy, because no one wanted to accuse the hero of Hungary. Lands on the river Imil, remote from the Mongol homeland, were allotted to him. This young scion of war rode off without protest, to exile; but he nourished an anger that would never leave him.

This scattering of the house of Ogadai was done in the year of the Pig, in 1251—nearly twice through the cycle of the years of the Twelve Beasts since the crowning of Ogadai.

And the next year Siyurkuktiti, the mother of Mangu and Kubilai, died of sickness. Mangu, the taciturn, bestowed on his mother at her grave the title of Empress. And she was buried beside Tului near the grave of Genghis-Khan in the valley beneath the Mountain of Power.

"She was the wisest woman in the world," Rashid says. "She

watched over her children until the time when the empire came to the hands of Mangu, by her skillful management. Although she supported the Christian people, she exerted herself greatly in gifts and bounties to Islam. Such was her way, until the year of the Mouse. And God, the All-Wise, knoweth best."

For Siyurkuktiti had wanted her sons to be educated, to learn wisdom so that they should no longer be nomads. Mangu had learned in the school of war—he was able to crush the enemies of the family like the Borjigun of old. And Kubilai had been Si-yurkuktiti's favorite. She had seen in him the wise calm soul that can pass through struggle undisturbed. And Kubilai had his mother's taste for finery. Because, secretly, she had longed to behold her sons in splendor, like the ancient head of her house who had been called Prester John of Asia.

Siyurkuktiti's overthrow of the house of Ogadai had broken the highest Mongol law, the Yasa. It had divided the Golden Family. And this feud between the house of Ogadai and the house of Tului was destined to last for generations—although for the time being it was quashed by Mangu's firm action. In the future, by a strange road, it would form a new Asia.

Because a subtle change was taking place in the Mongol thought. The nomads had looked up to the four sons of Genghis-Khan as the four Pillars, who had shared the conquests peaceably between them. Now only Mangu and Batu reigned, in the east and the west, as co-emperors.

In the minds of the Mongols the suldë of Genghis-Khan, the shadowy ancestress, the Blue Wolf and the ancestral Borjigun clan were losing substance.

The great battle standard still stood in the homeland by the Mountain of Power, the banners of the army were more numerous than before, the elder men still chanted their traditions. But with Mangu's ascendancy a new intelligence appeared to direct the Mongol world. In him tribal tradition struggled with the wisdom he had been taught. He relied upon reason, rather than force.

Mangu was the fruit of Yeliu Ch'u-tsai's long labor. And in him, the Cathayan triumphed over Genghis-Khan.

VI

The Book of Tsar Batu

VI

The Book of Tsar Batu

NOW BATU HAS WHAT HE WANTED. When the Sain Khan returns to his beloved Volga, at the turn of the century, he does not intend to go back to the east again. The disinherited one has obtained by patient striving and some good fortune a mighty heritage.

He rules in the west without hindrance. He must obey, it is true, the command of the Khakhan in Kara-korum; but this Khakhan is Mangu, his younger cousin and friend. He has raised Mangu to the Khanate, and he deserves well of him. Mangu's darugashi, or governor, sits in Batu's court and audits the census, selecting gifts to be sent back to Kara-korum, yet the rein of authority is lightly held.

Mangu has consented that Batu's family shall inherit this vast sea of grass in the west. Batu need no longer think of the Golden Family. He is head of his own, of the nomad dynasty known as the *Altyn Ordu*, the Golden Horde. Already his Russian subjects call him Tsar—their pronunciation of the imperial Caesar—Kaiser.

"He is kindly enough to his people," Carpini relates, "but they fear him much, for he is most sagacious in warfare, in which he served a long time, and he is cruel to others."

It matters not now that the Sain Khan is a bastard's son. Utterly different from the restless and savage Juchi, his father, he bears himself like a king—he never leaves his pavilion except beneath a scarlet, tasseled canopy. No one will mock him again, calling him an old woman. When he drinks, the wild Tartar pipes shrill and cymbals clash. He drinks from gold cups, but they are filled with mare's milk. He has a herd of 3,000 white mares to provide this milk. The covered wagons of sixteen wives follow his moving camp, and he has some difficulty in remembering the names of all of his sons.

At the Volga mouths he has ordered a city to be, and there one is: Sarai—the Court—with its mud walls and tents, a rendezvous for the merchants of east and west, a vast trading camp. In the spring Batu moves up the left bank of the gray Volga, while his sons follow the right bank to summer grazing where the ground is moist in the north. In the winter, when the river is frozen, they cross the ice to talk together by the fires.

He is careful not to wash his dirty hands in water, for fear of offending the spirits dwelling in running water. But he likes his girl slaves to rub musk on his stout limbs. And he puts the finest of his jewels in the two plaits of hair that hang down behind his broad, pallid head. Slippers of crimson velvet cover his gouty feet. Over his Chinese silks he wears wolfskins.

He carries a sword still, but its hilt is pure silver. His girdle is weighed down with shining gold plates. His skullcap is embroidered with pearls. For Batu has removed himself far from the Chinese *linya*. He is sufficient unto himself, a patriarch who enjoys prosperity, a nomad in a fertile paradise.

"Not a dog can bark," a proverb states, "without the consent of the Sain Khan."

And he rules like a nomad, from the eastern bank of the Volga, seldom venturing among his subject peoples. His *baskaks*, or collectors—the Squeezers, they came to be called—go out to all the villages, while the chieftains who dare look upon his face come with gifts, to kneel and press their foreheads to the carpet at his feet.

The Case of Great Prince Mikhail

These meetings sometimes have strange endings, because the subject princes know little of the Mongols. Prince Mikhail is sent for, in Kiev. Batu's messengers say to him, "It is not fitting that you should live in the land of the Khakhan, and of Batu, without doing homage to them."

Prince Mikhail goes, with his governor, Fedor, with dread of a shame that may befall them. Because it is rumored in the land that those who go to Batu are set upon by wizards and made to pass between fires, and to bow their heads to unseen idols in the dwelling of Tsar Batu. And it seems to the pious Russians that by submitting to the enchantment of pagan fires, and by bowing to unseen idols, they would destroy their souls.

(Actually, the Mongol shamans are accustomed to compel strangers to go between two fires so that any dangerous magic or invisible weapon they might carry would be rendered harmless by the action of the fire spirits. And visitors are asked to bow their heads toward the Khakhan in the east.)

Mikhail and Fedor are brought to the entrance where the fires are laid. Mikhail says: "It does not become Christians to go through fire, nor to bow to anything except the Father."

Then the shamans and Mongol guards go into Batu's presence and explain what the Russians have said. Batu, angered, replies: "Why have they put aside my command? If they will obey, they will receive their princedom from my hand, but if they refuse, they will die."

When this is told to the Russians, beyond the fires, they consult together, Fedor saying to Mikhail, "What shall it profit a man if he gain the sovereignty of the whole world, yet lose his own soul?" And they answer together, "To the Tsar I would bow, since God hath granted him sovereignty, but to these other things I shall not bow."

At this, Batu's household officer warns the prince: "Mikhail, take care. Thou art dead."

As he is silent, the guards rush on him and throw him down, stretching out his arms. Pounding him over the heart with their fists, they stamp on him with their heels, until his heart is stopped. (Since Mikhail was of royal blood, they are careful not to shed that blood.)

The March of the Barbarians

This tale is written in the Novgorod chronicle, which adds that the *Kniaz* Mikhail became a martyr.

Tsar Batu is careful in his overlordship. He prepares to mint coins, which the Russians lack, to aid them in paying tribute. And he investigates the yield of the salt beds along the southern rivers, as well as the silver mines in the Ural region. Meanwhile, he accepts five skins of animals as a tax upon every human head, each year. A skin of a white bear and of a black fox, a beaver, a sable and a polecat.

His treasure is laid up on the hoof—in growing flocks of fat-tailed sheep and herds of horses. The steppes are astir with captive animals—insurance against hunger.

In the outer world the specter of famine lurks. Floods of the Chinese rivers, or a drought, may starve those human animals, the peasants who dig the soil; along the Nile, low water may reduce the fellahin to eating the remnant of last year's grain; in Europe the serfs may grub roots or pound acorns to chew. Some of the tribesmen who come in to submit to Batu have been cutting up the bodies of their enemies to eat. The Turks in Asia Minor have been taking off their shoes and boiling them.

More than war, or even pestilence, famine is the dreaded destroyer of men in these periods of mass movements. When it invades a land, the common sort of human beings migrate away from it, trying to sell their children in slavery, so that the parents can eat a little, and the children survive. Or they attack the habitations in their path, to get at grain or flesh.

Now the Golden Horde is safe from hunger; its immense herds thrive on the grass of the steppes. Even in the hot summers, when the high grass is brown and wind sweeps dust over it, there is green growth by the rivers and their marshes. And these rivers, the Yaik, the Etzil and the Tana (the Ural and the Volga and the Don) do not fail.

Batu's camp is filled with curious animals. His hunters have captured gray buffalo and tigers in the Caucasus—his shamans have their trained bears. The Khan himself has the best of the falcons, the golden eagles, for his hunting. Visiting Moslem mer-

chants bring him curios from Egypt, giraffes that graze on tree=
tops, and miniature animal-men—monkeys. These monkeys make
the Mongols roar with laughter by their antics.

Solitary and powerful, Batu is welding his restless Turkish clans
into a single nomad nation. And he demands peace. He is following the saying of Genghis-Khan: "In war be like tigers—in peace,
like doves." Once the terrible Mongol conquest is finished, Batu
proceeds to save everything useful. He will allow no conflict, unless
it be of his own undertaking. Even the Russian princes may not
make war on each other without his consent, and he does not
choose to give it. So the strange nomad peace settles down on
eastern Europe, while the captive peoples wonder what next will
befall them.

One famous woman defies Batu's command. Rusudan, queen
of the Georgians, is much in the public eye. A beauty, among a
people noted for their beauty, Rusudan has the temperament of a
rustic Cleopatra.

She has many lovers, and when she tires of them, they are
thrown from a cliff near her tower. She has only jealousy for
her equally seductive daughter, Thamar. In anger, she can accuse
Thamar of incest.

Until the coming of the Mongols there is no one to challenge
her rule. Her nephew David is confined, like Joseph, in a stone
well, with vermin and snakes for his companions.

Batu hears of her beauty, and also of her temper. Perhaps he
feels that a woman is not good for the unruly Caucasus, perhaps
he desires the body of this Christian enchantress—most certainly
he is curious about her, and believes that she should come like
Mikhail and the others to make formal submission to him. So he
summons her, but Rusudan does not stir from her refuge in the
higher ranges, by the snows of Kasbek.

Then Batu adds entreaties and gifts to his summons, and still
Rusudan does not emerge. The careful Mongols discover the
nephew, buried alive in his well, and take him to the Khakhan at
Kara-korum, where he is given the kingship of the Georgians.

The March of the Barbarians

In the end, Rusudan does not obey Batu. She kills herself with poison—perhaps to escape being carried off to Batu's tents, perhaps because she cannot endure to see her nephew seated on her throne.

At this time the eldest son of the Sain Khan—Sartak—departs on his own account from the path of Mongol tradition. Sartak has been taught by two Nestorians, and he thinks favorably of the Christians, suffering their priests to perform ceremonies for him. To this, apparently, Batu does not object, although he himself remains a pagan. From the northern fringe of his empire, Batu can still see the lights that dance in the Gate of the Sky on winter nights, rising in cloudlike flames and then vanishing.

His brother Birkai, however, has turned another way. Birkai, the *Agha* who presided at the coronation of Mangu, with his foot carefully propped on pillows by Siyurkuktiti, has been governing the grazing lands along the Caucasus, where he has met bearded men of Islam. They have talked to him of Islam—submission—and the sword of the Prophet that will conquer all unbelievers. They have described the delights of Muhammad's paradise, and Birkai has become a convert.

He is the first of the line of Genghis-Khan to yield himself to a religion. Fearfully, he hides his conversion from his brother. Batu hears that Birkai is praying toward Mecca, and he summons his brother.

He inflicts no punishment on Birkai—only removing him from the vicinity of the dangerous Caucasus to the northern steppes, where he is out of touch with Moslems.

But something has entered within the limits of Batu's house that will change the nature of the Golden Horde.

The Journey of Friar William

Meanwhile the name of Batu has penetrated to the courts of Europe. The devout Louis of France, then on crusade in Egypt, sent a personal investigator, to learn what manner of man the powerful Khan might be, and whether he might not become an ally of the crusaders, against Islam.

The Book of Tsar Batu

This envoy, a barefoot friar, a Belgian named William of Rubruk (or Ruysbroek) had a stout body and a quick wit. And he had need of both, for his mission was simply that of a spy.

Another envoy had gone to Kara-korum before him—Friar Andrew, a priest who carried a scarlet chapel-tent as a gift from King Louis to the Mongol khakhan. As it happened, this scarlet pavilion had fallen into the hands of Ogul Gaimish, who was then in power, and she had taken it to be a sign of submission by the French king. She had said to those around her: "See what the king of the French sends as a token of submission to us."

When Louis had heard of this, he had been angered, and he had warned William of Rubruk on no account to let the Mongols think that he had come as an ambassador.

This made the adventure hard for Friar William, because the Mongols could not understand why one who was neither merchant nor ambassador should come from a Christian king to the great Khan. Moreover the stubborn Franciscan wore a shaggy robe like a beggar; he brought sealed letters but no gifts for the Mongols— only his own vestments, Scriptures, incense, fruit, biscuit and a certain muscatel wine that he liked. Friar William had need of all his wit.

"When we met Tartars for the first time," he relates, "I thought myself entered into another age."

He let them taste his muscatel wine, and he drank their mare's milk, which made him sweat, and he explained that he came from the king of the French, who was on pilgrimage, and he wanted to find Sartak, who was said to be a Christian.

They puzzled over him, but they gave him horses and sent him at headlong speed along the post stations, to the camp of Batu's son on the Volga. And there, instead of a horde of barbarians, he found keen minds, more aware of events than his own. He found a knight of the Templars from Cyprus and Armenians who read his letters, translating to Sartak, who listened with all his wives. They asked Friar William if his Bible held in its covers what he believed to be true.

Sartak gave his fat guest mare's milk and asked him to pronounce a benediction. Then he inquired who was the greatest monarch among the Franks. "The Emperor," Friar William answered.

"That is not so," Sartak corrected him. "It is the King of France."

Then Sartak's secretaries advised the friar not to speak of Sartak to Batu as a Christian, but as a Mongol. They were not, he discovered, willing to be called Christians, because the Christians seemed to them to be a nation of the west, while the name of Mongol was exalted above all peoples.

Friar William was ferried across the Volga to where the Golden Horde moved beside the river. And to the astonished friar the houses and tents of the encampment appeared like a city, stretching out to a vast length.

At once Batu's officers asked if the friar had come as ambassador from the king of the French.

"I have come," Rubruk answered boldly, "because my lord king is advised that you have become Christians. I have been sent to congratulate you—not from any fear of you."

Nor was he less bold when they made him kneel before Batu. For a space Batu, seated on a gilded couch raised above the pavilion floor, contemplated the stubborn Franciscan without speaking. Then he signed for Friar William to speak.

And Rubruk said a prayer, invoking the blessing of Heaven upon the Khan of the Golden Horde. "For," he added, "you may not attain to the beatitude of Heaven unless you become a Christian."

Batu smiled, and the Mongol noyans, listening, clapped their hands in derision. Then the Sain Khan allowed the Franciscan to rise, and he asked a question. He had heard that the king of the French had left his country with an army. Against whom did he go to make war?

"Against the Saracens," Friar William answered, "for they have violated the house of God, at Jerusalem."

Batu signed for a cup of mare's milk to be given the friar in a golden vessel from the table at the tent entrance—a mark of favor.

Soon thereafter, Friar William, passing through the encampment, was greeted in Latin—"*Salvete domini!*" Surprised, he discovered the speaker to be a Kipchak Turk, who had been taught by priests in Hungary. This Kipchak confided in Rubruk that he had been summoned by Batu to explain what manner of man the friar was, and what the Franciscan order might be; the upshot of it being that Friar William was told that he could not remain among the Mongols without going on to the presence of Mangu, the Khakhan. A Mongol noyan was appointed to lead him thither, and this aristocrat of the steppes examined the stout friar and his garments with misgivings.

"Think well," the Mongol warned him, "whether you will endure it, for the winter cold cracks trees and breaks rocks asunder."

When Friar William said he would go, the Mongol outfitted him for travel with sheepskin jackets and trousers, and footsocks of felt, with leather boots and hoods. So Friar William set out on the journey across the steppes that seemed to him like a great sea. When he crossed the invisible line between the domain of the Golden Horde and the Khakhan, in all the post stations he saw the people sing and dance in greeting to his Mongol conductor, "because it was their custom to receive the messengers of Batu in this way."

Gossiping on the road with the Mongol's secretary, Friar William learned that the careful Batu had written to Mangu saying that the friar must have come to beg the aid of a Mongol army to combat the Saracens! Batu had puzzled over Friar William's mission, and had decided it in his own fashion.

At Mangu's court, the Mongol secretaries demanded if Friar William had not come to make peace with them. ("For," he comments, "they are so filled with pride they think the whole world should make peace with them. But if I were allowed, I would preach war against them, as urgently as I could.")

Instead, Friar William had to struggle for his place in the foreign fellowship of refugees, adventurers and would-be miracle workers clustered in the felt tents and huts of the great Ordu. He stumbled into a small house and found a shrine and lamp tended by a black and lean Armenian monk with a hairy coat. He sat down by the fire of this monk, named Sergius, who fed him.

Another monk, who kept a private stock of dried fruit behind the altar, had made himself a bishop's folding chair and a cap of peacock's feathers and a small gold cross. Before the Mongols he posed as a bishop, but the astute Rubruk discovered that he was no more than a wandering weaver. The two of them rigged up a banner on a cane as long as a lance, and paraded it through the tents of the Ordu, singing *"Vexilla regis prodeunt,"* to the envy of the Moslem mullahs.

Friar William tried to go barefoot, in the winter cold, and a Hungarian boy explained to the amazed Mongols why the friar acted in this mad fashion. A crusader from beyond the Jordan told him the news of Palestine. A woman of Metz gave him supper and explained that she was now married to a Russian housebuilder and both of them were prospering. She sent him to one William Bouchier, a goldsmith of Paris who had married a good-looking Magyar girl.

This goldsmith was then finishing a work of art—a silver tree before the middle gate of Mangu's palace. At the roots of the tree four silver lions gushed mare's milk. Four gold serpents coiled along the branches of the tree, and out of the mouths of the serpents flowed wine, mare's milk, honey-mead and rice wine. Later, when Mangu held a solemn court, the goldsmith acted as butler—while a man hidden beneath the tree caused a trumpet to blow in the hands of the angel at the top of the tree.

When Bouchier fell ill, the monk Sergius dosed him with rhubarb and almost killed him. They were visited by the Princess Kutuktai, Mangu's favorite wife, who gave them presents and desired the monks' blessing on the cup she drank from. She bade the monks sing with a loud voice.

Nestorian priests brought slaughtered sheep into the chapel, to feast with this lady of Mangu. "And when she was drunk," Rubruk relates, "she got in her palanquin and went away, the priests singing all the while."

When this same Princess Kutuktai fell ill, Mangu summoned Sergius to cure her with a dose. The monk, weeping and praying, mixed rhubarb and holy water for her, Rubruk assisting doubtfully. The Mongol lady had been hysterical with constipation, and the mixture cured her—and saved Sergius' life. She heaped silver on Sergius, who took Rubruk's portion also, when the stout Franciscan refused payment.

Hearing of his lady's cure, Mangu summoned the monks before him and examined their cross curiously. "Without," William admits, "seeming to worship it in any way."

Friar William's keen eyes noticed that Mangu's pavilion was hung with cloth-of-gold, although the fire at his seat was fed with thorns and wormwood roots and dried dung. Mangu himself he found to be a silent man of middle height with a flat nose—about forty-five years of age. He sat high above the assemblage on a sealskin-covered seat, with a pretty girl at his knee.

Only the cupbearers ascended this dais of the Khakhan, going up one side and down the other. When Friar William excused himself for offering no gifts, Mangu answered thoughtfully:

"Even as the light of the sun falls everywhere, our power and that of Batu extends to every place. We have no need of your gold or silver."

But he requested the priests to work a miracle if they could, to bring to an end a blizzard that was taking toll of the nomad's herds. "For many beasts," he explained, "are in great danger, being heavy with young and about to bring forth."

Fortunately for the priests, the blizzard ceased. And Mangu, having listened to the exhortations of so many priesthoods, waxed curious as to the truth of what they argued. He had all a Mongol's keen curiosity about his spirit-life. Would he cease to be, at death? Would he become a kele, inhabiting water or fire? He summoned the Buddhists and Nestorians and the mullahs of Islam to debate before him, and Friar William joined the debate on behalf of the Nestorians—the son of the goldsmith interpreting for him.

The Franciscan silenced his adversaries by asking whether or not they held that God was all-powerful. When, after long thought, they denied this, the Moslems burst out laughing, and the Mongol judges of the debate had to enforce quiet. "No man can serve two masters," Friar William maintained. "How then can you serve many gods?"

The Mongols listened without denial but without consent. When

Mangu signified that the debate was at an end, Friar William relates that the Nestorians and Moslems sang together with a loud voice, while the Buddhists held their peace, and all drank together plentifully.

Mangu's Warning

Friar William was quick to seize upon the talk of the exiles in this desert city. David, an Armenian, and Basil, the son of an Englishman, told him that Mangu had sent envoys to the west to carry a bow so strong that two men could barely bend it, and silver arrows with a strange, pierced head. Mangu would offer peace to the western courts; if they refused peace, the bow was to be shown them, and the silver arrows fired into the air, to whistle in warning. And the Mongol envoys would say, "We have bows as strong as this, and signal arrows like to these."

He heard that the ambassador of the Kalif of Baghdad had been offered peace, if his Moslems would destroy their weapons and machines of war. And the ambassador had answered, "We will do that when you pluck the hoofs from your horses."

He noticed that every man of the steppe dwellers had work to do. Only the aged were spared this mobilization of labor, by order of Genghis-Khan. And he realized the meaning of the testament of Genghis-Khan. "They would long ago have resumed their war against Hungary and the west," he relates, "if their soothsayers had not advised against it."

It was not the soothsayers—the shamans—however, who decided this. Mangu was weighing the question in his own mind. He had the power to launch a new attack upon the European peoples with a word. No longer need Mangu, the Khakhan, invoke the testament of Genghis-Khan, or the family council, to decide this question. He meant to do so himself.

And the stubborn friar, his guest, did not realize what a vital part he was playing in shaping Mangu's thoughts. Carpini had puzzled the Mongols sorely when he had described the Pope as the viceroy of God upon earth. To the Mongols, this signified an earthly monarch of vast power—a khakhan of the west. But by degrees they had satisfied themselves that this viceroy—who happened to be Innocent IV—was an archpriest with peculiar attributes. Mangu paid little attention to him, or to the much-discussed German Emperor; instead, he studied carefully the saintly Louis of France. Friar William had come from that king; he had brought no message, and he appealed neither for aid nor for mercy. Why then had he come?

Mangu sent a secretary to ask why, again. Rubruk parried the question by asking if Batu had not explained in his letter. The secretary brushed this aside—the Khakhan desired to know from the friar himself. William, with his narrow shrewdness, parried this vital point—his King had sent only letters of friendship, and he himself had come merely to preach the gospel.

The secretary wrote all this down with care, and went to make his report to Mangu. The next day, another interview. Mangu knew that William had no message for him; he knew the friar had come to pray for him; but he did want to know if any ambassadors had come from Louis to the Mongol court before William.

And the worthy friar explained how David and Friar Andrew had brought hither the scarlet chapel before his coming.

Patiently, the secretary returned with Mangu's next question. Would William take Mongol ambassadors back with him to his country?

The friar refused, as Carpini had done before him. He was only a poor monk, and could not take it upon himself to guide an ambassador of the great Khan back through such dangerous country.

Then Mangu made his decision.

With the goldsmith's son to interpret for him, the stout Franciscan knelt before the Mongol khakhan. The boy warned him that it had been decided to send him back with a yarligh of the great Khan, and that he must make no objection.

"Have you said to my writers that I was a pagan?" Mangu demanded.

"My lord, I said not so," Rubruk objected boldly.

"I thought well you said not so, for such a word should not be spoken by you." Mangu thrust forward the staff on which he leaned. "Be not afraid."

Friar William smiled. "If I had been afraid, would I have come hither?"

Mangu spoke in a new tone, as if trying to express his conviction. "We Mongols believe there is no more than one God. We have an upright heart toward him."

"Without God's gift, that could not be."

Mangu thought for a moment. "God hath given to the hand its five fingers, and as many faiths to men. To you, he hath given the Scriptures, yet you keep them not. Certainly you do not find it written in the Scriptures that one of you should speak against another."

"No, and I made clear that I would not contend with anyone."

"I speak not of you. In like manner you will not find in the Scriptures that you should forsake justice for money."

When Friar William argued that he himself had refused to accept gifts of money, the Khakhan motioned him to be silent.

"I speak not of that," Mangu said. He drank thoughtfully from the cup in his hand. "God hath given you the Scriptures, yet ye keep them not. To us he hath given soothsayers, and we give heed to them, and live in peace."

While the friar waited to hear more of Mangu's belief, the Khakhan considered. "You have been here long," he announced, "and now I wish you to go back. You have said you dare not take my ambassador with you. Will you, then, take my messenger or my letters?"

"If my lord's words can be made clear to me, I will take them, to the best of my power."

Mangu then asked if the friar would have gold or silver, or fine garments. William would have none of these; he demanded only the expenses of his homeward journey, and a safe-conduct to Armenia.

"I will have you taken there," Mangu assented, "after which, look to yourself." For a moment he pondered. "There are two eyes in a head, yet both look to the same point. As one eye to the other is Batu to me. You came from Batu, and so you must return by him."

When Friar William protested again after his fashion that he was a man of peace, knowing nothing of the mind of his lord king, and that he wished to dwell among the Mongols to preach, Mangu heard him out patiently. Then, musing, he said, "You have a long way to go. Make yourself strong with food."

So, Rubruk explains, he departed from the presence of the Khakhan and returned not again.

It was a pity. For the zealot Franciscan apparently did not understand Mangu's anxiety to forge a closer link between himself and the adventurous French king. The Khakhan had a reason for that anxiety. But he had to express himself as best he could in written words to a monarch he had never seen:

"By the Command of the Everlasting Sky: As there is only one Sky, so on earth let there be one ruler. After Genghis-Khan, by the power of the Sky, this word is spoken to you, wherever men may hear or horses may go.

"The command of Mangu, Khakhan of the Mongols, to Ludovik, the king of the French, and to all other lords and priests of the great world of the Franks. May they understand these words.

"A certain man named David came to you, seeming to be an ambassador from the Mongols, but he was a liar; with him, your ambassador came to the Khakhan. Since the Khakhan* was dead, your ambassador came to this court, and Ogul Gaimish his wife sent to you a gift. But how could that evil woman, viler than a bitch, know the ways of war and peace? How could she settle the great world in quiet?

"The monks who came from you to Sartak were sent by Sartak to Batu; but as Mangu-khan is the foremost in the Mongol world, Batu sent them to us.

"And now that the great world of the Franks may live in peace and enjoy their possessions, and that the commandment of the Sky might be heard among you, we would have sent Mongols as ambassadors to you by your monk, but he could not take them. But if we could give our commands in letters to King Ludovik, he agreed to carry them. For this reason we have not sent our ambassadors; instead we have sent you this, the command of the Everlasting Sky, by your monk.

*Kuyuk.

"And when you shall hear and believe it, send your ambassadors to us, so that we may know if you will have peace or war.

"When, by the power of the Everlasting Sky, the whole world shall be at one, in peace and rejoicing, from the rising place of the sun to where it sets, then shall it appear what we will do.

"But if you see and hear the command of the Everlasting Sky and heed it not, nor will believe it, thinking that our land is far beyond great mountains and the sea—if you, thinking so, lead an army against us, then only he that renders the hard way easy, and the far-off near, only the Everlasting Sky knows what will befall."

In this letter a new thought is apparent. The wording is not the deceptive assurance of Batu, nor the rigid summons of Kuyuk. Mangu, groping for an understanding with the western world, offers the traditional alternative of peace or war. But he respects his European adversaries—he warns them against confidence in war, and he summons them to come to an agreement which will secure their possessions, under a Mongol peace.

He is thinking, not of war, but of the end of war. A strong intellect, in touch with events, is at work here. Mangu visualizes the unification of all peoples under one rule "from the rising place of the sun to where it sets." He is not concerned with enriching further the Golden Family, nor with seating the former tent dwellers in palaces. He ponders the fate of the civilized world under one emperor. He does not know what will come of it. "Then," he ends almost with despair, "shall it appear what we will do."

No ambassadors came to him from the unfortunate Louis of France.

On the road back to his king, Friar William passed another monarch bound for Kara-korum, to treat with Mangu. Haithon, king of the Armenians, acknowledged himself to be the vassal of the Mongol Ordu, and he was given a yarligh that protected himself and his people against war.

So, on the frontier of the west, the Armenians, Georgians, Alani

and Russians had become subjects of the Mongol rule, bound to
send contingents of armed men to the Mongol generals and to pay
taxes to the darugashis. That was the price of security.

The Grandson

Mangu, more truly than Genghis-Khan, held the destinies of
Asia and Europe in his hands. A strange nature—Mongol in
spirit, yet tempered by the wisdom of the outer world. Holding
fast to the Yasa, and the code of the nomads. Implacable, enduring, with all a steppe dweller's patience, he had the iron restraint
that Genghis-Khan had imposed upon himself.

A grandson of the conqueror, he had known only victory; he had
not shared the ordeal of campaigning with his father, Tului. And
he was much alone. He repaid his obligation to Batu with scrupu-
lous care, and Batu always acknowledged his authority. Yet the
cousins only met for a few months, after the European campaign.
Mangu had no other intimate. His favorite wife, Kutuktai, remains only a name in the chronicles.

No one person could influence Mangu—although he did not
domineer like the Mongols of two generations before, who had
dwelt in tents. He listened attentively to advice and formed his
own judgments. He gave the government of China to a Turk, the
aged and incorruptible Mahmoud Yelvadj, and to Mahmoud's
son the administration of mid-Asia. When they asked for scholars
to aid them, Mangu's curiosity was stirred.

"What are scholars?" he asked. "Are they as useful as physicians
and soothsayers?"

"More so," Yelvadj replied—and received permission to enlist
what brains he desired. But it was Mangu, not Yelvadj, who made
decisions. He gathered around him the hard souls of the tribes,
that had made a god of his grandsire, and he built a wooden
pagoda temple near the grave of Genghis-Khan.

He found relief in hunting. With his officers he would mount
the swift steppe mustangs and gallop out of the black walls of
Kara-korum to the open plain, tossing up the *bouragut*, the golden
eagles trained to take large game, when he sighted antelope. The
eagles would drive a beast from the antelope herd, and Mangu

and his riders would overtake the quarry while the eagles beat their wings about its head as the animals and men raced through the dust.

For Mangu hated to be pent in Kara-korum, sitting and listening to talk. Unlike Kubilai he had no patience with the extravagance of the women of the imperial house. He took from the women of the house of Ogadai their jewels and accumulated treasures. These he gave to the veteran officers of the home army. He even scolded his own women for buying too many precious things.

"What do they avail you?" he asked. And, thereafter he kept account of the expenditures of his ladies.

But he lacked the ordinary Mongol's itching fingers. When he examined the tax lists with Yelvadj, he lowered the tax payments in China and Turkestan, to one beast in a hundred, and silver in the same ratio. Teachers of religion and all those who could not earn a living he exempted from payment.

"I have it less at heart," he said, "to fill my treasury than to preserve my people."

Although he had detested Ogul Gaimish, he ordered all the assignments drawn by Ogadai's women to be paid in full. At the same time he deprived the hundreds of scions of the Golden Family of their privilege of giving out drafts on the treasury. No longer could they sign a paper, for others to pay. And he took away their tax exemption. Like Kuyuk, he detested luxury.

Unlike Kuyuk, he had no desire for festivals and the wine of life. Silent, and alone, he tried to forge the machinery of a world government. Yet his strange nature could feel the need of beasts, heavy with young, in the herds during a blizzard.

Mangu, however, could not rid himself of superstition. The tribal speakers to Heaven he countenanced as fully as the Moslem mullahs, although the Moslems had become traditional enemies of the Mongols. Had not Siyurkuktiti given money to build a mosque in Bokhara? He treated the five faiths as the five fingers of his hand. Secretly, the Buddhists said that Mangu believed Buddhism to be the palm of the hand, the one faith out of which the others sprang. But Mangu himself said not so.

The Book of Tsar Batu

In reality, the Mongols were discovering the attractions of new speakers to Heaven: the red lamas of Tibet. Their downright dealings with devils, their performance of miracles appealed to the steppe dwellers more than the renunciation taught by the Chinese. Mangu appointed such a lama, Na-mo, to be head of the faith in the empire. It was the first great lama from Tibet, the first *dalai*.

With incurable hope, Mangu summoned the different speakers to Heaven, to listen to their arguments. Was there in fact something within him that would live after death? Genghis-Khan had asked Ch'ang Ch'un bluntly for an elixir of life, and had dismissed the matter from his mind when Ch'ang Ch'un denied him.

But Mangu was losing trust in the Taoists, who made the greatest promises. From Tao, they said, was created the earth and human life, governed by the twin forces of Yin and Yang. And a man's spirit might rise again to Tao as a flame flies upward. But Mangu did not perceive that the miracles predicted by the Taoists came to pass. He issued an imperial edict forbidding their "false writings" to be made into books.

Wearying of this priestly disputation, Mangu turned both Taoists and Buddhists over to his milder brother Kubilai, who disliked the Taoists and placed his trust in a Chinese Buddhist. Kubilai, after a huge debate at Xanadu (Shang-tu), ordered the books of the Taoists to be burned.

Like many others before them, and since, the brothers Mangu and Kubilai found no guidance in the speakers to Heaven.

The Four Brothers

As with the four sons of Genghis-Khan, the four sons of Tului and Siyurkuktiti had become the heads of the Mongol nation. But in the generation between the sons and the grandsons, between 1227 and 1250, a change had taken place.

For one thing the Sain Khan Batu, their cousin, now reigned alone in the west, three thousand miles distant from the gilded halls of Kara-korum. For another, the three younger brothers did not pretend to hold authority. They deferred to Mangu, the

Khakhan. He alone sat on the felt-covered throne, and he alone could hold the loyalty of the elder Mongols, who still talked among themselves of the suldë of Genghis-Khan.

Except for these four, and Batu, the Golden Family had become a shadowy kind of assemblage. Owing to its swift breeding of children, the blood relationship had swelled from several hundred to more than two thousand—grandsons and great-grandsons. They had become pensioners of the throne. Besides, Mangu's purge had exiled Kaidu and other survivors of the house of Ogadai into the pastures of mid-Asia, where they kept themselves apart from all family councils. In the home grazing lands near Lake Baikal, the younger spirits of the Golden Family who had tasted the luxury of a few years before complained bitterly of the hard living Mangu enforced. The observant Friar William pointed out that the men of the home tribes were poor, and that they all had to work.

The four brothers had been educated by Siyurkuktiti, not by Genghis-Khan. After their mother's death, this difference in their minds appeared more clearly. They were loyal enough to the eldest, Mangu. But they had ideas of their own.

Hulagu, good-natured and warlike, was influenced by his first wife, Dokuz Khatun. She was a Kiraït, a niece of the great chieftain who had been called Prester John, and she had been Hulagu's stepmother before he married her. Being a Kiraït, she was wise in tribal law, and she prayed with the Nestorian Christians.

Kubilai had a love for things Chinese, and a mild spirit. He collected rare gems, and he liked to pass his time in gardens. He leaned on the counsel of Yao Chow, an ascetic.

Of the three, perhaps Arik Buka, the Little Man, was Mangu's favorite. The Little Man was the youngest. He had his father's recklessness, and a craving for the ancestral nomad life.

Mangu did not take long to make his decision. He would carry out the testament of his grandsire. He would divide the great Mongol army among his three brothers, to carry on the conquest of the known world.

"He proposed this plan himself," Rashid relates, "because there remained kingdoms which had not been conquered under the reign of Genghis-Khan. Since these kingdoms were at an immense distance, he chose to send one of his brothers toward each of them, himself remaining in the center of his empire, to administer justice to his subjects."

In this vast offensive against civilization, Mangu spared western Europe for the time being. That belonged now to Batu. And, besides, Mangu hoped that the armies of the crusaders might be of aid to his brother Hulagu.

The new attack went out, as Rashid says, almost to the full extent of the settled areas of the earth, to push Mangu's frontiers from the China Sea far along the shores of the Mediterranean.

An advance expedition struck through the mountains at northern India by way of Lahore. A second army moved into Korea. In 1253 Kubilai was ordered to march against the Sung empire in southern China that had never been invaded by barbarians.

The Mongol army in the southwest moved farther into Asia Minor, while Hulagu began his advance with a strong ordu against the remaining powers of Islam. Strangely enough, Mangu ordered him to eliminate the Kalif of Baghdad, and the Assassins—that secret fellowship of the Ismailites that held mountain strongholds from the Kohistan of Persia to the Lebanon and had not, until now, been attacked with success. Hulagu was to continue on toward the west, to reduce Egypt, the furthest citadel of Islamic military power.

The General Attack

The way had been prepared. By now the Mongols had pushed their roadbuilding to the far frontiers. The ancient road of the Barbarians had become a highway, with post houses a day's ride apart.

These post houses had sleeping quarters, food service and herds of horses for remounts in the corrals. A Chinese mandarin at each post checked in the travelers, and recorded the time of their departure in his books. Couriers of the army galloped in with despatches, handing them over to waiting riders to carry on. It was a medieval pony express.

The March of the Barbarians

It was called the *yam*, and the riders were the *chapars*. At times a Mongol horseman would appear with a dust cloud behind him—his body bound tight with leather bands, his greased face half covered. By the bells at his saddle, he would be known as a courier of the Khakhan, and a fast horse would be waiting for him when he pulled up. Then a Mongol noyan might arrive at the post station, bearing a yarligh of Khan, giving him authority to commandeer all horses for his own use.

These new post roads spread over the old Silk route and across mountain ranges where the gorges and rivers had not been bridged before. They offered easy routes to the long caravans that were moving now between west and east.

Over such a Mongol road stout Friar William was carried like an express packet back to Batu. "From Kara-korum to the court of Batu," he relates, "we journeyed for four months and ten days. During all that time we never saw a town, nor did we ever rest except one day when we could not get horses. Sometimes we had to go two or even three days with no other food than mare's milk."

Mangu was devoting most of his tax revenues to the finishing of these transcontinental routes, the building of army posts and the increase of the remount herds. The Mongols in the homeland were put again on military rations. Most of the able-bodied men in the former tribal areas were allotted to the new armies, which far exceeded the forces commanded by Genghis-Khan or Subotai.

Two men in every ten were requisitioned for Hulagu's ordu alone, and their work in the home yurts was turned over to the lads and elder nomads.

These recruits for the new armies journeyed to the frontiers to be mustered in, where the military commanders took them over. Here, grazing lands had been allotted for the new commands, and warehouses of grain and wine opened for them. They also received their arms here. For in the heart of Mangu's empire the Mongols no longer carried weapons.

Friar William relates that a guard of twenty Tatars was given him for escort on the road through the Caucasus where the mountain people still raided the Mongol herds. "I was glad of this, as I had never seen the Tartars armed. Yet of the twenty, only two had coats of mail which they said they had bought from the Alani."

The Mongol economy that had built up the roads and military supplies had done away with the old village economy. In these years when most of the men were requisitioned for service, the irrigation works and cultivation were neglected. A good deal of food had to be imported from agricultural regions outside. Moreover the famines and plagues that followed the major campaigns—although not affecting the Mongols themselves—had taken toll of life along the frontiers. Friar William passed over deserts where no water was visible for two days.

Slowly, the earth itself was depriving the Mongols of its support.

Mangu gave his younger brother a word of advice, at parting.

"Heed well the words of Princess Dokuz," he bade him, "and follow her advice."

And he asked Hulagu to send back to Kara-korum the celebrated astrologer Nasr ad-Din, who was then serving the Assassins. Perhaps Mangu hoped that the talented Moslem reader of the stars might reveal secrets that had escaped the Taoists, and even the red lama of Tibet.

At all events, there is no mistaking Mangu's intention to give a Christian ascendancy to this expedition. Dokuz Khatun, Hulagu's favorite, was a Nestorian; Hulagu himself was son of Siyurkuktiti, a Nestorian; Kit Boga, the chief general of the expedition, was a Christian. Mangu had just extended his protection to those warlike Christians, the Armenians and Georgians. And he had asked urgently for ambassadors from the Christian crusader, Louis of France, who was then supposed to be in the Holy Land. (Although, by the time Friar William reached Louis, that unfortunate monarch had returned, defeated, to France.)

Mangu had no intention of waging a religious war. He was simply making use of Christian fanaticism to gain useful allies in his movement to crush the remaining military force of Islam.

Hulagu departed with a great army of occupation—with a division of Chinese engineers, and some experts equipped with a new weapon: naphtha flame throwers; with geographers to draw the plan of the new conquests, and tax assessors, and road builders, to extend the post stations westward. And Hulagu followed his brother's advice. Breaking all Mongol precedent, he gave Dokuz Khatun a place beside him, in his council, and he listened to her advice.

Until then, the southwest had been a kind of military frontier. In 1229 a general of the Bodyguard, Charmaghan, had been sent there with three tumans to maintain order. Later, after the death of Tului, four officers representing the various houses of the Golden Family—including Siyurkuktiti—had been ordered out there to govern Khorasan. Meanwhile Charmaghan, an able commander, had found ideal winter quarters in the high grazing lands farther on, between the edge of the Caspian and the shore of the Mediterranean (Azerbaidjan, Armenia, northern Iraq, Arran.) He had punished Georgia, but left it self-ruled after the suicide of its Queen, Rusudan. Kerman and Fars had submitted.

In 1241 Charmaghan had become paralyzed. Turakina and Kuyuk then sent out another general, Baidu (or Baichu), to take over.

So the northern belt of the Islamic lands, above the hot irrigated regions, had become a military frontier administered by Baidu. Roughly, the Mongol conquest extended along the ancient Silk route. At the western end, a strange conglomeration of peoples struggled—the Byzantines of Constantinople at feud with the strong Turkish Seljuks, the remnants of the Khwaresmians driven back upon the Syrian Moslems still at war with the Crusaders on the coast. And beyond them, the growing power of the *mamluks*, or slave warriors of Egypt.

Toward this troubled west Hulagu moved as slowly as a juggernaut, but with the same implacable power; across the barrier ranges, skirting the snows of Tibet, hunting and holding high festival in his perambulating court—greeting the lords of the mountain clans who came in to pay tribute to such magnificence. Resistance would have been madness, and Hulagu had a way of laughing off wars.

In fact he laughed at most things. He relished the melons of

Samarkand, and he was insatiably curious about the mirages in the Red Sands desert, where lakes and fertile forests appeared to the sight that vanished when he rode up to them. He even let Dokuz Khatun bring along her traveling chapel with the wooden plaques that beat loudly to prayer.

All things that amused people seemed good to this conqueror with a sense of humor.

When he came to the strangest citadels of earth, the eagles' nests of the Assassins who had terrorized this region for six generations, he searched them out and obliterated them patiently. His riders broke into the artificial paradise of Alamut where the Old Man of the Mountain had drugged the youth of Persia to make knife-slayers out of them. And they hunted down the grand master of the Assassins, after burning his library of occult books. Hulagu thought that Mangu would like to see such a curiosity, and he started the captive Master on the journey back to Kara-korum when Mangu wrote that he had no wish to see him. So the Master was strangled like any ordinary man.

"Establish the laws of Genghis-Khan," Mangu reminded his wandering brother, "from Samarkand to the far side of Egypt. Be generous to those who submit to your orders. Humiliate those who disobey."

Hulagu's juggernaut found few to disobey it. Joined by Baidu with his veterans from Mosul, it moved down into the plain of the Tigris, down toward Baghdad that had been the city of the kalifs for five centuries.

And Hulagu sent a message of curious inquiry to the Kalif:

"You know the fate of the different nations of the world at the hands of the Mongol armies, since Genghis-Khan. The gates of Baghdad have never been closed to Seljuks or Khwaresmians. How then can you forbid entrance to us who have so much power? Take care not to struggle against the Standard."

The last Kalif of Baghdad tried to struggle. Calling helplessly for a holy war against the invaders, he gave battle and his army was obliterated. The Mongols rode into the gates of Baghdad and sacked its treasures. The Kalif himself was taken and brought before Hulagu, who had been struck by the wealth of the palaces on the Tigris and by the futility of their resistance. It seemed to him to be a faulty economy.

The tale is told that instead of offering the unfortunate Kalif food, he set before him his gold dishes and silver hand basins and jeweled incense burners, while he ate himself food from plain dishes.

"Eat what you have stored up for yourself," he urged the Kalif.

The master of Baghdad complained that he could not eat gold.

"Why have you kept it, then?" the matter-of-fact Mongol demanded.

The Moslem said nothing. Hulagu looked around at the great hall of the palace.

"Why have you not melted these iron grilles into barbs for your arrows? Why have you not paid these jewels to your men, and advanced with them into the hills to meet me and oppose me?"

"It was the will of Allah."

"Then what will happen to you is the will of God also."

Then he reassured the Kalif, saying that he would provide him with a house to dwell in where he would feel no cold and suffer no thirst. The Kalif was wrapped in a felt robe and trampled under the hoofs of horses.

Hulagu had been careful not to shed the blood of the head of Islam. But he had remembered that once the ambassador of this same Kalif had boasted that the Moslems would lay down their arms only when the Mongols tore the hoofs from their horses.

Ninety thousand Moslems were slain here, methodically, and the ruined Baghdad was burned. It never regained its importance as a center of the Moslem world.

Fear came again upon the cities of Islam. Caravans of refugees fled west to escape the Mongols. The price of dromedaries rose beyond reckoning.

"Never was Islam in such distress," a chronicler relates, "torn between the inroads of the Mongols and the Nazarenes."

Hulagu moved west, keeping to the cooler highlands where his horses could graze. And here Hulagu joined forces with Haithon of Armenia and the surprised Crusaders. The combined camps of the allies turned south, toward the Syrian desert, the lands of heat and poor grazing. Toward Damascus and Jerusalem.

Hulagu never came back to the Mongol homeland.

Kubilai's Heritage

Meanwhile Kubilai was penetrating into southern China, more than four thousand miles away.

"In the year of the Panther," Rashid relates, "Kubilai marched against the eastern lands."

It was his chance to escape into the gardens of Cathay. Kubilai, as silent and purposeful as Mangu, had come to crave a residence among the Chinese, whom he admired. Moreover the Lady Jamui persuaded him to give heed to the red lamas, and the Lady Jamui was the wife of his youth.

In 1252 Kubilai ordered the affairs of his new home province, Honan. He noticed that cultivation had gone badly during the last years, and he allowed the recruits of north China to return to the fields—even giving them seed and tools. And he cast about for the best spot to build a palace city of his own. His astrologer decided upon a fertile plain by a river north of the half-ruined Yen-king. They called it Shang-tu (the Xanadu of the medieval travelers). Here Kubilai ordered gardens to be built by the river. (Which was not, however, Alph, the sacred river, nor did he a stately pleasure dome decree.)

The sage Yao Chow, always at his elbow, warned Kubilai against his own inclination. "The Middle Kingdom is most to be desired of all. It holds the germ of culture and true richness. But, my prince, you must try to separate yourself from the people of the Middle Kingdom. It is wiser for you to assume only military government, and leave the administration to lesser officials."

Kubilai followed his advice, not realizing how timely it was. For Mangu commanded his brother to march against the Sung—the unconquered south of China beyond the Yang-tse—as his father Tului had marched against the Kin empire. Kubilai was to take 100,000 men and to make the almost incredible journey from the Mongol homelands, down past the ice plateaus of Tibet, into Yun-nan. Here, at the edge of tropical heat, Kubilai was to turn the flank of the Sung empire and advance into it from the south.

He gave Kubilai a Mongol general of the old type, Uriang-katai, the son of Subotai Bagatur, to share his command and see that he made no mistakes.

The two of them disappeared from sight for more than a year, passing into the long cold mountains—as the Mongols called them —and on into the hills of the *kara djang*, the Black People. These savage mountaineers, non-Chinese in race, had never faced an invader before—unless they had seen the Khmers of the jungles below them.

The chronicles say that when Kubilai came at last within sight of the Yun-nan encampment, that careful Chinese tutor, Yao Chow, persuaded him to advance with banners on which the symbols were written: "It is forbidden to slay."

The trick worked. At least for a while, and Kubilai was much interested in this method of breaking down resistance by proclamation. Not so Uriang-katai, who believed in liquidation of an enemy.

When they had penetrated far into Yun-nan, Kubilai rode north from the army to escape the tropical summer heat. Uriang-katai, left to his own devices, waged war in the usual fashion. In doing so, he found himself confronted by an array of war elephants for the first time. The armored elephants (the tanks of the medieval age) frightened the Mongol horses—until Uriang-katai ordered his riders to move back to covered ground and dismount, to fight the great beasts with flaming arrows. Maddened by burns, the elephants turned on the ranks of the Yunnanese and scattered them—the Mongols remounting to follow up their advantage.

But this intensive warfare in the heat caused heavy loss of life. Of the 100,000 who had set out with Kubilai, only 20,000 survived to follow Uriang-katai at the end of the summer. Mangu, however, was better content with the implacable tactics of Subotai's son—the old methods of his grandsire's day.

The chronicles say that when Kubilai and his companions camped at a place where they had won a victory, he and his attendants drank joyfully and danced so long beneath a tree that the earth sank in.

Kubilai's indulgence of the Chinese exasperated the older Mongols who thronged Kara-korum in their thousands. A certain Kurikchi dared to send a remonstrance to the Khakhan: "Kubilai Khan has taken many a city and fortress, coming back with stolen wars, while you have busied yourself only with meats and soup and wine."

Then, too, Kubilai failed to make any real progress against the Sung, from the north. Instead he watched the building of Shang-tu. His Chinese subjects, with abundant crops, freed from the decimation of intense warfare, prospered and gave honor in secret to the name of Kubilai. But Mangu was angered.

The Khakhan sent to his brother another Mongol, Alamdar, who carried an imperial yarligh. Mangu ordered Kubilai to give up his government in China to Alamdar and to return at once to Kara-korum.

Alamdar's first act was to execute many of the Chinese officials appointed by Kubilai, and to begin an examination of all the accounts of his administration. This roused Kubilai's resentment. When he summoned his own officers to his camp, fully intending to resist the order of his brother, Yao Chow remonstrated.

"You are the first subject of the Khakhan," he cried. "You can do nothing but set an example to the others. Send your wife and children to the ordu of your brother. Then go yourself, to say that all you possess, even to your life, belongs to him."

The wit of the aged Yao Chow sensed the danger to the Chinese in any attempt to rebel against Mangu. And his advice saved Chinese civilization from further destruction. Kubilai gave in to him and sent his household to Mangu's court.

When Kubilai came himself, alone, to face his brother, Mangu's suspicions vanished. Rigorously just, Mangu knew that Kubilai had committed no wrong. In very human fashion the two Mongols threw their arms around each other and sat down to talk happily as they had done in boyhood.

About this time, 1257, couriers came in from Hulagu to announce new victories in the far-off corner of the empire. And Mangu, characteristically, became impatient at his own inactivity.

"Our fathers and lords who were kings before us did a great work," he announced. "Each one of them seized a land and made his name shine before all men. Now I shall go in person to the wars, and make for the south of China."

It seemed fitting to him that he should aid Kubilai against the Sung. He was weary of the idleness and ease of the home encampment.

The Mongol princes of the blood who heard this objected, saying: "Why should he who reigns over the whole earth, and has seven brothers—why should he go himself to fight his foes?"

But Mangu went. To the Little Man, the youngest of them, he turned over the jade seal of the empire and the care of the home pastures. The Little Man, Arik Buka, was to be, as Tului had been, keeper of the hearth. Mangu himself rode, with beating drums, to place banners at the burial site of Genghis-Khan. He made a feast of his setting-out, and the elder Mongols got drunk with satisfaction. They felt this was in keeping with Mongol ways—the suldë of Genghis-Khan would accompany the standard of the nine yak tails when Mangu led his ordu to war again.

The two brothers moved down with their great camps to the Yang-tse that barred their way.

In the heat of the next summer, in the fifty-second year of his age, Mangu died of dysentery at the siege of Ho-chiu.

Mangu was buried near the grave of Genghis-Khan, where the pines grew on the slope of Burkhan Kaldun. The elder Mongols broke up the funeral chariot and burned the wood. Watching the smoke drifting up where the sunlight came through the blue pines, the shamans wondered in what place the suldë of Mangu would reside.

His name, which meant—like the name of the clan itself—either Silver or Eternal, was not spoken again by the steppe dwellers. The youngest of the four brothers, the Little Man, rode to the burial. But Kubilai and Hulagu were off in China and Persia engaged in the campaigns of conquest.

The Book of Tsar Batu

As in the case of his grandsire, Genghis-Khan, the death of Mangu arrested the activities of the Mongols. It came unexpectedly, and it found the members of the Golden Family scattered over the vast extent of the empire. And the family itself had ceased to be a unit. Instead of four blood relations, four emperors survived the death of Mangu.

He had been the tie that had held them together. Inflexible as his grandsire, he had been a true aristocrat of the steppes. The Yasa had been his code. He had been convinced that the hard life of the nomad was superior to the soft existence of civilization, and he had carried on the attack against the walled cities.

But more intelligent than Genghis-Khan, and perhaps better able to weigh advice, he had seen beyond the horizon of the grasslands. He had tried to guide himself by the wisdom of civilization. He had succeeded, but in so doing he had made himself, not the Yasa, the Law. And when he ceased to be, no one could take his place.

The King of the West

Batu, the eldest of the family, could not play again the part of king-maker. The Sain Khan, troubled by his gout and preoccupied by his desire for splendor, had died four years before his cousin Mangu.

And Mangu, the all-powerful, had failed to name Batu's successor. First he had selected Sartak—Batu's son and a friend to the Christians. But Sartak had died of sickness on his journey from Kara-korum to the west. Then Mangu had named a grandson, who had also died mysteriously within a few months. The two of them may have been poisoned, and if so, it must have been by Birkai's order.

For Birkai—Batu's brother—had been converted to Islam. And the merchants and muftis of Islam knew the efficacy of poison. Had Sartak or his son survived, the fortunes of the Golden Horde must have taken a different course. And this must have been apparent to the agents of Islam.

Whether or not he cleared his path to the khanship of the Golden Horde by poison, Birkai ruled in the west. And after Mangu's death, he rendered only lip service to the east. He felt himself to be emperor in his own right, and he desired only to be let alone by Kara-korum.

Outwardly, Birkai appeared to be Batu's very twin—a stout man afflicted with the family gout. He had yellow skin, and he coiled his black hair behind his ears. Like Batu, he had a fondness for jeweled earrings, high hats and green copper girdles gleaming with precious stones.

And, like Batu, he desired a city of his own. Batu's residence had been a tent town, bright with gilt—Sarai on the lower Volga. Birkai started building a new Sarai farther north on the river's bank. Instead of cloth, he built with bricks. It proved to be more comfortable in winter. The Russians today speak of these two nomad palaces as Sarai-Batu and Sarai-Birkai.

Here in his new quarters, the son of the bastard Juchi reigned at first without a rival even beyond the horizon. Merchants moving across his domain traveled for six months from east to west and three months from north to south. They brought to Sarai the glassware of Egypt, the carpets and fine stuffs of the south. Two Venetians, journeying from the Black Sea slave market, went to Birkai's Sarai to dispose of their jewels. They were members of the Polo family.

For Birkai, even more than Batu, had the shrewdness to follow the Mongol way of life. He never emerged from his lair in the steppes. It seemed to him infinitely better to let the luxuries of living flow to him than to venture himself among the complexities of civilization. He kept all a nomad's independence. He followed the advice of Genghis-Khan, at the same time ridding himself of the family obligations.

Birkai's independence of orders from Kara-korum had its effect on Europe. The stout khan of the Golden Horde failed to carry out his part in the general attack of the family on the frontiers of civilization. While his cousins Kubilai and Hulagu were pushing on the Mongol juggernaut thousands of miles away, Birkai only went through the motions of a new European campaign.

In 1258, just before Mangu's death, he sent a few tumans to raid the west. His swift-moving cavalry penetrated the Polish land as far as Kracow, following the routes that the Poles christened the *czarny szlak*—the "black roads"—burning and carrying off loot. In the winter other tumans moved through what had been Russia, to raid the warlike Lithuanians. Again they attempted to storm Kracow, only to be driven off by the valiant *voevod* of that city. These, however, were no more than routine frontier actions. Birkai was careful not to indulge in a major attack on the west.

So Birkai's treasury was kept full in a very simple manner. From the Russians he collected tribute; from the peoples farther west he took loot; from other monarchs in the shadow of his power he consented to receive gifts as the price of his friendship that granted them peace.

This state of affairs was very different from the general attack led by Subotai and Batu almost a generation before. While he fully intended to follow the traditional way of the Mongols, Birkai was actually becoming softened by luxurious living, and by religion. His raids into the west were simply for loot and for effect. It suited his purpose to keep only the Russians under the Mongol yoke.

This deliberate decision was the first departure from the plan of Genghis-Khan to break the armed forces of the civilized world, and to lay it under tribute to the nomads *in toto*. Undoubtedly at this point Birkai was influenced by the news from the east, where Mangu's death had led to the first open breach in the Golden Family. But already, in 1260, a change was taking place within Birkai's Horde.

First, the nucleus of native Mongols was growing thinner. Members of the house of Tului and of Ogadai were drifting back to the wars in the east. The preponderance of Turks in the Golden Horde increased, until it became a reincarnation of the earlier Turkish clans, the Betchenaks and Kipchaks. In fact, the Russians spoke of it as the Kipchak, or Desert, Horde—and called its members Tatars, not Mongols. Its language was Turkish, and nothing else. Its inclination was to settle down, after the Turkish fashion, in a fixed conquered area.

The Golden Horde began, as it were, to live on its income. And since Turks were never disposed to bother themselves with the routine of collecting taxes, the Turkish *baskaks* began to farm out the revenues to diligent Moslem merchants, notably to a group from Khiva. These were the ones the Russians called the Squeezers, for good reason.

Then Birkai's intention to settle down on the Volga to enjoy his mastery of the steppes was interrupted. A new power appeared in the south. Hulagu's juggernaut trundled by Samarkand, and then appeared farther west within sight of the Caucasus. Like Batu, Birkai felt himself to be an exile from the family. And he had no inclination to let another Mongol encroach on his new frontiers.

So between the years 1255 and 1260—the years of crisis for the Mongol empire—he was watching jealously the triumphal march of his cousin Hulagu.

Hulagu, it seemed, had the secret of success. Hulagu had loaded his kibitkas with the spoil of the Assassin citadels and Baghdad. Hulagu had slain under the hoofs of the Mongol horses the last kalif of Baghdad—and Birkai was a convert to Islam. "You have profaned a sanctuary," he wrote to Hulagu, "without first consulting the members of your family."

And he heard that Hulagu had been named *Il-khan*, or Lesser Khan, by Mangu, whose blood tie was closer to Hulagu than to Birkai. Moreover, Mangu had given a yarligh granting to this Il-khan the right to possess for himself and his children all the land he conquered.

Then, when winter came, Hulagu made camp in the uplands south of the Caucasus range, where he found good grazing for his herds—in the high valleys where the waters were sweet. That pastureland—even if it lay beyond the Caucasus—Birkai believed to be part of his heritage. Hulagu built an astronomer's tower there, and a treasure house for the gold of Baghdad. There Dokuz Khatun, that strong-willed lady, sounded her chapel bells, to the delight of the Armenians.

"Every religious sect proclaims its faith openly," angered Moslems reported to Birkai, "and no Moslem dares disapprove. Every Christian, whether of the common people or the highest, has put on his finest garment and gone forth to sing."

Christian Armenians, Jacobites and even Crusaders were flocking to Hulagu's ordu, looking upon the dreaded Mongols as providential saviors against the Moslems. "If you pray for me," the good-natured Hulagu said, "it will bring me good fortune."

The smoke of burning mosques rose from his line of march, but Christian sanctuaries were spared. A Moslem lord who resisted him was besieged and slain in unpleasant manner—pieces of his flesh cut from him and thrust into his mouth until he died. A Seljuk Sultan abased himself before the conqueror, presenting him with a pair of boots. On the soles of the boots the Sultan's head had been painted, and he besought Hulagu:

"Your slave dares to hope that his king will honor him by placing his august foot on the head of his slave."

It amused Hulagu, but Birkai did not relish it when he heard of it. Seemingly the Christian cross was being exalted beside the standard of Genghis-Khan.

Then, in the autumn of 1259, Hulagu turned south, away from the Caucasus. Aleppo was stormed by his tumans, its great mosque burned. His ordu swung down through Syria, entered Damascus. With it marched contingents of Christian knights from Antioch, led by Raymond VI, Georgians and Armenians—these last led by their king, Haithon. Hulagu was bound for the Holy Land, where the Moslems held Jerusalem. With Egypt occupied by the Mongols, the forces of Islam would be driven back again into the Arabian desert and the north African coast—the limbos of the known world.

"Such suffering had not come upon Islam," the chronicler Ibn Athir relates, "since the time of the Prophet."

Mongol advance patrols had reached the plateau west of the river Jordan on the road to Egypt when, early in 1260, Hulagu received the tidings of the death of Mangu. The courier from Kara-korum brought a summons to the Il-khan to journey back to the Mongol homeland.

Hulagu hesitated, as well he might. Mongol tradition called him back to the Gobi and the kuriltai of the blood kin, no matter how far away he might be.

But his brother was dead. He would not see the face of Mangu again. And had he not carried out scrupulously all Mangu's commands? He had earned his reward—the fair valley of Samarkand, the gardens of Baghdad on the gray river, Damascus, the queen of cities, Jerusalem the Golden, these were his, the appanage of the il-khans. A new world, to be the seat of the dynasty he would found.

In a few marches he would cross the desert strip to Cairo on the Nile. After that he would hold the mastery of the nearer east. The sons of his body would be il-khans, heirs of the vanished kalifs. They would have pleasure seats on the shores of the great sea, by the blue water. There was no doubt of success.

His army commander urged him to keep on. Why turn back at the last step? If Hulagu made the long trek homeward to the kuriltai, he would be gone for years. He would leave his new conquest exposed to Birkai, who had become antagonistic, who had gathered an army at the Caucasus.

Dokuz Khatun begged him to stay. Here he could rule unchallenged. In the Gobi he would be only one of three brothers, with no more than the memory of his great journey to hold to. Her Christian advisers—Haithon the Armenian, Bar Hebraeus, the Syrian patriarch—added their voices to hers. (For if Hulagu withdrew now, they would be exposed to the retaliation of the Mamluks of Egypt.) They urged him to give Jerusalem to them. Then the armed Crusaders on the coast, the Templars and Hospitalers, would become allies, and in time no doubt Hulagu might make them his subjects.

The Mongol officers for once agreed with the Christians. For the Mongol plan of conquest called for an avalanche advance—the men of the first conquered zone to be carried on into the next. Hulagu already had the Armenians and the knights of Antioch and the Georgian mountaineers. There could be no halt in such an advance.

Subotai, they reminded Hulagu, had refused to turn back when the princes of the Golden Family disputed in Russia. Instead he went on into Europe. Genghis-Khan himself had laid down the saying that an attack on an enemy must never be given up.

"The Khakhan who is now dead," they said, "gave command to destroy Egypt."

Hulagu pondered. In these days of his hesitation the future of the Mongol empire was not the only issue at stake. The possession of Egypt and the Nile, the Moslem mastery of the near east, and the ultimate fate of the Crusades hung in the balance.

And Hulagu turned back. He sent a message to his brothers saying that he would join them on the Kerulan.

With his horse herds and vast camp he started north. But he had no Subotai to advise him in this evacuation. He had to make his own plans.

In the end he left Kit Boga, his general, with one division and the Armenian and Georgian allies to hold the position by the Jordan. While the grass could still feed his herds he moved north, past the Caucasus. In the midsummer heat he reached the high ground by Tabriz.

There a courier from Palestine overtook him with incredible news. Kit Boga had been defeated and slain, and the Mongol army scattered and driven like sheep.

The Defeat at the Well of Goliath

If the news astonished Hulagu, it amazed western Asia no less. Not for thirty-seven years had a Mongol division been worsted in battle. The Moslems who had thought themselves to be at their last extremity greeted the victory as if it had been a miracle. Particularly as it had been gained by the army of Egypt, which had become the asylum of refugees, driven westward by the Mongol advance.

This Egyptian army had, in fact, grown out of slaves—the warriors known as *mamluks* (the possessed ones—the "Mamelukes"). In the beginning the mamluks had been boys bought as slaves and trained in arms, to serve the shadowy kalifs of Kahirah (Cairo) as a bodyguard—young Bulgars, Turks, Circassians and Georgians purchased in the slave markets of the nearer east. They were, therefore, scions of the white race—for the Turks were white— who knew no other profession than that of war. The most daring of them were known as the White Slaves of the River.

And, like those other Turks who had first served and then dominated the kalifs of Baghdad, the mamluks had soon made figureheads of the weaker kalifs of Kahirah. Their *corps d'élite* became the *halka* or Guard.

The March of the Barbarians

From the first inroads of the Mongols, the ranks of the mamluks had been enlarged by Turkish elements uprooted in Khwaresmia and the Black Sea region, particularly by those wayward souls the Turkomans of the White and the Black Sheep. One member of this turbulent fellowship had the hardihood to believe the Mongols could be defeated. And thereby hangs a tale as strange as any of the Thousand and One Nights.

It is, in very truth, a page from the Nights. Because the chief actor in it has inspired as many of its cherished adventures as Haroun the Blessed. (For much of the so-called *Arabian Nights* was written in Egypt; a deal of their coarse humor comes from the alleys of Cairo, and the river is the Nile, not the Tigris—the unruly slaves the mamluks, and the blacks of the Sudan.)

The man in question is indeed an actor, whose rare ability we have never appreciated. He is Baibars—the Panther—better known by his nickname of the Crossbowman. And Friar William of Tripoli, who knew much of him, relates that as a soldier he was not inferior to Julius Caesar, nor did he yield in malignity to Nero.
' In person he is a Kipchak Turk, more than six feet tall, with one eye whitened by the scar that blinded it. He wields his sword with his left hand, and he delights in covering his body with gorgeous silks. His dossier informs us that as a boy Baibars was conscripted by a Mongol army—taken captive, and sold by Venetian slave merchants in the market of Damascus for about ninety dollars, rejected by the purchaser by reason of his blind eye, taken as a slave by a mamluk amir. But Baibars knows the Mongol army and its methods, from bitter experience.

He finds himself in his element among the turbulent White Slaves of the River. His skill with a crossbow earns him respect, his lack of any scruples wins a way to promotion, his roisterous humor endears him to the multitude in the streets where wine shops ply their trade beside the hashish sellers, and the youngest harlots have to compete with Greek boys.

Baibars wastes no time in becoming amir of the *halka*, second-in-command to Kutuz, the mamluk who can call himself sultan because he has slain the last sultan. In his capacity as head of that oriental Foreign Legion, Baibars plays many roles.

The Book of Tsar Batu

Since he trusts no one but himself, he provides his own intelligence service by going about in disguise. Incognito, he raids the public baths to carry off the choicest women, and he sells his haul of them openly the next day, to build a hospital. He goes up the river with the fisherfolk and dreams of building a fleet. He leaves his cup companions and goes off unattended, to appear the next day in Palestine—the fourth day in the Arabian desert. For he has a steppe dweller's ability to ride both far and fast.

The crowds of Cairo worship him for his exploits, and fear him—because they cannot know where the Panther may be. He might be the tall mamluk watching them from the parapet of Saladin's citadel, or the tall rider hunting antelope with leopards beyond the sheep pasture, or the tall pilgrim from Samarkand rocking in prayer at the elbow of the kadi himself.

When he rides forth in state, Baibars is recognized by the horns and drums that go before him, and the black eunuchs in orange robes that guard his stirrup. To a soldier who strikes his fancy, he is capable of giving emeralds or Christian girls or an estate in Damascus. At a suspicion of revolt, he can behead one hundred and eighty lords of Cairo.

Since language is no barrier to this graduate of war and the slave market, he can talk intimately with Greeks and Arabs and the pagan blacks from the Nile's headwaters, while he does his own spying. He dictates, in another hour and role, his own letters to Charles of Anjou or the Venetians—he is gaining revenue by raiding the Venetian merchant craft, at the time that he is collecting port dues from their enemies the Genoese, and entertaining himself by playing the ambassadors of one proud city against the others until, to his vast amusement, he contrives a sea battle off the coast of the Holy Land between their fleets.

With a following of Turks he defeats the host of the allied Crusaders at Gaza. By the expedient of a counter-attack—a lesson learned from the Mongols—he has managed to break the heart of Louis, king of the French, and to repel a French crusade at Mansura. With Kutuz and a girl named Pearl Spray, he holds at his wayward disposition the nearer east—until the coming of his former masters, the Mongols.

The March of the Barbarians

Kutuz and Baibars took advantage of the terror caused by Hulagu's approach, to seize openly the throne of Egypt which actually rested in their hands. "Our one necessity," said Kutuz, "is to drive off the Mongols. To do that, a real leader is needed."

In due course Hulagu's preliminary summons came to Cairo: "This is the word of him who rules the earth. Tear down your walls and submit. If you do so, peace will be granted you. If you do otherwise, that will happen which will happen, and what it is to be we know not. The Sky alone knows."

The streets of Cairo were at that time filled with refugees, who spread tales of the Mongols' power through the bazaars. To make certain that his turbulent and fearful masses would resist, Kutuz killed the Mongol envoys, hanging up the bodies in the four quarters of the city. After that, he could be certain that Cairo must defend itself or be doomed.

While Kutuz, the Sultan-in-name, filled their war chest by confiscating the jewel stocks of merchants and appropriating the fortunes of lesser amirs, Baibars, in his capacity of commander of the Guard, recruited the fugitive bands of Turkomans and Arabs and summoned the wild Hawwarah of high Egypt, with the Bedouin clans. He drafted the fighting men of Cairo *in toto*, giving to the bastinado those who tried to hide. Between them they mustered an army of over 100,000. Of this host, the mamluk Guard was the only disciplined striking force.

Then—while they were preparing to defend Cairo—Baibars heard that Hulagu had withdrawn, leaving a Mongol army behind him in Palestine. He decided at once to do an unheard-of thing: to attack that army.

The mamluks moved up the coast cautiously to discover what the Crusaders in their fortified seaports might be doing about the situation. The knights, apparently in complete ignorance, and certainly without instructions from Europe, were doing nothing— except drive off Mongol patrols that ventured too near. Kutuz and Baibars satisfied themselves of this when they actually camped near the walls of Acre and bought food from the Crusaders there before moving up to the plain of Galilee, where Kit Boga was camped, near the Ain Jalut, the Well of Goliath.

The Book of Tsar Batu

In spite of odds of four to one against him, Kit Boga gave battle. Brushing aside the Egyptian light cavalry, the heavy Mongol regiments attacked from the right wing—the sweeping *tulughma* attack that had proved successful so often.

It prevailed against the Egyptians. Fearful at the beginning, they gave way before the weight of the Mongol sweep.

Baibars had counted on this. He had planned to use Mongol tactics against Kit Boga—holding back his best men, including the Guard, in ambush. His counter-attack took Kit Boga by surprise.

Heavily outnumbered, and affected by the late summer heat, the Mongols were broken and driven off at speed. The contingents of Georgians and Armenians on foot proved to be useless in this rapid maneuvering. Kit Boga was urged by his noyans to join the flight, but refused, saying "Someone else can tell the Khan how I died. And what is the loss of an army such as this to Hulagu Khan? Have the Mongol women ceased to breed sons, or the mares to drop foals?"

It was not a wise decision. Taken captive, Kit Boga was dragged before the mamluk leaders, and mocked. "You, who have broken so many empires—how does it feel to be bound in your turn?"

Kit Boga answered: "I know this. All my life I have served my master, while you have made yourselves great by slaying yours. After my death, all of you and all that belongs to you will be trampled under the hoofs of the Mongol horses. The Mongol horsemen will carry away the sands of Egypt in their saddlebags."

The mamluks cut off his head and fastened it on a pole. And his boast, which he believed to be a matter of simple truth, did not prove true. Kutuz and Baibars paraded the captive Mongols in triumph in the streets of Cairo before mutilating and killing them.

So Cairo had visible evidence that the invincible Mongols had been overthrown and scattered. The victorious mamluks pursued the remnants of the army across the Euphrates, and the strongholds of Islam rejoiced.

Kutuz distributed rewards and loot to his followers, but he neglected Baibars, to whom his success was due. And Baibars was not the man to endure neglect. While Cairo celebrated the victory, he assembled his mamluks and assassinated Kutuz. Criers went through the public places, calling upon the crowds: "O Believers, pray for the mercy of Allah upon the soul of the sultan Kutuz, and long life to your sultan Baibars ez-Zahir, Baibars the Victorious."

The Panther was much too popular with the crowds to be injured by the murder of Kutuz. Moreover, faithless and brutal though he might be, he was on this occasion the savior of Islam. Promptly, he proclaimed a holy war against Crusaders and Mongols.

Knowing perfectly that his defeat of Kit Boga's frontier force meant little—except retaliation by Hulagu's mighty ordu—he proceeded to war in earnest. Availing himself again of a Mongol expedient, he marched through Syria and evacuated the population from the northern part. Then he burned the grass to the Euphrates, cutting down the orchards and firing the villages—making sure that the Mongol ordu would find no grazing or food in this waste area. He compelled envoys of the Crusaders and Syrian Assassins to march with him, and to impress them with the advisability of remaining neutral, he castrated or put to death five hundred captive Armenians.

In these days Baibars kept close watch to the north, where Hulagu was. He provided his sentry posts with air mail—messenger pigeons—to warn him of any sight of the Mongols. When he camped for the night he never slept twice in the same tent, and he slept in his clothes, with a horse saddled at the tent entrance.

Then his outposts brought in some Mongols who were not from Hulagu's ordu. They were riders from the Caucasus, from the Golden Horde, bringing a message of peace and friendship from Birkai Khan. In the steppes Birkai had heard of the death of Mangu and of the surprising defeat of Hulagu's division in Palestine. It had seemed very advisable to Birkai to send his congratulations to the Panther.

Never, perhaps, had so welcome a message come to a man who could make such good use of it. Baibars saw instantly that the strongest allies he could have against the Mongols were the Mongols themselves. He feasted the riders from the steppes in Cairo, gave them girls and rank in his own *halka*—kept some of them to drill his mamluks, and despatched an embassy of his own with the others.

He also sent a few well-chosen gifts, after he had inquired as to Birkai's tastes: copy of the Koran wrapped in silk embroidered with gold, which he said was illumined by the Kalif Othman himself, a throne of ivory and ebony, gleaming prayer carpets, fine swords with silver handles, Damascus bows with silk cords, gorgeous parrots, Arab horses, swift-paced dromedaries, with a herd of wild ass, giraffes with painted saddlecloths, and a turban which had been on pilgrimage to Mecca—for Baibars hastily sent one of his officers there in Birkai's name. Also young girls skilled in cooking and singing, with a guard of eunuchs to attend them, and a menagerie of monkeys fitted out with silk garments.

Nothing could have been more to the liking of the Khan of the Golden Horde. Baibars himself wrote the letter to accompany the gifts—a missive from a humble Kipchak to the Khan of the Kipchaks, from one ardent Moslem to a mighty convert to Islam. The letter pointed out plausibly that Hulagu seemed to be waging no less than a campaign of extermination against Islam, while the insignificant Panther was striving to restore the Kalifate and to carry on a holy war against the pagans. Baibars added that he would have Birkai's name mentioned in the prayers of the Cairo cathedral mosque. And he suggested that Birkai might aid by attacking the rear of Hulagu's ordu.

It was all very politic and friendly, and it eliminated Hulagu as a threat to Egypt. For the first time a member of the Golden Family moved to protect an alien people against his own kin.

Baibars and the End of the Crusades

Hulagu never made the journey back to his homeland. The elder Mongols of his ordu—many of whom remembered the face and the words of Genghis-Khan—thought only of revenge for Kit Boga's death. Upon Hulagu lay the obligation, by every canon of the steppe dwellers, to crush Egypt and to pull down the brick walls of Cairo into the desert sand. This of necessity Hulagu prepared to do.

On his part, Baibars organized his growing army to meet the

attack, drilling his horsemen in Mongol tactics. He even indulged in a jest, to dispel the dread of the Mongols which still obsessed his Moslems.

Disappearing into the north, he wandered through Hulagu's domain in the guise of a tall minstrel. At a pastry shop where he fed himself and listened to the talk, he took pains to leave his signet ring behind in a cake where it would be sure to be found. Later, when he had gained his own frontier, he dictated a message to the Il-khan. "I left my ring at your roadhouse. Will you have the good will to seek it out and return it to me, because I value it?"

What Hulagu thought of this gasconade we do not know. But when the tale of it was told in the bazaars of Cairo, the listeners rocked with mirth.

And when, in the early winter of 1262, Hulagu prepared to advance with his ordu against Egypt, an army of the Golden Horde moved down to the passes of the Caucasus. Again Hulagu halted. He could not continue south with a hostile Mongol force at his rear. Turning sharply, he led an army of attack through the grazing lands and the Iron Gate where the high ranges meet the narrow edge of the Caspian.

Taking the encampment of the Golden Horde by surprise, beyond the river Terek, he drove his cousin's divisions northward into the steppes—only to be caught himself by a sudden counter-attack. Retreating over the ice of the Terek, he suffered heavy loss when the ice gave way beneath his horsemen and the rearmost division was cut off.

This clash of the mighty armies of invasion began a blood feud between the master of Sarai and the Il-khan of Persia. Hulagu's avalanche of invasion was checked. As they had struggled in merciless civil war in the Gobi before Genghis-Khan laid his restraint upon them, the new Mongol empires—no longer isolated clans—were locked in conflict.

The forested passes of the Caucasus barrier became the roads of the raiding armies. Contingents of Russians were enlisted by Birkai, while Hulagu sent his Georgian and Armenian allies north. The conflict spread to the eastward—because the Mongol armies had a vast range of maneuver.

Here Birkai gained new allies. The fanatical Moslems of Bokhara and Samarkand needed no encouragement to join in a holy war—and, obviously, Birkai was championing the cause of Islam against the pagan Il-khan. So Hulagu had to defend his inner frontier against his blood kin both west and east of the Caspian.

The civil war raged without decision. The Mongol commanders on both sides were too adroit to be caught again at a disadvantage. Their new empires covered too vast a territory to be invaded successfully. No great city could be besieged while a Mongol army remained at large within a thousand miles. So the nomad emperors reverted to their ancestral manner of raiding and plundering.

One power could have checked the conflict: a command from the Khakhan at Kara-korum. But now, owing to an unforeseen crisis in the far east, there was no khakhan seated in the Mongol homeland.

Then began a remarkable contest of strategy. Paying little attention to Birkai's raids, Hulagu set himself the task of finding new allies, in the west. For the first time a reigning khan of the Golden Family abandoned the war against civilization, to make an alliance with the strongest military power in the west, the kings of Europe.

This was precisely what Baibars dreaded. For all his boasting, the Panther had no desire to draw down on his head a general crusade—while the knights still held their Maginot Line of castles along the Syrian coast.

When Hulagu made advances for a marriage between his family and the imperial dynasty of Constantinople, Baibars advised the Khan of Sarai to do the same. Eventually both Mongols secured their wish. Hulagu's son Abaka was wedded to Maria, a bastard daughter of the Emperor of Constantinople, while Nogai, Birkai's young nephew—victor over Hulagu in the first battle in the Caucasus—received another daughter of the imperial Purple as bride.

Then Baibars, or his agents, attempted more direct action. Hulagu was much too dangerous to be allowed to survive.

"A comet appeared in the sky," Rashid ad-Din relates, "in the shape of a fiery pillar, and showed itself for several nights. When at last it disappeared there befell the great catastrophe."

Hulagu, it seems, had taken the comet for an omen as soon as he saw it. The Sky had made a sign appear to him. "He touched the ground with his head," another Moslem explains, "his fears increasing as the light of the comet diminished."

This sign, and the warning of his Moslem astrologers, however, did not serve to make Hulagu abandon the war. Whether he was poisoned by the Moslems, we do not know. But he died of sickness, and within a year Dokuz Khatun was dead as well.

"The grief of the Christians was great throughout the world," Bar Hebraeus explains, "at the loss of these two illuminators and protectors of the Christian faith."

And Stephen the Orphelin laments in stronger words: "The great king, the master of the world, the hope of the Christians, died in the year 1264, and he was followed by his wife Dokuz Khatun. They were both poisoned by the craft of a Moslem. The Lord knows they were not less in well-doing than Constantine and his mother Helen."

The irony of it is that the Mongol Il-khan had desired no religious war with the Moslems. He had tried to follow the ancestral tradition of religious tolerance—a policy incomprehensible to the western Christians. Abaka, his son, did likewise, with no better results.

He sent letters and embassies to Edward of England, and to the Pope at the Council of Lyons, urging an alliance of the Crusaders and Mongols against Egypt. In these messages, unlike the warning of Kuyuk's missive, there was no threat. Such an alliance might have been successful—it was favored by Rome. But the Christian chivalry, engrossed in its own quarrels, paid no heed to it.

Meanwhile Baibars had made a shrewder move. Instead of approaching the courts, he opened negotiation with the moneyed interest of the west—the Venetian merchant republic in particular. Since the caravan routes into Asia were thrown into turmoil by the civil war of the Mongols—in those years a young Venetian merchant, Messer Marco Polo, who visited Sarai with his uncles, had been obliged to go to the far east for a market because he could not reach the cities of the Il-khan—Baibars pointed out that Egypt was becoming the great *entrepôt* of trade with the east. There, in Cairo, the much-desired spices could be had by the Venetians. He offered those enterprising merchants concessions in the new Egyptian market.

With the merchants of Sicily he arrived at the same understanding. And he reached an agreement with Constantinople, to open the slave markets of the Black Sea to the mamluks. Thus fortified with trade pacts, he approached Charles of Anjou, of Sicily, one of the leaders of the Crusade then forming. The trade in slaves and spices was a source of wealth; the Venetian monopoly, the markets of Constantinople and Cairo—all these were too important to be disturbed. In the end, Baibars gained his point.

And the Crusade, led by Louis of France, John of Arragon and Charles of Anjou, when at last it set forth, was diverted from these markets to a futile attack upon Tunis along the African coast. There plague decimated the Crusaders' camp, and the saintly Louis died of it. With him vanished the moving spirit of the last Crusades. The dogged Edward of England, alone, reached the coast of the Holy Land, to be wounded there by an assassin's knife.

Later, in 1281, Abaka moved against Egypt without support from the Crusaders. His Mongol army—strengthened by Georgians and Armenians—was met in Syria and checked by the mamluk host commanded by Kalawun, who succeeded Baibars. The mamluks were able to scatter one wing of the Mongol formation and to wound its commander, and the Mongols retreated with their allies again beyond the Euphrates. "Many of them rode the Moslem horses," explains an English Crusader who witnessed the battle, "which were better than their own."

And this observer wrote earnestly to his liege lord, Edward of England: "The Holy Land was never so easy of conquest as now, with able generals and store of food, yet never have we seen so few soldiers of so little counsel in it."

The Mongol Il-khans, like the English knight, could not understand why no allies appeared from western Europe. They had inspected the line of Crusader castles on the heights along the Syrian coast—huge fortifications which had resisted attack until then, as formidable in their way as the Great Wall of China. But no armies of Crusaders appeared out of the sea.

The Il-khans persisted. Arghun wrote to Honorius IV a letter which has been preserved, in Latin translation in the Vatican. Asking once more for the help of a crusade, he ends his appeal: ". . . as the land of the Moslems lies between you and us, we can surround it and strangle it . . . we can drive out the Moslems with the help of God and the Pope and Genghis-Khan!"

Then Arghun sent a priest of his own to Rome, a Uighur Christian who had wandered out from China. This unusual emissary from the east journeyed faithfully from the Byzantine emperor to the Genoese merchants, and to St Peter's in Rome, where he was received by the See of Cardinals, who hardly knew what to make of him.

This envoy from Asia, Rabban Sauma, tells in his own words how he tried to make his mission clear:

"And after many days they came to Great Rome. And they entered the Church of Peter, where is the See of the Reverend Pope, where twelve men sat in council to elect a new Pope. Rabban Sauma sent word to them, saying, 'We are ambassadors from King Arghun and the Katholicos of the East.'

"And Rabban Sauma was bidden to enter to the twelve Cardinals, who did not rise in his presence, because they stand not before other men—such is the dignity of their See. But they sat Rabban Sauma by them, and one asked, 'Why hast thou come hither?'

" 'The Mongols,' he said to them, 'with the Katholicos of the East have sent me to the Reverend Pope with letters.'

"And they asked him, 'What is this region of the earth? Why hast thou come? Where does the Katholicos live?'

" 'In Baghdad.'

" 'What art thou there?'

" 'I am deacon of the Monastery there.'

" 'Who among the Apostles taught the religion you profess?'

" 'Mar Thomas and Mar Addai and Mar Mari taught us, and we hold to their teaching until now.'

" 'It amazes us,' they said, 'that thou, a Christian and a Deacon, hath come hither as ambassador of the King of the Mongols.'

" 'This same King,' Bar Sauma said, 'would like well to conquer the lands of Syria and Palestine, and asks your help because of the captivity of Jerusalem. And he sent me who am a Christian, that my word should be believed by you.' "

While the strange Rabban was honored by the Cardinals, he could not convince them of the reality of his mission. He was conducted on, to Paris and the French king, and to Edward I of England at Bordeaux—always greeted with surprise and delight, and accomplishing nothing. "A year has gone by," he laments, "and what have I to say to the Mongols?"

Arghun had no blame for the good Rabban. A last time the Il-khan wrote to Philip the Fair: "Here is our word. King of France, we ask you to depart from your country in the last month of winter of the year of the Panther, and to camp near Damascus the 15 of the first month of spring. If, on your side, you will send armed forces at this time, we will retake Jerusalem and give it to you. But it would be useless to move our forces if you are going to fail to be at the meeting place."

After that Mongol envoys were sent on a final round of the European courts. But they came back with only meaningless compliments. The princes of the west were too preoccupied with their own quarrels to venture again into Asia to attempt to reach Jerusalem. Ironically, in these last months, they wasted all the efforts of two centuries of the Crusades.

Baibars had saved Egypt from the Mongol invasion. More than that, the mamluks, his successors, liquidated the Crusaders' castles on the coast soon after Arghun's missions to Europe.

The Il-khans made no further attempt to reach the sea, or to establish contact with the Christian powers. They retired behind the frontiers of their new dominion, which stretched from Asia Minor to India. Nor did they return to the attack upon civilization.

They were surrounded by grandeur enough to satisfy even Mongols. After three generations the strong tribal instincts softened. Hulagu's descendants did not adapt themselves to cities and to labor. They believed themselves to be still hard and enduring, and free as the Golden Family had been. They still spent most of their lives on horseback—in the chase or frontier wars. They built cities of their own, levying heavy taxes on the agricultural populations to construct gardens and game preserves. To carry on the work of administration they relied more and more on the intelligent Moslem wazirs or ministers. And they were inclined to grant favors to those who came to their feet with the largest presents. Without realizing it, they were becoming enamored of the culture of Persia.

In the north, however, Birkai's dynasty remained isolated beyond the Volga, in the steppes. The Golden Horde, like the Il-khans, had abandoned the attack on the west. Served by subject Russia, it lived in barbaric luxury—taking delight in hearing its exploits made into songs by minstrels, and intermarrying with the princely Russian families.

Here, however, a sharp division was taking place. Nogai, the Mongol noyan who had forced Hulagu back from the Caucasus, had possessed himself of the fertile Ukraine—the grasslands almost deserted after the Mongol conquest. He chose to remain there with his army, and after Birkai's death in 1267 there was no khan of Sarai dominant enough to make him yield his conquest.

With a Byzantine beauty for wife, to guide him, he made an inroad of his own through the Balkans as far as the Aegean, becoming the master of the Serbs and Bulgars at that end of the steppes. In particular he took delight in the sun-warmed Krimea, where Venetian merchants appeared to buy slaves, and the débris of defeated peoples clustered in forgotten settlements—Greeks who had altered into nomads, long-haired Goths who still spoke their German tongue, Turks who had sought refuge from the earlier Mongol invasions.

There Nogai, son-in-law of the Emperor of Constantinople, established a dynasty of his own. His ordu became known as the Nogai Tatars, or the Krim Tatars. Of all the conquerors in the west, his people kept closest to the traditions of the steppe dwellers.

By then, in the third generation after the death of Genghis-Khan, the Mongols in the west had cast off all dependence on the Khakhan of Kara-korum. They struck coins in their own names, and sent no gifts to the kinsmen in the east. Because, by then, there was no khakhan at Kara-korum.

VII

The Book of Kubilai Khan

VII

The Book of Kubilai Khan

KUBILAI WAS STILL ON THE banks of the Yang-tse when the report of Mangu's sudden death spread through China, in that hot midsummer of 1259. He had with him the sage Yao Chow and the Lady Jamui of the Chestnut Horse tribe, and the famous Left Wing of the army.

Not without reason was Kubilai, the second brother, called *Sechen*, the Wise, by his Mongols. He listened to many rumors, saying little himself. It seemed to him ominous that men should whisper of happenings that might or might not be true. His Chinese advisers foretold that the Mongol dominion would be launched in a new direction, and that a change would take place on the continent.

Messengers came from Kara-korum to ask the recall of portions of his army. But they could give no reasons for recalling them. Kubilai refused to part with any of his Banners while he waited to learn what was behind the silence and the whispering.

Mangu's eldest wife wrote him that the Khakhan was gravely sick. She wrote again, saying that the favorite, Princess Kutuktai, talked much with Alamdar and the officers of Mangu's detachments. Kubilai waited, although, more than his brother Hulagu or his cousin Birkai, he had the ability to make decisions quickly. He merely wanted to know for a certainty whether Mangu lived.

"When he first heard the evil tidings of the sickness of Mangu

Khan," Rashid explains, "he said, 'I shall pay no heed to false rumors.' When he knew this thing for a certainty he came away from the army and went into mourning. He was then alone in the land of southern China, because Hulagu Khan was over in the west in the land of Iran. So the way was far between them and the throne-place (the Mongol homeland) where Arik Buka sat."

Arik Buka, the Little Man, youngest of the three surviving brothers, was then keeper of the hearth, at Kara-korum. He had in his keeping the ancestral grazing lands, and the bronze leaves of the Golden Book upon which the commands of Genghis-Khan had been inscribed.

"When he heard of what had befallen his brother," Rashid adds, "Arik Buka fixed his eyes on the throne and the kingship. The chieftains and princes of the blood egged him on to do this, so that he revolted against Kubilai Khan."

So Rashid says. But it was, in reality, Kubilai who revolted against his young brother. And perhaps in neither case was personal ambition the cause of the quarrel.

By the code of Genghis-Khan, the death of Mangu should have been followed by a gathering of the kuriltai of all the blood kin—all the members of the Golden Family. But Birkai was not expected to come, and Hulagu did not, while the formidable Kaidu remained apart in his pastures of mid-Asia. The issue of succession would then, in any case, have been decided by Kubilai and Arik Buka, both grandsons of Genghis-Khan and sons of the house of Tului.

And, inevitably, they were thrown into conflict by the influences that surrounded them. Around Arik Buka were gathered the elder Mongols, the pagans, the true dwellers in felt tents. Kubilai had with him only the officers of his own powerful field army and the bureaus of the Chinese mandarins. The ghost of Yeliu Ch'u-tsai haunted his ordu.

More than that, a change had been taking place in the Mongols themselves during this last generation. Those who continued to dwell in the steppes had built themselves small mud palaces. There they had enjoyed the spoils of vast conquests. While they remained

barbarians, life had softened for them. They no longer had to endure hunger and drought in the steppes.

At the same time the Mongols with Kubilai had occupied middle
China for most of that generation. They had been active in administration, and their desire was to increase their own well-being.
After experiencing the splendors of Yen-king, they had little desire
to return to the yurts of Kara-korum. Instead of being softened
by their contact with civilization, they looked upon themselves as
victorious and hard. They carried on the work while the steppe
dwellers reaped the loot of it. Their pride increased proportionally
—were they not carrying out the command of Genghis-Khan,
while the inmates of the Gobi were growing fat with "borrowed
victories"?

This pride of the former nomads was perhaps their most vital
impulse. The noyans in Kubilai's command did not realize how
they were changing, because in their own estimation they were,
as they had been, barbaric conquerors, living in the saddle.

On the other side of the frontier, the tent dwellers saw clearly
that the host in China was not destroying the ramparts of civilization in order to establish the steppe economy planned by
Genghis-Khan. Kubilai and his men were sparing Chinese civilization because they admired it.

Another change had taken place in the Mongol nation in this
last generation and a half. By throwing the old patriarchal tribes
into a national army, Genghis-Khan had been able to eliminate
the feuds between the tribes, but at the same time he had done
away with the tribes themselves. The former Kiraïts, Tatars,
Merkits, Oyrats, Uriankut, had been scattered among the various
armies of invasion, and a good proportion had been killed off. The
survivors felt themselves bound, not by the ancient clan ties, but
by loyalty to the individual members of the house of Genghis-Khan
who commanded them.

So the Mongol *ulus*, or nation, was fast disappearing. Individual
princes held authority by virtue of their pedigrees—those who were
closest in blood ties to the great ancestor had the more prestige,
and so the more numerous following. The stubborn loyalty of the
former barbarians now served individuals.

The March of the Barbarians

Genghis-Khan had been able to transform the steppe dwellers into an invincible mechanism of conquest. But he had not been able to foresee a change in the character of the Mongols themselves.

Before the grass came through the snow in the prairies, the adherents of the Yasa and the old Mongol tradition were riding in to Kara-korum, summoned to appear at Mangu's grave by the Mountain of Power. They were urging on the Little Man not to yield the khanship to Kubilai—a renegade, who had ceased to be a nomad. Couriers came in from Birkai at the Golden Horde and from Kaidu offering support to the youngest brother. Princess Kutuktai championed him, and Mangu's three sons swore fealty to him. Chieftains and noyans of the house of Ogadai—at feud with the house of Tului—journeyed toward the headwaters of the prairies to support him. Alamdar brought him a portion of the army.

Excellently informed of this, Kubilai acted without hesitation. Patching up a truce with the Sung dynasty beyond the Yang-tse, he ordered his Banners northward, to the homeland.

In June 1260, before he reached the edge of the desert, he called for a kuriltai to be held, in his pleasure city of Shang-tu. And there, surrounded by the officers of his army and Chinese officials, he had himself proclaimed khakhan of the Mongols.

This election held in a city of China, attended only by the Left Wing of the army, defied the law of Genghis-Khan. When word of it reached the Mongol homeland, Arik Buka's supporters held a kuriltai in the traditional spot by the waters of the Kerulan. They named the Little Man emperor, to succeed his brother Mangu.

And tidings of the dual election sped to the west and southwest. In the steppes of Russia, Birkai knew that civil war in Mongolia would free him from the overlordship of any khakhan, and he turned his forces at once against Hulagu.

In this way, in the early summer of 1260, began the civil war that was to last for forty years and to divide the Mongol empire beyond any hope of unification. Neither Kubilai nor Arik Buka had designed it; they did no more than drift with the forces already too strong to be altered by the will of one man.

Kubilai lost no time in advancing with his veteran tumans of the Left Wing and the Chinese against the reigning city of his people, where the keeper of the hearth awaited him. Taking the offensive at once, he kept it.

First driving out contingents of the Mongol armies in Shensi that had been Mangu's, he moved to the south of Kara-korum. Arik Buka's levies of the steppes were in no condition to oppose an active army like this. They retreated west to the tribal lands that had been Siyurkuktiti's.

This began a kaleidoscope of the swift Mongol maneuvering, in which the armies attacked and retreated without decision, as in the western campaign between Hulagu and Birkai. Such veteran armies could not be surrounded, or made to give battle at a disadvantage. Kubilai, however, withdrew from Kara-korum to the great metropolis of Yen-king.

"Let them go," Kubilai said, of the rebels. "They have lost their senses now, but they will be wiser later." To Arik Buka he sent word that he trusted in his brother's faith, and expected him to come in to yield himself before it was too late.

Arik Buka replied with a fresh attack, without being strong enough to recapture the nomad capital. And in 1264 he was caught with his army at the edge of the Gobi. A Chagatai prince from whom he had expected a reinforcement of men and horses turned against him, and the retreat of the Little Man was cut off. He was brought a captive into Kubilai's camp and made to kneel at the threshold of his brother's tent, the entrance flap thrown over his head. Then he was led to the secretaries' post, and Kubilai looked at him long without speaking.

"Well, my brother," Kubilai asked, "which of us has the right in this?"

"In the beginning," the Little Man replied, "I had. But now you have."

Kubilai spared his life and let him go free within the ordu. Defeated, the Little Man was not dangerous. But Kubilai had less mercy upon the chieftains and noyans who had advised his brother. Arik Buka urged that they were no more guilty than he.

"How are they not guilty?" Kubilai demanded. "The princes

and noyans who conspired against Mangu did not lift a hand against him, yet they were punished for their intention. These men have made civil war blaze up."

So he said. But he must have realized—because he did not try to deceive himself—that he had broken the Mongol law as much as the sixty officers he was condemning. He had merely had the greater force to prevail over them.

The noyans made no answer to him. One turned to the others, saying, "My companions, at the time we raised Arik Buka to the throne we swore to die for him at need. Now that time has come."

They were beaten or strangled to death. Kubilai had enforced his claim to the khanate. Yet outside of his own followers and the Chinese, he had no one of the Golden Family he could trust. Many of the steppe chieftains came in to make submission to him. Hulagu, from Syria, sent his recognition. And Birkai, to appease the new Khakhan, sent congratulatory gifts.

But Kubilai understood that he must rule alone. And he took a step that he must have weighed for a long time. It followed the path of his own inclination, and it changed the nature of the Mongol empire. He did not return to Kara-korum. With his court, he took the whole of his ordu back to China. He turned his back on the graves of his ancestors in the valley by the Mountain of Power. And at his departure the gray mud walls of Kara-korum became almost deserted.

Wiser than the elder Mongols, Kubilai understood that the desert city had outlived its purpose. It had served only as a meeting place for the Golden Family, a walled enclosure in the high prairies that came to be the nomads' warehouse for the loot of the outer world. Now, with the Golden Family divided, Kubilai as khakhan expected to gain his revenues from China alone. And he—steeped in Chinese culture—could not carry on the administration of Cathay from the prairies. Instead, he moved his court to Yen-king, within the Great Wall.

And this removal snapped the tie that bound his Mongols to their homeland. After that they ceased to be steppe dwellers even in spirit. Kubilai had faced them, for better or worse, toward the farther east.

And again, this decision was not entirely of his own making. He was only adapting himself to the circumstances created by the genius of Yeliu Ch'u-tsai and the tranquil persistence of Yao Chow.

The Irreconcilables

Another force pushed Kubilai Khan eastward. In the ranges of mid-Asia the survivors of the house of Ogadai had taken refuge, joining themselves there to the descendants of the Wild Horse (Chagatai) who still followed the ancestral way of life in the highlands remote from any direct contact with civilization. They found a man to lead them who was pure Mongol—Kaidu, Ogadai's grandson, the hero of the victories in Europe.

Kaidu was as much a master of war as Kubilai, his uncle. He had, moreover, a blood feud with the house of Tului. The elder Mongols saw in him the likeness of another Genghis-Khan, a hard soul indifferent to religion, determined to lead the steppe dwellers to war. When Kubilai sent to him to ask why he did not come in to submit, he answered laconically with the traditional excuse of the family, "My horses are sick."

"When Arik Buka went to Kubilai the Khakhan," Rashid explains, "Kaidu was seized with fear of Kubilai, and he turned from the Yasa and became a rebel. Because of that, many a Mongol and Moslem has gone to his death.

"At first Kaidu was master of few men, but he was clever and full of deceit and equal to any need. He got together two or three thousand men and set about making friends with the house of Juchi, until he was able to gather aid from every quarter."

Kaidu ranged from the forested Altai to the heights of Afghanistan, levying tribute on the Five Cities—allowing the Turk who was Yelvadj's son to administer these crossroad centers of sedentary people—while he raided Samarkand and Bokhara. He maintained no elaborate court, he welcomed the rebellious Mongol noyans as *andas*, companions in war.

And he waged war against Kubilai in the Mongol fashion—making surprise attacks when his horses were well fed and fit. Kubilai on his part was forced to stand on the defensive, as the

Chinese emperors had defended themselves against the nomads. Kubilai threw a screen of mobile cavalry units along his new frontier—the edge of the Gobi, and the midregion of the northern prairies. When Kaidu's attacks broke through this screen, the field army of the Khakhan would move against the invader, driving him back. The Khakhan could not pursue the rebels beyond the wastes of the Gobi, nor could he ever feel himself safe from surprise in north China.

Kaidu, like Kubilai, had the gift of inspiring loyalty. His followers were the descendants of the great Turkish clans, only gradually yielding to the influence of Islam. And he had a daughter so devoted to him that she refused a mate of her own. Like her father, she chose to spend her life in the saddle, and her skill in warfare became a tradition among the nomads who followed Kaidu.

Even the matter-of-fact Marco Polo, who ventured across Kaidu's dominion at that time, had a word to say of her:

"Her name was Ai Yaruk, which is to say the Bright Moon. This damsel was very fair, but also strong in feats of skill . . . and ye must know that her father never went away to war but she went with him. And gladly he took her. At times she would leave her father's side, and make a dash at some enemy, as deftly as a hawk pouncing on a bird."

Rashid had a clear impression of this daughter. "She went about like a boy with the army, and her father honored her, although her brothers cried out against her, saying, 'Your work is with sewing knife and needle—what have you to do with our ruling and our following?' When they said that, she was angered.

"Her father honored her. He would give her to no man, and people slandered him, saying that surely he was in love with his own daughter. After many years Kaidu felt shame of the mockery of his people and gave her to wife to a man of Cathay."

It is known that this Bright Moon made her father's cause her own. Legend relates that Ai Yaruk took tribute of horses from would-be husbands, but refused to give up her army life for any man. Her courage gave a romantic hue to Kaidu's indomitable revolt, and between them they held the grazing lands of mid-Asia for nearly forty years.

This campaign of the irreconcilables had consequences that grew decisive with time. Since the area of Kaidu's raids covered both main caravan routes across the continent, the traffic between east and west was interrupted. The ancient Silk route especially was becoming hazardous. And since communication between the new empires of the Il-khans and the Golden Horde and Yen-king had almost ceased, the Mongol conquerors in the west felt themselves free to act independently of the authority of the khakhan in Yen-king. The Mongol empire was dismembering swiftly into its four quarters, and the homelands had ceased to have any significance.

Xanadu

While Kaidu rode with his herds, his bagpipes and minstrels beyond the Gobi's sands, Kubilai felt free to rule at last as he wished. He entered Cathay not as a barbarian Mongol, come to squeeze the land, but as a well-wisher, a benevolent conqueror intent on founding a dynasty of his own. The *Sechen* had seen the defects of Mongol supremacy.

He had cast his lot with the Chinese. And—first of the Mongols to do so—he understood them. He understood them too well to trust them, much as he admired their culture. He did not mean to yield to this persuasive culture, as the Kin had done before him. With all a nomad's great personal pride, he felt that he could rule as a Mongol over the Chinese.

It was a daring ambition, to try to dispense with the evils of the Chinese system and the failings of simple Mongol autocracy, to find a happy medium of his own. But Kubilai had great courage and stubbornness, as well as the Mongol's natural instinct for statesmanship.

His new residence of Shang-tu (the Xanadu of Coleridge's laudanum dream) began to take strange shape. Within a palisade sixteen miles in circuit parks grew beside lakes that were man-made. Trees—which were Kubilai's pet obsession, after his early life in the dust-driven prairies—began to rise by the lakes. He rode through the Shang-tu park, to watch his hawks in mew. And at times he carried a hunting leopard behind his saddle—loosing the leopard at any animal that took his fancy. Xanadu was really a huge game preserve.

Satisfied with shade and running water, the Mongol who was designing the structure of an empire planned a new kind of palace. It stood in the wood of Shang-tu, built of canes gilded and roped together with silk cords—so that it could be taken down and moved elsewhere at his pleasure. He spent most of his time, at first, in a pavilion of leopard skins. But the skins were lined with ermine.

Not content with that, Kubilai ordered a marble court to be raised by the lake—the marble to be gilded and painted with forms of hunters, birds and beasts. And trees. He did not feel at ease in a Chinese yamen that was like a prison. Yet to please his Chinese counselors, he decreed the building of a temple to Confucius beside the marble court.

And before then, he erected elsewhere, at the suggestion of the Chinese mandarins, a strange structure—a palace for his dead ancestors. In this palace, called by the Chinese *Tai-miao*, he placed tablets for each of the Golden Family—for Yesukai, Genghis-Khan, Ogadai, the bastard Juchi, Chagatai, Tului his father, Kuyuk and Mangu. Upon these he bestowed honorific names in Chinese (with the exception of Juchi and Chagatai, who were not Kubilai's direct ancestors, and who had not reigned).

Before these name tablets, incense was burned. And Kubilai came at intervals to bow before the distinguished dead—who would have been vastly surprised in their lifetime to contemplate such ceremonial. Kubilai was neither the first nor the last self-made man to sublimate his ancestors.

And he gave a name to the dynasty he meant to found. It was to be the Yüan—the Outland.

Straightway he commissioned a group of Han-lin scholars to write the history of the Yüan dynasty. And it seemed fitting to order an astronomer, Jamal ad-Din, to make a new calendar to inaugurate his reign. And, to increase the skill of his scientists, he ordered the casting of new bronze instruments for the astrologers' tower—a globe of the sky, an armilary sphere, a gnomon. This task kept his seven chosen scientists occupied for years—because Kubilai was ever hungry of omens that had a mathematical basis.

The Book of Kubilai Khan

It was a great convenience to know the fortunate moons and lucky days, and also the hours when the Star of evil omen was ascendant.

He made a habit of pitting the Chinese against the Moslems in such endeavors, being much too shrewd to trust one of the many peoples subject to him. To translate works that he wished to read, he gathered a coterie of Uighurs, Persians, Tibetans, and Turks of the Bokhara academies at his court. He had an insatiable curiosity, and he was avid of the wisdom gleaned from books. Being a Mongol, he could be deceived, but it was most dangerous to attempt to deceive him. In fact he established what amounted to a clearing house of the scientific knowledge of that time.

He discovered that strangers who joined his court could be trusted to serve him, and he made a practice of rewarding them greatly. At the same time he was pitiless if imposed upon. Once, listening to a reading from the Koran, he discovered that it laid a command upon Moslems to kill unbelievers. Summoning the chief mullah to him, Kubilai asked if this were so. The teacher of Islam admitted it.

"And you believe that this Koran has been given to you by God?" Kubilai demanded.

The mullah assented.

"Then why do you not obey its command and slay those who do not believe as you do?"

"Because the time has not come, and because we are unable to do it yet."

"But I am able to do it," Kubilai assured him, and ordered the execution of the mullah. A terrible persecution of Moslems followed throughout Cathay, until a sage of Bokhara was able to convince Kubilai that a Mongol like himself could not in any sense of the word be an unbeliever, because he put the name of God at the head of all his utterances.

Kubilai shocked the ritual-minded Marco Polo by the freedom of his reasoning. "There are four prophets," he declared, "to whom people pray and give reverence on earth: Jesus Christ, Muhammad, Moses, and Sakya-muni. I bow to all of them, and also before *him* who of them all is the most great in the Sky. I pray him to give me aid. Why then should I make myself a Christian? You see well

[267]

that the Christians in this land are ignorant, while the servants of the pagan gods can do anything they desire!"

And he gave Messer Marco a demonstration of the miracle-working of the Tibetan lamas, who managed to move a goblet filled with wine through the air into Kubilai's waiting hand. "They can conjure up storms," the Khakhan added, "and direct them where they please. They can speak to their pagan gods."

To such a red lama out of Tibet, Kubilai gave the spiritual headship of his domain. However much Kubilai really believed in the tantric rituals of the shamanists, he seemed to have a strong liking for this lama, Phags-pa, from the long white mountains. To Phags-pa he gave the title of "King of the great and precious Law, and Creator of the Emperor."

But he put Phags-pa to useful work, requesting him in his wisdom to devise a universal alphabet, in which the spoken Mongolian could be combined with the written Chinese and Tibetan—this to relieve the plague of tongues and scripts at the Mongol court. Not even a dalai lama could devise one script to satisfy all tongues —although Phags-pa made a brave attempt.

This authority enjoyed by a Tibetan offended the Chinese intellectuals, who were Taoists in imagination and Confucianists in scholarship. Perhaps that did not displease Kubilai, who was attempting to build a world state upon the foundation of China. He was struggling against the very culture he most admired. For in the placidity and ritualism of Chinese life he observed a force that could not be broken by weapons.

In his system of government—shrewdly devised to extend to all classes of his subjects—he gave no race a controlling hand. His native Mongols held the commanding positions in the army, and over the darugashis, the judges, provincial commands, and heads of departments. The more subtle Moslems were appointed to secondary authority, and served also as financial agents. The Chinese controlled the schools and the heads of corporations. So, in rough outline, Kubilai kept the police power in the hands of the Mongols, the treasury under the aegis of the foreigners, and the education under the Chinese.

Each race, under this plan, could do the work it was best fitted for, and each would act as a balance to the others. For Kubilai intended to bring about no less a thing than an administration of peace that should eliminate all suffering among the lower classes of his peoples.

To do this, it was necessary for him first to conquer the south of China where the Sung dynasty reigned. Convinced by Yao Chow and his Chinese advisers that the Mongol plan of conquest was too bloody—resulting in obliteration of man power and in rebellion— he set about this task in a manner of his own. The campaign against the Sung, he argued, should be waged without slaughter. Cities, he told his commanders, could be taken more easily by humanity than by pyramids of dead bodies.

In the end this new method of conquest was carried out as Kubilai wished. But it took twelve years.

The Fall of the Sung

The heart of China beat below the Yang-tse's swift waters. And this heart was formed of human multitudes. Barbarians had raided and ruled the north—Cathay—since the early dynasties. But the south had remained untouched by invasion. It had isolated itself from migration and world conflict. And to that extent it had stagnated. The blood of the heart was thinned, pulsing slowly.

The rulers of the Sung had the memories of eighteen dynasties. Their own society had endured for three centuries. And the eyes of that society had turned inward—to contemplation of spiritual values, to appreciation of a painter's brush strokes and the delicacy of lines that suggested lakes in twilight. Increasing melancholy touched the spirits of the Sung.

They had made for themselves an earthly paradise among the southern mountains, a paradise where the foliage of trees turned an autumn red, and an old moon hung over drowsy villages, "Upon a terrace in a motionless land," the poet Sung Po-jen wrote, "in the evening light, to watch the rain clouds passing across the sky, while the light swallows are carried away by a distant wind . . ."

To such a feeding upon the inward spirit had their long isolation reduced the Sung. In their thoughts the advance of the Mongols beyond the frontier was no more than another raid of the horse nomads from the steppes.

During these centuries the Sung empire had perfected an economy of peace in which the agriculture of the countryside supported the gigantic centers of city life. In turn, the trade of the cities sustained the workers of the soil. But it was a fragile economy, breeding the extremes of wealth and poverty. The members of the imperial family, close to the Son of Heaven, were remote as the clouds of the poet's sky from the fishermen of the Yang-tse gorges.

The strength of the Sung lay in these immense walled cities. Lin-ngan itself enclosed sixteen hundred thousand families. It was a metropolis built of a dozen city centers. Vassaf the chronicler says that it had sixty-four public squares, and seven hundred temples walled like fortresses. Its river was intercut with canals, over which the population moved on 360 bridges—Marco Polo, with his love for mighty figures, says twelve thousand!—some, of stone, so huge that ocean-going junks could pass under them.

Paved with brick and stone, the streets were drained into the canals. Each street had a fireproof tower in which grain could be stored. Each house, ornamented with paintings, had its inhabitants listed on a tablet hanging by the door. Police guarded the barriers of the different quarters, under command of the Great Quieter— serving also as firemen at need.

And Lin-ngan was shaped for the enjoyment of life, with its central community park, its lake surrounded by the palace and temple districts—where gondolas and pleasure barges gave greater quiet than the streets.

In this we recognize the outline of a modern metropolis, without skyscrapers or a factory district. It even had an outer, encircling boulevard—chariots could drive around the summit of the vast city wall.

Toward Lin-ngan the armies of Kubilai advanced in their new method of attack, avoiding bloodshed. Fortunately for Kubilai he had commanders who were men of genius. Achu, a grandson of Subotai, had the sagacity of the elder Mongols, while Bayan—the

Gifted—had nothing less than genius for arriving at his ends. In fact the war after the first years became less Kubilai's than Bayan's.

For Kubilai did not lead this invasion in person. The Mongol commanders as it happened had a just grievance against the Sung, because the Sung minister had taken advantage of the truce hastily agreed upon by Kubilai when he marched back to Kara-korum to deal with Arik Buka. This minister represented the truce, within his frontiers, as a victory gained against the Mongols in the field, and never enlightened the imperial family of the Sung as to the terms they were obligated to carry out. He had profited further by the Mongol civil war to liquidate the Mongol frontier detachments, and so to claim new victories. The people at home believed the Mongols had been defeated.

And when envoys were sent from Kubilai's court to protest, the Sung minister had them assassinated. Other Mongol officials he imprisoned—preventing any word of the actual situation from reaching Lin-ngan. But he found himself unable to cope with the new Mongol armies of attack—supposedly defeated long since. And his treachery caused several of the ablest commanders of the Sung to desert to the more responsible Mongols. So Bayan presently had under his command not only contingents of the north China engineers and crossbowmen, but some of the best units of the Sung frontier infantry.

He advanced by methodical stages, besieging a city only when necessary. Although he could not escape costly battles—and at times he would enter a captured town to find the wells choked with the bodies of the Sung families that had committed suicide—he spread before his advance a propaganda of pacification instead of the customary Mongol terrorism.

He took pains to go himself to make public prayer by the bodies of Sung commanders who had killed themselves after a defeat. This gesture of respect earned the appreciation of the Sung people. Passing through a plague-ridden countryside, Bayan sent physicians from his command into the affected villages. Some of his regiments carried plows and hoes, to help the field workers of the countryside to get their crops sown.

Nor did he yield to the diplomatic trickery of the Sung ministry.

The March of the Barbarians

Envoys were sent from Lin-ngan to his camp to protest against the invasion of a country which was then ruled by a boy Emperor and his mother, the Empress Dowager.

"Your master is young, you say," Kubilai's generalissimo replied. "But have you forgotten that the Emperor of the Chou, from whom your founder wrested the empire, was also a child? Do you find it strange that we do likewise to you?"

A deft answer like this, making the Sung envoys lose face—not for the first time—weighed more with the Chinese spirit than a victory in the field. Not that Achu and Bayan abandoned military expedients. They called for experts in the manufacture of siege engines from Abaka, the Il-khan of Persia, and these Moslem engineers were able to construct mangonels—the heavy artillery of the day—casting stones so large that they shattered any defensive wall and crushed buildings within the cities. Achu even devised a navy—and the Mongols were always reluctant to enter boats—on the lower Yang-tse. He manned a chain of boats with Chinese crossbowmen, and when he was attacked from leeward by a Sung flotilla, he opened fire with flaming darts from the crossbows that started a conflagration in the attacking junks. The fire carried down the wind, breaking up the flotilla. (Another account has it that the fire was started by inflammables shot from ballistae.)

When the grandmother of the seven-year-old Emperor sent letters broadcast through the lands of the Sung, urging the feudal nobility to join in the defense of the capital, Lin-ngan, Bayan despatched his officers over the countryside with sacks of coins to be distributed where the campaign had impoverished the towns.

On his approach to the immense walls of Lin-ngan, he gave orders prohibiting Mongol soldiers from stealing any property or requisitioning food. No armies of field workers could be assembled to resist such an advance. Some of the devoted Sung commanders committed suicide, and Bayan gave them solemn burial, with benefit of ritual. The war, in fact, was won.

When the banners of the Mongol advance reached the river of Lin-ngan, Bayan halted, spreading his encampment along the horizon facing the centuries-old ramparts. The Dowager Empress, realizing more clearly than her ministers and commanders that resistance was useless, sent a request to Bayan to come into her presence. Wisely, he excused himself, saying that he was ignorant of the proper ceremonial to be employed in approaching a presence of such distinction.

His only move to take possession was the despatch of an officer who advised that the imperial court ceremonial should be ended from that hour, and the Empress and the seven-year-old reigning monarch should make ready for a journey to the court of Kubilai the Khakhan.

In this way, in the third moon of the year 1276, the dynasty of the Sung made submission to the Mongol.

The Empress dismissed memories, and refused to heed the urging of those who could think of nothing but suicide or resistance. She ordered the child emperor to kneel and beat his head nine times against the floor.

"The Son of Heaven grants you life," she said. "It is fitting to render thanks to him."

When the imperial cortege started on the long journey to the north, it was followed by a long procession of families of the blood and scholars of the Academy. Bayan appointed four officers to enter Lin-ngan and to preserve under seal all libraries, registers, geographical maps, paintings, historical registers and edicts of the tribunals.

The heart of China still beat, and the treasures of Lin-ngan remained intact for Kubilai's edification. And rumor brought to Kubilai's ears the saying of the Dowager Empress who had named him, the grandson of a barbarian conqueror, the Son of Heaven.

When specimens of the treasures of Lin-ngan were arranged in his palace, he brought Jamui Khatun to see the delicate porcelains, the cloth-of-gold embroidery and the ivory and coral work. Jamui Khatun had received the dowager of the Sung kindly, and had arranged for the maintenance of a miniature court about the child who had been emperor. When she looked at the captured treasures, she wept. "The thought came to me," she explained to Kubilai, "that the Mongol empire will end like this one day."

The March of the Barbarians

The fall of the capital and the capture of the boy emperor did not end the resistance of the Sung. The millions of souls in the extreme south were incapable of realizing that the end of the dynasty had come. The war-wearied armies of the Mongols were forced to new campaigns, their losses replaced by contingents of prisoners released by Kubilai's command from chains. Fu-kien was invested, and finally the huge trading center of Canton.

Even after the loss of Canton, the Sung adherents carried on the war by sea. The Mongol generals were obliged to outfit a fleet and to invade the islands on which the Sung war junks were based. This conflict on the sea ceased after the sinking or capture of eight hundred junks. When the Sung admiral jumped into the sea, after drowning the members of his family, no leaders remained to carry on the struggle.

The two halves of the ancient Middle Kingdom were now united under the hand of a stranger. And the wars and revolutions of the next centuries did not break this unity. China had become a whole, by the conquest of Kubilai.

The City of the Khan

The Chinese called Kubilai *T'ien tsu*, the Son of Heaven. At the same time Kubilai was conqueror of the world, overlord of the Golden Horde and the Il-khans—did not Abaka, at the far ends of the post roads, keep an empty throne beside him, raised higher than his own, while he made public acknowledgment to his courtiers that he did nothing without the assent of Kubilai the Khakhan, for whom alone the empty throne was reserved? Kubilai was then fulfilling two destinies. As Mongol khakhan, he occupied China, no more than a quarter of the domain of the heir and successor to Genghis-Khan. As the Chinese emperor, the Son of Heaven, he could look upon the distant Russian steppes and the Persian plateau as no more than provinces.

Kubilai, apparently, was satisfied by the two roles he played. His appreciation of grandeur was growing with the homage paid him. He had no misgivings.

He felt confident that he could give China an administration not only of peace but of reform. And his ideas of reform were both radical and monumental. Actually that, because the dark son of Tului thought in terms of building. He wanted to create new things, not to repair the old.

Even while the campaign against the Sung was passing through its last achievement, Kubilai was remodeling the northern areas. When he rode along the imperial highways—and he had elephants now to carry his throne seat with its cloth-of-gold—he ordered lines of shade trees, sal trees, to be planted. He resumed work upon that vast public enterprise, the Grand Canal, that would carry shipping from Yen-king down to the plains watered by the Yang-tse. This canal was to be excavated, lined with stone—its edges to become stone-paved ways leading past orchards and markets, watered by side cuts and shaded by the inevitable trees.

It seemed to him possible to check the three great sorrows of China, plague, drought and famine. He ordered hospitals built in the different areas. And he revived the old idea of storing grain —the surplus of a year of good crops to be sealed in granaries against a year of drought; and the reserve of grain in an abundant district to be lent to a neighboring countryside where crops had failed—or prices had been raised too high.

Kubilai had the imagination to deal with the mass of agricultural workers—who would have become the slaves of a Mongol of two generations before. He, or his Chinese co-planners, doubled the allotment of land to each peasant and arranged for seed grain and plow animals to be distributed from the public supplies. To gather information as to agriculture, he despatched a bevy of officials to note down the state of the crops in the villages and the condition of the workers.

Naturally this investigation brought before Kubilai the problem of the poverty-ridden peasants. He granted relief on a large scale, distributing rice, millet, cloth and huts. After a little of this, he found it necessary to provide for the aged poor, for orphans, and the sick and crippled, by aid from officials. Within Yen-king itself, he signed a decree ordering 30,000 poor to be fed from the public kitchens. (It was against the traditions of the steppe dwellers to take from the strong, to aid the aged and incompetent.)

He heard appeals from the frontier districts. A family at the

Gobi's edge complained that the year before they had given food to a party of Mongol officers weather-bound there. And in this year the same Mongols had come by, demanding food. The peasants feared that if they gave it again, it would become a yearly exaction. Kubilai sustained the peasants and required his Mongols to repay them in damages.

His eager idealism was fed by the Chinese mandarins, who had vision to see farther into the future. And Kubilai found that to carry out his public works and his agricultural reforms, he needed larger bureaus of educated Chinese.

This machinery grew to massive proportions. Besides his chief ministers of the Left and Right, ten others were appointed. Under these came the Inspectors of Departments, with two Assessors of the Right and two of the Left. Then the State Reporters, and the Great Council that had been created at first to advise the new emperor. Beneath the Council, six tribunals administered the departments of War, of the Post, and others.

Outside this vast central administration, the twelve prefectures had their own councils and governors. Once Kubilai asked his mandarins why, when the peasants worked so constantly and were given so much aid by the State, they remained so poor.

"Because the State," the Chinese answered, "encouraging the workers in the soil, draws its chief wealth from them. The laborers themselves have little left, because the greater part of their earnings goes to pay overseers and taxes, together with the cost of collecting taxes."

Confronted with the world-old problem of farm relief, Kubilai altered his government as a potter moves wet clay under his fingers on the ever-turning wheel. He had the inflexible determination of his grandfather and a Mongol's instinctive knowledge of the earth, of animals and of men who worked at the mercy of weather. And, more than Genghis-Khan or Mangu, he was ready to accept criticism. His impetuous orders startled the methodical Chinese— who were urging him along the course he followed, but were not prepared for his amazing inclination to combat difficulties as if he were fighting an army of enemies.

The Chinese pointed out truthfully that the vast military machine he maintained absorbed the bulk of their tax receipts. Kubilai would not scale down his armaments, but he began to put—as Yeliu Ch'u-tsai had attempted to do under Ogadai—civil authorities on par with the military. Civil judges were given authority to overrule the darugashis. Chinese mandarins were appointed to head the administrative departments of Crime, Rites, Public Works and War. Also, the ancient and peculiar office of Censors was restored.

These Censors were, in modern phrasing, secretaries without portfolio. They were privileged to petition the Emperor when they believed they had discovered maladministration in the vast machinery of the State. They could even petition the Emperor against his own failings. On the other hand, if evils went unchecked, the Censors lost honor. At times in the past Chinese of high integrity in this office had committed suicide when they were unable to remedy what they believed to be wrong.

Kubilai had reached a rather brilliant solution of his dilemma. Without reducing his armed forces, he had made the Chinese objectors personally responsible for the well-being of the multitudes. He even agreed to put the immense classes of Mongol princes and army and palace officers under strict regulation. And to publish all legislation, so that any scholar could read the new laws.

For a while the Chinese civil authorities did not clash with the Mongol military. The new industrial activity kept the multitudes well fed, and universally occupied. The decade after the final conquest of China became, in fact, an era of prosperity. The omens, the astrologers on the tower reported, were favorable.

Under such circumstances Kubilai Sechen was the last man in the world to deny himself the family hobby of palace building. A new palace would be the most important of public works—it would be a necessary setting for the majesty of the new Mongol Son of Heaven. Kubilai made his plans with the diligence of a great love; it would be his gratification, his imperium within the Empire, his sanctuary from worries and the ideal spot for the ultimate in tree culture.

He laid down its outer wall of clay brick as early as 1271, and he christened it Tai-tu or the Great Court. Naturally, people called it Khanbaligh in Mongolian, the City of the Khan (the "Cambaluc" of the western visitors).

Because it was in fact a new city. Since Yen-king had been ruined, and neglected besides, by the Mongols of the Left Wing, Kubilai selected a site outside the old walls. The ramparts of Tai-tu enclosed a lake and an inner residence, policed by the Mongol Guard, the tower of the astrologers and barracks for the personal army of the Khakhan. Foreign merchants had their quarters outside, with the native Chinese—quarters administered by the Great Quieter and supplied with 20,000 prostitutes to serve the extraneous population. At least so Messer Marco Polo says, and he spent a decade of years in the court of Kubilai.

For by now Kubilai had enlisted the shrewdest of the foreigners to serve him. Bayan himself had spent his youth in Persia and Syria; the personal Guard of the Khakhan was recruited from Christian Alani whose homeland lay in the far Caucasus; two Germans served as chief huntsmen of the court, and the all-important Minister of Finance was a Persian, Ahmad by name.

Some years before, Kubilai had sent the elder Polos back to the west to bring out to his court missionaries and scientists from Rome. The Venetian merchants had been unable to do this, but they had reappeared with young Mark Paul.

Between the devout and feudal-minded Marco and the aging Kubilai a strong friendship grew. The young merchant, with no more imagination than a counting machine, amazed by the luxury he found around him, felt convinced that his greatest profit lay in serving Kubilai's person. Marco made notes of all he found unusual in his business trips around Cathay, and Kubilai liked to hear him relate his observations when he returned to Tai-tu. Marco, dizzied, tried to enter his glimpses of this dream world in a merchant's ledger. And Kubilai put him to work as financial adviser of the great Council, while Marco stored away his growing profits in the more precious jewels, sewn into the padding of a heavy Mongol coat. So if he lost the favor of the Khakhan, Messer Marco might at least hope to escape from Cathay with his wealth by wearing the great coat. But so methodically were the post roads policed that no foreigner could expect to leave the empire without Kubilai's permission. And Kubilai would not give the young Venetian permission to depart until the best years of a generation had passed. Meanwhile, Marco's stock of precious stones increased.

So he became by circumstance the medieval Boswell of a whimsical Johnson. He saw the inner palace of Tai-tu with admiring merchant's eyes:

"It is enclosed by a great square wall, each side a mile in length. In the middle of the second enclosure stands the Lord's great palace with a terraced walk around it by which people come and go. Its walls are plated with gold and silver, and adorned with figures of dragons, beasts and birds. On the lofty ceiling as well, you see nothing but gold and silver and painting. Outside, it is covered with vermilion varnish, shining like crystal.

"The hall of the palace is so vast that 6,000 persons can sit at table there."

Kubilai had a native Mongol's delight in feasting his people. But his banquet hall was done in the Chinese manner.

"Near the table of the great Kaan there is placed a buffet about three paces on each side, beautifully wrought with figures of animals, carved and gilded and holding a mighty vessel of pure gold from which wine, flavored with spices, is drawn."

Kubilai had improved on Ogadai's drinking fountain, but he contented himself with little wine and much mare's milk brought from the imperial herd of white mares—the milk that no one could drink who was not of the blood of Genghis-Khan.

"And you should know," the methodical Venetian adds, "that those who wait upon the great Kaan with his drink are some of the high lords. They have their mouths and nostrils covered with napkins of fine silk and gold so their breath may not taint the drink. And when the Kaan is about to drink, musical instruments begin to play. When he raises his cup all the lords and the others of the company drop on their knees and bow down to him, and then he drinks."

Outside the hall as many as 40,000 spectators might gather, to render similar obeisance to the name tablet of Kubilai in the courtyard. The splendor of the Son of Heaven was increasing.

"When all have eaten and the tables have been carried out, then come in troops of jugglers and players, making great mirth so that everyone is merry."

For Kubilai had a love of music and theatricals that was not satisfied by the dry artistry of the Sung court. The matter-of-fact Mongols expected to be entertained by the players, and out of this expectation grew the famous theaters of the Yüan dynasty.

Messer Marco observed, but did not appreciate, the parks and lakes outside the Khakhan's palace. He notes down faithfully the fruit trees, the herds of white stags and fallow deer, the gazelles and roebucks—even to the squirrels, and the fish in the artificial lake.

But a corner of this park Kubilai ordered planted with the high grass of the steppes. And to this corner of earth and grass he took his sons at times. "This," he said, "is your true heritage. From this you have come."

Kubilai could say that. Yet he had abandoned the life of the steppes for Tai-tu.

He had another sanctuary. When he wanted to be alone he would go there—and no one has explained the instinct that made him want it.

"About a bowshot to the north side of the palace," Marco relates, "there is a hill made by men's hands, about a hundred paces high and a mile around. This hill is overgrown with trees that never lose their foliage but remain ever green. And I swear to you that wherever a fine tree is found and the Emperor hears of it, he sends for it. Then it is transported hither with its roots and earth, and planted on this hill of his. No matter how big the tree may be, he gets it brought by his elephants.

"And he has also covered the hill with blue-green ore. Thus not only are the trees green but the earth also—hence it is called the Green Hill. And atop it is a dwelling just as green, inside and out. The great Kaan caused all this to be made for the comfort of his spirit."

Whatever impulse may have led Kubilai to build himself an artificial mountain wherein everything was green, he found re-

The Book of Kubilai Khan

laxation also in the family passion for hunting. Being afflicted like the others with gout, he devised for himself a way to hunt game without exertion.

From March to May he would set out with his noyans and the regiments of his huntsmen and beaters—dogs, leopards and hawks of various kinds—to the edge of the northern grasslands, where game preserves had been established. But he went out to hunt in a compartment on the backs of four elephants!

"He is carried," Marco relates, with appreciation, "upon four elephants in a fine room of timber plated inside with gold and lined outside with lions' skins. Beside him he keeps a dozen of his chosen gerfalcons. Several of his barons [Mongol noyans] ride by the elephants. And at times as they may be going along, and the Emperor in talk with these barons, one of them may cry out: 'Lord, look out—for cranes!'

"Instantly the Emperor commands the top of his chamber to be thrown open, and he selects whichever of his gerfalcons he chooses. Marking where the cranes fly, he casts the gerfalcon. Frequently the quarry is taken within his range of view, so he has the grandest sport as he sits or lies there within his traveling compartment. So I tell you that there is not another man in the world with such enjoyment of sport as he has."

Kubilai had another obsession, almost as strong. With him, the Mongol acquisitiveness took the form of collecting. He craved precious and gorgeous things—a ruby from Siam as large as a man's clasped hand, carved elephants' tusks, massive smooth jade from Khotan, and matched pearls as large as birds' eggs. These *objets d'art* he lodged in his private treasury within the Khan's palace, beside the harems of his women. For Kubilai not less than Ogadai had a healthy lust for shapely girls. The brides of his earlier years he quartered in miniature palace suites, giving each an entourage of her own. But he took pains to make certain that he would be able to select yearly a few additional girls for his own quarters.

"He has four wives that he keeps as his lawful consorts. Each of them has a court of her own, very grand and large—none of them having fewer than 300 handmaidens to serve them. With the boy pages and eunuchs, one of these ladies might have 10,000 persons waiting on her.

"When the Emperor desires the company of one of these consorts he goes sometimes to her apartments, and at times she comes to his own. He also has a great number of concubines, and I will tell you how he gets them found.

"You know there is a Tatar tribe called *Ungrat* [Konkurat—the Chestnut Horse—Jamui Khatun's tribe] who are noted for their beauty. Now every year a hundred of the most desirable girls of this tribe are sent to the court of the great Kaan, where they are given to the care of certain experienced old women.

"And these old ladies have the girls sleep with them to discover if they have sweet breath, without snoring, and are round and supple in all their limbs. Then a selected number of them are allowed to wait on the Emperor by turns. Six of the most beautiful of these damsels attend him for three days and nights, waiting on him when he is in his bedroom and watching while he is asleep, to obey any orders he may give. At the end of the three days another six take their place. So throughout all the year reliefs of these maidens wait upon him.

"The Emperor has twenty-two sons by these four wives of his . . . and also twenty-five other sons by his concubines. The great Kaan, their sire, is the wisest and most gifted man, the best to rule an empire that has been among the tribes of Tatars."

Kubilai's Paper Money

It was inevitable that Kubilai should finance his needs by printing currency. He knew of the Chinese experiments with bank notes, and in the first year of his reign—when his treasury needed filling—he printed an issue of bank notes as an emergency measure.

He had no Yeliu Ch'u-tsai to convince him of the danger of issuing paper like this. He needed huge sums for his public works and his farm projects, as well as for his enormous establishment at Tai-tu.

Meanwhile, instead of deriving yearly treasure from the west, he had to meet the drain of the frontier war with Kaidu. And Kubilai could not understand why he should lack a continuous supply of money when the Chinese printing presses were able to make it for him. Dreaming of enlarging the activities of his empire, it seemed to him that the money itself was no more than the means to the end he desired. The shrewd brain of his Minister of Finance, the Persian who had been raised to office by the favor of Jamui Khatun, devised a scheme to satisfy the Khakhan. And the Chinese advisers, wiser than the Persian Ahmad, made no objection. So long as taxes were kept down, they did not care what the Yüan dynasty might do with finances. Certainly they could visualize the end of it better than Kubilai.

Ahmad's plan was to issue bank notes payable in silver to the amount of only half their face value. (The unit of Chinese currency was the ounce of silver.)

These printed notes were known as *pao chao*—precious paper.

The price of this new paper currency was fixed by law. The bank notes had to be accepted at face value. So, while the government took its tax toll largely in silk, crops, furs and animals, it paid its expenses with paper. Marco Polo, coming in contact with such financing for the first time, was in ecstasies over the magical ease with which it functioned.

"I shall tell you," he relates—almost with emotion—"of the Mint which the Emperor hath in his city. Tell it how I may, you will never be convinced that it is actually true. The Emperor's Mint is so wrought that you would say he hath found the Philosopher's Stone, and you would be right.

"For he makes his money after this fashion. From the bark of a tree, the mulberry tree, the leaves of which feed the silkworms, the fine inner skin is taken. This is made into something like sheets of paper. These sheets, which are black, are cut up into different sizes—the largest being worth ten Venetian bezants [about ten *liang*, or ounces of silver]. All these pieces of paper are printed with as much care as if they were actually pure gold or silver. On every piece officials write their names; then the chief officer of the Kaan puts red vermilion on the State seal and stamps it upon the paper. The money is then authorized. And anyone forging it may be put to death.

"And the Kaan causes such a vast amount of this paper money—

which costs him nothing—to be made every year that it must equal the other treasures of the world.

"These pieces of paper he makes pass wherever his sovereignty extends, in all territories, and with them he makes all payments on his own account. Nobody, however great in rank, dares refuse them. And, indeed, the people take them readily because with them sales and purchases of goods can be transacted as well as with coins of gold or silver.

"More than that, merchants arriving from India or foreign lands, bringing with them gold, silver, precious stones and pearls, are forbidden to sell to anyone but the Emperor's treasurer. He has twelve expert appraisers to buy in this way, at liberal prices, with these pieces of paper. The merchants accept his price willingly, because they would not get so good a figure elsewhere—and they get it quickly. . . . It is true that these merchants bring in valuables to the amount of 400,000 bezants several times in the year. So the Kaan buys up such a quantity that his treasure grows beyond count, while the paper money he pays out costs him nothing!

"And more—at times throughout the year public proclamation is made that anyone having gold or silver or gems or pearls may take them to the Mint and get a handsome price. The owners are glad to do this, because they can find no one else to give so good a price—though those who choose may let it go unheeded. In time, in this way, most of the valuables of the empire come into the treasury of the Kaan.

"And if any baron hath need of gold or such in order to make plate or ornaments or the like, he goes in turn to the Mint and buys what he wishes, paying in this paper money. When any of the pieces of paper are spoiled—and they are not flimsy by any means —the owner carries them to the Mint and, by paying 3 per cent charges, gets new paper money for the old."

What Messer Marco does not mention is that the precious paper could only purchase bullion to half its nominal amount.

Without doubt, Kubilai paid no attention to the working of his financial scheme—or rather Ahmad's—so long as things could be bought with the notes. But the amount of precious metal outside the treasury grew less each year—while the government's expenditures kept on scaling up, with the costs of new wars. The issue of 1269 was 228,960 ounces of silver (and silver had a purchasing power in Asia, at that time, of many times its value today), while in 1290 it rose to the amazing figure of 50,002,500 ounces.

So while the treasure of the Khakhan grew to vast proportions, the country as a whole was flooded with increasing amounts of paper. Not any law of the Minister of Finance, or the death penalty, could maintain the value of paper which was issued each year in increasing amounts. Sellers, inevitably, asked more paper for goods. Kubilai's ministers had no trouble in finding a solution of this difficulty. The paper currency was devalued. The new price was set at one fifth the old, and financing went on as before.

The consequence of this inflation was not felt for a generation— not until after the death of the persuasive Kubilai. And he lived to a full old age. In his eighty years he was destined to see the final conquests, the grandeur and the beginning of the disintegration of the empire of the Golden Family.

Messer Marco's narrative of these years echoes a curious excitement. We feel that the man is exaggerating, and at times this is true. But in the main he is giving us a life portrait of Kubilai against the background of China. We may think it strange that he does not mention what appears to us today to be notable—the Great Wall, the drinking of tea, the bound feet of the secluded women. But the merchant of Venice has an appraiser's soul, and he is intoxicated with statistics of trade and ever-swelling profits. He thinks in terms of foreign exchange, in this Utopia of commerce. He mentions only casually the ghosts of the Gobi; he is much more concerned with the numbers of remounts kept by the great Khakhan at the post stations along the desert routes. In fact, Kubilai is the real adventurer, and Messer Marco his man of business.

Marco dismisses the other Mongols as gentlemen of leisure, although he is a little envious of their life of luxury and facilities for sport:

"They are brave men and hardened to war. They live like gentlemen, troubling themselves about nothing but hunting and looking after their falcons—unless it be war. . . . They have more children than other men because they have more wives."

Without being aware of it, Marco has drawn a portrait of the aristocrats of the steppes who have moved into an environment of civilization. Work is intolerable to their pride, and they occupy themselves with leisure, sport and women.

But the Venetian speaks reverently of the prosperous trade of Cathay; of cities in which the suburbs of a dozen gates are each one larger than the whole of Venice; of rivers which 200,000 cargo boats ascend and leave each year—more than the merchant fleets of all the European west; of the ships themselves, with four masts and crews of three hundred men, laden with tons of the coveted pepper and spice. Of the black stones that are burned within houses for fuel (coal), and the black moisture in the earth that gives birth to flame (petroleum), and the miraculous tissue (asbestos) that is cleaned and not consumed by flame.

Of Lin-ngan he says: "They have there so many merchants and such great riches, yielding a trade so important that no one can value it! Know for truth that the masters of the trades—who are the promoters—and their women never lay their hands to labor, but they lead a life so rich and splendid that you could call them kings."

At "Zaiton" (Chinchau) he marvels over the varieties of silks loaded along the docks. Raw silk, silk of damask, "Camocans," and brocades of gold, samites and the heavy silks of luxury—satins.

A thousand carts of these silks enter the City of the Khan each day, he calculates, on their way to the finishing factories. "And I tell you that for one ship laden with spice that voyages from India to Alexandria or a port of the Christian world, a hundred set out for Zaiton."

He swears—knowing that few people will believe him—that the ships of the great Khakhan import from Java spices still unknown in Europe, "black pepper, white walnuts, Java cubebs and cloves." And the merchant fleets coming from Ceylon bring cargoes of ginger, cotton and muslins of Hindu manufacture, as well as the pearls of the ocean and the diamonds of the Dekkan. A few of these, penetrating to the markets of Alexandria and Venice, were setting up new standards of luxury in the west.

Ironically, when this ardent economist returned at last to the Polo establishment in Venice, his story was disbelieved until he displayed the jewels stored in his traveling coat.

And Marco's words bear testimony to a new and vital change. The intermittent civil wars of the Golden Family interfered with the transcontinental land routes. It was becoming easier to go by sea, coasting down to Pahang and across to Ceylon and up the Persian Gulf, or to Egypt. Interocean traffic, which had been carried on only by a scattering of adventurous Arabs, was now in its birth throes. And it was moving from the civilized east toward the still-barbaric west.

Among the Chinese inventions that found their way westward by slow stages were two that the Mongols employed without making much of them. But these two innovations had a vital effect upon the future of the west.

Gunpowder and the Printing Press

Powder had been known to the Chinese for some time—both its fusive and explosive qualities. They made use of it as a military weapon in a left-handed way, setting off makeshift bombs that terrified by flame and smoke. These bombs, lowered over the wall of a Kin city in 1233, startled the Mongol besiegers, and it is certain that Subotai and other commanders studied the strange Firecasters for their own ends. In the European campaign of 1238–41, the Mongols used these flaming bombs in their attack on the Hungarian camp at the battle of the Sayo. And their armies of occupation made use of searing flame from powder—with its resulting smoke screen.

Moreover the Franciscan friar, Carpini, who visited Kuyuk's court mentions a flame-thrower used in a Mongol attack.

Now it cannot be coincidence that the Franciscan Berthold Schwarz is supposed to have invented gunpowder in the portion of eastern Europe in the years when these same Mongol armies were posted there. The other inventor of tradition, Friar Roger Bacon, is known by his own words to have talked with Friar

[*287*]

The March of the Barbarians

William of Rubruk, who visited the court of Mangu, a dozen years after the Mongols had made acquaintance with gunpowder. Both Carpini and Rubruk were keen observers of the military inventions of the Mongols.

Roger Bacon may have hit upon the formula of explosive powder before his meeting with Rubruk. But the fact remains that the Mongols were making active use of gunpowder at the same time.

They did not, however, invent any workable cannon. In the campaigns of Kubilai the siege engines used were of the mechanical type, casting stones. It remained for the Europeans to make the first destructive firearms, and to develop artillery in which gunpowder could annihilate human beings in numbers and destroy cities.

At the same time a gentler art was making its way westward. The Franciscans who flocked toward China after Messer Marco's journey ended became acquainted with the delicate painting of the Sung and the Yüan dynasties. And the memory of these paintings, with their movement and their realism, seems to have accompanied the friars homeward—because the first traces of this more human delineation appears within the walls of Assisi, the headquarters of the Franciscan order, early in the fourteenth century.

Long before then the Chinese had printed their classic texts with wood blocks. In Kubilai's day an edition of the Buddhist sacred texts was published—as well as the laws of his ministers, and the bank notes that so intrigued Messer Marco. Not long after that, the Chinese experimented with movable types of metal. The knowledge of printing certainly reached the court of the Il-khans. Here a fine paper was made in Samarkand of silk floss.

Whether the Mongols of the Golden Horde availed themselves of this invention, we do not know. But Chinese printed pages were circulating westward. The first crude attempts at using type and inking and paper in Europe bear resemblance to these Chinese pages, which were printed only on one side.

Messer Marco may have had a hand in this—because one Pamphilo Castaldi saw in Venice some books made from Chinese wood blocks brought back from the east by Marco Polo, while Gutenberg was still a boy. The later work of Faust and Gutenberg was no more than an improvement on the Chinese process.

Through the court of the Il-khans and Egypt knowledge of the eastern oil fields reached Europe—to be ignored for centuries. Arab seamen showed the Europeans a strange invention that guided their navigation in fogs and dark nights, replacing a sight of the stars: a magnetized needle floating in water in a bamboo case. It came originally from China, where the "south-pointing needle" had been more than a curiosity. It had served to guide caravans across the barren parts of the Gobi where landmarks did not exist.

With this embryo of the mariner's compass came specimens of fine blue porcelain and delicate bronze from Chinese workshops. Such discoveries challenged the ingenuity of western minds. It is hardly by mere chance that the age of inventions began in Europe when the early voyagers came back from Cathay.

Kubilai began to remove himself from active administration as his age advanced. He built himself a new hunting lodge in the prairies and allowed affairs at Tai-tu to take their course—being more desirous to prolong his own years. He had chosen his heads of administration with discernment, and had the good sense—rare among autocrats—to let able men run their departments without interference. "He loved his people," the Chinese chroniclers relate, "and he had only one grievous failing—he placed foreigners in supreme authority over the people."

Inevitably this led to conflict—especially as Kubilai's sons resented the influence of the foreign ministers. The conflict, however, burst around one individual. Ahmad, the adroit financier, had managed to make a fortune for himself not much smaller than the treasure of the Khakhan. And Kubilai could not, or would not, believe this. Leaders of the Chinese faction acted to right the wrong. Instead of committing suicide, they killed Ahmad. Messer Marco was a witness of the event.

"The Kaan held Ahmad in such esteem," Marco explains, "that he could do what he pleased. This person had power to dispense government offices and pass sentence on evildoers. When he wished to be rid of anyone, with or without just cause, he would go to the great Emperor and say, 'This one hath acted against your imperial dignity.' Then the Kaan would say, 'Do what you think to be right,' and thus Ahmad would have the person put to death. High rank did not safeguard anyone from him, because if a man were accused of crime by Ahmad, the accused could not bring testimony to prove his innocence. No one dared stand by him in opposition to Ahmad.

"More than that, if he desired a beautiful woman, he managed to get hold of her. If she were not a wife, he forced her to marry him; if she were married, he compelled her to submit to him. When he heard of a lovely girl of some father, his agents would go to the father, saying: 'What do you say? Give this daughter of yours to the Viceroy Ahmad, and he will make it possible for you to have a certain office for three years.'

"Then Ahmad would go to the Emperor, saying 'This man is a proper candidate for that office, which will presently be vacant.' And the Emperor would answer, 'Do what you think to be right.' And the father would be appointed to the district, and the girl would belong to Ahmad. In this way, through fear of the minister, most of the beautiful women were at his summons, either to be wives or mistresses. Not only that, he had twenty-five sons who conducted themselves in much the same manner.

"This Ahmad had collected a great treasure, because men who wanted office made him heavy presents. In such power did he continue to rule for twenty-two years."

The Chinese, wearied of bribing the minister and submitting to the dishonor of their women, decided to get rid of him while Kubilai was off hunting in his new game preserve at Chagan Nor, where he had begun to raise partridges. The conspiracy was led by a certain Cheng-y whose mother, wife and daughter—according to Marco Polo—had all been possessed by Ahmad. A commander of an army division, Wang Chu, supported Cheng-y, and there was a sorcerer in the plot which was aimed at an overthrow of the Mongol garrison in Tai-tu. At the signal of a lighted beacon the Chinese were to take to the streets—which were cleared every night after the curfew—and kill all bearded men. This meant the Moslems and foreigners, and probably the Mongols. The *putsch* began well and might have succeeded, if it had not been for the alertness of the commander of the Mongol guard, Kogatai.

"Wang Chu and Cheng-y entered the palace at night," Marco relates. Wang Chu sat down in the hall and ordered a number of lanterns to be lighted in front of him. Then he sent a messenger to Ahmad who lived in the Old City, to summon him to the hall. He pretended that Chingkim, the great Kaan's son, had returned unexpectedly. When Ahmad heard this message he was surprised, but he hurried toward the palace because he feared Chingkim.

"When he reached the gate he found Kogatai there, who was captain of the guard in the Khan's City.

" 'Where do you go, so late?' Kogatai asked.

" 'To Chingkim, who has just now arrived.'

" 'How could he arrive?' Kogatai asked. 'How could he get in secretly without my knowledge?'

"Because of this doubt he followed the minister in, with a detachment of soldiers. Now the idea of the Cathayans was that if they could get rid of Ahmad they could manage the rest of it well enough. As soon as Ahmad stepped into the palace hall he saw the lights of all those lanterns before him. And he bowed down hastily in front of Wang Chu, thinking him to be Chingkim. And Cheng-y, who was standing by ready with a sword, cut him on the head.

"Kogatai had stopped at the entrance. As soon as he saw this happen, he shouted 'Treachery!' Instantly he loosed an arrow from his bow, wounding Wang Chu. At the same time he shouted to his men to seize Cheng-y. Then he sent to proclaim through the city that anyone found in the streets would be killed without warning.

"The Cathayans knew then that Kogatai had an idea of the plot, and they no longer had their leaders, so they kept quiet in their houses. Kogatai at once sent riders to the Emperor with a clear report of the incident, and the Kaan sent back an order for him to investigate carefully and to do what he thought right about punishing the guilty.

"In the morning Kogatai examined the Cathayans and put a

number of them to death—those whom he found to be leaders in the conspiracy.

"After the great Kaan had come back to Cambaluc [the City] he was anxious to find out all he could about what had caused this. Then he learned about the iniquities of Ahmad and his sons. It was proved that he and seven of his sons—for they were not all bad —had forced innumerable women to become their wives, besides the ones they had ravished.

"The great Kaan then gave orders that the treasure Ahmad had gathered together in the Old City be transported to his own treasury in the New City. It was found to be enormous. When the great Kaan realized this, he ordered Ahmad's body to be dug up and thrown into the streets for the dogs to tear apart. Those of his sons who had been evil were flayed alive.

"Now when all this happened, Messer Marco was there on the spot."

Like all Messer Marco's narrative—dictated years later to a French writer when both of them were in a Genoese prison—this terse account of Ahmad's end is bald but true. Messer Marco makes no comment on the vigilance of the Mongol officer who stopped a state conspiracy in an hour—nor upon the amazing speed with which a report was written out, carried the distance of two days' ordinary march out of the City, answered by Kubilai and the answer brought back, all between the early hours of the night and morning.

Reading between the lines, we can realize how reluctant Kubilai was to interrupt his hunting, how he left a vitally important decision to his divisional commander, yet held an inquest of his own when at last he returned. And the laconic Venetian fails to tell us that he himself gave the evidence that enlightened Kubilai as to Ahmad's character.

Because the Chinese annals of that year yield this evidence: "The Emperor, returning to Shang-tu, desired Po-lo, Assessor of the Privy Council, to explain the motives that had led Wang Chu to commit this murder. Po-lo spoke boldly of the crimes by which Ahama [Ahmad] had oppressed people and which had made him detested through the Empire. The Emperor's eyes were opened, and he praised the conduct of Wang Chu. He complained that those who surrounded him had feared Ahama more than they had desired to serve the interest of the State."

Kaidu, Khakhan of the Steppes

Ahmad's crime, it seems, was not that he had debased the currency of the empire, but that he had made a private fortune almost as great as Kubilai's. He was besides convicted after his death on a morals charge by Messer Marco's testimony. Straightway the astrologers in their towers—for Kubilai by then had erected a second tower for the Moslem experts—predicted that Kubilai would find another Ahmad.

He did this—in spite of the objections of Chingkim and the Chinese, who foresaw only disaster in withdrawing silver from circulation and in opening vast channels of speculation. The man appointed by Kubilai was Sanga, a Buddhist who succeeded both Phags-pa and Ahmad.

The first attempt to raise the revenues of the empire to the vast amount of 15,000,000 ounces of silver yearly failed, by the opposition of Kubilai's sons and the mandarins. The advocate of this scheme was put to death.

Not that Kubilai was merely avaricious or stubborn. His scale of expenditures had to be met by growing revenues. It is doubtful if he could have reduced his expenditures even if he had been willing to do so. And Kubilai saw no reason to do so. He demanded only that the mass of the common people be protected against poverty, and that the necessary revenues be raised by the minister.

Accordingly, a new system was devised—a clever compromise that took into account Kubilai's heedless idealism, the opposition of the now conservative Mongol families of imperial blood, and the objection of the Chinese mandarins to a fluctuating currency.

A new coinage was to be established, a kind of token money. The various treasuries would be empowered to mint and distribute copper coins, worth little intrinsically but with a fixed nominal value. This coinage could be paid out in relief payments to the peasants impoverished by drought or locusts, and would also be used to pay foreign merchants. From the copper coinage it was calculated that the Emperor would derive a profit of seven parts in ten. With a portion of this profit, grain reserves could be bought up and sold cheaply to the masses.

Also the government was to appropriate all forges owned by the noble Mongol families. With these forges, arms were to be manufactured and sold at a profit.

And the government was to have a monopoly of the wine business. The tax on the sale of wine was increased.

To compensate the Mongol families, they were to be given the right to dispose of certain raw products of their herds—wool, hides, etc.—at a profit of two parts in ten.

This new scheme, like most compromises, accomplished little. A few years later the paper currency had to be devalued to a fifth. Kubilai's treasury was kept filled and emptied at the same time.

In compensation, the splendor of the ritual at the court of Tai-tu increased yearly. On the feast of his birthday, thousands of the Mongol and Chinese nobility appeared in robes of cloth-of-gold. The pearls and jewels on such robes sent Messer Marco into amazed calculation—he estimates that some of the costumes were worth ten thousand bezants. But at this birthday festival the nobles were expected to make gifts to the imperial treasury (ostensibly to the person of the Khakhan himself). And the amount of all gifts was carefully graduated by the imperial assessors.

The celebration of New Year's became a greater event. Then the imperial elephants were paraded in their housing, and the strings of camels. The assembled courtiers—who in a previous generation had been the chieftains and noyans of the tribes—made prostration before Kubilai at the cry, "Bow and adore!"

"They bow down," Messer Marco explains, "in adoration toward the Emperor as if he were a god. Then they go out to the splendid altar, which is decorated. They incense the altar with a gold censer, bowing to the tablet of vermilion with the name of the Kaan inscribed upon it."

Kubilai accepted such homage without protest. When one man is enveloped by the ritual of a deity, he must keep himself apart from his fellows. He is dependent upon those who carry out his orders, and they in turn can have no personal relationship to him.

The Book of Kubilai Khan

Not by any craving for ceremony but by the inevitable process of Chinese ritual, Kubilai was being changed from a victorious Mongol khakhan to a benevolent Son of Heaven.

It was impossible for him to free himself from the pressure of Chinese opinion. When he asked a commission of Chinese savants to explain the cause of earthquakes to him, he was answered in characteristic fashion:

"Earthquakes occur by five causes. First, when a monarch allows thievery to be protected. Second, when he takes too many women into his palace. Third, when he punishes too rigorously. Fourth, when the men about him intrigue against the public interest. Fifth, when he makes war thoughtlessly, without inquiring into its justice."

The change in Kubilai became more marked after the death of Chingkim and his first wife, Jamui Khatun. From the far south, Bayan dared to send him a message of warning. In the years of Kubilai's grandeur, the brilliant general reminded him, Kaidu had knit together the ancestral dominion of the Mongols in the steppes. Kaidu, in the beginning no more than a rebel, had become the *anda* of the descendants of the house of Chagatai. The elder Mongols had given him the title of khakhan.

In the eyes of the chieftains of mid-Asia, Kaidu was the true heir of the house of Genghis—Kubilai had become a monarch of China.

And twenty-one years after the outbreak of the civil war, Kaidu made his most dangerous attack upon north China, an attack that seemed destined to succeed. Bayan was down in the tropics with the armies of conquest, and Kubilai himself had not taken the field since the surrender of his brother. This time, the Mongols of the steppes had allies. The Manchu-Tatar tribes of the Amur region were armed and moving toward the site of Kara-korum, while Kaidu advanced eastward toward them from the Altai pastures. These two armies might invade the region within the Great Wall, or they might join forces at Kara-korum. Already they had taken possession of the valley of the graves of Genghis-Khan and the earlier khakhans—a circumstance that disturbed Kubilai greatly.

He sent couriers to recall Bayan with the army of the south, knowing that Bayan would need time to make the march north. Kubilai ordered him to intercept Kaidu if possible. He acted himself with a decision that startled Marco Polo and the multitude of courtiers—although first he took the opinion of his astrologers.

Gathering all armed men in Tai-tu, Kubilai started a forced march to the north, to strike the Manchu army before it could unite with Kaidu's. Rounding up his regiments of huntsmen and kinsmen, with the imperial Guard, Kubilai had himself transported at the head of this scratch army in his traveling compartment with the four-elephant motive power. He ordered the spearmen to ride behind the horsemen, and he lugged along a fire-p'ao, or bomb-thrower. For twenty marches he crossed his yearly hunting grounds, and he gained touch with the rebel army somewhere near the Liao river. He was with the advance, moving forward into the darkness, and when he found his elephants in the midst of the Manchu mounted units, he did not withdraw.

On their part, the rebel commanders suspected that Kubilai's unexpected appearance was a trap, and they did not attack. By the first daylight, Kubilai's main body had come up. And Kubilai himself attacked, ordering the saddledrums to sound through his lines. Chanting to this music—which may have been the customary Mongol method of signaling in the near-darkness—Kubilai's forces penetrated the rebel camp. The surprise of the attack was increased by the blast of the fire-p'ao, which dismayed the Manchus.

Kubilai gained a complete victory—an old man incapacitated by gout, lying on his couch above his elephants. The rebel commander was taken and executed promptly, before anyone could beg for mercy for him. The Manchus retreated to their forests. Not until Bayan arrived with the Emperor's field army did Kubilai retire from the campaign, to celebrate his victory in the pavilions of Shang-tu. Eventually Bayan was able to force Kaidu back to the western pasturelands, and Tai-tu was not again threatened by the rebels.

"And when the great Kaan had gained this battle," Messer Marco relates, "all the people and tribes of the north declared their loyalty to him."

The Book of Kubilai Khan

The New Frontiers

Actually, Kaidu was getting a firmer grip on the steppes. Bayan
had to be summoned again, to drive him off from the home pastures near Kara-korum. He had knit together the lands of the
house of Ogadai—his own—and the house of Chagatai. His empire
in the unsettled west served to separate Kubilai from the Russian
and Persian dominions. So it was not entirely by his own volition
that Kubilai was becoming an emperor of China alone.

Barred from the west, Kubilai set about extending his frontiers
in the other directions: up into the headwaters of the Yang-tse
beyond the gorges, through the barbarian tribes on the slopes of
the Tibet massif. One expedition penetrated as far as the Brahma-
putra River, as it felt its way toward India, only to be turned back
by the impenetrable mountain ranges. Kubilai then sent other
armies to go around the impregnable ranges, by the edge of the
southern sea. They brought back reports of dense jungles where the
heat of the Sky slew men—and of elephant-riding people and the
forgotten temples overgrown by this strange forest life.

And for the first time, Kubilai heard that his armies had been
defeated. They had penetrated to Yun-nan, where sickness and
bad water had taken toll of them, so that the next season they were
driven out. They had managed to overpower the elephant army of
Mien (Burma) with flaming arrows, but they could not survive in
such a tropical climate.

Kubilai could not understand this. Years before, he had forced
a way himself through the edge of Yun-nan. Merchants brought
him ivory from there, and rhinoceros horns and drugs from Tong-
king. He would not acknowledge that his armies could not bring
into submission such lands which obviously were not defended by
military forces as great as his own.

But the jungle folk of Tong-king were able to retire into their
forests and harass the Mongols with poisoned arrows. It was no
country for the maneuvering of horsemen. Kubilai, however, refused to believe that, and his stubbornness cost the lives of two
favored generals. New armies were mobilized for this tropical
front. Seventeen battles did not make the Mongols masters of the

country. In the end the lords of Tong-king saw wisdom in making formal submission and sending a statue of pure gold to Tai-tu.

There were silver mines in the hills, and gold and silver towers in Mien, and Kubilai ordered that the whole of the southern peninsula be brought into subjection—although the regiments of his Alani had been massacred when they were drowsy with wine and heat in a city known as the River Guard.

His Mongol generals struggled with the small brown folk who could not be penned in the open. Their fleets, sailing down from Canton, raided the Malaya coasts, and officers in disguise explored the distant island of Sumatra.

A Mongol fleet felt its way out to Java, to invade the shore of that almost unknown island—successfully at first, then to be checked and decimated in the forest. The casualty lists of these tropical campaigns grew to tens of thousands in each year.

The result of it was that Kubilai could call himself ruler of Koryu (Korea) and Tibet, Liao, Malaya, Sumatra, Yun-nan, Tong-king, Thai (Siam) and Pegu. But the Mongols were not able to colonize the tropics or to draw more than a slight tribute of treasure from them. At the same time the Mongol armies tended to become more and more drafted contingents of foreigners, commanded by both Chinese and Mongols.

A group of islands little-known then refused to render any allegiance to Kubilai. They were called the Place of the Sun's Rising—*Jih pen kuo* in Chinese (which we now pronounce as "Japan")—and "Nippon" in the native speech of the islanders. Korean merchants told Kubilai that the palaces of Nippon were plated with gold, while large rose-tinted pearls were drawn from the Nippon seas.

Envoys were sent from Tai-tu to the Japanese islands with a conciliatory message: "The Mongol power will be kind to you; it does not desire your submission, more than that you should become part of the great Mongol empire."

The feudal and courageous warriors of Nippon did not even receive the envoys of the Khakhan. After a lapse of years, Kubilai ordered the despatch of a small fleet which failed to subdue the outlying islands of Tsu-shima. Angered by this check and the heavy losses suffered, Kubilai prepared a greater armada after a lapse of years. In 1281 some 30,000 Mongols embarked in a great armada with twice as many Chinese and Koreans, and apparently took horses with them.

And they accomplished little more than the Spanish Armada against the English islands. Landing and beginning to fortify themselves in camps, they were beset by feudal bands of warriors, experts with bows and long swords and in no way terrified by the Mongol attack. Meanwhile a typhoon scattered the transport junks, sinking the greater part of them. For some days the Mongols fought their way along the shore, trying to construct new boats. The attacks of the Hojos' men exhausted them. The Japanese put to death the Mongols who surrendered, and kept as slaves the Cantonese and Koreans, whom they thought to be slaves of the Khakhan. There were few survivors.

Kubilai ordered another fleet to be mobilized, while he sent bonzes to serve as spies in the adventurous islands. And the seamen of the ships threw the bonzes into the ocean.

At the Korean ports there was silent rebellion against another expedition. Korean sailors deserted, captains of war vessels turned pirate and made their own fortunes along the coast; mandarins who were to supply the fleet held back the rice and money. Kubilai's generals warned him that there would be open rebellion if he persisted in his attempt to send the fleet to sea. At last even Kubilai realized the uselessness of another attempt, and yielded to advice.

The constant campaigns had exhausted the Mongol soldiery. Kubilai, at last, contented himself with the homage paid him in the foreign courts.

Yet the stress of the frontier wars had not affected the lands of China itself. The country, united under one unquestioned authority, prospered.

While Sanga wrestled with the ever-troublesome finances, Kubilai occupied himself with letters. He had managed to have a new set of astronomical tables published. Now he watched the progress of printing at the Imperial College, and ordered work to begin on the grand canal at the Shantung end.

The March of the Barbarians

While Bayan stayed at Kara-korum to hold off Kaidu's raids, Kubilai made a journey on his elephants down to inspect the massive tombs of the Sung dynasty, his forerunners.

When the Polos begged again for permission to return to the west, he released them from their long service, allowing them to serve as escort of honor to the Princess Kokachin. "A maiden of seventeen," Messer Marco says, with rare feeling for him, "a very beautiful and charming person."

Kubilai was sending her to Persia where the Il-khan Arghun had lost his first wife who came from the Chestnut Horse people, and so desired another to be sent him from the same stock. His envoys had approved the Lady Kokachin, and welcomed the three Polos who knew so much of the southern seas. Because the war with Kaidu made the land routes hazardous, with many detours, Kubilai routed them by sea. "At last," Marco explains, "he gave them all permission to depart from his presence." Kubilai urged Marco to give his greeting to the western powers and especially to the King of England, and then to return to Cathay.

They sailed in a ship of state down the coast to Sumatra, and on to the Indian Ocean.

In the first moon of the year of 1292 the dwellers in Tai-tu were troubled by an eclipse of the sun, a bad omen. The Chinese astrologers urged Kubilai to examine his conduct in those last months, to propitiate Heaven. And Bayan persuaded him to name Ching-kim's son his heir. In the tenth moon of the next year a comet crossed the sky, frightening the multitudes.

The Chinese astrologers warned Kubilai to examine how he had governed people. Instead, sick in his chambers in the inner court of Tai-tu, unable to visit the Green Hill or to ride forth on his elephants, Kubilai summoned Bayan back from the prairies to comfort him.

The great Mongol general rode north along the new roads, and dismounted within the gates of the new imperial city. Bayan, who could no longer win victories, found Kubilai lying helpless on a balcony where he could turn his head to see the pines of the Green Hill. And Bayan, standing on that balcony, saw wall upon wall, the barriers of civilized men, shutting in this aged monarch who had been born in the steppes.

Nothing of the steppes remained to Kubilai. Jamui Khatun, the young wife of the Chestnut Horse tribe, had become a plaque with written words upon it hanging in the temple of his ancestors; Chingkim, his son, who had had the strong spirit of the steppe dwellers, was a ghost, wandering in the spirit world. And Chingkim's son, with the bright face, was already, in his body and spirit, a Chinese emperor-to-be.

Kubilai died in the first moon of 1294, in the eightieth year of his age and the thirty-fifth of his reign.

His body did not remain in Tai-tu. It was carried back, by his command, to the valley beneath the Mountain of Power, where the headwaters of the Kerulan flow, and where the graves of his family surrounded that of Genghis-Khan.

To Marco Polo and the westerners he had been a glorious monarch, knowing and courageous—a friend to men of letters, who loved wealth for its own sake as well as the public good. The Chinese say of him that he was influenced by excessive superstition, by love of women and silver, by his ridiculous attachment to the lamas of Tibet. His failing was to sacrifice such multitudes in the war with Kaidu and in the Yun-nan and Japanese wars.

Before Kubilai conquered China, he had been conquered by the Chinese. The truth, perhaps, is more than that. Kubilai attempted to govern the Chinese as a Mongol. He kept a nomad's pride in leadership and personal magnificence. In fulfilling this personal ambition to become the master of the Chinese, he alienated himself from the old clan life and from the Mongol ties. At his death he was alone.

He may not have realized, or he may not have cared, that in uniting China he had brought the empire of the steppe dwellers to its end.

VIII

The Consequences

VIII

The Consequences

KUBILAI DIED WHEN Messer Marco Polo was voyaging homeward, in the last years of the thirteenth century. And at the end of this century a change took place as decisive as the fall of a curtain.

The Mongol empires were penned within their frontiers. The waves of migration out of northern Asia had ceased. For some two thousand years the steppe dwellers had marched south and west. Now this human tide had turned back. The invasion of civilized centers had come to an end.

In the far west the Seljuk Turks, driven into Asia Minor by the Mongols, were to move with increasing power into Europe, to become the Othman or Ottoman Turks of Constantinople. And in the far east, the Manchus, kinsmen of the Mongols, were to advance from their forests into the yellow-earth region of north China. But these were isolated currents, the length of the continent apart.

The year 1300 marks the full of the tide. Until then, the barbarian invasion had altered all civilizations in different ways. The greatest danger had been from the Mongol inroad. And this inroad had consequences both rapid and far-reaching.

First in China:

The Lament of the Khakhan for Shang-tu

Genghis-Khan had said that his descendants would eat dainty foods, and clothe their limbs in fine stuffs, and press lovely women in their arms, and forget to whom they owed such things. So it happened, in China.

Timur, the grandson of Kubilai who reigned after him, had some fine natural qualities. A drunkard and reveler in his youth, he lived a temperate life when he came to the Dragon throne. He passed a law that no one was to be put to death within the empire unless he himself had first passed on the sentence. Officers who allowed their soldiers to loot or damage the crops of the peasants were punished.

This quality of mercy was a far cry from the plan of the nomad conquest. In fact Kubilai's descendants were doing the opposite of the earlier Mongol method. Nor was there then any Yao Chow to warn Timur to adhere to military rule and not to surround himself with satellites. Timur had the strength of character to remove from office more than 18,000 mandarins who did not practice the virtues they preached, but he had no one to advise him.

Surrounded by rigid ranks of courtiers, bound to a court routine of ceremony and pageantry, he lost touch with his officers. His only recourse was to favor those who seemed most loyal. He had lost the energy and simplicity of the barbarians. Heir to thirteen dynasties, he was becoming a figurehead of empire, serving the memory of ancestors not his own. The Buddhists imposed on him in their desire for privileges.

"Like the sun and moon," they said, "the Khakhan and the Dalai Lama should hold ascendancy over the earth, not together but in succession."

To a khakhan like Mangu this would have been unthinkable. But Timur had ceased to be khakhan except in name; he had become a candidate for the title of Son of Heaven, the second of the Yüan dynasty.

Not that his days were without glory. The Mongols who loved music that excited them had improvised orchestras with stringed instruments and the wailing tribal pipes. Lightness and gaiety transformed the older Chinese harmony of the Confucian odes.

And, since the Mongols liked to be entertained—and not educated—by plays, the full-bodied drama of the Yüan dynasty humanized the roles of actors. There were even clowns. Romantic stories were written, to be read in court—forerunners of long Chinese novels.

The truce that prevailed within the frontiers made for enjoyment, and the Chinese, ever quick to seize on it, had their share of it. Timur and his successors were by no means "fools of the north." They were simply confined to palace routine.

So with the painter's art. The mysticism of the Sung artists did not vanish under the Yüan. A new realism appeared in it, producing some fine portraits of hermits and emperors, and scenes of nomad life full of movement and vitality. The galloping horse appeared under the painter's brush as in the vigorous art of the T'ang. And the Buddhist influence of mid-Asia crept into the painted figures.

In spite of their adaptability, the Mongols could never become Chinese by instinct, or make themselves accepted by the Chinese. Nor were they able to fit themselves into the Byzantine environment of Tai-tu.

Three things the Chinese never forgave them: the favoritism shown the lamas of Tibet; the foreigners in high office; the breakdown of the Mongol economy. For Timur's generals were Turks and Tangutis, his engineers were Uighurs and Syrians, his leading merchants Arabs and Italians.

The second collapse of the paper currency led to new devaluation and to heavier taxation. This in turn squeezed the multitudes —for the burden of taxation was passed on by the officials to the mass of the population. Food reserves failed, owing to misconduct of administrators. Famine was felt again in the south. Floods took their toll. Bands of refugees and rebels settled upon outlying districts like swarms of locusts.

Timur's successors lacked the energy of Kubilai and Timur. The imperial army was scattered in garrison at frontier points; the outlying steppes were hostile, and the descendants of the multitudinous branches of the Golden Family had become little more than pensioners of the Crown.

The risings spread through the agricultural south. The reigning khakhan gave command to defend the line of the Yang-tse, but the barrier of that river had already been crossed. In the south the leaders of the rebellion had been able to restore order. One of the leaders was a bonze, the son of a workingman. As usual, in China, the poverty-ridden peasantry rallied to the new command in expectation of loot, and it became apparent to the rebels that the Mongol yoke could be broken.

The khakhans, changing as intrigue went on within the palace area, did nothing to restore the Mongol prestige. One of them could organize a fête in honor of Buddha with musicians and danseuses—and build a pleasure barge on the palace lake in the shape of a dragon with moving head and tail—while the war of rebellion went on.

The Chinese rebels hit upon a slogan: "These barbarians are made by destiny to obey and not to command a civilized nation."

For the first time an armed Chinese citizenry was able to gain supremacy, from Yun-nan to Manchuria. For the first time they had no need to defend themselves against the nomads of the steppes.

When the Mongol officers of the last khakhan urged him to defend Tai-tu, Kubilai's city, he made his escape without battle into the prairies. On the way he composed a lament:

> *"Oh thou, my great city of Tai-tu!*
> *Oh thou, fresh summer palace of Shang-tu! Green prairie of Shang-tu*
> *where the lords my ancestors lived in happiness!*
>
> *My revered city of Tai-tu, built without flaw by the power of Kubilai.*
> *Place of never-satiating repose, sustaining the rigor of winter and*
> *the summer's heat.*
>
> *And you, my grandees and companions, faithful in all your works!*
> *My people, simple and well loved!*
> *All these, which were my all, have been snatched from me!"*

The new dynasty of China proper was called the Ming, or Bright. This was in 1370. Within a generation the armies of the Ming dynasty invaded the steppes, took Kara-korum, and defeated the Mongols decisively near Buyar Lake, driving the remnants of them across the Kerulan.

Seldom, even in Asia, has there been such a complete reversal of power. The Ming expeditionary forces, trained in Mongol tactics, cleared the desert frontier with a terrible blood bath and drove the survivors of the Mongol tribes far beyond the Gobi, where they pressed in turn upon the Chagatai and Oyrat groups—the first now converted to Islam.

What Genghis-Khan had dreaded now took place. Deprived of guidance, and with the frontiers of civilization closed to them, the surviving nomad tribes began to struggle for the life-giving pasturelands. They were reduced to living again on their herds, and in their felt tents.

The Chinese frontier armies now in possession of the area beyond the Great Wall and the oases around the Five Cities seized their opportunity to set tribe against tribe. For some two centuries this internecine struggle went on.

The effect of the Mongol conquest upon the China of the Ming dynasty has been disputed. Beyond doubt, it knit together the greater empire that endured until the twentieth century. It also increased vastly the contact of this new empire with southern and mid-Asia. The heavy trade of the Yüan period continued into the Ming.

Then, too, the Mongols had thrown open the courts and schools to nearly all languages and religions—especially to the Tibetan, and to Buddhism. The impact of the Persian, Turkish, Italian and Uighur adventurer-ministers quickened Chinese thought. And for a while the Ming emperors, succeeding to the throne of the kha-khans, claimed the sovereignty of a larger Asia.

Naturally, a strong reaction against foreigners and foreign thought set in. Tibetans were expelled, with the Franciscan missions. To some observers it seems as if the new China had been endowed with increased vitality by the invasion. Others hold that the shock of the Mongol conquest exhausted the Chinese spirit and caused its revival under the Ming to be cautious and weak—the vital China of the past becoming imitative, fearful of new invasion and particularly of the westerners who now began to arrive on its shores in ships.

As before, the life of its civilized centers tended to stagnate. The workers had no period of rest, the farmers had no escape from striving against time and weather, while beyond the Great Wall the nomads, regaining by degrees a freedom of life, grew stronger physically.

Once more the tribes of the Altai region and Lake Baikal became isolated. They were forced to live again on the meat and the milk of their animals, or to barter for food with Chinese traders. They thinned out in numbers because they were once more subject to the hardships of an unproductive earth. If they migrated, it was over small areas—up toward water, or down from the snow.

Some of their leaders, like Altan Khan, were able to raid within the Great Wall. But not to unite them again. They separated into wandering *aimaks*.

Their mild Buddhism became a barrier between them and the western clans who were now devout Moslems. But the growing lamaseries tended to enervate them. A Chinese, observing them, wrote to his government: "Buddhism forbids the shedding of blood and the doing of harm. That is why this belief should be fostered by all means among the nomads."

Meanwhile the discovery of the ocean routes took trade away from the caravan routes. The old trails through the Five Cities only served from town to town, and the encroaching sands of the Gobi began to cover the half-deserted crossroad cities.

The noyans, descendants of the Golden Family, repeated the name and tradition of Genghis-Khan. They had not forgotten the age of their conquests. Some of the Mongols visited, in the spring, the valley where the graves of the Golden Family had been, where the graves themselves had been lost to sight.

No longer did the nomads read the books of Kubilai's time. Their life continued without change.

In these centuries, outside of central Asia, firearms were being improved and printing presses perfected. Neither arquebuses nor books penetrated into the steppes. Nomad life was sufficient without them.

The steppe dweller, cherishing his freedom, thought himself to be above the city dweller who had no respite from work, and above the farmer who dared not leave his fields. He still found his contentment in riding over the grasslands on his shaggy pony, his falcon on his wrist. In his mind, an arquebus was a clumsy hunting contrivance, and a book—unreadable in any case—a useless thing.

Unnoticed by him, a change was taking place. The long supremacy of the horse archer had come to an end. The greater physical endurance of the nomad did not give him any advantage over a man with a gun. The mobility of his horse did not accomplish anything for him against cannon and blockhouses.

For the first time, and also forever, the balance of power was shifting from the barbarian to the civilized man.

What Happened in Persia

The ocean-going junk of the Polos was lost at sea more than once. It waited out the monsoon on strange coasts, being long delayed at Sumatra and Ceylon. Of the hundreds of souls on it, only eighteen survived the two years' voyage up to the head of the Persian Gulf. But the Polos lived, and the Princess Kokachin, who had become fond of them and who—the chronicles say—wept at parting from Messer Marco. The story of that voyage and of his guardianship of the princess of Cathay, Messer Marco never wrote. He delivered her to the court of the Il-khans, and because Arghun had died during the time of the voyage, Kokachin became the bride of the younger prince, Ghazan.

Ghazan, insignificant in person, became the force that separated the Persian dominion from the overlordship of China. Alone of the imperial family, he had refused to let paper money be circulated in the district he ruled. "The climate here," he said curtly, "is too damp for paper, and it cannot endure." And he burned the bank notes, with the printing presses that had been sent to him.

When Ghazan became the fourth Il-khan, he did not put the name of the Khakhan in Cathay on his coins. A man of keen intellect, he understood that the overlordship of the Golden Family had ceased and that the Mongol military power was a thing of the past. He exerted himself to bring about a truce between the empires and so far succeeded that his successor could write that the civil war had ceased.

The March of the Barbarians

Ghazan, converted to Islam, built an Islamic state, himself the autocrat. An amateur of science—a skilled botanist, chemist and steel worker—he had patience with neither military pageantry nor with experiments in government. His purpose was to live in peace and develop the caravan trade, although he led his great army on Hulagu's path, beyond Aleppo, down through Syria, to drive the Mamluks back toward Egypt.

In this march he found no trace of the Crusaders who had been driven out of their citadels on the coast of the Holy Land. "Instead of destroying," Rashid says of him, "he built up a civilization." And Rashid had reason to praise his lord—for Rashid ad-Din was now a minister of the Il-khan, laboring at Tabriz, with a staff of Chinese and Mongols, to write the long history of the family of Genghis-Khan, the work that he called the Collection of Chronicles, and from which portions have been translated to be quoted in this book.

Rashid, a Persian physician, could not have had access to the leaves of the Golden Book, the secret history of the family which had been entrusted to the sons of Genghis-Khan and kept in the Buddhist shrines of the east. But he did have with him as he worked the aged Pulad Chingsang, a Mongol who carried the genealogies of the imperial family in his head. And Ghazan himself knew more of the Mongol saga than anyone except Pulad.

Ghazan, while he built palaces and gardens in Tabriz, in the mountain region, was more concerned with putting in order a dominion that would last. He forbade armed conflict and prohibited his grandees from confiscating the goods of the peasants. "You like to pillage," he told them, "but what will you do when you have driven off the cattle and taken the crops of the men on the land? You will then come to me to be nourished—but you will have only punishment."

Impetuous and practical, Ghazan saw no gain in conquests; he learned from the failure of the Golden Family. And he set himself to make his lands fertile by irrigation works, taxing his people only in proportion to the fertility of their land. But in this vast endeavor he was ahead of his time. His death ended the protection of the land workers.

The Consequences

His successors followed the easier way of leaving administration to a wazir, while they occupied themselves with hunting. They patronized skilled painters. And these, learning much from the Chinese who had migrated there with the Mongols, began that new art of the Persian miniature—which is Chinese in its origin.

Musicians themselves, the Il-khans encouraged guitar players and singers, holding tournaments of music. Because they desired their gardens more splendid, they paid the tile-makers lavishly. Delicate and whimsical porcelains, fashioned in Ray, appeared on their tables. Their gaiety encouraged the poets.

Two generations more, and the successors of these Il-khans had become cup companions with a gift of observing and enjoying life. So it happened that when Tamerlane came down from the northern mountains, he found a Persia in which all trace of Hulagu had been lost, and Hafiz had been born.

Ironically, the domination of this southwest of Asia by the house of Hulagu had fostered the very elements which Hulagu had set out from Kara-korum to destroy—the religion of Islam, the agricultural Iranian peasant life and its old heritage of Persian civilization.

This heritage has been the enduring life of Persia. Joined to Greek artistry in the far distant past, it survived the inroads of Alexander's barbaric Macedonians, the Turks of mid-Asia, and the Mongols themselves. It survived the degeneracy of its own rulers and the blood bath of Tamerlane's coming. In the great age of Shah Abbas it flourished to the full. (Today, confined to Persia proper, and dominated by the military caste of the present Reza Shah, it still remains characteristic of the nation. The Persians as a whole are agriculturists and intellectuals. They still read Sa'adi and Hafiz in their desert gardens.)

What the Turks Did

The Mongol Il-khans had pushed the Seljuk Turks on, into Asia Minor, and had added to them various refugee Turkoman clans. So by Ghazan's day the Black Sea had become a rendezvous of the Turks. No longer curbed by the Crusaders' settlements or the great Mongol armies of invasion, these Turks proceeded to new frontiers, away from the Il-khans. This migration-attack passed around Constantinople, into the Balkan ranges, and, eventually, as far as the gates of Vienna.

But these Othman Turks, as they came to be called, did not lose the chief characteristics of their ancestors. In their minds, they were still horsemen ruling over subject peoples. Sulaiman the Magnificent was a pure Asiatic, reigning in Europe.

(Today, confined to Asia Minor again, they keep their military characteristics, their indifference to culture, and the traditions of their origin. Under Kemal Ataturk—Father of Turks—they restored emblems of their past, the Gray Wolf and the Blacksmith of the myths. This Blacksmith was in fact the figure of a tribal memory, of their escape from a slave life in the dawn of history by forging metals from the mountains that hemmed them in. And the minds of the older Turks identified this Blacksmith with Kemal Ataturk himself.*)

Like the Persians, the present-day Turks keep to the national life best suited to them.

Central Asia

As with Ghazan in Persia, the death of Kaidu in mid-Asia in 1301 had deprived the descendants of the Mongols of the personality that held them together. Kaidu had been the last of the house of Ogadai and the last of the true Mongols. He had held to the Yasa of Genghis-Khan. The chroniclers say that he was the cause of forty-one battles—he died in the saddle, after an unsuccessful attempt to recapture Kara-korum.

If he had lived a generation earlier, Kaidu might have knit the Golden Family together again. But in his time Kubilai had become

*The emblematic gray wolf and blacksmith have appeared on the new Turkish postage stamps and currency. The present writer was consulted, when he visited Istanbul in 1928, by Turkish scholars. They were trying to sketch, under the direction of Sami Bey of the ef-Kaf museum, a shield-of-arms for the new Turkish republic. They wanted to combine in this design, as I recall it, the gray wolf's head, a Fascist mace, the blacksmith and the head of Kemal Pasha as he was then called. A difficult problem for an artist.

On another visit, I discovered that the newspapers of Istanbul were publishing serially translations of my life of Genghis-Khan, and of Tamerlane—the latter under the heading, "Every Turk should read this life of Timur-i-lang." It was part of the government's endeavor to make the people conscious of their past in Asia.

too strongly intrenched in China, and the other branches had come under the counter-influence of Islamic and Persian culture. They no longer saw a purpose in the nomad empire.

Kaidu did maintain the rule of the house of Chagatai in the center of Asia. So that his people were known thereafter as the Chagatai Turks.

His successors reverted to the earlier clan life of raid and pillage. Being too weak to venture elsewhere, they raided their own cities, like Samarkand and Kashgar.

Kaidu's death, however, had one unexpected consequence in the outer world. He had been the last member of the family to try to carry out the dream of world conquest. With Kaidu in his grave, the feud between the house of Ogadai and the house of Tului died out. The Mongol khans no longer struggled for the now-visionary central power.

This in turn brought about a truce. Between the years 1301 and 1339 the civil wars in the Mongol-governed dominions died down to scattered forays.

The nomad peace again prevailed in Asia and eastern Europe. The caravan routes were still open. Mongol tolerance still made existence easy for the followers of various religions. And that meant for *all* the populations.

This world truce was the Indian summer of the Mongol rule. Ghazan, perhaps, inspired it more than any other man. He demanded it. When a distant cousin, Nogai, who wandered between the Krimea and the Balkans with his Byzantine princess and slaves, invited Ghazan to unite with him and to drive the powerful Golden Horde northward, Ghazan refused. Nogai offered to share the Volga region between them, after driving out the house of Juchi. Ghazan still refused.

"The law of Genghis-Khan," he reminded the aged Nogai, "forbids war within the Mongol nation."

If Ghazan had launched himself into this civil war, it might have had a decisive effect on the future of Russia, because it would have broken the Mongol yoke upon that captive people.

As it happened, the veteran Nogai was defeated by the Golden Horde in the steppes, and slain. Nogai was the last leader of what might be called the war element among the fourteenth-century Mongols. Ghazan, wiser than he, had seen clearly that the future of the Mongols lay in the caravan trade and an economy of peace.

After their defeat, Nogai's sons and followers withdrew to the steppes around the Krimea. There they kept to the ancestral way of living and allowed, for the time being, Venetian and Genoese merchants to use their ports. They became known as the Nogai, or Krim Tatars. They ruled over that strange peninsula, the refuge of exiles, for some four centuries.

The truce prevailing from 1301 to 1339 proved a happy circumstance for Europe rather than for the Mongol khans. By this time, after the return of Marco Polo, the papal council realized the tremendous significance of the east. Groups of missionaries were sent across Asia. In fact this interval is called the time of the missions. The westerners were looking toward the east with open eyes.

Also, merchants had the freedom of the east for nearly two generations. The trade in spices, paper, pearls and fine textiles grew larger. In 1325 we find one Savignano of Genoa commuting back and forth between China and the Krimea as both envoy and merchant. Goods out of Ceylon were shuttled through the Persian Gulf. Ships reached Java and Sumatra—that had been Kubilai's objectives. A certain Messer Francesco Pegolotti, acting for the great house of Bardi in Florence and for Edward of England, wrote out his Practice for Merchants in the years 1335–43. "You will travel a safe road," he testified, "from Tana [the port for slaves near the Krimea] to Cathay, even at night. Such is the evidence of merchants who have used it."

The truce, however, did not last. Before Messer Francesco had finished writing his advice to eastern salesmen, the caravan routes became not so safe. The clans of the Chagatai Turks were becoming zealous Moslems in mid-Asia. In 1339 they eradicated the Christian settlement in Almalyk. Perhaps this was the first religious persecution in any Mongol-dominated lands. Then, when the descendants of Kubilai were driven out of China in 1370, the Christian religion was proscribed and foreigners exiled.

The Mongol-built transcontinental roads began to fall into ruins, and the Chagatai clans began to drift away from these trade routes.

They had to retreat from the once-fertile valleys. During the long civil wars most of the men were kept in the saddle. The cultivation and irrigation of the dry valleys fell to the women and unfit men, who could not cope with the labor. So the clans—which still kept together—withdrew by degrees to the hills where natural grazing could be found and water in the streams coming down from the snow areas.

With this withdrawal, and the decline of the great caravan traffic, the cities of central Asia sank into stagnation. Desiccation went on unchecked, and at the Gobi's edge, towns were invaded by the encroaching sands. Particularly in the area of the Five Cities, where the rivers were drying up in their beds. Elsewhere caravan cities, half deserted, began to yield to ruins. This wasting heart of Asia became known as Turkestan, the Land of the Turks. And a voyager could write of it: "Hardly anything is to be seen now in Turkestan but ruins more or less complete. From far off, as you approach, you see a settlement that looks well built, surrounded by fertile fields. But near at hand you see that the houses are empty and the ground overgrown with grass. You do not find any people, because they are nomads who live elsewhere and do not practice agriculture."

It was out of such a Turkestan, with its ghost cities and memories, that Tamerlane emerged. He was a pure Turk, an adventurer, an individual soldier. By his attack, in the middle of the fourteenth century, he shattered the remnants of the Mongol-controlled trade routes and the hierarchy that had held Asia in fee for a century.

Tamerlane, the Individual Soldier (1336–1405)

This scion of the Barlas clan of Turks, the Iron Limper—Timur-i-lang—dreamed of the conquest of Asia. Not being a descendant of the house of Genghis-Khan, he could claim no hereditary right to dominion. Instead, he placed upon various thrones from Delhi to Angora puppet figures, the distant grandsons of the Mongol conqueror. He took for himself only the surname of Amir al Kadr, the Great Lord. He aspired to military conquest, and perhaps no man in the record of history, unless it be the spectacular Alexander of Macedon, achieved so much of his ambition in his lifetime.

He was in almost every respect the Napoleon of Asia. Insignificant in body, limping from a wound after his early years, he drove himself to achievement by irresistible will power. Like Napoleon, he assembled his first army from bands of disorganized men surrounded by stronger enemies. The Turkish clans of that day had not lost the military instincts of the Mongol era. Tamerlane had Napoleon's personal magnetism. He could influence masses, and his versatility was equal to any problem. He had, besides, Napoleon's memory for detail, and rare ability to take advantage of opportunities. Like Napoleon, he organized a striking force that proved to be irresistible.

Perhaps Tamerlane—when his campaigns are studied and understood—will be recognized as the most brilliant leader of cavalry known to history. His career was one spectacular *chevauchade*, an uninterrupted ride to victory, after the struggles of his first years with the Chagatai Turks—a ride of terror, leaving behind it the pyramids of skulls that were the milestones of his victories. No force, and no natural obstacles, could check his course. He was fortunate in that he lived while the Asiatic horsemen were still the most formidable striking force of warfare.

He had the secret of victory. For he marched without preconceived plan, his host of wild horsemen little drilled. Like Napoleon, he kept his army of perhaps a hundred thousand soldiers in constant readiness to maneuver.*

*Timur-i-lang usually formed his veteran Tatar cavalry on the right wing. It had its own advance and reserves, and Timur's most gifted amirs commanded it. It made a formidable striking force, answering to the shock battalions of today.

The Tatar strategist was apt to hold his left wing refused, and to make his attack with the powerful right wing, in a sweeping movement like the Mongol *tulughma*, the "standard sweep." When his right had broken through the opposing line, he would then allow the left to advance.

He himself commanded strong reserves in the rear of the center, which was intended to hold fast to its ground. In this way it acted as a pivot for the two wings. It was seldom in motion, until the end of a battle, after the smashing impact of his splendid cavalry.

Timur was capable of swinging his whole front, on the pivot of his reserves, to advance obliquely after the right wing—the left *following* the center. The formation of his army was a permanent one, each regiment knowing its position and duties.

At least once, in his terrible defeat of the Othman Turks at Angora, Timur disappeared from the sight of the enemy with his entire command—to reappear far behind

The Consequences

His secret, perhaps, was that he kept his forces in motion while he waited to profit by an enemy's mistake. He relied on his own ability, and, at his own chosen time, he was able to throw his stronger units against the weakness of an adversary. So Napoleon seems to have done.

Tamerlane's victories, like Napoleon's, were the achievements of his genius. As Napoleon enriched Paris with the souvenirs of his victories in other lands, Tamerlane rebuilt Samarkand from the spoils of India and Persia, until his magnificence became a legend in Europe.

There the similarity ceases. For Napoleon ended his career in St Helena, dazed by fatigue, endeavoring to write out a vindication of his wars. Tamerlane was never defeated, and he died on the march toward China, before he reached the outposts of the Ming beyond the Gobi. But the conquests of the Amir al Kadr endured no longer than those of *l'Empereur*. Both were military enterprises, dependent on the genius of one man.

When Tamerlane had subjugated the Chagatai khans, and over-ridden the remnants of the Il-khans, he found the Golden Horde in his way.

Apparently this *beau sabreur* of Samarkand desired simply to destroy the Golden Horde as a feat of arms. With his veteran Tatar regiments he marched north into the steppes to hunt the Horde in its own lair—a feat no one else had cared to attempt. It was a march in the grand army style. In all the splendor of their silks and gold-inlaid armor, his amirs crossed the Hunger Steppe, holding parade every evening when the sun was red over the high grass —riding past Tamerlane's pavilion, with cloaks tossing, spurring their horses, while the massive *kourroun* trumpets blared.

The Golden Horde had vanished into the north like a hunted wolf. The Tatars of Samarkand searched for traces of it, knowing

the enemy's lines, in possession of his camp and supplies. The Turkish army had become disorganized, first in trying to get in touch with Timur's forces, and then in marching back to its own base where he awaited it.

Timur availed himself of one expedient of Genghis-Khan's. His divisions attacked in much closer formation than the customary loose alignment of the time. So in actual contact he threw the weight of two men against one. And such divisions were more easily handled.

that in this wilderness the Horde was never so dangerous as when retreating. It was really very much like Napoleon's advance on Moscow with his grand army.

Half starving, the Tatars had to ride down wild game for food. They found the first trace of the elusive Mongols at a river where the ashes of a half-dozen fires still smoldered on the far bank. Not even shadows of men.

The half-pagan Horde and the Tatar cavalry met as wolves clash—both sides attacking. The khan of the Horde had waited until he was certain that hunger and hardship would not decimate the Tatars; then he had turned at bay. Tamerlane's mastery of maneuver was too much for the riders of the Horde, and they broke in headlong retreat, losing heavily as they fled.

Tamerlane kept on to Sarai, along the Volga. He found there the citadel of the descendants of Birkai, made pleasant by water channels running along terraces, turning huge water wheels. Courtyards of tiled walls and mosaic floors, carpeted gardens— ceramic furnaces, great shops of garment workers and jewelers had given the khans the luxury they required. Even to a new drink which became known later as coffee.

Tamerlane's troopers tore down and fired both the old Sarai and the new, leaving only skeleton ruins. The twin Sarais, the metropolis of the merchants and desert khans, were never rebuilt. Only recently have their ruins been explored.

Riding off with their haul of slaves and loot, Tamerlane's horsemen held one of their savage celebrations after victory. "This place on the Volga," his chronicler relates, "had been the residence of Juchi, the son of Genghis-Khan. And here Tamerlane had the satisfaction of mounting to sit on their throne. The most beautiful of the captive women of the serais were led before him and his lords who sat there cup in hand. The garments were stripped from the women, and their hair let down. All the army shared in this festivity which helped the soldiers forget the hardships of the war. For twenty-six days they amused themselves, as fate permitted them."

Tamerlane passed on with his regiments, a strange apparition in the steppes—an invincible soldier without a purpose. But in his sweep through the Ukraine he scattered the Mongol encampments to most of the points of the compass.

The lord of Samarkand saw nothing in the bare steppes to appeal to him. He did not return. Nor did the remnants of the Golden Horde gather again at Sarai. Instead, the steppe dwellers collected around Kazan in the north, and down at the Volga mouths where Astrakhan was building by the sturgeon fisheries, along the caravan track that had been a portion of the road of the Barbarians. And the Nogai Tatars remained unharmed in the Krimea.

Tamerlane's spectacular career had little in common with the methodical advance of Genghis-Khan from the steppes. The Iron Limper welcomed battle for its own sake—the cautious Mongol avoided risk, looking ahead to the ultimate gain. Tamerlane was much too civilized to desire a change in the city civilization that lay in his path. Ostensibly a Moslem, he cared too little for religion to arouse the fanaticism of the Islamites. Although his conquests enriched his soldiery with loot, he had no plan of government to offer them.

And the multitudes of Asia are intolerant of those who cannot protect them. The steppe dwellers who came under Tamerlane's sway reverted to their natural life, the cultivators of the soil returned to their quest for food.

Tamerlane was able to bequeath Samarkand to his children, and under Ulugh Beg, a grandson who was himself a skilled astronomer, a revival of culture took place during the period now called after Timur, the Timurid.

His magical career, however, had two vital consequences. His humiliating defeat of the Othman Turks within their hills did not postpone their advance into Europe and Constantinople for more than a half-century. But his march past the Black Sea destroyed the trading centers of the Venetians and Genoese, especially at Tana. He took those worthy slave merchants and sold them as slaves. This blow to their overland traffic helped to turn the two merchant republics toward the sea, at the end of the fourteenth century, to seek new markets.

In this march Tamerlane's host passed almost within sight of Moscow, without destroying that enterprising city. The Russian communities suffered little damage. Tamerlane gave them new hope by breaking the yoke of the Golden Horde. He did this for his own interest, and gained nothing tangible by it, but he prepared the way for the emancipation of Russia.

Babar, the Adventurer (1483–1530)

Not as yet, however, were the Russians able to break their chains. The khans of the Krim, of Kazan and Astrakhan still dominated that captive people. A century passed, and the power of the three khanates still endured.

But in the hills above Samarkand a man was making himself felt. He was Babar, the Tiger, who counted both Genghis-Khan and Tamerlane in his ancestry, a poor relation of the still-celebrated Chagatai khans, an adventurer by force of circumstances, who relished both melons and poetry. He had a gift for saving his life by running away, and then winning battles.

Taking his roost in the Afghan hills, he led his tribal following down into the plains of India. There, rather to his own surprise, he became the first of the great Moghuls (or Mongols) of India. Babar himself fell homesick for the melons and the cold winds of Samarkand; but he had in him a Mongol's ability to persevere and to rule. "My family," he admitted, "has always adhered to the law of Genghis-Khan."

(This conquest and long domination by the Chagatai Turkish strain intensified the hold of Islam, and of the descendants of the steppe dwellers, on the north of India—leaving a line of cleavage between Moslem and Hindu India. A line of cleavage so wide that it remains today the great problem of India.)

Ymago Mundi

To understand what happened now, it is necessary to look once more at Messer Marco, his father and his uncle. After their return to Venice in 1295—unrecognized and at first suspected after their long absence of twenty years—Messer Marco found himself, with his stock of jewels, again a merchant in a Christian world.

He did not find the change a happy one. He had been the envoy of the great Khan, with messages to the Pope and to the King of

The Consequences

England—now his fellow Venetians listened incredulously to his tales of Cathay. The voyage of his ocean-going junk, the Princess Kokachin—all that seemed to them to be the stuff of minstrels' tales. In truth, Messer Marco had been away from home too long. When he tried to adapt himself to life in Venice he found himself embroiled with women and burdened by taxes. Then he was drafted into a war.

It seemed that the distinguished Signory of Venice was then at war with the hated Genoese. Marco Polo was not only liable for war taxes, but he was pressed to serve—or he volunteered—in the Adriatic fleet. In this service, the Venetians being disastrously defeated by the Genoese admiral Doria at Curzola, Messer Marco found himself a prisoner in the internment camp at Genoa which was nothing less than a dungeon.

Here he was persuaded by the Genoese, who scented a profit in it, to dictate his story of Cathay and Kubilai Khan. Or he may have been urged by a fellow prisoner, one Rusticiano of Pisa, to do so. At all events he did dictate the story of those eventful years, and Rusticiano—who seems to have been a romantic space writer of the day, addicted to the style of Round Table legendry—added a good many flourishes of his own, being careful to whet the appetite of the public with such a preamble as this:

"Great princes, emperors and kings, dukes and marquesses, counts, knights and burgesses and people of varying degree who desire to gain knowledge of all the many races of Mankind and of the sundry regions of the Earth . . . ye shall find herein all kinds of wonders, and divers histories such as that of Persia and the Land of the Tartars and of Ind and many another country of which our Book doth speak, according to the description given by Messer Marco Polo, a wise and most knowing citizen of Venice, as he saw them with his own eyes!"

And the good Rusticiano ended with this flourish:

"For, as was said in the beginning of this Book, there never was a man, be he Christian or Saracen or Tartar or Heathen, who ever traveled over so much of the world as did that noble and illustrious citizen of the City of Venice, Messer Marco, the son of Messer Nicolo Polo."

The March of the Barbarians

In spite of such an excellent appeal both to the curiosity and the patriotism of the Venetians, the Polo opus did not find belief. He had been too long in Asia, and the book was not the stuff that traveler's dreams are made on. For he had failed to see the Tree of Life and the ramparts of Gog and Magog; he had almost no anecdotes to relate of the marvelous Prester John of Asia who dwelt in a palace built on golden sands, and he explained the Old Man of the Mountain as a real personage instead of the magician that popular fancy insisted he must be. In fact, because Messer Marco told the truth, he was not believed.

Not, that is, by the mass of people. Not despite the fact that he had brought back a Tatar servant, who it seems was not willing to leave his master. Because he insisted, perhaps too heedlessly, upon the enormous statistics of the empire of Kubilai Khan, his fellow citizens christened him Millions Marco. When he went out of his door at the Ca' Polo, in the little square by the canal, he was besieged by beggars demanding silver coins from his millions.

On his deathbed a worthy priest urged him to recant the fables he had told, and to confess that he lied. Then, for the first time in the record of his life, Messer Marco spoke a word for himself. He said he had not lied. "And more," he added, "I have told but half of the whole truth."

By his will he left one hundred lira and freedom from bondage to his Tatar servant Peter. And thereafter, in the Venetian puppet shows, he appeared in mockery—a comic fellow named Il Milione.

There was adequate cause for disbelief in the narrative of the conscientious Venetian. As late as 1300, western Europe looked upon the outer world with the eyes of superstition. From Biblical tradition, and from the words of the early Fathers, from Greco-Roman philosophers, those who thought at all about the farther spaces of the earth were convinced that their world was round, and flat, and immovable. The sun and planets revolved about it in fixed cycles, and it was encircled by vast ocean.

Beneath this terrestrial orb ran the river Styx, and burned the fires of hell; above it extended the unknown geography of heaven, about which there was much speculation. More precisely, the Garden of Eden was supposed to be on a height somewhere in northwest Asia. Out of this region ran the rivers of Paradise. To the north and south stretched zones of uninhabitable cold and heat, the antipodes.

Knowing souls, it is true, had begun to doubt that the Elysian fields could be found in the first strata beneath the earth's surface —or that the races of Amazons and Pygmies (who battled for their lives against the cranes of the upper air) really existed as the early Greek imagists had supposed. Herodotus remained their authority upon the marvels of Asia, and Alexander's conquest of that vast unknown terrain had been magnified into tales of treasure found and magicians combatted that would have delighted the good Rusticiano who had written much of Merlin.

So western thought still clung to its belief in the Sea of Darkness, the monsters that inhabited the deeps, the dog-headed people and that other race of the giant feet which were used as parasols against the heat of the midday sun. Prester John, the land of the Magi, were—in the popular conception—the main points of interest in the farther east, where perhaps Eden might not, after all, be visible to mortal eyes. Jerusalem remained the center of the habitable earth. Was there not a knob of marble in the Holy Sepulcher that marked the exact center of the round world?

In general, the accurate summing up of Strabo and the scientific calculations of Eratosthenes were little heeded. The known facts of the campaigns of the Romans into eastern Parthia and the Caucasus were ignored, and the carefully devised geography of Ptolemy of Alexandria attracted little attention in the west. The much more accurate map of Idrisi, etched in Sicily, seemed to be unknown; while the knowledge of the Arab scientists had been discounted at first because the Arabs were pagans and worse, followers of that arch-fiend "Mahound." So the geography of fable still prevailed over the recording of science.

But opinion was changing, in the lifetime of Messer Marco. The remnants of the Crusaders drifting back from the east brought with them a much more accurate picture of the nearer half of that unknown expanse, together with an appreciation of the Arab cosmographers. Roger Bacon had discussed the real shape of the eastern earth with Fra Rubruquis. One Marinus Sanutus drew an outline of the near east in discussing ways and means to recapture Jerusalem. The Venetian and Genoese merchants, thriving on the Kipchak slave trade of the Black Sea and the diamonds of Golconda—the spices of the far Indies—made clear the course of the trade routes into the farther east. In spite of the disbelief in Messer Marco's detailed account of China and its seas, the more enterprising spirits realized that Cathay must exist where the Garden of Eden had vanished without trace. The grand "Kaan" did rule where Prester John seemed not to be. The Fortunate Isles might be the spice-giving islands. There were, indeed, incredible things beyond Thule.

This growing awareness of the richness of reality came at a time when the spirit of venture was stirring in the west. The furs of "Muscovy"—for Moscow had become known as a trading point—were priceless ermines and sables, worn by the Tatar khans of the Golden Horde. The medicinal rhubarb and ginger, once cultivated by Yeliu Ch'u-tsai, healed many ills of the meat-gorging western-ers. The Chinese silks that Birkai had liked—when he was bartering for jewels with those jewel experts, the elder Polos—were becoming the fashion among the ladies of the small western courts. The spices of Java helped to make dishes of too ripe meat palatable. It was all real, and in time the keen, bargaining western minds perceived that more profit lay in reality than in fable.

And those careful mercantile minds did not arrive at the conviction of reality with any flash of enlightenment. They were drowsy with long stagnation and the nepenthe of superstition. But the small bearded presence of the Nestorian Bar Sauma in Rome did dispel the illusion of Prester John; letters of the khakhans and Il-khans did make clear that the Mongols ruled over actual dominions both vast and wealthy.

Never before had there been such a contrast between the resources and culture of the east and the poverty and superstition of the west. And never again would the contrast be so great. It was Messer Marco's misfortune that he tried to make clear the one to the other. So he suffered the common fate of prophets who returned home.

The enterprising westerners were beginning to restore the balance. And they were enabled to do so because the Mongols had perfected the caravan and post roads from the edge of Europe all the way through to Tabriz, Delhi, Samarkand, Almalyk and across that blind spot of the Gobi to "Cambaluc" and "Zaiton." Their post stations, with the equivalent of hotels and remount herds, had made travel speedier than along the trails of Europe. No bandits infested the *yam* of the Mongols, especially in the opening of the fourteenth century, when the Ghazan-inspired truce prevailed, with its profound sense of security.

In this linking of west to east during the century from 1275, when Messer Marco arrived at the court of Kubilai, to 1375, when communication was broken down, was born the modern west. The natural inventiveness of western minds was fed by contact with the actual achievements of the east. The ever-progressing German brains were studying the explosive qualities of black salt-peter and sulphur and charcoal—together with the possibilities of ink applied to a wooden slab and pressed against a sheet of the new paper. The first printed books were a-making. And at the same time the first cannon were beginning to roar against stone walls. While the Franciscans of Assisi painted Chinese-inspired frescoes on their refectory walls.

This awakening, or Renaissance, of the west, drew its stimulus from the east.

Messer Marco had not written his last testament "In the Name of the Eternal God Amen" when Europeans awoke to the full realities of the unexplored east. For a few keen minds had begun to compare the growing mass of evidence that markets existed in the east and could be reached. Marinus Sanutus was writing his Secrets for the Faithful of the Lord. The good Franciscan, Odoric of Pordenone, was being carried eastward on the stages of the Mongol roads—although he was detoured around the Afghan country where Chagatai clans were raiding the northern plain of India. And Odoric was writing of "Kinsai" that had been Lin-ngan: "It is the grandest city of the world, with its two lakes and canals like Venice . . . and it is a wonder to me that within it so many races could exist in peace, administered by one power."

The March of the Barbarians

This same Odoric found a Christian archbishop in Tai-tu. For the papal advisers at long last had realized the urgency of sending missions into the east—missions for which Mangu and Kubilai, Bar Sauma and Marco Polo and other envoys of the Mongol courts had asked in vain for nearly fifty years. Friars Minor were making the eastern journey in groups, establishing bishoprics from the Krimea to "Zaiton," building cathedrals and monasteries—one of them near the palace of the great Khakhan. John of Montecorvino was to spend his lifetime there, and to earn the respect of the last Mongols.

This was the half-century of truce, the Indian summer of the nomad peace (1300–50).

And now the Europeans were beginning to realize the shape and extent of the world. Pegolotti's book followed Messer Marco's, and the work of Marinus. When this truce ended, and the Venetians and Genoese were driven from the Black Sea region, the Catalan map was drawn giving the first crude semblance of the real world. Then, by aid of this new knowledge, the Portuguese and Spanish navigators began to feel their way down the African coast, to find a sea route to Asia. They found that Africa stretched interminably to the south.

Messer Paolo Toscanelli of Florence drew up a plan, showing how he believed the shore of Asia could be reached by sailing west across the Atlantic. He had read Messer Marco's repetition of the Mongol tale about Japan—that plates of gold covered its palaces, and gold and pearls abounded in this fabulous isle. "That island," Toscanelli wrote, "could certainly be reached."

An ambitious man of Genoa, Columbus, also read Messer Marco's book. And he sailed, in the service of the King of Spain, to find these islands with a letter for the Khakhan of Cathay. When he returned from the land he had discovered, he wrote that they lay favorably for commerce with "the great Khan." He never knew that he had made his landfall on the North American continent. He had reached a new world and thought it to be the outlying islands of Asia.

The Consequences

But other ships found their way around Africa. Miniature, clumsy caravels, armed with cannon. Gunpowder, loaded into these cannon, had become an improved weapon of civilization. These ships came seeking the spices, the precious things of Asia. Yet they came armed.

The era of sea commerce had begun. And with it the invasion of Asia by Europe.

While the exploration of the North American coasts went on, with the voyages of the Portuguese to India, a third movement was taking place as vital as these. Unheeded by the western Europeans, it progressed slowly into the east.

Russia was freeing itself from the Tatar dominion and advancing toward the steppes. The Russians were moving into the forest of Sibir toward the homeland of the nomads, to repeople northern Asia.

IX

... *Of All the Russias*

. . . *Of All the Russias*

SINCE 1238 the Russian peoples had been kept under the Mongol yoke. They were shut off from the west for two centuries and a half.

When they broke free from the yoke, something unexpected occurred. The new Russia faced east instead of west. And it rebuilt, to its profit, the empire of Genghis-Khan.

To realize how this happened it is necessary to look at Russia as it was under Batu and Birkai, in the mid-thirteenth century.

The Mongol Yoke

It was a strange rule—strange at least to the western spirit. Russia had become the *ulus* of the house of Batu. Its lands pastured the nomad's herds. Its people worked, in the settlements, for the enrichment of its nomad masters.

The free, democratic land that had been taking shape before the invasion of Batu and Subotai disappeared forever: the land of the stalwart *drujina*, the Variag lords, the independent councils of freemen, and the turbulent, bickering cities. The elder civilization of Kiev, the heart of that Russia, had ceased to be.

Kiev had become a city of ruins. Fra Carpini, passing that way, counted no more than two hundred families hiding in the ruins. And he found the steppes beyond whitened by human bones. "The bravest of our men," a Russian chronicler laments, "had fallen, and the survivors wandered about like strangers. Mothers wept for their children, lost under the hoofs of the Tatar horses. The living envied the quiet of the dead."*

Farther north, the fertile Suzdal region, with its newer settlements, recovered when the storm had passed. But here men turned to the soil rather than to arms. It was necessary to glean from the earth the food that sustained their lives. So they began to collect in hamlets by the streams, avoiding at first the sites of the burned cities—where the walls had been destroyed by the Mongols, who forbade the Russians to fortify their towns.

Of these survivors the methodical Mongols of Batu's day made a census. They counted the living heads of men and laid a tax upon every head. Poor or rich were obliged to pay the tax—the *vyhod*—in furs, hides or coins. Batu and Birkai minted coins in the name of the far-distant Khakhan, to make payment easier. But the burden lay heavy upon the poorer sort, the *smerdis*.

If a man failed to pay the *vyhod*, his children were seized to be sold as slaves. And he might be taken himself. To escape this payment to the Squeezers, many of the free land workers bound themselves as serfs to richer men. They became *chlops*, animals. The wealthier landowner paid the tax for his new serf or animal.

Being sturdy souls, the unfortunate peasants often revolted against the Mongol taxgatherers. Then the dreaded horsemen of the Horde would appear, to drive off the cattle and carts of the rebels, and then to lay waste the villages with fire and sword.

The Russian princes were obliged, on such occasions, to intercede for their liegemen. They went before the Khan to ask mercy for their people. And in time they were forced to beat down rebellion among their *smerdis*, to escape an inroad by the Mongol horsemen.

Meanwhile both princes and common men were becoming

---

*Kiev never was rebuilt, in its old splendor. When this writer visited it, in July 1939, Soviet archeologists were excavating the site of the Church of the Tithe where the Russians had made their last stand against Batu's attack. They said that a mass grave had been uncovered, in which the skeletons bore evidence of a massacre by weapons—the skulls were split and crushed. This grave dated from the sack of the city by Batu. The Soviet excavators, however, denied that the "Tatars" had broken open the tombs of that time, to search for loot in the graves, as tradition has so often related.

accustomed to the absolute authority of a distant tsar, like Birkai, against which rebellion meant death. There was no loosening of this authority.

The Mongols called these Russian princes the servants of the Khan. When Russian nobles appeared at the encampment of the Khan, they had to kneel and bow their heads to the carpet at his feet.

But they were no longer sent to Kara-korum with their petitions. Birkai heard their petitions and accepted their gifts. Russia had become his *ulus*—no longer an appanage of the east. The *yarligh*, or Khan's command, that he gave to the petitioners was signed by his own name.

In all this lay the germ of a hardy agricultural people, dependent upon the wealthy families of its princes, and by slow degrees becoming accustomed to utter obedience to the command of a never-visible khan whom they called tsar.

This concept of servitude was not exactly strange to the Russian mind. Before then, it had known the majesty of the distant Byzantine emperors—emperors sublimated above ordinary mortals.

Contact with the steppe dwellers of the Horde changed nothing in the Russian spirit. For one thing, the conquerors remained apart in the eastern grasslands. They did not indulge in trade, nor did they interfere with the *smerdis*' routine of life. At times they carried off quotas of Russian women, but these were taken into the steppes, where they remained—their children went into the Mongol stock, not the Russian. Not until a generation after Birkai did intermarriage begin between the wealthier families of the Horde and the *boyarin* nobility. And such marriages were rare.

True, the Russians of the better sort sequestered their women. But this was a custom derived from the Byzantines, who guarded their women closely. The women of the Golden Horde went about freely, unveiled, in these first generations.

Nor did the Mongol yoke make life in the Russian villages brutish. The nomads seldom appeared, and never remained, in the villages.

The superstitions of the pagans fitted well with the vagrant mysticism of the Russian spirit. There was no clash of cultures

The March of the Barbarians

between conquerors and conquered. The Mongol who feared the Everlasting Sky had much in common with the Slav who dreaded an angry God; the tent dweller who took care not to offend the master spirits by touching fire to iron or upsetting a vessel of water could understand the *choutar* dweller who sprinkled salt where the horses were tethered, to keep out the stable goblin. They both walked warily where the spirit of the woods followed.

The yoke of the Mongol was, in effect, a business measure. It called for a census—a tremendous task, and a novelty to the Russians—for an increase in coined money, the use of the Asiatic counting machine (which, by the way, the Soviet workers still use in the most modern offices). Mongol words that have crept into the Russian language more often than not bear on trade: *bazar* (market), *tovar* (goods), *puto* (copper money), *denga* (silver).

But, beyond that, it laid the shadow of terror on the Russian land. Peace could only be had by obedience to the unseen horsemen. The Russians were cut off for more than two centuries from contact with the vigorous feudal growth of the west. They passed from vassalage to despotism without being aware of freedom. Batu and Birkai and their successors of the Golden Horde sequestered Russia and forced it to face east instead of west.

The Russians had one refuge during the centuries of isolation: the monasteries and churches. After the first attack, the superstitious tolerance of the steppe dwellers spared all religious property. The gold altar vessels and holy pictures went unmolested.

The nomads, with their shrewd political sense, realized that the clergy would serve to control and influence the Russian masses. They exempted the churches from the *vyhod*, and the "white ones" and the "black," as they called the priests and monks, from harm.

This had a natural effect, unforeseen at first. A *smerdi* who could not pay the tax could take refuge in a monastery. A wealthy *boyar* could bestow his goods upon a church, and there live a life of contemplation untroubled by the distress outside.

"For its sins," the clergy preached, "God hath brought this punishment upon the Russian people." They spoke of the Mongol yoke as the *Bozhi batog*, the cudgel of God.

So ardent souls devoted their lives to penance, within the cloisters, to expiate the sin. There, where the figures of the Apostles stood in mosaic and gilt upon the walls, they could cling to a hope that did not exist in the grim land outside. The population within walls grew apace; the power of the Church went unchallenged. The bearded clergy became arbiters of disputes. The lands of the monasteries extended farther beyond the walls. And the Metropolitan, who had had little influence in the turbulent twelfth century, spoke with more authority than any great prince. His voice became that of the Russian land.

Another peculiarity of the Mongols aided the Church. The khans demanded that the Russian princes keep peace among themselves. Civil wars could only be waged by permission of the khan. The Mongols had the right to commandeer one man in ten to serve in their own campaigns, but they seldom called upon the Russians for this levy. The churches were freed from the depredations of internal war. In return, the clergy prayed for its new master. Birkai Khan even ordered a bishopric to be established in his city of Sarai that was a-building.

In this way the Russian Church gained a power, under the Mongols, that it did not relinquish until the twentieth century.

The Sun of Russia

One corner of the Russian land escaped ravage by the Horde. Up in the north where the birch and fir forests meet the first lakes of the arctic *taiga*, Novgorod the Great survived. At first the Mongol armies had been too preoccupied to venture into the damp forest region. But Batu Khan had not forgotten that within the forest by the Baltic's edge this rich republic of merchants endured.

It remained sturdily independent, with its Slavic culture. But not without an ordeal by battle. At the first coming of the Mongols, the northern neighbors of Novgorod—the Scandinavians—and the Livonian and Teutonic Knights took up arms. Not, as the chronicler of Novgorod relates sadly, to aid the free city, but to despoil it. The Finns as well, retreating before the Mongol advance, raided the lands of the republic.

The March of the Barbarians

A young Russian prince, Alexander, became the hero of the north when he fought off these Christian invaders at the line of the river Neva. His people, exulting, christened him Alexander Nevski.

But the tale of his exploits along the Baltic came to the ears of Batu, who remembered that Novgorod alone of the Russian city-states had not made submission. He recalled too that Yaroslav, great prince of Vladimir and Alexander's father, had yielded to the Mongols and had made the journey to Kara-korum, dying in the desert on his return.

And Batu sent this reminder to Alexander Nevski: "The Sky hath subjected uncounted peoples to me. Why do you alone refuse to recognize my power? If it is your wish to keep your land, come to me yourself, that you may see my glory."

Alexander had the alternative to resist like the other princes—to become a heroic figure in the traditional manner through the sacrifice of his people—or to go to abase himself at the feet of the Khan. The burghers of Novgorod were determined to defend their wooden walls against the pagans. Alexander knew the folly of that, and made his decision to submit to the Mongols.

The *posadnik* who announced this decision in the streets was killed by the Novgorodians, and Alexander's son cried out against a father "who put the chain of slavery upon freemen." It needed iron restraint for Alexander to imprison his son and execute the leaders of his people in revolt. Then Alexander went to play a coward's part and beat his forehead against the carpet before Batu's slippers.

"I see well," that sagacious Mongol remarked, "that you are superior to the other princes of this land."

He despatched Alexander and his brother to the great Khan Kuyuk, who announced that the leader of Novgorod would be the "oldest" of the Russian princes, and would reign under Batu, from the ruins of Kiev to the northern ice.

But again the citizens of Novgorod rebelled, saying, "This is well for the nobles, who keep rank and riches. But we simple men have lost what we held most dear in life."

They gathered in the great church, determined to resist. Alexander cajoled them again, swearing that he would ride off with his men if the citizens tried to defend Novgorod. He placed himself between the Mongol *baskak* and envoy, to keep them from being slain when they rode from house to house to make the census—a new sin, in the judgment of the superstitious Russians. He persuaded the clergy to preach submission, and he forced the payment of the *vyhod*. When, in 1262, the Suzdal region rebelled against the tax, he went to prostrate himself before Birkai to beg that the rebels might escape annihilation.

He won Birkai's favor as he had won Batu's, and the north escaped a new purge. But Birkai kept Alexander at Sarai until his death.

With their naïve emotionalism, the people lamented the death of Alexander Nevski as loudly as they had reviled the part he played in life. "My children," the Metropolitan proclaimed at Vladimir, "the sun of Russia has set." And the listeners cried out, "Who is to save us?"

No one man could save Russia. The princes of the next generation had grown up under the Mongol yoke. Their initiative could no longer break the invisible bonds of servitude to the Khan. Alexander had refused to allow his people to be commandeered for the army of the Horde, but his son Andrei marched with his *drujina* to aid the Mongols to pillage Vladimir. Another prince, Gleb, took a daughter of the Khan to wife, and joined an expedition of the Horde into the Caucasus. Like the riders of the Horde, the Russian men took a portion of the loot for their pay.

From this subservience it was only a step to calling upon the Mongols for aid in settling their own feuds. A Christian prince would petition the lord of Sarai to grant him bands of the dreaded Mongol horsemen to raid a neighboring city. And—since each petition was presented with a gift of gold and precious things—the khans began to realize that they could make a profit from the disputes of the Russian princes. Civil war paid them better than the early general peace. They no longer objected to the internecine conflict of the Russian nobility.

The March of the Barbarians

Naturally, in this state of affairs, the prince who brought the largest cup of gold to Sarai received the highest favor of the Khan. Their fortune lay at the feet of the Khan at Sarai.

This in turn led to a change in the collection of the *vyhod*. The yearly tax which had been gathered by the Moslem *baskaks* was given to the Russian princes to collect. At the same time the Mongols were careful to make a new census each generation, to count the living heads so they could be certain of the amount due them. Their own agents made this census.

As a result they were inclined to be well disposed toward the prince who brought a large tax to Sarai. So the nobles of the Russian land became the Squeezers—the taxgatherers and police of the Khan at Sarai. And in this lay another germ of a tsarist Russia.

The land was mutilated, the high culture of Kiev forgotten. It became a vast prison in which serfs, no longer vassals, labored for masters who were in turn subservient to an autocrat. There was no escape from servitude.

In the north, Novgorod fell more and more under the influence of the Teutonic Baltic. Novgorod traded with the Swedes, and felt the effects of Swedish culture. To the south of Novgorod, the savage Lithuanians harried the western frontier—there the Russians existed without change in a twilight of barbarism. The spirit of the earlier centuries was lost. No Prince Igor led the Russian *drujina* against the steppe dwellers.

In this twilight—little lighted by the stiff Byzantine figures of martyrs and kings—the Russian spirit became hard, to endure. Silence and deceit helped the leaders to survive. Because they were themselves slaves they came to be callous of servitude. Their lives never safe, they cared little for loss of life in others. They could watch torture without flinching.

But they endured.

Beyond them, in the west, the other Slavs, the Poles, progressed in knowledge while the Russians remained as they were. Poland, now free from the Mongol inroads, became the nucleus of a new Slavic world. The fire of the Renaissance touched the Poles, but not the Russians. Nicholai Kopernik (Copernicus—1473-1543) began to teach in the University of Kracow. Kracow became in time what Kiev had ceased to be.

The Building of the Kremlin

During this time of stagnation, Moscow rose to its ascendancy. On the forest height over the Moskva River—the name means Troubled Waters—the wooden settlement begun by the Finns had been burned by the Mongols in their first campaign.

A son of Alexander Nevski received the site as part of his appanage, and it began to thrive as a trading post, because the grain and honey of the south passed up the river to the Novgorod merchants. Churches were built in the forest—one of them known as the Saint Savior of the Pines.

The princes of Moscow became, like others, *baskaks* of the Khan of Sarai. More politic and more merciless than the others, they shaped their ambition to the whims of the Mongols and escaped destruction. The site of Moscow was washed often with blood. It needed both treachery and an iron determination to gain other appanages for the dynasty of Moscow, to double the head tax in order to pay greater sums to the Mongols, and by their aid to overthrow the rival districts.

But Suzdal and Novgorod became tributary to Moscow. Cathedrals were built on the height of the Kremlin overlooking the gray river—the Cathedral of the Assumption, the *Uspensky Sobor*. And the Metropolitan came to take residence at these sanctuaries. There the princes were placed in their tombs.

Until the ruler of Moscow could call himself Great Prince of All the Russias. So in the Kremlin was formed the nucleus of resistance to the Mongol yoke.

Moscow Faces East

It was now the sixteenth century and the time of Ivan called the Terrible.

The energies of the grand princes of Moscow were directed to one end, the breaking of the military yoke of the Tatars. Although the Golden Horde had dissolved, these Tatar khans were still masters at Kazan and Astrakhan and in the Ukraine.

The March of the Barbarians

A curious thing had happened. The Tatars had not changed during the last two centuries. And the minds of the Russian masses had stagnated during this long captivity. They were, in fact, the disinherited people of Europe. They still thought longingly of the golden Kiev of the past. The Russian folk had loved Kiev; they feared Moscow.

Another influence helped to bind people and grand princes to the past. Elsewhere—outside the limits of Tatar dominion—Constantinople had fallen to the Othman Turks. Those Moslems had put an end to the Patriarchate of that Byzantine city. In consequence, the head of the church of Moscow, the Metropolitan, now became the successor to the Patriarch of Constantinople. More than that, the Tsar of Moscow was acknowledged by the orthodox Church to be heir to the emperors of Constantinople, to the ghostly figures, half divine, that had worn the imperial purple since the days of Rome. Ivan III of Moscow married Zoe-Sophia Paleologue of that imperial house, and in 1492, when Columbus was exploring the seas, the Metropolitan proclaimed him to be "lord and autocrat of all the Russias, and Tsar of the new city of Constantinople, Moscow."

Meanwhile, the incoming of the Turks had driven Byzantine scholars and scientists away from Constantinople. These educated souls took refuge in the west, especially in Italy, where they aided in the revival of learning that created the Renaissance. The Byzantine scholars did not go east, into Russia.

The rulers of Moscow were surrounded with the archaic splendor of Byzantium. The sleeping chamber of a tsar had no windows, for what need had such a sublimated being of the ordinary light of day? This chamber might lead down to the torturer's room, where the tsar could watch offenders stripped of their flesh—but what need had a tsar of mercy? He could smash his own son with a steel-tipped staff, or brood himself into madness. He was still the tsar.

Moscow fell heir to the superstitions of Byzantium. Its rulers took the double eagle of Byzantium for their emblem, adding three crowns—that of Moscow and, before long, the twin khanates of Kazan and Astrakhan.

They surrounded themselves with crude Byzantine imagery—

importing Italian architects to design buildings of painted brick and stone about the Kremlin. The towers that rose along the Kremlin wall had neither meaning nor use; they were, like the cupolas of the Saint Vasili, dream-grotesques, savoring of Venice and gingerbread. As twisted as the minds within the Kremlin. And not very different from Kubilai's walled city of Tai-tu.

It was a strange prospect that opened before the eyes of the Moscow tsars. They were surrounded by the universal dominion of the Tatars, their minds indelibly marked by servitude to the khans. At the same time they felt themselves to be endowed with a divine right beyond other monarchs. They were never able to free themselves from these two influences.

Meanwhile the unrest of the Russian masses had found a voice: "Why have you brought the Tatars into the Russian land, and given them land and settlements? Why do you love the Tatars and their talk more than is proper, and why do you oppress the peasants more than is necessary? And why do you give gold and silver and all good things to the Tatars?"

In the hamlets, women sang this cradlesong:

> "*Baiu, baiuchi, baiu!*
> *Small child, sleep—dream you are fierce and brave!*
> *To take your arms from the wall,*
> *Gird your sword, load your pistol,*
> *And go!*
> *To bind and kill the godless Tatar*
> *And all his Tatarchiks!*"

Songs have a way of anticipating destiny. The Russian horsemen made use of their pistols.

The situation of Moscow had altered. In Birkai's time there had been one Golden Horde, opposed to the scattered Russian principalities; now there was one Moscow, mistress of the central Suzdal region, facing three or four khanates. And the khans had been obliged to ask the aid of the Moscow grand dukes in their own rivalries. Ivan IV was able to attack them individually, and to push the nascent Russian empire eastward to the Volga, capturing both Kazan (1551) and Astrakhan (1556). In so doing he scattered the Finnish population of the upper river and the old Bulgar-Turkish tribes of the steppe region.

The actual warfare was on a small scale compared to the operations of the great Mongol armies. But it made a vast change in the rulers of Moscow. From vassals they became autocrats, in the fullest sense of the word. Like Tamerlane, they had possessed themselves of Juchi's throne. Unlike Tamerlane, they kept it.

The Westwall and the Road to the East

They acted, however, almost without volition of their own. They yielded to popular pressure to get rid of the *vyhod*. They were drawn toward Kazan because it was a rich trading center. And the Volga itself was a mighty artery of traffic leading to the east. Each objective drew them on to another.

They could not expand in any other direction. To the southwest the growing power of the Turks held the Balkans. In the west the Polish state was at its greatest expansion. Beyond, the Lithuanians held the marsh and forest areas. In the northwest Novgorod was still fighting off the Germans—and making treaties with them. "Fear Lord Novgorod and God," an old proverb said. But the Muscovites feared German firearms more. The shores of the Baltic were closed to them by the Swedes.

At the edge of the northern forests the Finns held fast to their ancestral heritage, the lakes and the long peninsula extending up into the arctic. The half-pagan Finns, with their magicians, hunted around the shores of Lake Ladoga and over the site where Petersburg was yet to be built.

So the west was closed to the Russians. More civilized and much better armed, the western nations could not be invaded by the Tatarized forces of Moscow. For the time being, the Nogai Tatars along the Black Sea were too formidable to attack. Ivan IV turned to the east.

The capture of Kazan rid the Russians of their fear of the Asiatics. They had taken their first step toward the east with little effort and vast profit. It was a simple matter to break down the earth and log fortifications of the Khan's city, but to the Russians it meant emancipation after those three centuries. Ivan's strange nature could mock at the heads of the western nations. As heir of the Caesars and conqueror of the Khans, he felt himself superior to them.

"You are a monarch made, not born," he assured the Polish king, who had been elected as usual by the nobility. "Because your peers elected you, you owe your sovereignty to them." He called the king of the Swedes a functionary. And he reproached Elizabeth of England—although he wrote to her presently to demand an asylum in that country if he had to flee from Moscow—for not governing like a monarch but letting herself be advised by jobbers.

Himself he held to be tsar by the will of God and not by the connivance of human beings. His only equals were the sultan of the Turks and the khan of the Krimea. He looked upon Tatars of the blood of Genghis-Khan as more exalted than his own boyars. A descendant of Batu was named a prince of Russia.

Ivan's nobles were more than willing to marry women of the Khan's family. And they secluded their brides as rigorously as the Moslems had done. They rode Tatar horses, with jeweled scimitars at their hips. When these Russian horsemen were seen along the western frontier, the Poles and Swedes did not recognize them as Christians.

There is no doubt that Ivan the Terrible and his successors felt gratified to think of themselves as rulers of the Golden Horde. At the same time they were faced by obstacles they could not sur- mount on the other three sides—they had to face east. By taking Astrakhan, at the Volga mouths, Ivan had opened the way to intercourse with Persia and the Turkish clans.

The Tatars, however, although willing enough to swear alle- giance to the "White Tsar," were quick to counter-attack. To maintain his new frontier on the Volga, Ivan had to draft his feudal nobility with their armed serfs into a permanent army. He found himself compelled to do what the khans of the Golden Horde had done before him, to hold the steppes by armed force. He com- mandeered horses and men for this task, calling his boyars into a council of war and putting to death those who refused to obey his orders.

The March of the Barbarians

Moscow, under such a regime, was able to make small headway toward the west. In the time of troubles, so called, after Ivan's death, the Swedes penetrated to Novgorod, and a Cossack posing as tsar in the Kremlin called for a bride from Poland. Outlaws ranged along the rivers, and the bells of the churches ceased ringing. The boyars were divided in rebellion, some of them bought by foreign gold.

In this time of troubles (1584–1613) the Russians turned their backs toward European culture. They knew nothing of the Renaissance and the Elizabethan age.

And this strife in Moscow turned the ambition of the next tsars decisively toward Asia. Fortunately for them a great part of their new empire was offered them as a gift by a band of outlaws.

Ataman Irmak

They were Cossacks—a new breed of men in the steppes. For generations lawless elements had been drifting from the Muscovite settlements out to the frontiers—men with a thirst for wandering, men with a price on their heads, men who were tired of servitude. In the southern steppes they had intermingled with the Tatars and nomad Bashkirs. Gradually they formed a brotherhood of wanderers and exiles, and in time this brotherhood grew into a combative people, hunting and fighting along the marches of the Ukraine, giving allegiance neither to Polish *voevod* or Russian prince or Turkish sultan. They were known as Kazaks, Wanderers.

A group of them, outlawed, drifting east with their Ataman, or headman, Irmak, quartered themselves in the lands of the Strogonofs—one of the feudal families reigning over the new lands of the east. The Strogonofs were slave owners, fur traders, and autocrats of the frontier, residing in log palaces, attended by their own priests and Moslem merchants. They sent the unruly Cossacks on into the forests above the Kama. In that quarter the Tatars of Sibir had been raiding the Strogonofs' settlements. It was good policy on their part to rid themselves of the Cossacks and Tatars at the same time.

What happened, however, was unexpected. The Cossacks kept on going, hunting as they went, building long boats on the rivers.

Irmak and his outlaws fought and subdued the Tatar khan, Kutchun. They became masters of the forested mid-region of Sibir. It occurred to them to make a gift of all this, not to the Strogonofs, but to the Tsar in Moscow, and so to earn release from their outlawry. This gift was accepted in 1582.

It seemed to the tsars to be their due, as successors of the khans of the Golden Horde. And it opened the way to the vast extent of the farther east. Sibir, "the Gate," actually the gateway, gave its name to this new heritage, Siberia. Kutchun Khan revealed to the exploring Cossacks the line of the Urals, with their crude silver mines.

Here lay a new vista of grassy hills, blue lakes that reflected their fringe of pines, marshes alive with wild duck and swans. Here grew maple thickets by swift rivers and the dark mass of timber stretching into the purple distance—very different from the sluggish waters of the west or the sea of dry grass in the steppes. The next generations of Cossacks went on exploring.

Meanwhile on that other frontier where Father Dnieper ran down past Kiev, other Cossacks had formed themselves into war bands. They had their great camp known as the *Siech* in the islands of the Dnieper, and they moved this camp about to escape the attack of their enemies. They came to be called the Zaporoghian Cossacks—Below-the-Rapids Cossacks. They shaved their heads in the Tatar fashion, and they raided the settlements of the Catholic Poles and the Moslem Turks not because they were devout themselves but because religion offered them the best pretext for war, in which they most thoroughly believed. At times their long boats raided the shores of the Black Sea.

Under an ambitious *khoshevoi ataman*, Bogdan Khmielnitski, they raised the peasants of the Ukraine in revolt, and allying themselves with the Nogai Tatars they became a turbulent political power in the mid-seventeenth century. This revolt of the common sort had the effect of driving the more civilized Poles from the Ukraine, but it also raised the Cossacks to a political eminence in which they were not at home. Before long they decided to declare themselves subjects of the Muscovite tsars.

The March of the Barbarians

So for the second time the tsars received a slice of empire without volition of their own. The Cossacks, however, did not take kindly to the rule of Moscow, and they drifted east across the steppes, where the grass-grown kurgans marked the thoroughfares of the earlier nomads. They reached the waters of the Don and the foothills of the Caucasus.

Behind them colonists moved into the rich black-earth region. The Cossacks themselves preferred to leave agriculture to their women, and they moved on to new frontiers.

"The Tsar reigns in Moscow," they said, "the Cossack on the Don."

In time these wild Cossacks became tamed to the extent that they served as the military force of the advancing frontier. Their *stanitzas* or settlements were fortified posts. The mounted warriors of these *stanitzas* formed a mobile cavalry force that could cope with the Tatar ordus. The tsars found in them a key to open wide the gateway to the east.

Peter the Builder

One man, Peter the Great, tried to arrest this drift into the east. He endeavored to remold both his army and his people along the lines of western progress. Peter did object violently, for his was no gentle nature, to the traditional stagnation of Russian minds. He banished, as it were, the ghost of Byzantium from his court. He melted down church bells into cannon and imported Germans to drill his soldiery. He faced west decisively when he drove his people to build Peter's city—Petersburg—on the gray waters of the Neva with its outlook toward the Baltic. He built with brick as well as logs, and he launched the first ships of a fleet upon the Baltic. And Petersburg, built upon Finnish soil, became a menace to the Finns. Peter's army pushed them northward, beyond Lake Ladoga. And that same army, with its new cannon and tactics, overthrew the Swedes.

The new Russian empire had taken a foothold upon the Baltic. But Peter in no way forgot his heritage of the east. While he waged defensive warfare along the Baltic's edge, he began the active penetration of the Ukraine. His frontier forces seized on Azov and reached the Caspian. His hastily constructed ships on that inland sea explored the coast of Persia. He even attempted to enter the Caucasus and to take under his protection the Khan of far-off Khiva.

That he failed to reach these objectives is no indication that he did not desire them. Within two generations the talented Catherine took firmer hold on their Asiatic heritage—or what they believed to be such. She did arrange, with Frederick the Great of Prussia, and Maria Theresa of Austria, the total division of Poland, extending Russia's western frontier past Vilna and Warsaw, and putting a stop to the growth of Polish culture. But she also finished the conquest of the Nogai Tatars in the Krimea region, and advanced the frontier *stanitzas* into the foothills of the Caucasus. With the entourage of her favorites, she made a triumphal procession through her new Asiatic dominion, escorted by runners with torches, and costumed Mamluks. It was more barbaric than the pageantry of Kubilai Khan.

So much for the ambitions of these successors to Batu. A truer picture of the Russian movement eastward would be the new life astir on the Volga then. Timber rafts floating down to Astrakhan —condemned men hung up on hooks on the masts of other rafts, a bell tolling over them as they drifted, a warning to lawbreakers. Volga *burlaki*—rivermen—working their fishing boats up against the current. Tatar horsemen moving through the high grass of the steppes, skirting the blockhouses of the settlements. Mud and logs of a fur trader's post. The sails of the masterless men, Stenka Razin's river pirates, with rushes tied to their boats to hide them, moving over the gray waters at sunset. The cry of Stenka Razin's bands, *"Sarin na kitchka*—kindle up and burn: death to the white hands."

Stenka Razin, who smelled, the Cossacks say, like a wolf eating garbage, and who was branded with the mark of Cain—"for good reason," he admitted—is still more truly a maker of the new Russia than the Empress who received her court in rooms of amber and Chinese lacquer and lapis lazuli. The cry of Stenka Razin, the pirate, was heard again thereafter, and the song of the Volga rivermen has endured.

The March of the Barbarians

For Stenka Razin was shaped by the Volga and the prison where he spent his younger years. He was a descendant of the east more than of the west. And this was true of the mass of the Russians who moved eastward.

At that time the Volga, more truly than the Mississippi of a century ago, was the channel of mixed races. The Volga rivermen were the sons of Slavic fathers and Tatar mothers.

In their period of supremacy the Mongols had little effect upon the Slavic stock; but now in their decadence, when they had lost their type, they were changing the Russian stock by interbreeding. And this change was to become greater as time went on.

An insatiable hunger for land, and more land, was driving the Russian colonist eastward, and as he went, he bred his sons from the women of the Asiatic tribes.

The Eastern Empire

The first Russian advance beyond the Volga took a northern route, avoiding the more warlike of the Asiatic tribes. At first the people of Finnish stock offered little resistance. The Cheremisse and Mordvas fled east through the forests with their pagan gods. They would not be converted nor would they work for Russian masters. So the Russian proprietors imported agricultural workers of their own, who filtered among the Mordvas, cultivating their fields, marrying their women.

Meanwhile the bands of adventurers pushed ahead, still keeping to the north. The Samoyeds and reindeer people of the forests were peaceful, offering no resistance. Moreover the northern way was easier for the Russians than the heights of central Asia. And they advanced swiftly.

By 1609 the Cossacks have reached Tomsk, near the Ob. A few years later they are on the banks of the Yenisei. In 1632 they are building the log forts of Yakutsk on the Lena, whence one of them descends to the mouth of the river at the border of the Arctic Ocean. The khan Altan promises them that he will accept the presents of the White Tsar. In four years they advance a thousand miles farther, and begin to descend the Amur. This brings them into contact with the Chinese frontier forces, and they retreat, to

[350]

build Irkutsk. But within a generation they are exploring Kamchatka and the Pacific shores.

This is a vast territory—it is two and a half times as far from Moscow to Kamchatka as from New York to the California coast. Aided by the arctic tribes, the Cossacks even cross from island to island to Alaska. And Russian fur traders follow them, to descend the coast of North America and to come into sight of California before American settlers take possession there.

The Tribes of Central Asia

Until now the lands of the great clans of mid-Asia had been avoided by the Russians. The nomad horsemen were still formidable with their bows. They had all their old pride in their freedom, and no least desire either to submit or to pay tribute to the *Urusse* traffickers and soldiers. Early in the seventeenth century the tribes of the Chagatai area had coalesced under the leadership of Batur, and then Galdan, khans of the Dzungars (or Jungars, the East Wing)—Turks who still followed the yak-tail standard. The rise of this Turkish power drove out—as usual in the steppes where the movement of one group presses on another—the smaller tribes. When the Dzungars emerged from the Altai passes, the surviving Mongols did not feel themselves strong enough to resist. They would not become subjects of the western clans whom they had once ruled. Instead, these surviving Mongols bound themselves to the Manchus and Chinese—yielding in 1691 to the Manchu emperor.

The firearms of the Chinese armies drove back the Dzungars—pursued them into the mountain ranges, giving the great Manchu emperors a foothold along the T'ian Shan and in the Five Cities. Meanwhile the Mongols proper clung to their prairies south of Baikal, no longer a sovereign people, but preserving their customs and their pride, weakened by the indolence of Buddhism.

One more move outward was made by the western clans, now much stronger than the Mongols. The Oyrats or Kalmuks—the Exiles, as the Russians called them—struggled with the Manchu armies, their bows opposed to guns. A part of them, the Torguts, migrated westward to escape the pressure of the Chinese and settled in the Russian steppes. They were, in the eyes of the Russians, pagan Buddhists, intractable to government. "The Kalmuks," their chieftains said, "have always been free; they have not been slaves to anyone, nor will they ever be."

When Russian colonists closed in around them, the Torguts could no longer endure the rule of the westerners. Without warning, when the rivers were frozen in the winter of 1770–71, they decamped and started the long trek back to their homeland. Seventy thousand tents moved slowly eastward across the Volga and Ural in this last migration of nomad power. The Moslem Kara-Kirghiz followed the retreat like wolves, cutting off stragglers to be sold as slaves. Cossacks, ordered by Moscow to bring the fugitives back into the Tsar's frontiers, attacked the rear of the Torguts, and drove back a portion of the horde, to convert them by force to Christianity and compel them to occupy their old pastures.

But these enemies could not check the flight of the Torguts. Instinct drove them eastward toward their ancestral grazing lands. The remainder of the great trek pushed on, across the deserts to the waters of Lake Balkash. Those who survived found grazing lands in the valleys that had once belonged to the Chagatai Mongols.

After the breaking up of the Kalmuks, the nomad tribes remained in their home pastures, where the advancing Russians encountered them.

Behind the Russian explorers came the fur traders, behind the traders the Cossack *stanitzas* and the first colonists, working the soil in a slipshod way, but holding fast to the land.

The colonists and Cossacks had firearms that blasted away the resistance of the nomads, who still rode horses and used bows. The colonists, more dangerous to tribal life than the Cossacks, interbred with the tribal women.

These Russians were moving into the caravan routes of Asia, over the road of the Barbarians. In spite of the resistance of the Moslem Kirghiz and the Turkomans, they were advancing toward the silk route. Where they came, they repeopled the lands. At first they changed the tribal life little, because they had mixed Asiatic blood in them; in culture they were inferior to the begs and amirs of clear Turkish strain.

At times the Russian soldiery escorted droves of prisoners, to be quartered in the wastes of Siberia, as the Mongols had once driven in captive labor gangs.

The Russian advance penetrated to the homelands of the Mongol tribes. These, living quietly around the Baikal pastures, had separated from the Turkish clans to the west. Now, along the line of the Khingan range, they were feeling the pressure of the Manchus—a vigorous people of the old Tungusic stock, who were already penetrating north China from the Liao-tung peninsula.

When the Manchus became masters of Tai-tu, now Pe-king, or the North Court, the Mongols became their allies, in 1644. No Genghis-Khan had appeared, to lead them to new victories, and it seemed better to become the allies than the foes of the Manchu-Chinese. Especially when the new Manchu dynasty began to extend its armed forces around the Gobi.

For the Mongol nomads had become a remnant of the past. They still lived and armed themselves as they had done three centuries before, when driven out of China. They began to trade with the Russian settlers, appearing around Lake Baikal.

The Prophecy

At first the Russian movement had been merely a reflux, into the territories of the Tatar khans. Then it had advanced slowly toward the Pacific, and the China trade.

After 1800 it quickened with a new impulse. The power of the Russian armies had grown, in avalanche fashion, by the subjection of peoples who were in turn drafted into the army, after the plan of Genghis-Khan. At the same time improved firearms and cannon gave the Russian regiments greater superiority over the Asiatics. Their advance now came with irresistible power—a blind, inexorable force.

The Russian government had become aware of the mineral wealth of Siberia and the fertility of its soil. And its advance over that soil became an attack, to gain and hold as much land as possible. This attack began to radiate toward all points of Asia.

After 1800 the conquest of the Caucasus was pushed, through the Tatars and Georgians of those mountains. North of the Black Sea, Russian armies drove the failing Turks back toward Constantinople—reoccupying Nogai's domain.

Western Europe went through the throes of the Napoleonic wars, emerging exhausted from the last campaigns. Russia, comparatively unharmed, and militarized now, with vastly increasing numbers to feed its armies, was in a position to dominate the western nations—almost as Batu and Subotai had dominated the west from the Danube. The military force of the new Russia had become gigantic. It had taken Finland from a weakened Sweden.

But the Romanof tsars, ruling from St Petersburg, still faced east. Their Cossack *stanitzas* moved down through the Hunger steppe, past the Sea of Aral. By ruthless force the Kirghiz and Kara-Kalpaks were subdued. Then the valley of Samarkand. The khans of Khiva submitted, and the Russian outposts climbed into the barrier ranges looking down on India.

The Romanof tsars saw unlimited expanses of land in the east, to be colonized, and held by force. They were obeying the instinct that drove both peasants and Cossacks down toward warmer valleys and the southern seas. Their outposts moved into the ruins of the Five Cities and paused at the edge of the Gobi's sands. Masses of settlers advanced past the Altai. Cities grew up along the transport lines. Irkutsk was built at the edge of Lake Baikal.

The outposts reached the Amur, that river of conflict whose name means Peace, then Sakhalin island. A railroad followed the colonists' path across the continent, Manchuria was taken from the Chinese—the now-pacific Manchus subdued—and the Russians looked across the Great Wall at Pe-king. In 1898 they forced the Chinese to yield the port at the end of the Liao-tung peninsula and fortified it as Port Arthur. They prepared to advance into Korea.

Then in 1904–05 an Asiatic power struck back. The Japanese islanders had learned to use, if not to make, the weapons of the Europeans. For the first time the European invaders were defeated, with modern weapons.

Tsarist Russia, in 1905, had almost regained the geographical structure of the empire of Genghis-Khan, peopled with the same racial elements. If it had not been for the counter-stroke of the Japanese, the dominion of the Tsars would have passed the Great Wall and enveloped Pe-king.

In this new coalescence of humanity the Russians, not the Mongols, dominated the military force. The empire was ruled from its western sphere, not from the east. It had, like the Mongol empire, the vast natural reservoir of Siberia to draw from. But the Siberian region yielded it resources of timber, metals and fertile soil, instead of human beings.

The mild autocracy of the religious Tsars and the nobility ended in the revolution of 1917–18. Out of the revolution came the merciless but rational rule of Lenin, soon to be supplanted by Stalinism. Curiously enough the capital is again Moscow, as in the medieval period. The eyes in the Kremlin look again toward Asia. Stalin himself is more Asiatic than European.

Under a thin surface of western customs and catch phrases, the dominating power is again Asiatic, as in the days before Peter the Great. It is a pure dictatorship, supported by military force.

This military force has been harnessed again to the task of war. Already it has seized upon the lands of the Poles that it once held; it has penetrated into the small Baltic states, holding in subjection the once-independent Lithuanians.

It has been driven against the liberty-loving Finns, who had withdrawn, after centuries, into their peninsula in the far north. Stalin, in casting aside the doctrines of the revolution, has turned back to the medieval policy of military conquest.

Now, as after the death of Genghis-Khan, western Europe waits to learn what direction the new empire will take, and in what quarter its force will be driven.

As for the nomads of mid-Asia, their herds were taken from them, and they are now being transformed into workers of the soil and factories of the Russians, although they exist in name as independent republics.

Not so the surviving Mongols. Destiny has placed them in a strange position. Their ancestral lands, the prairies south of

Baikal, lie between frontiers. Until now, they have escaped the railroads and settlements of Russian colonists. Their way of life has not greatly changed. They still guard what they believe to be the site of the grave of Genghis-Khan.

Those prairies are the only pathway for armies between the wastes of the northern Gobi and the line of the Amur, fortified by both the Japanese and Russians. And those prairies are flanked by the guerrilla forces of the Chinese, now arming in earnest.

So, regardless of their quietude in these last centuries, the star of war still hangs over the Mongol prairies. Upon this battlefield, the fertility of Manchukuo, the still-untouched resources of Siberia, the access of trade through Asia to the Pacific hang in the balance.

The Mongols are waiting in their felt tents for the issue to be decided. They are grouping around their yurt fires. And they are repeating a legend.

They say: "When that which is harder than rock and stronger than the storm wind shall fail, the empires of the North Court and the South shall cease to be. When the White Tsar is no more, and the Son of Heaven has vanished, then the campfires of Genghis-Khan will be seen again, and his empire will stretch over the earth."

Afterword

Afterword

MORE THAN A CENTURY AGO the first scholars began the attempt to translate the documents dealing with the Mongols and their time. Pétis de la Croix assembled Persian and Arabic texts in Paris. The gifted sinologue Abel Rémusat translated portions of the Chinese annals. Baron d'Ohsson, in Constantinople, wrote the first connected narrative of the Mongol empires.

Later, the first field explorers undertook their work of examining what lay beneath the surface of the lands. The Russians, Prjevalsky and Peter Kozlov, began, with Radloff, the exploration that had been left off by the Franciscans five centuries before.

The work of this small group of linguists and archeologists was carried on by others. The group always remained small, its labors exacting. And it became, perhaps more truly than any similar group, an international fellowship in work. Even the Scandinavians had their part, with the work of Sven Hedin and Czaplicka.

A list of their published works, as I have collected them on my shelves, follows.

I have little of the high qualification of such scholars. Twenty-three years ago, while searching for more information about the Mongols, I found that the search always ended in the name of Genghis-Khan. And that name, in turn, revealed little more than the figure of a barbaric conqueror, or an inhuman destroyer of lives. On the other hand, it soon became evident that to his Mon-

gols Genghis-Khan had been a demigod. At that time I could not
find out what kind of man he really was, or how he had lived.
In searching for more information I became fascinated by the
Mongol world. The quest for more knowledge led inevitably
toward Marco Polo and the Old Man of the Mountain, and
Xanadu, and then to all the scene of medieval Asia. This proved
to be an irresistible temptation, to a storyteller.

So the greater part of the last twenty-three years has been spent
in this quest for knowledge of the Mongol world. Being able to
read only French and Latin at first, I had to learn what I could
of the oriental languages—Persian, which afforded some inkling
of Arabic and Turkish. In south Russia I made acquaintance with
the medieval Ukrainian, and picked up a smattering of Manchu-
Tartar. Now it was necessary to attempt Russian, and Mongolian
itself.

Meanwhile I have been able to travel over and examine more
than half the lands occupied by the Mongols. In such trips my
work was made easy by the kindness of such well-wishers as Bayard
Dodge, at the American University of Beirut, and Itimadaulat,
the former Minister of Education in Iran (Persia). The great
courtesy of Monsignor—now Cardinal—Eugène Tisserant helped
my two years of reading at the library of the Vatican. Such friend-
ships have been an undeserved reward for work that must be lonely,
and often fruitless, owing to its difficulties.

In preparing this book, I am indebted to the skill of Marzieh
Gail in translating with me a large part of the Persian chronicle of
Rashid, with the co-operation of Professor William Popper of the
University of California. And to the members of the Archeological
Department of the Polska Akademia Umiejetnosci of Kracow for
their aid in finding references in the Polish ecclesiastical chronicles
to the invasions of the Mongols, as well as information as to the
little-known stone *babas*. This aid was given unselfishly in the
weeks when the Poles themselves were aware of the danger threaten-
ing them from the invasion of the Reich.

Before then, at Leningrad, Professor Vasily Struve of the Institute of Ethnography kindly discussed with me the origins of some of
the Turco-Mongol clan groups in Siberia, and made it possible for

Afterword

me to meet with the translators of the Institute of Oriental Studies.

I am indebted, above all, to the findings of the brilliant linguists, Edouard Blochet, B. Y. Vladimirtsov and Vasily Barthold. The work of Paul Pelliot has cleared away many of the problems of Central Asia that defied lesser minds.

The Sources

It is only possible today to reconstruct in broad outline the lives of these Mongol khakhans, these "savages of genius," as Professor Vladimirtsov calls them. The details of their time, and actions, are scanty. It is necessary to disregard hearsay and depend upon established facts. These facts are, however, sufficient to trace in shadowy outline the personalities of the Golden Family and the consequences of their attempt to dominate the world. The sources yield us more detail for the descendants of the conqueror than for Genghis-Khan himself.

This record of their lives has nothing to do with present-day morality. They were nomads of the thirteenth century. They were influenced by their own environment and by the different cultures with which they came in contact. Modern militarists can see in them a supreme accomplishment of warfare, and pacifists can visualize them as inhuman shedders of blood. I have only tried to draw the men themselves, as they existed against the background of their time, as it was then.

"Chingiz [Genghis] Khan," Professor Barthold points out, "considered the organization of the empire only from the point of view of the dominion of nomad conquerors over civilized peoples whom God Himself had delivered into Mongol hands in order that they should derive revenues from the labors of the conquered, and for this object alone should protect them. . . . Agriculturists and artisans were to form the raw materials from which it would be possible for their owners, the Mongol leaders, to derive advantage. Chingiz Khan worked only for himself, his descendants, and his closest adherents; there is no evidence of any sort that he was open to the idea of laboring for the good of the whole nation."

The terror caused by the Mongol attack—and it was caused deliberately—did not enter into their home life. It was a means to an end, a weapon to be used against the outer world. Within their own *yurts* the Mongols were more often than not amiable, hospitable and carefree. Assassination and treachery—and even theft—were rare until the influences of the outer world crept in after two generations. The discipline established by Genghis-Khan over the new army was inflexible in its severity. But he schooled himself to exercise that same rigid control over his own actions. Chagatai and Kuyuk did likewise.

"Like all conquerors," Barthold reminds us, "Chinghiz Khan could calmly exterminate people by the thousands if he considered it necessary . . . but in none of his actions of which we have at all reliable information is there any sign of useless or stupid cruelty."

His inflexible will stifled the emotions of those close to him, and his descendants reflected either that remorseless severity or the natural reaction from it. Chagatai and Kuyuk never allowed themselves to smile, and they inspired terror wherever they went. "Others," Barthold adds, "gave way to the natural vivacity of the nomad, manifested most strikingly in the desire to live and let live. . . . They allowed themselves a gaiety that passed into debauch (Ugudai)."

This is the explanation of the Jekyll-and-Hyde conception of the Mongols that has persisted for so many centuries—wherein they appeared to outside enemies as a kind of demoniac invaders, and to their own people as inspired, if severe, benefactors. Even the Chinese, who both feared and understood Genghis-Khan, admit that "he led his armies like a god."

The Mongolian Sagas

So we have in the accounts of the Mongols themselves, at that time, a record of the heroic type. Before then the Mongols had no written documents. Their sagas are echoes of the spoken word, making no difference between legend and fact, and tinged with mysticism. Little of these early records has survived.

The sayings of Genghis-Khan (the *bilik*) were written down, probably by Uighurs. Also his commandments, in the form of the Yasa. They were kept by members of the Golden Family, and brought out, to be read at the kuriltais. They are all lost.

Afterword

We have only portions of them quoted by different chroniclers, and a version of the Yasa written by an Egyptian Moslem, Makrisi, two hundred years after the death of Genghis-Khan. (A text and translation is in De Sacy's *Chréstomathie arabe*. A fresh translation was made for use in this book. Makrisi's version is colored by the author's leaning toward Islam.)

The earliest Mongolian writing, known to them as the *Altyn debter*, the Golden Book, appears to be lost. Bits of it appear in the work of later writers.

A later writing, again apparently by Uighurs, has survived in a Chinese and Mongolian version. This Secret History, as it was called by the Mongols, dates from 1240. It has been translated from the Chinese into the Russian by the Archimandrite Palladius (in *Trudy Rossiiskoi dukhovna missii v Pekinye*—Texts of the Peking Mission). The Chinese version is known, I believe, as the *Yuan c'ao mi shi*. I was told at the Academy in Leningrad in July 1939 that a translation of the Mongolian text was being made by the Oriental Institute. This saga is in the nomad vein, with accounts of the individual exploits of Genghis-Khan and his companions. It has, apparently, little to say about his descendants or the external wars after the first conquest of north China.

A well-known Mongol annalist, Ssanang Setzen, compiled a legendary account of the ancestors, the life and the sons of Genghis-Khan, in the mid-sixteenth century. It was translated into Russian by Father Hyacinth, and thence into a faulty German version by Isaac Jacob Schmidt (*Chungtaidshi der Ordos*, 1829). It is distorted by Buddhist myths, yet gives many traditional details of the struggle of Genghis-Khan against his enemies.

The Chinese Histories, and Travelers

The Chinese point of view was quite different from that of the Mongols themselves. They saw the Mongols in perspective as nomad invaders; they were under fear of the Mongol attack. Yet they understood the Mongol character much better than the Moslems or the Europeans.

Their *Yüan shi* or Annals of the Yüan dynasty was compiled in the fourteenth century, and has not yet been translated in full from the Chinese. A brief version was made by Father Gaubil—*Histoire de Gentchiscan et de toute la dynastie des Mongous, tirée de l'histoire chinoise, par Anthony Gaubil*, Paris, 1739. I have made use of this version. It is accurate in the main, and gives full details of Kubilai's reign, up to his death. The Chinese had almost no knowledge of the geography west of the Gobi region, so their accounts of events in the farther west—when they give any particulars at all—are apt to be a real puzzle.

During the life of Genghis-Khan a Chinese envoy named Meng Hung visited him and left an interesting account of his trip and his impressions of the Mongol character. He observes the change from their nomad state, when "they existed for generations without care, being sufficient to themselves." His journal has been translated into Russian (Texts of the Peking Mission).

Ch'ang Ch'un, a Taoist, also visited Genghis-Khan in the west. He was a friend of Yeliu Ch'u-tsai, and his journal gives a good picture of the Mongol roads, the great encampment of Genghis-Khan. Translated into English by Arthur Waley—*Ch'ang Ch'un: The Travels of an Alchemist*, London, 1931.

Extracts from some other Chinese travelers are given in Dr Bretschneider's *Medieval Researches from Eastern Asiatic Sources*, London, 1888 and 1910. The most interesting is an account of the start of Hulagu's journey.

The *T'ung kien kang mu*, or history of the imperial dynasties, compiled by Ssi ma Kuang, has little to say about the early Mongol rulers. It is available in an old French translation, the *Histoire générale de la Chine, traduite du Tong-Kien-Kang-Mou par le Père Joseph Anne-Marie de Moyriac de Mailla, dirigée par M. le Roux des Hautesrayes*, Paris, 1777–78.

Biographical accounts of Tatatunga, Subotai, Yeliu Ch'u-tsai and Sartak have been translated from the Chinese sources by Abel Rémusat—*Nouveaux Mélanges asiatiques*, Vol. II, Paris, 1829. These agree very closely with Gaubil's and Rashid's versions.

The Persian and Arabic Chroniclers

These differ markedly from the Chinese. The earliest Moslem writers saw, or heard about, the terror of the Mongol attack. They paint a horrifying picture, but it is a true picture. They knew less, at first hand, about the events in China or Europe. But they were cultured minds, capable of fuller expression than the Chinese and the Europeans.

The earliest is the famous chronicle of Ibn al-Athir, who knew little of the Mongols himself but gave many anecdotes from eye-witnesses.

The *Ta'rikh-i-Jahan Gushai* (History of the World Conqueror) of Ala ad-Din Ata Malik, called Juwaini, was written in 1260, and the author was an eyewitness of events in Khorasan and Afghanistan. His account of the Mongols themselves seems to be brief but accurate—his work ends with the coming of Hulagu. (The greater part has been published in the Persian in the E. W. Gibb Memorial Series.)

By all odds, the most valuable work is that of the Persian physician, Rashid ad-Din. His *Jami at-Tavarikh*, or Great Collection of Histories, was made about 1300 under the direction of the Il-khan Ghazan. Rashid, a gifted chronicler, had the aid of older Mongols who remembered the events of the generation before him, and he used both Chinese and Mongolian written records—even the lost *Altyn debter*, or Golden Book.

So he had a clear perspective of the events around him, even in Europe. His account of the sons of Genghis-Khan are drawn, apparently, from Mongol spoken tradition or writing. Often, in his pages, he uses Mongolian words instead of the Persian equivalent, as in his names for the twelve beasts of the calendar. In his description of the tribes and ancestry of the Mongols, he uses their terms—*yusun, uruk,* etc.—and he is very accurate in his family relationships, which the Chinese and westerners never mastered.

Upon Rashid's volume dealing with the ordu of Genghis-Khan, the earlier portion of the present book is largely based. (A translation of the parts dealing with Ogadai, Tului, Siyurkuktiti, Kuyuk, Mangu and Kubilai was made at the University of California, from the text edited by Blochet, in the E. W. Gibb Memorial Series. This text had many lacunae and errors—not all of them noticed by Blochet.)

I was fortunate in being able to discuss many points of this

The March of the Barbarians

translation with the oriental scholars of the library of the Leningrad Academy, in the difficult days of July 1939. They did not consider the Blochet text too reliable, and they were making a translation into Russian of the whole *Tavarikh* from the Leningrad manuscript, and photostats of several others.

Rashid's history is most detailed in the account of Hulagu's expedition and the affairs of the Il-khans. This portion has been translated by Quatremère—*Histoire des Mongols de la Perse, par Raschid eldin, traduite, accompagnée de notes*, Paris, 1836. The notes are valuable.

In the introduction to his first volume, dealing with the history of the Golden Family, Rashid strikes a modern note:

"Until this time, we have had only unsatisfactory accounts of the nations of the Mongols, of the structure of their tribes, the events of the life of Changiz-Khan and the reigns of his successors. The writers of these accounts have consulted only popular recitals, and have arranged those according to their own inclination.

"The small amount of actual facts they relate are denied by the princes of the house of Changiz [Genghis-Khan] and by the chieftains of the Mongol nation.

"However we have in our archives [of the Il-khans] historical fragments that are recognized as authentic, written in the Mongol speech and script. But few people have access to them. To place these materials in the hands of the public, our sultan Gazan Khan has wished that they be written out in historical form, and he has confided this work in the year 702 (Hegira) to the most humble of his servants, Faz'l-allah the son of Abu'l Khayir, surnamed Rashid the Physician, of Hamadan. This servant has been ordered to consult—to round out these materials—the Chinese sages, and the Hindus, Uighurs and Kipchaks who are at this court, and especially that great noyan, generalissimo and administrator of the kingdom, Pulad Chingsang, who knows better than anyone else in the world the origins and the history of the Turkish peoples, and particularly of the Mongol nation . . . because few persons nowadays recall the events of a century ago, and the greater number of the younger Mongol lords have forgotten the names and the exploits of their ancestors.

Afterword

"But now that the greater part of the earth is under the rule of the descendants of Changiz-Khan, and a multitude of learned men, of Chinese astronomers and historians, as well as Hindus, Kashmiris, Tibetans, Uighurs, Arabs and Franks [Europeans], is gathered here at this court, it is needful that I make an outline of the history of all those nations as well, and add to it an account of the lands they inhabit."

Rashid was the first, but not by any means the last, to realize that, to write a clear history of the descendants of Genghis-Khan, he would need also to describe most the peoples and the territories of the world at that time. So he worked, with his associates, at his great collection of annals. It was to have been in four parts, with a geography. He labored for more than nine years. And he tried to make certain that his masterwork would be circulated among readers and preserved for all time. He translated his Persian writings into Arabic, and vice versa. And he created a fund for recopying his books each year.

In spite of his desire, and all his precautions, much of his splendid work has been lost. When a grandson of Tamerlane tried to assemble a complete version a century later, he was unable to do so. This loss now appears to be irreparable.

During the time Rashid was at work at Tabriz, another Persian Fadlallah, surnamed Wassaf, or the Praiser, was writing a chronicle that begins with the death of Mangu. It is known as the *Ta'rikh-i-Wassaf*, and it is written in the pompous style popular in the Persian courts.

Much later, Mirkhwand compiled his history of Genghis-Khan. He seems to have used the works of Juwaini, Rashid and Wassaf, with bits of added material. His text has been published by Jaubert, Paris, 1841. A casual examination of it reveals no original contributions, although his account of Kaidu is full and interesting.

While the viewpoint of the Moslem writers is utterly different from that of the Chinese, they make it possible to see the Mongols, as it were, with two eyes—the characters of the Golden Family become more rounded under their writing. They knew little, or

The March of the Barbarians

cared little, about the Chagatai khans in mid-Asia. Juwaini gave a brief account of the successors of Chagatai, which has been translated by Defremery in the *Journal Asiatique*, 4 ser., t. 20.

They had slight information, apparently, about the Golden Horde or the campaigns in the west.

The Eastern Christians

At the end of the Mongol empires, a Syrian patriarch, Bar Hebraeus (Abu'l-faraj), completed his *Chronicon Syriacum*. This chronological summary of the various kings of the east has much to say about the Mongols, especially the house of Hulagu. It has been translated by Budge recently—*The Chronography of Bar Hebraeus*.

During the years from 1220 to 1300 the Mongols were in close contact with the Georgians in the Caucasus, and the Georgian annals give interesting accounts of Batu, Birkai, Hulagu and his successors, and speak sometimes of the reigning dynasty in Kara-korum. They have been translated by M. Brosset—*Histoire de la Géorgie depuis l'antiquité jusqu'au XIX siècle, traduite du géorgien*, Petersburg, 1849.

An Armenian, Haithon, brother of the reigning king of that country, made the journey to the court of Mangu with his wife and child. He dictated an account of his mission, and added an account of the Mongol khans up to that time. His information is garbled, but his narrative is interesting. Translated into Latin in 1305—*Haytonus, Flos Historiarum Terre Orientis* (published in the *Recueil des Croisades, documents arméniens*, Paris, 1906).

The account of the journey to the west of the Syrian patriarch Mar Yaballaha, with Bar Sauma, was translated from the Syriac by J. B. Chabot—*Histoire de Mar Jabalaha III: Revue de l'Orient Latin*, 1893-94. It appears also in a newer English edition—*The History of Yaballaha III, Nestorian Patriarch, and of his Vicar, Bar Sauma*, by James A. Montgomery, New York, 1927.

Other material from the Syriac is found in the Assemani collection—*Biblioteca orientalis Clementino-Vaticana*, Rome, 1720. This has an account of the Nestorian Church under the Mongols.

Afterword

Other material for the Christian churches at that time is found in J. L. Mosheim—*Historia Tartarorum Ecclesiastica*, Helmstadt, 1741. (This gives Mangu's letter to Louis of France.)

The texts of the narratives of Carpini, Rubruquis (Rubruk), and Odoric are published in *Sinica Franciscana, Volumen I, Itinera et Relationes Fratrum Minorum Saeculi XIII et XIV*: P. Anastasius van den Wyngaert, Firenze, 1929. This also has the brief later account of Marignolli. The vital journal of Rubruk is published in the Hakluyt Society—*The Journey of William of Rubruck*, by W. W. Rockhill, 1900 (a distinguished work). Also, *The Texts and Versions of John de Plano Carpini and William de Rubruquis*, by C. R. Beazley, 1903.

The narrative of Roger, Canon of Varadin (*Carmen Miserabile*), is found in *Scriptores Rerum Hungaricum, I*. Other references to the Hungarian campaign are in Eccard, *Corpus Historicum medii aevi, I*. And in Matthew of Michow, *Cronica Polonica*.

A French Crusader has left in his journal an account of the messengers sent by Louis of France to the Mongol khakhans—Sire de Joinville, *Histoire de S. Louis*. Wailly; Paris, 1874.

The narrative of Marco Polo is dealt with in great detail and with complete notation in *The Book of Sir Marco Polo*, by Colonel Sir Henry Yule and Henri Cordier, London, 1921. A new edition with translation and notes by Paul Pelliot is now being published in Paris.

Colonel Yule's *Cathay and the Way Thither*, Hakluyt Society, 4 vols., London, 1876, gives excerpts from most of the early medieval travelers, including the informative Pegolotti. Other source material is presented in Hallberg—*L'Extrême Orient dans la littérature et la cartographie de l'occident des XIII, XIV, XV siècles*, Gotenborg, 1906.

For this period, many of the decrees and documents of the khakhans of the Yüan dynasty have been collected, published and translated: Bonaparte—*Documents de l'époque mongole (XIII et XIV siècles)*, Paris, 1895. And Devéria M. G.—*Notes d'épigraphie mongole-chinoise*. (*Journ. As.*, 1896.)

Almost the only Russian source for the period of the early

Mongol khans is the well-known *Novgorod Chronicle*. (Available in an English version edited by Charles Beazley.)

A full bibliography for these first contacts between the east and west is to be found in Van den Wyngaert's *Sinica Franciscana*.

The Standard History

The only reliable history of the Mongols—of Genghis-Khan and his descendants—was written before 1824 by M. the baron C. d'Ohsson. He was a diplomat, of Armenian descent, born in Constantinople. His work was guided, apparently, by the previous research of Pétis de la Croix; and he read his way painstakingly through nearly all of the Moslem chronicles known to us today (chiefly Juwaini, Rashid, Wassaf, Mirkhwand). These manuscript copies he must have found both at Constantinople and the national library of Paris. He seems to have used only single copies, and these naturally contained errors.

At that time the Mongolian sources had not been uncovered, and D'Ohsson had access to the Chinese histories only in the French summaries and translations of Da Mailla and Gaubil. Using only Moslem and European sources at first hand, he is biased naturally in judging the Mongols. They seemed to him essentially cruel—sacrificing other peoples in every respect to their own purposes. But in the main, he is very sound, using Rashid as his chief source. Time has shown the value of his work, while proving him to be mistaken in very few details.

At such a vital point as his description of Tului's act in drinking the wooden cup of the shamans' potion, when Tului was nursing his sick brother Ogadai, D'Ohsson consulted Rashid and Juwaini, with Mailla and Gaubil. So D'Ohsson's relation of the incident comes very close to the Mongol account, unknown to him, which describes Tului's act as a heroic sacrifice to save his brother's life.

What Rashid actually said is this:

"Then it chanced that the Qaan [Khakhan] was taken with a sudden sickness, and as it is their way the concubines [women of the house, and the shaman women-men] gathered together, and

they did a sorcery and set a spell upon his sickness and were wash-
ing it into water, when Tuluy Khan entered. Then he raised his
face as a suppliant toward heaven [i.e. the sky] and said: 'O great
and everlasting God [*tangi*—the Mongol Turkish Power, or Sky
Spirit], if Thou dealest out punishment for sin, my sin is more than
his, and at the wars I have killed more men than he, and have
snatched away their wives and children, and made the mothers
and fathers of those captives to weep. And if Thou seekest to draw
into Thy presence a slave fair in shape, and wise—then I am the
better fitted. So, take Thou me in Uktay's [Ogadai's] place,
and fix his illness upon me, so that he may be healed of this
evil.'

"He spoke with all humility and took up the bowl of water
wherein the women had washed the spell of the sickness of the
Qaan, and he drank it down. Then, through the power of the Sky
the Qaan was healed, and Tuluy Khan, having requested his leave,
went on ahead to his own *urugh* [the encampment of his family].
And on the way he fell ill and he died. This was in Mughay-yil,
which is the year of the Snake, during the months of the year 630
of the Hegira."

(Notice that Rashid uses the Mongol word, *mokhoi*, or *mughai*,
instead of his native Persian *mar*, for the serpent.)

Now Rashid, a Persian physician and administrator under the
enlightened Ghazan in that country, three generations later could
not have believed either in the efficacy of the shamans' sorcery or
a sacrifice to the power of the Sky. But he relates it as it was
written down, or told him by the Mongols. And D'Ohsson relates
it so, adding on his own account: "Superstitious spirits did not
fail to believe that Tului was the victim of his love for his brother,
although his death was caused by excessive drinking, to which they
[both] were habitually addicted." Which is very close to the truth,
as we see it. But there is no doubt that Tului did drink down the
shamans' cup, and in the opinion of the superstitious Mongols
that amounted to a sacrifice of himself.

D'Ohsson's fine work was published in four volumes: *Histoire des
Mongols depuis Tchinguiz-Khan jusqu'à Timour Bey ou Tamerlan*, La
Haye and Amsterdam 1834–35. (Unfortunately very rare today.)

His history is much more accurate than the vast compilation of Sir Henry Howorth in four volumes and an appendix: *History of the Mongols*, London, 1876–88. Howorth did not work directly from any oriental source; he did assemble an enormous amount of detail without coherent plan.

The very recent historical summary of René Grousset is an important and authentic treatment of the Turko-Mongols during the two thousand years from their first appearance, to the last of the steppe dominions: *L'empire des steppes: Attila—Gengis-Khan—Tamerlan*, Paris, 1939.

General

Abu'l-Ghazi: *Histoire de Mogols et des Tatares, publiée, traduite, et annotée par le baron Desmaisons*. St Petersburg, 1874. (An interesting later account of the Mongol empires, written by a Khwaresmian Turk.)

Backer, Louis de: *L'Extrême Orient au moyen âge*. 1877.

Baddeley, John F.: *Russia, Mongolia, China*. London, 1919. (Maps, and narratives of the first Russians to venture east.)

Barckhausen, Joachim: *L'Empire Jaune de Genghis-Khan, preface et traduction de Dr George Montandon*. Paris, 1935.

Barthold W. (Vasily): *Turkestan Down to the Mongol Invasion*. London, 1928. (A masterly work on the Turks of Central Asia, with important notices of the Mongols.)

Batuta: *Voyages d'Ibn Batoutah texte arabe et traduction par Defremery et Sanguinetti*. Paris, 1853. (Account of the Arab who journeyed through Asia toward the end of the Mongol dominion.)

Bachfeld, George: *Die Mongolen in Polen, Schlesian, Bohmen und Mahren*. 1889.

Beauvais, Vincent of: *Speculum Historiale*. Duaci, 1624. (Important for the European knowledge of the Mongols and the east.)

Beazley, Charles: *The Dawn of Modern Geography*, II and III. London, 1901.

Blochet, E.: *Introduction à l'histoire des Mongols de Fadl Allah Rashid eddin*. (Gibb Memorial Series.) 1910.

— *La mort de khaghan Koyouk*. (*Revue de l'orient chrétien*, 1922–23.)

Afterword

Bréhier, L.: *L'Eglise et l'Orient au moyen âge—les croisades.* Paris, 1928.

Cahun, Leon: *Introduction à l'histoire de l'Asie; Turcs et Mongols, des origines à 1405.* Paris, 1896. (The work of a brilliant linguist, too credulous of Turkish legends and Mongol sabers.)

Chavannes, Edouard: *Documents sur les Tou-kiue (Turcs) occidentaux.* —*Le cycle turc des douze animaux T'oung-pao.* Série II, Vol. VII, No. 1.

Czaplicka, M. A.: *The Turks of Central Asia, in History and Present Day.* Oxford, 1918.

Douglas, R. K.: *The Life of Genghis-Khan.* London, 1877. (A life of the conqueror from Chinese sources.)

Dulaurier, Edouard: *Les Mongols d'après les historiens arméniens.* (*Journ. As.,* 1858.) (Brief source material, important for the house of Hulagu.)

Encyclopedia of Islam: Articles on Batu, Birkai, Hulagu, Karakorum, etc.

Feer, Léon: *La puissance et la civilisation mongoles au treizième siècle.* Paris, 1867.

Fox, Ralph: *Genghis-Khan.* New York, 1936.

Grousset, René: *L'empire des steppes.* Paris, 1939. (See above.) —*Histoire de l'Asie, III, Le monde mongol.* Paris, 1922.

Grum-Grzhimailo, G. E.: *Zapadnaya Mongoliya.* Leningrad, 1926.

Hammer-Purgstall, J.: *Geschichte der Goldenen Horde in Kiptschak.* Pest, 1840.

Heyd-Raynaud: *Histoire du commerce du Levant au moyen âge.* Leipzig, 1885.

Howorth, Sir Henry H.; *History of the Mongols.* London 1876–88. (See above.)

Jordain, Catalani P.: *Mirabilia Descripta Sequitur de Magno Tartaro.*

Kara-Davan: *Chingis-Khan, Leader in War and His Heritage.* (In Russian.) Belgrade, 1929.

Klaproth: *Aperçu des enterprises des Mongols en Géorgie et en Arménie.* Paris, 1833.

Kliouchevsky, W.: *History of Russia,* 5 vols.

Korostowez: *Von Tschingis-Khan zur Sowjetrepublik.* 1926.

Kousnietsov: *La lutte des civilisations et des langues en Asie centrale.* Paris, 1912.

The March of the Barbarians

Lamb, Harold: *Genghis-Khan*. New York, 1927.

—*Tamerlane, the Earth Shaker*. New York, 1928.

—*The Flame of Islam, the Later Crusades*. New York, 1930. (The relations between the Mongols and Crusaders, Baibars and Saint Louis.)

Lattimore, Owen: *The Mongols of Manchuria*. (Their tribal divisions, geographical distribution, historical relations with Manchus and Chinese and present political problems.) New York, 1934. (A brilliant work, laying bare the conditions of life among the Mongol tribes of today and the historical causation of those conditions.)

Le Coq, Albert von: *Buried Treasures of Chinese Turkestan*. New York, 1929.

Le Strange, Guy: *The Lands of the Eastern Caliphate*. London, 1930. (The physical geography, caravan routes and intercity trade of western Asia, in the medieval period. A painstaking work from the Moslem sources.)

Levchine, Alexis de: *Description des hordes et des steppes des Kirghiz Kaissaks*. Paris, 1840.

Lot, Ferdinand: *Les invasions barbares (et le peuplement de l'Europe)*. Paris, 1937.

Ma-Touan-Lin: *Ethnographie des peuples étrangers à la Chine: ouvrage composé au XIIIe siècle de notre ère*. Genève, 1876–83.

Makrisi: *Histoire de l'Egypte, trad. par Blochet*. (*Rev. Or. lat.* 1898–1906.)

Marinus Sanutus: *Secrets for True Crusaders to Help Them to Recover the Holy Land*. Pal. Pilgrim Text Soc., 1921. (Map and description of the nearer east, after 1300.)

Matthew of Paris: *Chronica majora*. Ed. Luard, 1872–83.

Palladius, the Archimandrite: *Elucidations of Marco Polo's Travels in North China, Drawn from Chinese Sources*. (*Journ. North China, Br. Roy. As. Soc.*, 1875.)

Parker, E. H.: *A Thousand Years of the Tartars*. London, 1924. (The Turco-Mongols until the generation before Genghis-Khan.)

Pelliot, Paul: *Chrétiens d'Asie centrale et d'Extrême orient*. *T'oung pao*. 1914.

Afterword

Pelliot, Paul: *Mongols et papes aux XIII et XIV siècles.* Paris, 1922.

Prawdin, Michael: *L'empire mongol et Tamerlan. Trad. du Dr George Montandon.* Paris, 1937. (A study of the Mongol attack on Europe, and the decline of the house of Genghis-Khan after the rise of Russia.)

Rémusat, Abel: *Mémoires sur les relations politiques des princes chrétiens et particulièrement des rois de France avec les empereurs mongols. (Mémoires de l'Académie des Inscriptions et Belles-Lettres, VI–VII, Paris, 1822.)*

Ross, Sir E. D. (with F. H. Skrine): *The Heart of Asia.* A history of Russian Turkestan and the Central Asian khanates from the earliest times.

Smirnow-Boyer: *Les populations finnoises des bassins de la Volga et de la Kama.* Paris, 1898.

Stein, Sir Aurel: *Serindia.*

—*On Ancient Central Asia Tracks.* London, 1933.

Stübe, R.: *Tschingiz Khan. (Neue Jahrbücher für das Klassische Altertum.* 1908.)

Wolff, O.: *Geschichte der Mongolen oder Tataren.*

—(Works of the Peking Mission.) In Russian.

Vladimirstov, B. Y.: *The Life of Chingis-Khan. Translated from the Russian by Prince Mirsky.* Boston and New York, 1930. (A scholarly and vitally important study of the social structure of the Mongol and kindred clans, and of the life of Genghis-Khan, from Mongolian sources and some Chinese.)

Yule, Colonel Sir Henry: *Cathay and the Way Thither.* Hakluyt Society, London, 1876.

Special bibliographies are to be found in Bréhier and Lamb (*The Flame of Islam*) for the Mongols and Crusaders in the nearer east. Czaplicka for the origins of the Turkish clans. Yule and Cordier have a full bibliography for the medieval travelers to the east. Prawdin, for the Mongol campaign of 1236–41 in Europe.

Note

All but one of the works cited by Prawdin on the Mongol military campaigns are in German. One, by Strakosch-Grassmann—

The March of the Barbarians

Einfall der Mongolen in Mittel-europa, 1893—is the classic study of the conquest of Europe. Another German work on the Tatar method of attack was published in 1915 during the first European war. The translation of my brief life of Genghis-Khan into German in 1928 has sold heavily and steadily ever since.

There are other indications than these that readers in the Third Reich have made a close study of the Mongol campaigns and especially of the Mongol technique of attack.

Professor Pelliot now believes that the date of the birth of Genghis-Khan was 1167, not 1157. This would mean that the Mongol conqueror died at the age of sixty, not at seventy, as we had thought.

A rereading of Rashid's chronicle makes clear that there were two branches of the Urianguts. One, the Mongol branch, had become nomads. It is to this clan that Subotai and his sons must have belonged.

The other branch of the Uriangut remained in the northern forests and took little part in the wars. They clothed themselves in skins and hunted wild animals for food, having no herds of their own. These forest Urianguts were the true reindeer people of northern Siberia, and their descendants still survive in the highlands of the Syansk—a peaceful people, devoted to the reindeer that they call "Reem."

Rashid says of the thirteenth-century forest Urianguts that they never left their woodlands, where they moved about, carrying their belongings on the backs of beasts. "They believe that there is no happier life than their own. Their country being very cold, they hunt much over the snow. They bind to their feet long lengths of wood that they call *chana*, using a staff in their hands to push them along the snow, like the pole of a boat. They shoot down mountainsides so swiftly that they catch up with animals. Anyone who is not accustomed to these wooden skates is apt to hurt his feet, especially in descending. But those who are accustomed to them can travel great distances speedily.

"This is something you must see, in order to believe it."

Afterword

The Transliteration

In this volume the names of persons and places are given in the best-known forms. "Genghis-Khan" is written instead of the newer transliteration, "Chingiz Khan." Translators and writers in so many European languages, dealing with so many oriental languages, have followed varied spellings—which at times make for confusion in the reading.

In general, however, my transliteration of the oriental names follows the early Turkish of Central Asia. So "Ugadai" is written instead of "Uktay," "Mangu" instead of "Mongkë." Most of the place-names in the oriental sources are in Turkish. So "Betchenak" is used instead of the more familiar "Petchenegue" for that Turkish clan.

"*Yasa*" is written, for the law code of Genghis-Khan, rather than the purely Moslem "*al-Yassak*." I have written "Khakhan" instead of the "Qa'an" of Rashid, or the "Ka'an" of Marco Polo. At the same time I have kept the harsher form of the early Turkish "*kagan*" for the pre-Mongol period. This title, signifying great khan or emperor, was—and is—pronounced more softly by the Chinese and Persians, and appears in their written records as "Qa(h)an" and "Han." "Khakhan" was selected as the best way out of the difficulty. Although Genghis never used this title, the Mongols who spoke of him after his death did use it—so Ogadai, for instance, speaks of his father as Genghis-Khakhan, after he himself received that title.

Index

Index

Abaka, 272, 274; Egypt attacked by, 251; marriage of, 249; policies of, 250

Abd ar-Rahman, 167, 178, 180; execution of, 189

Achu, 270 ff.; navy devised by, 272

Ahmad, 278, 283 ff.; killing of, 289-93

Ain Jalut, battle of, 244

Ai Yaruk, 264

Alamdar, 233, 257 ff.

Aleppo, storming of, 239

Alexander the Great, 12, 13, 27, 325

Alexander Nevski, 338-9, 341

Almalyk, destruction of, 316

Altan Khan, 310

Altyn Ordu (*see also* Golden Horde), 205

Amir al Kadr—*see* Tamerlane

Andrew, Friar, 211, 217

Arabia (*see also* Arabs), chroniclers of, 364-8

Arabian Nights, 242

Arabs, 31-2, 35, 36, 228 ff., 238

Arghun, Amir, 183, 252, 300; death of, 311

Arik Buka, 234, 258, 271; Kubilai's conflict with, 258

Arlats, 103

Armor, use of, 129

Arragon, John of, 251

Art: Chinese, 27-8; Five Cities, 27-8; Mongol, 41, 265 ff.; nomad, 28; Sung dynasty, 288; Yüan dynasty, 288

Aryans, 12, 13-4, 24, 27-8

Assassins, 227, 229, 238, 246

Atabegs, the, 29

Athir, Ibn—*see* Ibn Athir

Attila, 16-8

Austria, invasion of, 163 ff.

Avars, 17; Constantinople attacked by, 18

Babar, 31n, 322 ff.

Babas, 14, 16

Babylon, 4

Bacon, Roger, 287-8, 325

Baghdad: capture of, by Hulagu, 229; Kalif of, tortured and killed, 230, 238

Baibars, 242 ff.; army formed by, 244; character of, 242-3; Crusaders won over by, 250-1; defeat of Crusaders by, 243; joke of, 248; Kutuz assassinated by, 246; trade pacts of, 250-1; Venice courted by, 250-1

Baichu—*see* Baidu

Baidar, 133, 141

Baidu, 228 ff.

Banners, described, 55, 129

Bashkirs, 346

Batu (Tsar), 121, 131 ff., 182 ff., 190, 205 ff., 221 ff.; Bouri executed by, 200; character of, 132-3, 205-6; death of, 235; European campaign sustained by, 170; Kuyuk's quarrels with, 140-1, 190 ff.; letter forged by, 158-9; letter to Hungarian king, 144-5; Mangu proposed for Khanate by, 195-6; origin of, 84; quoted, 140-1; Russia under, 143, 172-3, 205-10, 333 ff.; taxation by, 334; western empire given to, 104, 132

Batur, 351

Index

Index

Index

Index

Index

Mohammedanism—*see* Muhammadanism

Mohi, plain of, defeat of the Hungarians by the Mongols in, 151 ff.

Money: Cathayan, 117-8; Kubilai's, 282-5, 293; paper, 294, 307, 311; Russian, 334

Mongols (*see also under specific headings*), 9, 20, 24, 31n, 32n; Buddhism among, 223; campaign of, against Middle Europe, map facing 148; decline of, as nation, 358 ff.; grazing lands of nomad clans of Lake Baikal region, which formed confederacy under Genghis-Khan, map facing 52; present-day situation of, 355-6; primitive—*see* Horse nomads; religion of (*see also* Shamans), 54, 76, 215 ff., 309-10, 315, 335-6; sagas of, 362-3

Montecorvino, John of, 328

Moravia, invasion of, 148

Moscow, burning of, 136; rise of, 341 ff.

Muhammadanism (*see also* Arabs; Egypt; Religion; Turks; *etc.*), spread of, 30-2

Naïmans, 29, 55

Na-mo, 223

Nan-king, siege of, by Subotai, 113 ff.

Nan lu (South Road), 26

Napoleon, Tamerlane compared with, 318-9

Nasr ad-Din, 227

Navy, Achu's, 272

Nestorian Christians, 101, 210 ff., 224, 326; coming of, 27-8; Mangu's attitude toward, 227; rituals of, 179, 189, 192, 214; Wang Khan among, 79

Nevski, Alexander—*see* Alexander Nevski

Nile, early civilization of, 3

Nogai, 254, 315-6; marriage of, 249

Nomads—*see* Horse nomads

Normans, 34

North Gate, 6, 15

North Road, 25-6

Novgorod, 337 ff., 344; chroniclers quoted, 135-6, 137, 208, 369-70, 337; trade of, 138

Noyans, described, 37

Odoric of Pordenone, 327-8

Ogadai (Khan), 68, 141, 178 ff., 196 ff.; army of, described, 127 ff.; Batu given western empire by, 132; character of, 85, 92; coronation of, 92; death of, 169;

decline of, 166 ff.; extravagance of, 94-5; house of, broken up, 197 ff.; Khanate given to, 81 ff., 90-2; rule of, 93 ff., 116-7, 277; Tului's sacrifice for, 107-8, 370-1; wars of, 102 ff.; wives of, 95-6, 281.

Ogul Gaimish, 190, 219, 222; execution of, 199-200; rule of, 211

Old Man of the Mountains (*see also* Assassins), 229, 360

Oleg the Handsome, 143

Ordus, described, 11, 13

Othman Turks, described, 31n, 313 ff.

Oyrats, 100-1, 103, 351

Painting, Chinese, 288, 307

Panther, the—*see* Baibars

Pegolotti, Francesco, 316, 328

Pei-ping (*see also* Tai-tu), early, 7

Peking—*see* Tai-tu

Pelliot, Paul, 79n, 361, 369, 376

Pe lu (North Road), 25-6

Persia—*see* Iran

Peter the Great, 348-9, 355

Petersburg, building of, 348

Phags-pa, 268, 293

Philip the Fair, 253

Pig people—*see* Tungus

Pila, 119

Plano Carpini—*see* Carpini

Poland: division of, by Catherine of Russia, 349; invasion of, by Mongols, 146, 236-7; Renaissance in, 340-1; Russian invasion of, in 1939, 355

Polo, Marco, 172, 236, 311, 360; Ahmad described by, 289-92; death of, 324; European career of, 322 ff.; general remarks on, 285-7; influence of, 316, 328; Kokachin described by, 300; Kubilai's friendship for, 278-9; Kubilai's paper money described by, 283-4; Lin-ngan described by, 286; New Year's celebration described by, 294; printing types possibly introduced into Europe by, 288; purpose of visit of, 250-1; quoted, 264; religion of, 267-8; Tai-tu described by, 279 ff.; voyage to Europe, 311; writing of story of, 323; writings of, 369

Polos, the (*see also* Polo, Marco), 172, 236, 311

Ponce d'Aubon, 148

Postal system, Mongol, 225-6, 327

Index

Index

Index

THE MONGOL DOMINIONS

The following end-sheet map gives the frontiers of the empire actually governed by the Mongols. The area of their conquests extended beyond these frontiers. Such states as Mien, on the Bay of Bengal, and Novgorod, near the Baltic, paid tribute to the Mongol khakhans.

Mongol armies in their attack upon civilization penetrated to Nippon (Japan) and Java in the far east, and to Bohemia and Egypt in the west. In northern India the Mongols advanced periodically as far as the Indus and Lahore.

Of the area shown in this map only the sheltered peninsulas of India, Arabia and Italy were free from Mongol influence.

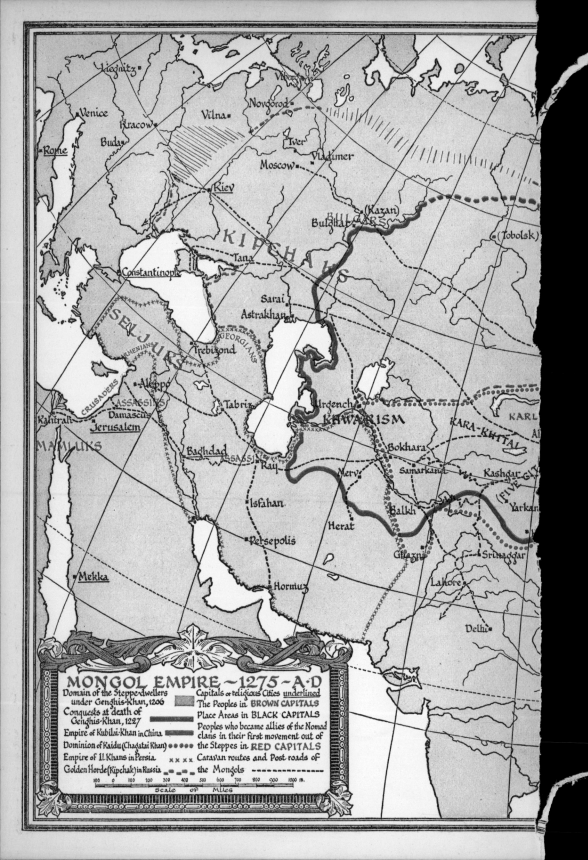

MONGOL EMPIRE ~ 1275 ~ A·D

Domain of the Steppe-dwellers under Genghis-Khan, 1206

Conquests at death of Genghis-Khan, 1227

Empire of Kubilai-Khan in China

Dominion of Kaidu (Chagatai Khan) ● ● ● ●

Empire of Il-Khans in Persia ✕ ✕ ✕ ✕

Golden Horde (Kipchak) in Russia ‒ · ‒ · ‒ ·

Capitals or religious Cities <u>underlined</u>
The Peoples in BROWN CAPITALS
Place Areas in BLACK CAPITALS
Peoples who became allies of the Nomad clans in their first movement out of the Steppes in RED CAPITALS
Caravan routes and Post roads of the Mongols ‒ ‒ ‒ ‒ ‒

100 0 100 200 300 400 500 600 700 800 900 1000 m.
Scale   of   Miles